Robert Eisenberg

Sams **Teach Yourself**

Windows®

Workflow Foundation

in 24 Hours

SAMS   800 East 96th Street, Indianapolis, Indiana 46240 USA

Sams Teach Yourself Windows® Workflow Foundation in 24 Hours

Copyright © 2009 by Pearson Education, Inc.

All rights reserved. No part of this book shall be reproduced, stored in a retrieval system, or transmitted by any means, electronic, mechanical, photocopying, recording, or otherwise, without written permission from the publisher. No patent liability is assumed with respect to the use of the information contained herein. Although every precaution has been taken in the preparation of this book, the publisher and author assume no responsibility for errors or omissions. Nor is any liability assumed for damages resulting from the use of the information contained herein.

ISBN-13: 978-0-321-48699-8

ISBN-10: 0-321-48699-4

Library of Congress Cataloging-in-Publication Data:

Eisenberg, Rob.
   Sams teach yourself Windows workflow foundation in 24 hours / Robert Eisenberg. – 1st ed.
      p. cm.
   ISBN 978-0-321-48699-8
   1. Windows workflow foundation.   2. Application software–Development.   3. Microsoft .NET.
   I. Title.
   QA76.76.A65E38 2008
   006.7'882—dc22

                                                        2008049304

Printed in the United States of America

First Printing December 2008

Trademarks

All terms mentioned in this book that are known to be trademarks or service marks have been appropriately capitalized. Sams Publishing cannot attest to the accuracy of this information. Use of a term in this book should not be regarded as affecting the validity of any trademark or service mark.

Warning and Disclaimer

Every effort has been made to make this book as complete and as accurate as possible, but no warranty or fitness is implied. The information provided is on an "as is" basis. The authors and the publisher shall have neither liability nor responsibility to any person or entity with respect to any loss or damages arising from the information contained in this book.

Bulk Sales

Sams Publishing offers excellent discounts on this book when ordered in quantity for bulk purchases or special sales. For more information, please contact

   U.S. Corporate and Government Sales
   1-800-382-3419
   corpsales@pearsontechgroup.com

For sales outside of the U.S., please contact

   International Sales
   international@pearson.com

Editor-in-Chief
Karen Gettman

Executive Editor
Neil Rowe

Development Editor
Mark Renfrow

Managing Editor
Kristy Hart

Project Editor
Betsy Harris

Copy Editor
Barbara Hacha

Indexer
Lisa Stumpf

Proofreader
Williams Woods Publishing

Technical Editors
David Franson
Richard Olson

Publishing Coordinator
Cindy Teeters

Book Designer
Gary Adair

Senior Compositor
Jake McFarland

Contents at a Glance

Table of Contents

About the Author

Robert Eisenberg, principal, RE Associates, has more than twenty years of application development, consulting training, and management experience. Robert is currently an analyst and consultant specializing in WF, WCF, SharePoint, SOA, BizTalk, and Oslo. Robert's past experience includes the following: CEO and CTO, U.S. operations of the largest Internet professional services firm in Europe; acting director of enterprise systems at a publicly traded manufacturing company, where he architected and implemented all key business systems; founder and president of a software services company that installed and customized midmarket ERP solutions and created custom systems for Fortune 500 and midsize corporations. Clients included SBC, Ameritech, the Federal Reserve Bank, US West, and Cushman & Wakefield. Robert writes articles and frequently speaks about the topics he consults on at CodeCamp, *Integration Journal*, and *Intelligent Enterprise Magazine*.

Dedication

To my wife Patricia and son Matthew.

Acknowledgments

This book started out as a high-level conceptual book and morphed into a hands-on detailed book. There were actually close to two books written to arrive at this one. Therefore, writing this book was a lot of work. I thank my wife, Patricia, and son, Matthew, for their patience and understanding! I look forward to spending weekends and nights with both of you again. I also look forward to spending weekends playing baseball, basketball, and football with Matthew again. Again, thank you to both of you.

I also want to thank the people at Pearson, who are far more patient than anyone else I have ever known. They somehow remained steadfast through this project. In no particular order I would specifically like to thank Mark Renfrow, Neil Rowe, Joan Murray, and Karen Gettman for their patience and confidence. I would also like to thank Barbara Hacha at Pearson for copyediting the book and making it more readable. I would like to thank David Franson and Richard Olson for technically reviewing the chapters and many of the labs. I would also like to thank Kai Middleton for stepping in at the last moment and reviewing a couple of chapters and labs. Finally, I would like to thank Betsy Harris for managing the copy-edit process and getting this book to you.

We Want to Hear from You!

As the reader of this book, *you* are our most important critic and commentator. We value your opinion and want to know what we're doing right, what we could do better, what areas you'd like to see us publish in, and any other words of wisdom you're willing to pass our way.

You can email or write me directly to let me know what you did or didn't like about this book—as well as what we can do to make our books stronger.

Please note that I cannot help you with technical problems related to the topic of this book, and that due to the high volume of mail I receive, I might not be able to reply to every message.

When you write, please be sure to include this book's title and author as well as your name and phone or email address. I will carefully review your comments and share them with the author and editors who worked on the book.

E-mail: feedback@samspublishing.com
Mail: Neil Rowe
          Executive Editor
          Sams Publishing
          800 East 96th Street
          Indianapolis, IN 46240 USA

Reader Services

Visit our website and register this book at informit.com/register for convenient access to any updates, downloads, or errata that might be available for this book.

Introduction

I have spent half of my career focused on business and the other half focused on software development. I am—through my business persona—driven by efficiency. Whereas software has led to tremendous efficiency gains, to say the least, it has also left tremendous room for improvement. Applications are hard to create, understand, and change. My quest for more efficient ways to create software led me to business process management a few years back. After watching the BPM and workflow industry for a couple of years, I was very excited when I learned of Windows Workflow Foundation (WF). After learning more about WF, I became more excited and decided to write this book.

I am convinced that we are entering a new phase of software development and that—on the Microsoft platform—WF lies at its core. Let's look at the key benefits WF will drive:

▶ Simplified development and improved process comprehensibility are delivered because workflows are graphically created and therefore inherently self-evident.

▶ There is a built-in infrastructure to monitor running processes that supplies runtime transparency. The same graphical diagram that runs the workflow is used to illustrate its current step, previous executed steps, and potential completion paths.

▶ There is improved runtime flexibility because WF processes can be loaded at runtime from a database and executed without precompilation. Running processes can be changed. An individual running order, for instance, can have an additional approval step added to facilitate unexpected regulatory concerns.

▶ Simplified and powerful state management is provided. The workflow engine keeps track of the current process step, idles and persists as necessary, and restarts the workflow when appropriate. The workflow engine also allows for interrupting the prescribed process flow and skipping or redoing a step. For instance, it offers tools to transition an order to the earlier customer service step from the shipping step.

▶ Domain-specific languages can be created by adding a collection of custom activities (WF building blocks) and potentially a custom workflow designer as well.

▶ Cloud Service Infrastructure is provided. WF's integration with WCF permits it to expose itself across the cloud and to access cloud services securely and reliably. When accessing multiple cloud services from a workflow, it becomes a cloud service composition platform.

The goal of this book is twofold: first, to explain what WF is, its value, and how and where its features fit into the product's overall goal; second, it drills these concepts into you with pervasive hands-on labs. At the end of this book, you should be well-schooled in the "why" and the "how" of WF.

Book Target Audience

This book is targeted at all levels of .NET developers. It covers most aspects of WF. The labs walk you through the exercises step by step. It is appropriate for beginning .NET developers because of the step-by-step nature of the labs. It is appropriate for inter-mediate and advanced .NET developers because it covers a substantial amount of material that more advanced developers can take time to digest more thoroughly. All developers will also much better understand the "why" of WF. It is much more than a tool to use to create executable diagrams.

How This Book Is Organized

Each hour in this book, with the exception of Hour 1, is packed full of hands-on labs. When a new topic is introduced, it is first explained. The first time an item appears in a lab, you walk through each step and the item is explained in or near where it first appears. When the item appears again later in the hour or in a new hour, it is generally not re-explained. The lab, however, will almost always walk you through the steps to perform the task—although maybe in less detail. The reason I walk you through steps again (and sometimes again) is based on my own experience. I frequently am absorbed learning a new topic and do not want to divert the mental resources from learning the task at hand to remembering or looking up past topics. A contrary viewpoint is that *not* rewalking through the steps each time a topic reap-pears in a subsequent lab provides a better learning experience, because readers must learn how to perform the task on their own. This viewpoint is perfectly valid; when and if you want to take this approach, I recommend attempting to perform repetitive actions without reading step-by-step instructions.

If you copy and paste code from the electronic version of this book, double-check how the quotes paste. Depending on your program, you might need to manually alter the quotes to make them compatible.

Hour Summary

In Hour 1, "Understanding Windows Workflow Foundation," a conceptual overview of workflow is provided first. Then WF, the product, is covered in whole. Finally, WF's main components are covered individually.

In Hour 2, "A Spin Around Windows Workflow Foundation," you learn how to build a basic sequential workflow by dragging and dropping activities (WF's building blocks) onto the workflow designer. You also learn to create workflows declaratively using XAML.

In Hour 3, "Learning Basic Hosting," you dig into hosting a workflow. WF workflows run in the process spaces of another application, referred to as a host. You learn to register events to interact with the host and to register runtime services to change the host's behavior.

In Hour 4, "Learning Host-Workflow Data Exchange," you learn how to send data from the host to the workflow and vice versa. Workflows send data to the host via synchronous methods, and hosts send data to the workflow via asynchronous events.

In Hour 5, "Creating an Escalation Workflow," you learn how to create a workflow that is accessed by two different hosts, which is a very likely scenario. The first host invokes the workflow and allows approval or rejection to be specified. If the process requires further (managerial) approval, the workflow is accessed from the second host.

In Hour 6, "Creating Basic State Machine Workflows," you learn how to create StateMachineWorkflows. StateMachineWorkflows hold a series of states that each contains a collection of valid events. They are the second most popular type of work-flow style (behind sequential workflows).

In Hour 7, "Creating Advanced State Machine Workflows," you learn how to interact with the state machine workflow using capabilities available only to state machine workflows. These include accessing the current state and overriding the current state to perform the skip and rework pattern.

In Hour 8, "Working with Parallel Activities and Correlation," you learn to perform tasks concurrently. The workflow runtime handles the logistics of performing the tasks in parallel (or interleaved, as you learn in the hour). You then reconfigure the approval workflow to call for concurrent approval, which requires learning about correlation.

In Hour 9, "Working with the Replicator and While Activities," you learn to use activities that perform a task n number of times, where n is specified at runtime. The Replicator—one of WF's advanced control flow activities—can perform the tasks sequentially or in parallel and also features an early termination clause. The `While` activity is similar to the C# while statement.

In Hour 10, "Working with `EventHandlingScope` and Strongly Typed Activities," you learn to use the `EventHandlingScope` activity that allows one or more events to be received throughout the lifetime of the workflow, such as cancellation and approver maintenance.

In Hour 11, "Creating Data-Driven Workflows," you learn to use the `ConditionedActivityGroup` (CAG) activity. The CAG is another advanced control flow activity. It allows concurrent processing, like the `Parallel` activity, with a few additions. Most noteworthy, each branch has a `When` condition, and the CAG has an overall `Until` condition.

In Hour 12, "Working with the WF `RuleSet`," you learn to use WF `RuleSet` technology and add-on products to access `RuleSets` from a database. `RuleSets` are a collection of rules that can be prioritized and configured to reevaluate in case a dependent rule changes. Each rule in a `RuleSet` has a `Then` and an optional `Else` action. The first is executed when the rule evaluates to true and the second when it evaluates to false. You then work with third-party add-ons that allow `RuleSets` to be stored and analyzed in a database and loaded at runtime.

In Hour 13, "Learning to Track Workflows," you learn to monitor running workflows. First, the tracking architecture is covered. Then you learn to create custom tracking profiles to filter the information that is tracked. Then you learn to augment the extracted information with business information, such as the order number and order amount. This information is useful to produce more meaningful reports and create alerts when, for example, the order amount falls below a threshold amount.

In Hour 14, "Working with Roles," you learn to control access to the workflow. Each incoming event can be wired to an Active Directory or ASP.NET role provider. Then only users existing in the role provider are permitted access.

In Hour 15, "Working with Dynamic Update," you learn to modify running workflows. Activities can be added and removed, and declarative rules can be changed. Changing running workflows are one of WF's primary capabilities. Using this capability in conjunction with WF's tracking is particularly intriguing.

In Hour 16, "Working with Exceptions, Compensation, and Transactions," you learn to trap and handle errors and to create transactions. Exceptions and transactions work similarly to the way they work in standard .NET. Compensation is a WF-only capability that is used to correct already completed work in WF.

In Hour 17, "Learning Advanced Hosting," you learn to use most workflow events to control the workflow from the host, add additional capabilities to alter the workflow runtime, and invoke another workflow from a workflow. You will experiment with the suspended, aborted, and other events. You will add runtime services that control transactions, threading, and other functions. Finally, you learn to call a workflow from another workflow.

In Hour 18, "Working with Web Services and ASP.NET Hosting," you learn to expose a workflow as a web service, call a web service from a workflow, and to run workflows from ASP.NET.

In Hour 19, "Learning WF-WCF Integration," you learn to integrate WF with Windows Communication Foundation (WCF), Microsoft's new distributed technology. WCF can expose WF workflows as services accessible in the cloud and can be used to call out to services from WF workflows. These two products appear to be merging into one unified application server.

In Hour 20, "Creating Basic Custom Activities," you begin to create your own custom activities. In WF, you are not limited to the activities provided out-of-the-box. Custom activities are a major part of WF. Therefore, five hours are devoted to them. In this hour you will create `Customer` and `CreditCheck` activities that encapsulate this "domain" functionality in activities that can be placed on workflows just as can be done with the activities that ship with WF.

In Hour 21, "Creating Queued Activities," you learn to create activities that execute in multiple bursts and to work with WF's queuing system, which underlies all WF communication.

In Hour 22, "Creating Typed Queued and `EventDriven`-Enabled Activities," you learn to strongly type the data accessed in queues and to create a special type of queued activity called an `EventDriven` activity.

In Hour 23, "Creating Control Flow Activities Session 1," you learn to create activities that serve as placeholders for child activities and that schedule their child activities for execution. You can create your own control flow patterns that match the need of your domain. You can also implement general workflow patterns like those found at www.workflowpatterns.com.

In Hour 24, "Creating Control Flow Activities Session 2," you also learn to implement compensation at the activity level. Then you implement activity validation. Finally, you learn to use attached properties that allow a property, such as a condition, to be passed down from a parent activity to a child activity.

PART I

The Basics

HOUR 1

Understanding Windows Workflow Foundation

What You'll Learn In This Hour:

▶ What workflow is in general

▶ What Windows Workflow Foundation (WF) is

▶ The main components of WF one-by-one

▶ Installation instructions and requirements

This hour begins with a general description of workflow because many definitions exist. It then covers Windows Workflow Foundation (WF), first with an overview and then by diving into many of its main elements. Finally, it provides installation instructions and requirements to get you ready for the next 23 hours that are packed full of hands-on exercises.

Describing Workflow and Workflow Systems

This section provides a general overview of workflow and related topics. In addition to offering a general overview, it is intended to give you an understanding of Windows Workflow Foundation's goals as you continue through this hour and the rest of the book.

A Conceptual Description of Workflow

Workflow is another overloaded technological term. One reason for this is that its meaning has been defined by companies with a vested interest that it matches the features of their products. Another reason is that it is commonly bound to current technology capabilities. These reasons prevent it from being objectively defined. A workflow is logic—consisting of one or more steps that are predicated by one or more conditions—that a system or person must perform to complete a function. Because the logic or process automated by a workflow generally consists of more than one step that may occur over a period of time, it must track the state of the overall process. Here are some examples of workflows: an order process, an expense report, and rescheduling a missed meeting.

The order process is almost always automated using a traditional computer language. Its control flow is supported through `if`, `while`, `foreach`, and other statements in the C# language. The expense report may be automated using a traditional computer language or a workflow product with a graphical designer. The rescheduling is almost always performed manually. All of these are workflows, or logic. Why, then, are they automated differently? Expense reports are generally routed and escalated to people that must act on them. These touch points are called human intervention. Workflow systems are generally well suited at handling these scenarios that call for human intervention. Therefore, systems with prevalent human intervention are prime workflow system targets. The rescheduling is not automated, or rarely, because for the most part, systems are not yet ready to automate these types of tasks.

Both the order and expense report would generally have lifetimes that span hours, weeks, or months. Therefore the system used to automate them must be able to track their progression, or state. Rescheduling a meeting may only require logic to change the meeting, unless it must also await confirmations. In short, workflow consists of both logic and managing the process state.

A Sample Expense Report Workflow

A sample expense report workflow can make concrete some of the concepts about process discussed so far. Figure 1.1 illustrates a simplified workflow. The process is described directly following the figure.

The workflow receives an expense report and checks the amount; if it is less than or equal to $500, the expense report is approved. Otherwise, manager approval is required. The workflow then removes itself from memory to free resources, and the workflow product waits for the response. The manager may either approve or reject the expense report. In either case, the workflow product reactivates the workflow. If the manager approves, the expense report is marked approved and an approval email is sent to the submittee. If the manager rejects, the corollary rejection process occurs. If the manager does not approve in time, the timeout option is triggered and manager approval is rerequested, which is depicted in the line going back to the Request Manager Approval shape.

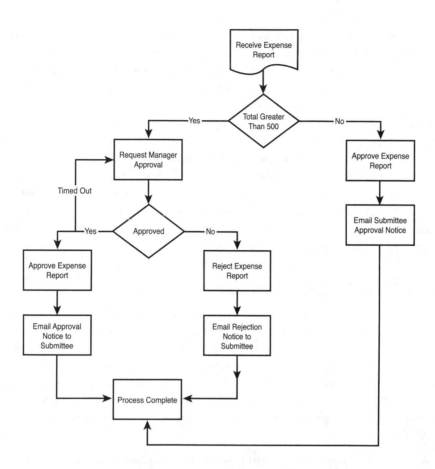

FIGURE 1.1
Sample expense
report workflow.

Let's look at some of the benefits gained by using most workflow systems to automate this process:

▶ **Design-time transparency**—It is clear what the expense report process does just by looking at it.

▶ **State management**—The workflow system manages keeping track of the current step, removing the process from memory when waiting for manager approval, and going back to the approval step when required. A workflow system provides these state management features for you. In contrast, a process automated via a traditional computer language generally requires the developer to create tables and fields to manage the state themselves.

▶ **Runtime transparency**—The workflow system can also visually show the current step and the execution path of the process. This feature is generally referred to as *tracking* (you will learn more about it in the "Tracking" section of this hour).

Many think that there is no way to graphically model application logic because any complex process will have so many control flow statements the diagram will be unreadable, eliminating the promised transparency. A process automated with a graphical workflow application should be self-describing. It should serve the same benefit that a flowchart currently supplies (or at least most of it). Just as a flowchart does not include every single control flow statement, neither should a graphical workflow. Figure 1.1 provides a solid understanding of the process without detailing every control flow statement or diving into the individual steps. Some of the detail held is not relevant to understanding the process and does not need to be added to a workflow at all. Other steps, such as approve order, may be their own workflows with their own detail. They still show on Figure 1.1 as one step, which is appropriate because the details of the expense report approval step aren't needed to achieve a general understanding of the expense report process.

Workflow Segmentations

Workflow is also frequently segmented along in-application, human, and integration lines. Traditional languages, like C#, are generally associated with in-application workflow. Human workflow systems arose from the desire to better support human-centric scenarios. Integration systems or integration-centric workflow systems arose from the need to better automate integration scenarios using dedicated integration systems. Let's look a little closer at the human- and integration-centric workflow and the tools created to support them, because they are the roots of modern workflow systems.

Human workflow generally describes processes that require substantial human involvement and escalation. Human processes are also frequently nonlinear. A proposal, for example, may go to final approval only to be sent back to initial approval. Tasks and forms to request feedback are critical components of human workflow systems. The tasks and forms will generally be delivered to the requisite people via email, as Outlook tasks, or via a portal (such as SharePoint).

Integration-centric workflow systems are frequently used when connecting systems. Deciding whether an order should be added to SAP that is received from Microsoft CRM, for instance, may require a number of validations, such as whether all the required fields are filled out. These validations are logic, and logic is workflow.

Human workflow systems generally have better form and task support, and integration-centric ones generally process faster and have better transactional support. Although traditional computer languages are still used to automate many human and integration workflow scenarios, these other purpose-built systems have arisen as alternatives.

What Is a Business Process Management System?

The purpose of a business process management system (BPMS) is to create a system that manages processes more completely than human workflow and integration workflow systems and traditional computer languages. There are largely two, potentially overlapping, paths to this process completeness. One is to combine the strengths from human workflow and integration workflow systems. In the previous Microsoft CRM to SAP integration example, a BPMS could be used to integrate the systems and then call on its human workflow support to request human intervention in case of an exception.

The second path is application life cycle and human workflow driven. The application life cycle features generally include tools to deploy the process. Strong monitoring tools are frequently referred to as business activity monitoring (BAM). BAM builds multiple graphical views, portal integration, and business intelligence integration on top of tracking (mentioned in the "A Sample Expense Report Workflow" section) to provide enhanced analysis and monitoring of running processes. BPMSs sometimes allow running processes, such as an order, to be changed. An additional approval step, for instance, could be added to an order. Depending on their roots, human workflow or integration, a BPMS will generally be stronger at either human or system workflow. The human workflow element is gaining market momentum as the ability to interject people into processes is key to increased flexibility, a BPMS staple.

BPMSs also promise businesses better visibility into their processes. That the processes are graphically created and therefore visible combines with BAM to help achieve this visibility. They also frequently promise that business analysts can use their design tools to create processes without IT assistance.

Many BPMS proponents predict that a BPMS is a better way to do all workflow, including in-application. A mass move to using a BPMS for all workflow hasn't occurred, although this idea has attracted much interest and this may change.

This is one perspective of workflow and BPMSs. If you are interested in learning more or gaining additional information, Wikipedia is a good place to start.

.NET Framework 3.0 and 3.5

Windows Workflow Foundation (WF) is part of the .NET Framework 3.0 and 3.5. The .NET Framework 3.5 is a newer version of the .NET Framework 3.0. Both the .NET Framework 3.0 and 3.5 are add-ons to the 2.0 Framework (see Figure 1.2). Neither

FIGURE 1.2
.NET 3x stack.

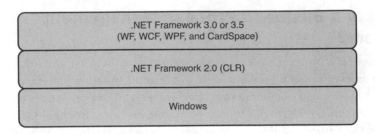

replaces the 2.0 Framework. They simply add new namespaces that make up WF, Windows Communication Foundation (WCF), Windows Presentation Foundation (WPF), Windows Cardspace, and other new features.

WCF unifies Microsoft's current messaging technologies: web services, .NET Remoting, and Enterprise Services/Com+ .WCF is significant to WF because it provides a resilient way for WF to communicate with other applications, inside and outside of the firewall. Hour 19 covers WF and WCF integration.

WPF is Microsoft's new forms technology that looks to unify and improve on its current web and Windows forms capabilities while simultaneously adding multimedia and other features. WF and WPF can both be created using the same markup language, XAML (described in the "XAML Workflows and Serialization" section of this hour), which may prove interesting when creating applications that utilize both.

Windows Cardspace is Microsoft's new consumer-oriented authentication technology and has no underlying connecting to WF.

WF is very similar across the 3.0 and 3.5 Framework versions. The main difference across framework versions is there are two WCF modeling activities in WF 3.5 that are not in 3.0 (covered in Hour 19 "Learning WF–WCF Integration").

Overview of WF

All applications have workflow, no matter how they automate it. Many applications also look to offer tools to allow others to build custom workflows on top of their product. WF's goal is to support both of these scenarios and do so at mainstream scale. If you are building an application on Windows that tracks orders, it is WF's goal to power this workflow. It doesn't matter if it is an ASP.NET, Windows Forms, Windows Service, or other application. If you are building a platform, like SharePoint, where people build their own custom workflows on top of it, WF's objective is to provide the tools for this as well. WF also intends to serve all three types of workflow: in-application, human, and integration-centric. WF includes all the foundational elements to create all three types of workflow.

WF must play well with others if it expects other applications to use it to power their workflow and potentially to permit custom workflows to be built with it on their platform. WF has to offer its services in such a way that the applications can use its services and cannot make assumptions about what elements will be available to the application. For instance, if WF is hosted (called from) in a Windows Forms application on a client, there may not be access to SQL Server. It therefore cannot build a hard dependency on storing idled workflows to SQL Server.

These higher-level functions, such as where to store idled workflows, how and if tasks should be stored, and functions such as BAM, are up to the host application to implement, as needed. An application using WF for in-application workflow support, for instance, may not need BAM. The host application can generally start from one of WF's building blocks to add higher level functionality. The host, for instance, can choose to use WF's persistence service that stores idled workflows to SQL Server out-of-the-box (OOB), or with minimal effort to another medium, such as Oracle. Likewise, the host can build on WF's tracking service to supply BAM. It is critical to WF that these building blocks are extremely powerful so that it will be embraced by other products looking for workflow support. Therefore, many WF features may not include the final user interface, but they will be based on an extremely strong infrastructure, as both the persistence and tracking services are.

SharePoint provides a fully functional WF host, as described in the "SharePoint Workflow" section of this hour. Many use SharePoint's WF implementation just for its hosting capabilities, even those not interested in SharePoint. Microsoft CRM also provides a host. Microsoft is in the process of building a "generic" host based on the combination of WF and WCF. WCF hosting of WF was added in the .NET Framework 3.5. Going forward, this tandem is likely to form a standard host that can be used by any Windows application that chooses to employ workflow functionality. Third parties, such as K2 BlackPearl, have also built hosts on top of WF.

By the end of this hour you will have a better understanding of the rich and powerful capabilities WF offers to create workflow applications and products. These concepts will be expanded on throughout this book.

Next, let's look at the fundamental pieces of WF.

Standard Modeling Activities

Activities are the unit of design and execution in WF. WF comes with a set of modeling constructs that it calls activities and a workflow designer (see Figure 1.3). The activities are dragged and dropped from the toolbox onto the workflow designer. The properties of the activities are then set. A workflow is the composition of the activities placed on the workflow designer.

FIGURE 1.3
Workflow designer and activities.

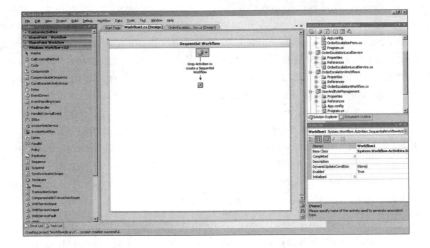

WF ships with approximately 30 activities. It calls these activities the Base Activity Library (BAL). The activities are largely segmented as follows: control flow activities, activities that facilitate data exchange between the workflow and the application running the workflow (a Windows Forms application, for example), one that permits arbitrary code to be written, and another group that supplies exception handling.

The control flow activities include a Sequence activity that is a shell for other activities. It is equivalent to {} in C#. It is a block where activities may be added. A Sequence activity can hold a tree of activities, as you will see in Figure 1.10 when its sequential workflow cousin is discussed. Figure 1.4 shows a Sequence activity that contains two other activities.

FIGURE 1.4
The Sequence activity.

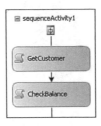

The `While` (Figure 1.5) activity loops while the condition associated with it remains `true`. There is a condition not seen in the figure. Conditions are discussed in the "Rule Capabilities" section of this hour.

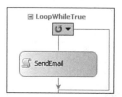

FIGURE 1.5
The `While` activity.

The `IfElse` (Figure 1.6) activity holds one or more branches that are each governed by a condition. The first branch to return `true` is executed; no other branches are executed.

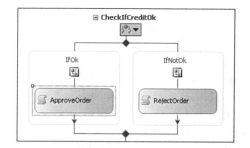

FIGURE 1.6
The `IfElse` activity.

Another control flow activity is the `Listen` (Figure 1.7) activity that allows two or more branches to be added that each wait for an external event. The left branch, for instance, may wait for approval and the right branch for rejection. A timer may also be placed in a `Listen` activity branch. The branch that receives the first event executes unless the timer goes off first, in which case the timer branch executes. The `Listen` activity supports a prototypical workflow pattern to wait one or more responses and then timeout if response is not received within a specified duration.

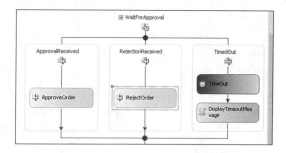

FIGURE 1.7
The `Listen` activity.

A Parallel activity executes two or more branches concurrently. (Branches are actually executed in an interleaved fashion as described in Hour 8, "Working with Parallel Activities and Correlation.") The Parallel (Figure 1.8) activity will wait for all branches to complete before completing.

FIGURE 1.8
The Parallel
activity.

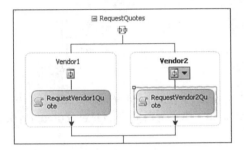

Advanced control flow activities include the Replicator activity, which can process a number of elements specified at runtime and can do so in serial or parallel. It is similar to the C# foreach statement with the additional capability to process in parallel as well as sequentially. This activity is critical to document approval and other scenarios that have different numbers of approvers on different instances and therefore require the number of approvers to be specified at runtime. The EventHandlingScope activity is similar to a Listen activity but it allows the events to be received multiple times. The combination of the Replicator and EventHandlingScope activities power much of the OOB SharePoint workflows that require the number of participants (approvers) to be specifiable at runtime and must be changeable throughout the workflow life cycle.

The data exchange activities include CallExternalMethod and HandleExternalEvent. The first is used to send data from the workflow to the application running the workflow (the host). The latter allows data to be sent from the host to the workflow. There is also a set of activities to expose a workflow as a web service (WebServiceOutput and WebServiceInput) and call a web service from a workflow (InvokeWebService). Finally, Send and Receive WCF activities exist that can be used only with .NET 3.5. The Send activity is used to connect to a WCF endpoint (or any compatible endpoint) from a workflow. The Receive activity is used to expose a workflow as a WCF Service.

The Code (Figure 1.9) activity points to a handler with standard .NET code. It can be used to add custom functionality to a workflow, although in many cases it is better to use a custom activity, as discussed in the upcoming Custom Activities section.

```
private void DisplayTimeoutMessage_ExecuteCode(
    object sender, EventArgs e)
{
    MessageBox.Show
        ("Order number: " + OrderNumber + " timed out.");

}
```

FIGURE 1.9
The Code activ-
ity and handler
code.

Multiple Workflow Styles

WF ships with OOB support for three styles of workflows: sequential, state, and data. The third, data, is powered by an advanced control flow activity called the ConditionedActivityGroup that can be placed on both sequential and state machine workflows. It is not a standalone workflow style like the other two. It is included here as a separate workflow style because it is well suited for certain types of processes, as you will soon see. It is therefore sometimes referred to as an activity and at other times as a workflow.

Let's first start with sequential workflows (Figure 1.10), which is summarized following the figure.

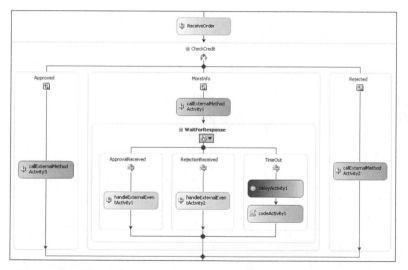

FIGURE 1.10
Sample sequen-
tial workflow.

A sequential workflow, like a Sequence activity, serves as a container for a tree of activities. A sequential workflow lays out a process in a linear form from top to bottom. It is similar to a flowchart. The general convention is that sequential workflows are best suited for processes that have a linear path and that are not highly dynamic. The notion is challenged because advanced control flow activities (like the Replicator, EventHandlingScope, and ConditionedActivityGroup that you will learn about shortly) allow sequential workflows to handle some highly dynamic processes. All three styles of workflow are covered, so you can make your own decision.

The process begins with receipt of an order. It is then automatically approved, sent down the more information required path, or automatically rejected. If more information is required, it waits for manual approval or rejection with an option to time-out. As you can see, the process starts at the top, then branches, and continues to move down until completion. Sequential workflow coverage begins in Hour 2, "A Spin Around Windows Workflow Foundation." You will also want to look at many other hours that cover the different activities because it is these activities, placed on the sequential workflow, that dictate the workflow's behavior.

State machines are a very common modeling technique—for creating both executing programs and static diagrams—built on process milestones and events. State machines are largely predicated on the notion that processes are dynamic and take many divergent paths to completion. This is why state machines are frequently associated with human-centric processes. In fact, one reason WF proclaims to have the capability to support human workflow is that it includes state machine workflow modeling. Figure 1.11 illustrates a state machine workflow. Directly following the figure is a description.

FIGURE 1.11
Sample state machine work-flow.

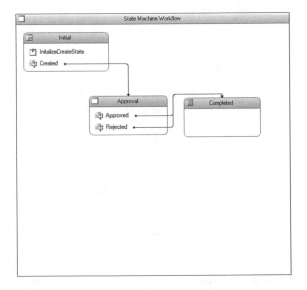

The business milestones are the states (Initial, Approval, and Completed). The events are the text within the states (Approved, Rejected). This means that in the

Approval state both the Approved and Rejected event may be received. The lines from the event to the state represent the transition that occurs when that event is received. For example, when the Created event is received and the workflow is in the Initial state, the workflow transitions to the Approval state. When either the Approved or Rejected event is received in the Approval state, the workflow transitions to the Completed state. It would be just as easy to send the workflow back to the Initiation state from the Approval state if necessary. Processes with many states and many possible gyrations are solid state machine workflow candidates. No prescribed order exists. Each state is autonomous and equally accessible. Hours 6 and 7 describe creating state machine workflows.

Behind each event is a Sequence activity that holds the activities that process the work for the selected event. Figure 1.12 shows the sequential logic executed when the Approved event is selected. In essence, a state machine workflow is an inverse sequential workflow. The events are on top and the sequential logic embedded when using a state machine workflow. In a sequential workflow it is the opposite. Look at the sequential workflow and you will see the Listen activity and event embedded in the sequential logic.

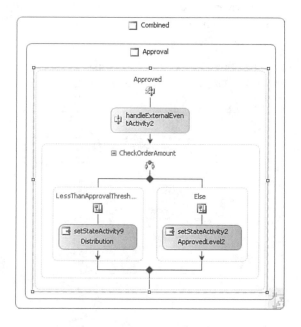

FIGURE 1.12
Approval event logic.

Way

The activities behind the events are actually slightly constrained Sequence activies, as you will learn in Hour 6.

The `ConditionedActivityGroup` (CAG) activity is an advanced control flow activity that can be placed on either a sequential or state machine workflow. From a process standpoint it can be viewed as an alternative style of workflow to the better-known sequential and state machine styles. Generally, sequential workflows are recommended for deterministic processes that have a well-defined beginning and end. State machine workflows are best suited for dynamic processes that iterate through states without a guaranteed order. Data-driven workflows, on the other hand, are best suited when the data determines the process execution order. Many pricing and promotional algorithms exist that may not execute a branch based on the data at the beginning of a process, but will do so later when other parts of the process change the data the branch depended on. For instance, the order may not be subject to a discount until after tallying the line items.

Depending on your needs, the CAG activity may be the only activity on a sequential workflow. In this case, all your child activities will be embedded in the CAG, and you will have created a data-driven workflow. In other cases, you may embed a CAG into a larger sequential or state machine workflow. In this case, only a subset of your workflow will be data driven.

The CAG (Figure 1.13) has three lanes. Each lane will execute one or more times during the lifetime of the CAG. The lanes execute when their When condition is true dur-

FIGURE 1.13
Conditioned
Activity Group
sample.

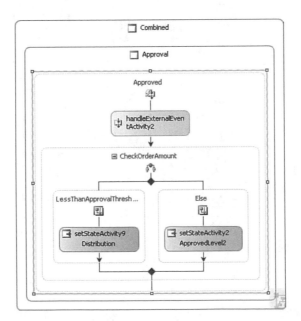

ing the CAG lifetime (lanes with no When condition execute exactly once). The CAG is covered in Hour 11, "Creating Data-Driven Workflows."

Hour 2 begins covering sequential workflows. State machine workflows are covered in Hours 6 and 7. The CAG is covered in Hour 11. However, workflows are a composition of activities, so you will need to be familiar with the OOB activities, custom activities (covered in the forthcoming "Custom Activities" section of this hour), and other WF functions to create workflows of any type. These topics are interspersed throughout the book.

Hosting

WF is not a standalone application. WF is an engine that executes workflows on behalf of a host application. A Windows Forms, ASP.NET, Windows Service, or other Windows application starts the workflow engine running. The host application is then responsible for managing the life cycle of the workflow engine. The host application must remain active while workflows are running and communicate with the workflow engine. If the host application terminates while workflows are running, they will stop running. The host application needs to know the status of workflows the workflow engine is running on its behalf. It achieves this by subscribing to a number of events the workflow engine makes available to it. Three of the most common are completed, terminated, and idled.

The completed event is fired when a workflow completes processing successfully. The terminated event is fired when the workflow completes unsuccessfully. The idled event means the workflow is not complete but inactive. The workflow in Figure 1.10 would enter the idled state when waiting for a response. In a state machine workflow, the only time the workflow is active is when processing the logic behind an event (Figure 1.12). At other times, it is idle waiting for the next event.

How do the workflows receive events if they are idle? This is the job of the workflow engine. It passes the incoming event on to the correct workflow instance. If the workflow is idle, the workflow engine will reactivate it first. This is important because many workflows run for hours, days, or longer. They are generally active only for very short bursts during their lifetime.

In addition to being embeddable in different hosts, the workflow engine must also be configurable to meet the needs of different host applications. For example, when a workflow idles, it should be serialized and stored in a storage medium. If not, a server would hold countless workflow instances over their entire lifetimes. This would devastate scalability and be very risky. If the server went down, the workflows would be lost because they are in memory. This is actually the default behavior of WF because it is not aware of the hosts' needs or capabilities. There may be some scenarios where all workflows have very short life cycles, and no need exists for storage during inactivity. In some environments, such as client scenarios, no SQL Server is available to store the current state of the workflow. For these reasons, WF ships with a number of pluggable services that can be added to the runtime as needed. WF ships with a SQL Server persistence service that can be added. When the persistence service is added, idle workflows are saved to SQL Server. This meets the first criteria—that the service should be available when necessary. It does not meet the second criteria—that the storage medium the workflow is saved to should be flexible. The second option requires extending the base persistence service. It is not available OOB but is an anticipated extensibility point and can be done in a straightforward manner.

Hosting in WF requires starting the engine, choosing which runtime services to add to the runtime, and subscribing to the events you are interested in.

The `WorkflowRuntime` type in the `System.Workflow.Runtime` namespace is the workflow engine. The following code demonstrates instantiating the workflow engine (`WorkflowRuntime` type), adding the persistence service to it, subscribing to the closed event, and starting the workflow engine. This code would be the same regardless of whether the workflow engine was hosted from a Windows Forms, ASP.NET, Windows Service, or other application.

```
WorkflowRuntime workflowRuntime = new WorkflowRuntime();

workflowRuntime.AddService(sqlPersistenceService);

workflowRuntime.WorkflowCompleted +=
    new EventHandler<WorkflowCompletedEventArgs>
        (workflowRuntime_WorkflowCompleted);

workflowRuntime.StartRuntime();
```

Hosting is covered in Hour 3, "Learning Basic Hosting," and Hour 17, "Learning Advanced Hosting."

Tracking

Tracking allows workflow information to be extracted from running workflows. The information is usually saved to a storage medium for monitoring or analysis. Tracking is not added to the WF runtime in its default configuration; it is an optional, pluggable runtime service (just as the persistence service is). WF ships with a SQL Server tracking service that stores running workflow information to SQL Server. If you need to store the information in a different storage medium, you can customize the tracking service to do so. WF also ships with the WorkflowMonitor SDK sample that reads the information in the SQL Server tracking database and graphically displays it. Figure 1.14 shows a running sequential workflow graphically displayed (the same one displayed at design time in Figure 1.10). The checkmarks illustrate which activities executed. The left pane allows you to select the workflow model and specific instance you are interested in. There is also a filtering mechanism at the top that can be used to select which workflows to show.

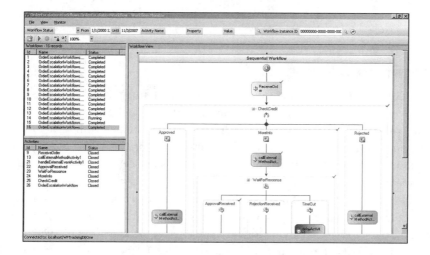

FIGURE 1.14
Workflow Monitor sample.

WF's very powerful tracking capability is used to extract the tracking information from running workflows. The information can be stored to any medium. WF's SQL Server tracking service is used to store the information to SQL Server. Then the WorkflowMonitor SDK application is used to graphically display and interact with the information that is extracted from the workflow and stored in SQL Server.

If the objective were to compare orders to target and display pie charts and trigger alerts for problem orders, another front-end application would be developed to do this. A BPMS would generally have more tools as part of its BAM offering that simplify developing user interfaces that show workflow information in analytical formats. WF's focus is to make sure the information can be extracted and not on the tools that control the output, although the WorkflowMonitor application is useful in and of itself.

Tracking is covered in Hour 13, "Learning to Track Workflows."

Rule Capabilities

WF has two types of rules, and it stores rules in two different formats. The first type of rule, a conditional rule, is bound to a control flow activity and is used to determine how the control flow activity processes. For example, which branch of an `IfElse` activity should execute? The second type of rule in WF, a `RuleSet`, executes a collection of rules and adds prioritization, reexecution, and other capabilities to the collection of rules.

The next sections look at conditional rules first in both formats and then at `RuleSets`.

Conditional Rules

The `While` and `IfElse` activities covered in the "Standard Modeling Activities" section are both governed by conditional rules. The `While` activity's `Condition` property holds a rule that determines whether the `While` activity should continue iterating. Common conditions in a `While` activity are counter < 3 or IsValid = true. In the first example, the `While` iterates until the counter value is 3 (or more). In the second example, it iterates while `IsValid` is true. The `While` activity's `Condition` property is evaluated at each iteration to determine whether it should continue iteration. The `Condition` property can be set as a Declarative Rule Condition or as a Code Condition. Declarative Rule Conditions can be created using the Rule Condition Editor and are stored in an XML format in a `.rules` file. Figure 1.15 shows the Declarative Rule Condition being created in the Rule Condition Editor.

FIGURE 1.15
Rule Condition
Editor.

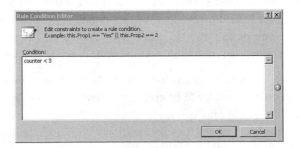

Figure 1.16 shows the `While` activity `Condition` property set to Declarative Rule Condition and pointed to the rule created (named `CounterDeclarative`) in Figure 1.15. The `CounterDeclarative` Declarative Rule Condition is now bound to the `While` activity `Condition` property, which ensures iteration will stop when counter is 3 or more.

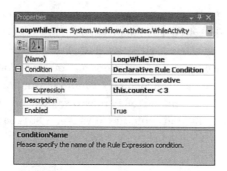

FIGURE 1.16
While activity condition property.

Declarative Rule Conditions are stored in an XML format in a .rules file. The file is extremely verbose and hard to read. The advantage of creating rules declaratively is that they can be changed at runtime without recompilation, stored in a database, and more general tooling support exists for them.

See Hour 12, "Working with the WF RuleSet," for details on loading rules from a database. See Hour 15, "Working with Dynamic Update," for details on changing rules at runtime.

The alternative is to set the While activity Condition property to Code Condition. It then requests a method name. You would insert counter<3 in the method and if the value is less than 3, the method would return true, otherwise it would return false. The method replaces the verbose XML file as a storage medium. Code Conditions do not receive the same level of tooling support as Declarative Rule Conditions in WF.

RuleSets

A RuleSet permits a collection of rules to be created that each has a corresponding action. The rules in the RuleSet can be prioritized and configured to reevaluate if a dependent item changes. Reevaluation can be explicitly set on an individual rule or defined overall by setting the RuleSet Chaining property (or both).

When the RuleSet Chaining property is set to Full, rules that have a dependent value changed downstream are automatically reevaluated. Think of a pricing scenario where a discount is applicable if the customer reaches a year-to-date-sales threshold. This discount rule can be reevaluated every time the year-to-date-sales change. The neat part is that WF can do much of this detection automatically via clever CODEDOM programming (a .NET serialization capability) in contrast to forcing the developer to attribute the dependencies.

Figure 1.17 shows a `RuleSet` with three rules. It is set to Full Chaining, so it will automatically reevaluate. The selected `DiscountPercent` rule checks if the `OrderAmount` is larger than the `DiscountThreshold`. If so, it applies a 5% discount. The other two rules in the `RuleSet` have their own conditions and actions. Notice that the other two rules (`YearlySales` and `TotalOrderAmount`) contain information likely related and relevant to calculating a discount. `RuleSet` rules also have an optional `Else` action that executes if the rule condition evaluates to `false`. A `RuleSet` is a collection of related rules that solve a common problem such as pricing.

FIGURE 1.17
`RuleSet` dialog.

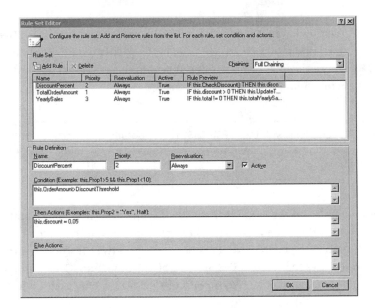

In WF, `RuleSets` are always stored in `.rules` files. WF does not add any tools management, central rules storage, or other common functionality found in a commercial rules engine product. However, some add-on products provide some of these capabilities. One of the add-ons stores `RuleSets` in a SQL database and retrieves them at runtime. Another does some analysis on the rules (Hour 12, "Working with the WF RuleSet").

`RuleSets` can be added to a workflow via the `Policy` activity, which has a `RuleSetReference` property that binds a `RuleSet` to a `Policy` activity. The `Policy` activity then executes the `RuleSet` from the workflow.

See Hour 2 for more details on Declarative Rule Conditions and Code Conditions. See Hour 12 for more details on `RuleSets`.

Custom Activities

This section first describes the reason for custom activities and then describes their technical characteristics.

Reason for Custom Activities

You are not limited to the OOB activities in WF. You can create your own. Creating custom activities is as core to WF as any other capability.

This section discusses three reasons to create custom activities: to improve on an OOB activity for usability reasons, to create domain specific activities, and to create custom control flow patterns.

Improve on OOB Activities

In Hour 17, "Learning Advanced Hosting," a third-party created synchronous InvokeWorkflow activity is explored. It is looked at because the OOB InvokeWorkflow activity only calls workflows asynchronously. Many scenarios call for calling workflows and waiting for the called workflow to return a response. Some may even choose to create an entirely new set of OOB activities. Improving the OOB activities is a viable scenario for custom activity development, but is not anticipated to be the primary motivation behind creating custom activities.

Create Domain-Specific Activities

The OOB activities provide general functionality. They are host agnostic and know nothing about any vertical domains or any individual enterprise. Many who use WF will find that its value grows proportionally to the amount of domain activities added. If, for example, you want to use WF to model the credit process, you could use the OOB activities for control flow and then augment them with standard code to perform the actual credit process. Alternatively, you could create Customer, CheckCredit, SendNotification, and other custom activities that augment the credit process. Figure 1.18 shows custom activities on a toolbox, and Figure 1.19 shows the custom Customer activity on a workflow and its properties.

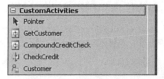

FIGURE 1.18
CustomActivities toolbox.

FIGURE 1.19
Customer cus-
tom activity on
workflow and its
properties.

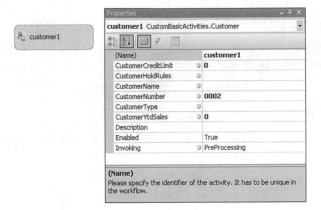

Create Custom Control Flow Patterns

A large portion of WF's utensil and ability to attract a wide range of authors is predicated on there being control flow activities that simplify modeling the respective
process. The CAG activity, for instance, makes it possible to model data-driven workflows. The StateMachineWorkflow (workflows are themselves activities) allows for an
event-driven style of workflows to be modeled. When nondevelopers are included as
authors, there needs to be control flow activities appropriate for them.

Types of Custom Activities

Five types of custom activities exist in WF: basic, long-running, event-driven, control
flow, and compound.

Basic activities are similar to standard components. They are called, and then execute, complete their work, and return in a finished state. A sample basic activity is a
Customer activity that retrieves customer data. When creating a basic custom activity, you will override its execute method to tell it what to do. You may optionally also
customize the activity's appearance, add it to the toolbox, and validate it. The next
code snippet shows the code from the custom Customer activity discussed in the last
section (variable declarations are omitted for brevity). You will create custom basic
activities in Hour 20.

```
[Designer(typeof(CustomerDesigner), typeof(IDesigner))]
[ToolboxBitmap(typeof(Customer), "Resources.Customer.jpg")]
public partial class Customer : System.Workflow.ComponentModel.Activity
  {
     protected override ActivityExecutionStatus
Execute(ActivityExecutionContext executionContext)
     {
```

```
            // Perform preprocessing.
            base.RaiseEvent(Customer.InvokingEvent, this, EventArgs.Empty);

            SqlConnection dbConn = new SqlConnection(ConnectionString);
            SqlCommand getCustomer = new SqlCommand("GetCustomer", dbConn);

            getCustomer.CommandType = System.Data.CommandType.StoredProcedure;
            getCustomer.Parameters.AddWithValue("@CustomerNumber",
CustomerNumber);

            dbConn.Open();


            using (SqlDataReader custReader =
getCustomer.ExecuteReader(CommandBehavior.CloseConnection))
                {
                    if (custReader.Read())
                    {
                        CustomerName = custReader["CustomerName"].ToString().Trim();
                        CustomerCreditLimit =
double.Parse(custReader["CustomerCreditLimit"].ToString());
                        CustomerType = custReader["CustomerType"].ToString().Trim();
                        CustomerYtdSales =
double.Parse(custReader["CustomerYtdSales"].ToString());
                        CustomerHoldRules =
custReader["CustomerHoldRules"].ToString().Trim();
                    }
                }

            Console.WriteLine
                ("The customer number is: " + CustomerNumber);
            Console.WriteLine
                ("The customer name is: " + CustomerName);
            Console.WriteLine
                ("The customer credit limit is: " + CustomerCreditLimit);
            Console.WriteLine
                ("The customer type is: " + CustomerType);
            Console.WriteLine
                ("The customer YTD sales is: " + CustomerYtdSales);
            Console.WriteLine
                ("The customer hold rules is: " + CustomerHoldRules);
            return ActivityExecutionStatus.Closed;

        }
    }
```

Following is a summary of the additional custom activity types in WF. These activities build on the steps necessary to create a basic activity.

Long-running activities do not complete on initial call. They continue processing on another thread. They return control to the workflow while the processing occurs. When the processing completes on the other thread, the long-running activity notifies the workflow that it is complete (via WF's internal queuing system). The same Customer activity can also be coded as a long-running activity. The reason is that if the database call to retrieve the customer information was to a local database and was fast, it would make sense to do all work in the execute method. If the call was across the firewall and not so fast, it might be better to return control before the customer data is retuned. Hour 21, "Creating Queued Activities," demonstrates modifying the `Customer` activity, shown in the previous code listing, that currently executes in one part to execute in two distinct parts.

Event-driven custom activities can wait for external events inside of a `Listen` or other activity. Custom event-driven activities are described in Hour 22, "Creating Typed Queued and `EventDriven`-Enabled Activities."

Composite or control flow activities, as previously mentioned, allow you to create your own control flow patterns. These activities are responsible for determining which child activities should execute and then scheduling them for execution. Creating custom composite activities is discussed in Hour 23, "Creating Control Flow Activities Session 1," and Hour 24, "Creating Control Flow Activities Session 2."

A compound activity is prepopulated with other activities. It is useful when a pattern of activities is commonly used. Figure 1.20 demonstrates a `CreditCheck` compound activity that uses the custom `Customer` activity to retrieve customer data; then it uses the `CheckCredit` activity to determine if the customer is on credit hold. Finally, it evaluates the return results in an `IfElse` activity. The left branch processes the order, and the right branch rejects it. You will create this compound activity in Hour 20.

FIGURE 1.20
Compound credit
check activity.

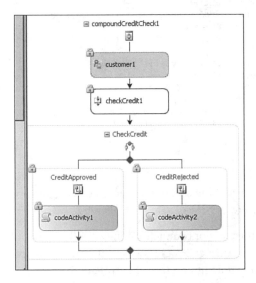

All noncomposite activities derive (directly or indirectly) from `System.Workflow.ComponentModel.Activity`. Composite activities all derive from

`System.Workflow.ComponentModel.CompositeActivity`. These are the same classes the BAL activities derive from.

Custom activities are covered in Hours 20 to 24.

XAML Workflows and Serialization

XAML (pronounced "ZAML") is an XML language used in both WF and WPF. It allows a hierarchal collection of objects, their relation to .NET types, and input and output data to be described. In WF, XAML can be used to describe the tree of workflow activities, the .NET types that encapsulate the logic, and the data sent to and received from the activities. In WPF it does the same for the user interface controls.

WF supports specifying the tree of activities in both code and XAML. Why the need for XAML? As an XML dialect, XAML receives the benefits of the investment being made in XML by Microsoft and others. These investments include the capability to store XAML workflows in SQL Server. WF will load a XAML workflow at runtime without requiring precompilation. If the workflows are expressed in XAML, each workflow instance can be stored in a database. Calculating the difference to the baseline process and between individual workflows is as simple as using XSLT, XQUERY, or other XML manipulation languages.

If no compilation occurs, can't invalid workflows be loaded? No, WF's validation capability, which you learn about in Hours 15 and 24, validates workflows when they are loaded. It checks the workflow for structural fidelity. You are free to extend the validation on any workflow to add business-specific checks, such as if a `BankBeginTransfer` activity exists on the workflow, ensuring there is also a `BankEndTransfer` activity.

As a whole, storing workflow models in a database and then retrieving them at runtime to execute is a compelling possibility. The capability to then store each workflow instance is also compelling.

No matter what format you choose, the graphical workflows are saved in a format that can be seen and edited. This means you can modify the code directly if needed.

The next listing shows a simple workflow with one `Code` activity expressed in XAML. The one immediately following shows the same workflow expressed in code. If you are familiar with Windows Forms development, you will notice that the code representation matches the format of a Windows Forms application.

```
<SequentialWorkflowActivity x:Name="Workflow2XOMLOnly"
    xmlns:x="http://schemas.microsoft.com/winfx/2006/xaml"
    xmlns="http://schemas.microsoft.com/winfx/2006/xaml/workflow">
```

```
    <DelayActivity TimeoutDuration="00:00:00" x:Name="delayActivity1" />
</SequentialWorkflowActivity>.
```

The same workflow expressed in code:

```
        this.CanModifyActivities = true;
        this.delayActivity1 = new System.Workflow.Activities.DelayActivity();
        //
        // delayActivity1
        //
        this.delayActivity1.Name = "delayActivity1";
        this.delayActivity1.TimeoutDuration =
System.TimeSpan.Parse("00:00:00");
        //
        // Workflow2
        //
        this.Activities.Add(this.delayActivity1);
        this.Name = "Workflow2";
        this.CanModifyActivities = false;
```

XAML workflows and serialization are covered in Hour 2.

Dynamic Update

Two of WF's primary goals are to support long-running processes and to provide increased process agility. One common denominator to both these goals is the ability to evolve processes. It is a simple fact that processes change. If software cannot handle it, the changes are implemented out-of-band. This not only diminishes the efficiency of the process itself but reduces reporting accuracy because the data used to compile reports does not include the out-of-band operations. With dynamic update, activities can be added and removed from workflows (a change can be implemented via an add-remove combination). Declarative rules can also be changed.

The next code listing demonstrates adding a Delay activity to a workflow. The details will be covered in Hour 15, "Working Dynamic Update," but this is all the code necessary to change a running workflow.

```
        // use WorkflowChanges class to author dynamic change and pass
        // it a reference to the current Workflow Instance
        WorkflowChanges workflowTochange = new WorkflowChanges(this);

        // Crete a new Delay, initialized to 2 seconds
        DelayActivity delayOrder = new DelayActivity();
        delayOrder.Name = "delayOrder";
        delayOrder.TimeoutDuration = new TimeSpan(0, 0, 2);

        // Insert the Delay Activity to the TransientWorkflow collection
        // (the workspace) between the two Code Activities
        workflowTochange.TransientWorkflow.Activities.Insert(1, delayOrder);
```

```
// Replace the original Workflow Instance with the clone
this.ApplyWorkflowChanges(workflowTochange);
```

Although the capability to change a running workflow is powerful, it is also unnerving. WF has controls in place to make changing running workflows more palatable. The first is that each workflow can be set to stipulate when and if dynamic update should be permitted. The default is always. Workflows have a `DynamicUpdateCondition` property (Figure 1.21 shows it set to a Declarative Rule Condition). This property can be set to determine when and if dynamic update should be permitted. If you want to disallow it completely, return `false` from the Condition property. If you want to selectively permit it, for example, to be allowed at one part of the workflow that changes from instance to instance, apply the appropriate condition.

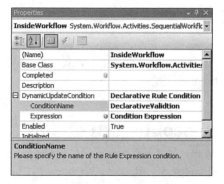

FIGURE 1.21
Declarative
update rule con-
dition.

The second is that two ways exist to store per-workflow instance changes. If using XAML workflows, each instance can be saved to a database and changes can be compared to other instances and to the baseline process. If trends are noticed, the baseline process can be changed. If using tracking, it will store the changes, and the mechanism you use for displaying tracking information can include them. The WorkflowMonitor SDK application, for instance, will show changes made when viewing the workflow instances. It is not always appropriate to view each and every workflow. However, if you store each XAML workflow instance in a database or use tracking, the information is there and available to report on.

The third is that WF's validation is called when dynamic update changes are applied. This prevents erroneous changes from being made to running workflow instances.

Dynamic update is an extremely powerful feature that goes hand-in-hand with WF's per-instance tracking capabilities. It seems feasible that processes will continually be changed going forward with WF and controlled with strong reporting tools that leverage tracking. The capability to change running workflows is common in BPMSs, and

WF provides a solid set of tools to do it and build even more powerful solutions to change running workflows and track these changes.

XAML and dynamic update can appear to overlap. XAML can be loaded at runtime without precompilation but cannot be changed on a running workflow. XAML is good for tools and for database loading. Dynamic update is used to change an actual running process. Dynamic update can be performed on workflows expressed in either XAML or code. Rules are a little different. Declarative rules (those expressed in `.rules` files) are also more tool friendly than their code counterparts and can also be loaded without precompilation, which makes database storage compelling. Only declarative rules can be changed with dynamic update, though. Hour 13 demonstrates loading declarative rules from a database. Hour 15 covers Dynamic Update.

WF and WCF

The first subsection in this section provides an overview of WCF and conceptually describes using WF and WCF together. The second subsection discusses the product features that integrate the two.

WF and WCF: Conceptual Overview

WCF, WF's counterpart in the .NET 3.x Framework, is Microsoft's preferred technology for hosting and accessing network endpoints. WCF and WF have a symbiotic relationship. By leveraging WCF's core strengths, WF workflows can be securely and reliably exposed across the network. WF workflows can also access network endpoints. Let's look at a couple of examples. If you have a workflow that performs a credit check, and you want to expose it to clients within and across the firewall, you can expose it as a WCF service. Likewise, if you wanted to access a remote service to receive a client's credit score from a workflow, you would use WCF to access the remote service from the workflow. A workflow hosted by a WCF host is referred to as a WorkflowService.

WCF provides one programming model and runtime for distributed computing on the Microsoft platform. It subsumes all previous Microsoft distributed technologies, including web services, web service enhancements, .NET remoting, and enterprise services. WCF supplies the most thorough web service standard support on the Microsoft platform. WCF can listen for and access network endpoints via HTTP, TCP, named pipes, and just about any other protocol.

WCF services (endpoints) are protocol and host agnostic. For example, a service communicating across the firewall can choose the WCF HTTP binding, which sends standard SOAP over HTTP using basic security. If the service needs additional security, it can use WCF's sibling HTTP binding that includes WS* (special web service security) security. Finally a service communicating behind the firewall can utilize the TCP binding that uses compiled SOAP. Therefore, the same service can support all three communication patterns. There simply needs to be one WCF endpoint created for each communization pattern the service supports.

WCF separates the service (the application logic) from the endpoint. The service can be implemented in standard .NET code or as a WF workflow. It is up to you to choose whether to use standard .NET code or a workflow to provide the service logic. Leveraging WCF, WF could expose the same workflow over HTTP to remote clients and TCP to local clients.

Like WF, WCF can be hosted in any .NET 2.0 plus application domain, such as a Windows Service, IIS, or Windows Activation Service (IIS in Windows Server 2008) process. Unlike WF, there is a WCF project type for IIS that simplifies hosting in IIS. This enables WCF services to take advantage of IIS's message-based activation, security, process pooling, and other capabilities. There really is no reason not to use WCF for distributed computing on the Microsoft platform.

WF and WCF: Integration Specifics

Two activities are designed to support WF-WCF integration: Receive and Send. The first is used when exposing a WF workflow as a WCF endpoint. The second is used to access a remote client from a WF workflow. The Send activity is host agnostic—it can be called from any WF host. The Receive activity is not. It can be used only when WF is hosted by WCF.

The remote client does not actually have to be a WCF client. It just must be exposed using a protocol and binding that WCF can communicate with (see Hour 19).

By the Way

There are also two WCF workflow projects in Visual Studio 2008 (Figure 1.22). The first contains a sequential workflow project and a WCF contract (interface). The second holds state machine workflows and an accompanying contract. These project types are relevant when exposing a workflow as a service.

The Send and Receive activities are very powerful. They both provide synchronous and asynchronous communication capabilities. The Send activity has a very similar structure to a method call: expected return type, method to call, and parameters to pass. The Receive activity has a very similar structure to a called method. The WF

FIGURE 1.22
WCF Project
types.

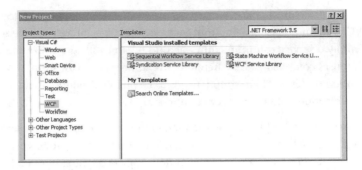

communication activities made available in the .NET Framework 3.0 do not offer such a natural way to call out from and into a workflow.

Many prefer to host all WF workflows in WCF for the following reasons: the robust communication implementation of the Send and Receive activities, the IIS and Windows Activation Services hosting support offered to WCF, Microsoft's apparent emphasis toward WCF as WF's hosting apparatus, especially going forward and the expectation that WF and WCF will continue to be interweaved until they look like one.

WCF and WF integration is discussed in Hour 19, "Learning WF-WCF Integration."

SharePoint Workflow

This section on SharePoint workflow and the next on designer rehosting and external modeling discuss topics not covered in later hours. They are discussed in this hour because they are important to the overall WF vision and understanding them will help you understand WF's goals. SharePoint workflow is not covered because it is not part of the base WF product. It is built on top of the base WF. Following the hands-on labs would also require that you install SharePoint, which is no small task. The reasons for not including designer rehosting and external modeling in a subsequent hour are described in the next section.

This section contains three subsections. The first provides a conceptual overview of SharePoint workflow, the next describes the Visual Studio version of SharePoint workflow, and the last the SharePoint Designer version.

SharePoint Workflow Overview

SharePoint is Microsoft's collaboration, document management, and general information environment. Many companies use SharePoint to implement departmental and event-specific sites for groups of people to share information and work together.

A common site may have document libraries, tasks, form libraries, a calendar, and other data specific to the site's purpose (Figure 1.23). SharePoint can also be described as a portal. SharePoint also features business intelligence and much more. For our purposes, SharePoint is an information hub where groups of people collaborate.

FIGURE 1.23
Sample Share-
Point site home
page.

Workflow is a common requirement for SharePoint because the vast information in it needs to be routed. Expense reports and documents stored in it, for example, need to be approved, rejected, and escalated. SharePoint tasks (which can be integrated with Outlook tasks) also provide a great destination for workflows to assign work. If Jane, for instance, must approve John's expense report, a task can be assigned to Jane. Jane can then access this task in her SharePoint or Outlook task list, or, depending on configuration, it may be emailed to her.

SharePoint can be customized by both technically savvy business users and developers. One of its selling points is that its sites and other items can be created and configured without the need for IT. There are three levels of customization performed in SharePoint. The first is performed via SharePoint configuration forms, the second is performed in the SharePoint Designer, and the third in code. For the most part, both users and developers can configure SharePoint via the forms. SharePoint Designer (FrontPage's replacement) configuration is generally performed by power users. Changes requiring code are performed by developers.

SharePoint workflow features both Visual Studio and SharePoint Designer workflow authoring options. Additional custom activities are targeted at the SharePoint host in both offerings. A tighter relationship exists between the workflow and the forms used to collect its data. The most common forms are task and initiation. The first is used to collection information for tasks that are assigned by the workflow. Remember that approval requests, for example, are assigned via tasks. The second is used when the workflow is started to collect information. SharePoint Workflow (in the Microsoft Office SharePoint Server offering) also includes a number of OOB workflows that support approval and other common scenarios. They are highly flexible and good to work with to get an idea of the types of workflows that can be created in SharePoint work-flow.

SharePoint Workflow Visual Studio

In Visual Studio SharePoint workflow, developers use the same Visual Studio environment used in standard WF development. The main difference is a collection of additional activities tailored to the SharePoint host. A couple of project templates also reference SharePoint assemblies and simplify deployment to the SharePoint host. Figure 1.24 demonstrates the Visual Studio SharePoint workflow. The toolbox shown is specifically for SharePoint. It contains a number of task-centric and other activities specific to the SharePoint host.

FIGURE 1.24
SharePoint
Visual Studio
Project.

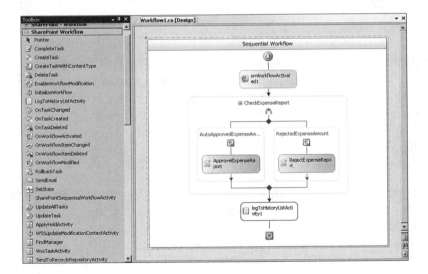

The capability to add a collection of custom activities specific to a domain, in this case the SharePoint domain, makes WF much more useful. It is also demonstrates how effectively you can extend WF by adding a collection of activities specific to your business and/or host. The SharePoint custom activities are used in addition to the BAL activities. WF's BAL activities provide the general control flow and other generic capabilities, and the SharePoint custom activities provide host-specific functionality.

SharePoint Workflow SharePoint Designer

The Visual Studio version of SharePoint workflow allows developers to create work-flows to run in SharePoint. However, SharePoint allows technically savvy business users to customize many aspects of SharePoint. Consistent with this premise, workflows can also be designed in the SharePoint Designer. The SharePoint Designer includes a similar collection of activities to that found in Visual Studio SharePoint workflow and packages them in a different design environment. Figure 1.25 shows the SharePoint Designer workflow designer.

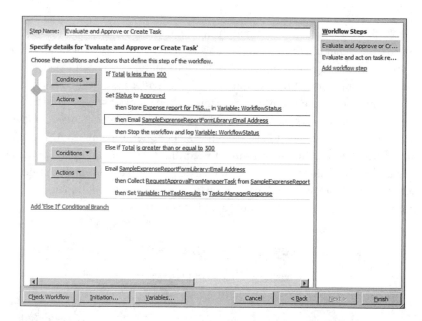

FIGURE 1.25
SharePoint Designer workflow.

It is rules driven because Microsoft thought it preferable to a graphical one, which is a controversial decision. However, the big picture is that it takes a similar set of base functionality and exposes it in a different designer targeted at a less technical user. Custom activities can be added to the SharePoint Designer as well. Adding a collection of domain-specific custom activities to this designer significantly increases the potential for technically savvy business people to create workflows by themselves. The SharePoint Designer saves the workflow in a XAML format, which is then loaded by WF and executed.

Designer Rehosting and External Modeling

At times you may need to graphically create workflows outside of Visual Studio and graphically monitor and interact with them at runtime. The most common reason to author workflows outside of Visual Studio is to allow nondevelopers to author workflows. There will almost always be a need for a collection of domain-specific custom activities in addition to the custom authoring experience if business users are to create workflows. There are two ways workflows can be authored outside of Visual Studio. The first, referred to as designer rehosting, permits the design tools used to create workflows in Visual Studio to be rehosted in another application. The second is to use an external modeling tool to produce a workflow model that can be executed by the WF runtime.

Figure 1.26 shows the workflow designer hosted in a Windows Forms application. If the current designer is sufficient and you want the authoring performed outside of Visual Studio, rehosting the designer is likely appropriate. The design experience consists of a combination of the designer and the activities used in the designer. For instance, moving the Code activity to a custom designer does not eliminate the need to write code to support its execution. You should therefore use or create activities appropriate for those targeted to use the rehosted designer. You can even create custom control flow activities if you think the configuration requirements of the OOB ones are not appropriate to your target audience. The WorkflowMonitor application (looked at in the "Tracking" section) demonstrates rehosting the designer for monitoring and interacting with running and previously executed workflows.

FIGURE 1.26
Workflow designer rehosted in a Windows Forms application.

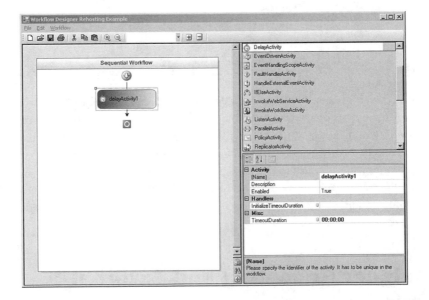

If there is a need for an entirely difference experience, then using a different tool altogether is probably more appropriate than rehosting the designer. Maybe Visio has the required authoring tools because that is what the business people know. Maybe a rules-driven designer, such as the SharePoint Designer, is called for.

When rehosting the designer, you can also include its serialization tools to create the XAML or code, depending on which format you choose. When using external tools, it is up to you to serialize the information, which will almost always be to XAML.

Designer rehosting and using an external modeling tool are not covered in this book. They are included in this hour because they are important to WF's overall vision, but they are advanced topics, especially external modeling. By the end of this book, you will have experience in custom activity authoring (to create your domain activities) and WF in general, readying you for one of these two alternative authoring options. I will post a sample of external modeling that I have worked on some on my blog at www.reassociates. net and will try to do the same for designer rehosting. You can also see http://msdn. microsoft.com/en-us/library/aa480213.aspx for an example of designer rehosting.

> The business users do not have to create an executable workflow. It is possible to allow them to lay out the process using a rehosted designer or external modeling tool. Their work can then be loaded by a developer and completed. This may be a better approach, in some cases, than producing static requirements that are not leverageable by the developer who created the process or not connected to the final executable application in any way.

By the Way

Summary

This hour first outlined workflow in general, discussed common workflow categorizations, and looked at BPMSs. It then provided a brief overview of WF. Then it covered a number of WF's capabilities. Let's now look at six of the main benefits offered by WF, having gone through its capabilities:

- ▶ **Design-time transparency**—This is intrinsic because the workflow that executes also graphically describes the process.

- ▶ **Runtime transparency**—The tracking infrastructure and tools built to leverage the infrastructure supply visibility to running processes.

- ▶ **Runtime flexibility**—XAML allows processes to be run without precompilation and be retrieved from databases, and dynamic update allows processes to be changed at runtime.

- ▶ **State management**—The workflow keeps track of the current step, idles and persists as necessary, restarts when appropriate, and can even skip or redo steps.

- ▶ **Domain-specific languages**—Domain-specific languages can be created by adding a collection of custom activities and potentially a customer designer to go along.

▶ **Participate in network**—WF's integration with WCF permits it to expose itself across the network and to access network (cloud) services securely and reliably.

These benefits combine to form a better way to create application logic.

The rest of this book consists of explanations and accompanying labs that walk you through most areas of WF.

Installation Instructions

You should install Visual Studio 2008 and .NET Framework 3.5 to follow along with the hands-on labs in this book. If you are using Visual Studio 2005 and .NET Framework 3.0, you will not be able to complete the hands-on exercises in Hour 19, "Learning WF-WCF Integration." There are also other minor incompatibilities. The two known differences, creating projects and dependency properties, are pointed out the first time they are encountered.

You should also install the WF, WCF, and CardSpace samples that can be found at http://msdn2.microsoft.com/en-us/library/ms741706.aspx. These samples include the aforementioned WorkflowMonitor application that is used in exercises in various hours. These samples are also generally useful for you to explore and are referred to for topics not covered in the book or to obtain more information on topics that are covered.

To follow the hands-on labs, download the samples from my website at www.reassociates.net. I recommend that you unzip them to your root directory to create the following directory structure: `c:\SamsWf24hrs\Hours`. Each hour and the associated labs will be appended to the base directory. Retaining this structure will make it easier to follow the labs. Each hour will have at least one completed solution in a Completed subdirectory. Many will have more granular solutions to help you follow along throughout the hour. See the readme.txt file included in the root directory of each hour's labs for details for each hour.

See the next section for Visual Studio 2005 installation instructions and the one immediately following for Visual Studio 2008 instructions.

Visual Studio 2005 and .NET Framework 3.0 Installation Directions

Visual Studio 2005 and the .NET Framework 3.0 require the following to be installed:

▶ Windows 2003, XP, or Vista. (The .NET Framework 3.0 should already be installed if you have Vista.)

- SQL Server or Express 2000 or later.

- SQL Server Management Studio for SQL Express or SQL Server.

- Visual Studio 2005.

- .NET Framework 3.0 runtime components available at www.microsoft.com/downloads/details.aspx?FamilyID=10CC340B-F857-4A14-83F5-25634C3BF043&displaylang=en.

- Windows SDK for Vista and the .NET framework 3.0: http://www.microsoft.com/downloads/details.aspx?familyid=C2B1E300-F358-4523-B479-F53D234CDCCF&displaylang=en.

- Visual Studio extensions for the .NET Framework 3.0 (Windows Workflow Foundation): www.microsoft.com/downloads/details.aspx?familyid=5d61409e-1fa3-48cf-8023-e8f38e709ba6&displaylang=en.

Visual Studio 2008 and .NET Framework 3.5 Installation Requirements/Directions

- Windows 2003, XP, or Vista.

- SQL Server or Express 2000 or later.

- SQL Server Management Studio for SQL Express or SQL Server.

- Visual Studio 2008 and the .NET Framework 3.5. (The .NET Framework 3.5 should be included with Visual Studio 2008.)

HOUR 2

A Spin Around Windows Workflow Foundation

What You'll Learn in This Hour:

▶ Creating a workflow with basic activities and rules

▶ Adding parameters to a workflow

▶ Creating a XAML + code workflow

▶ Creating XAML-only workflows

In this hour, you will create a sequential workflow using selected Base Activity Library (BAL) activities. You add both code conditions and declarative rules and run and debug the workflow. Then you re-create the workflow as a code-separated workflow, edit the XAML, and run it from the console host as an XML text reader.

As this hour's name implies, its intent is to give you a basic understanding of many of WF's features.

Creating a Basic Workflow

The basic concept of developing a workflow is covered in this section. This will be expanded on in later hours when, among other items, you learn more about advanced host-workflow data exchange options and workflow events. The goal here is to get you up to speed with the WF basics.

Creating a Workflow Project

There are six workflow project types in Visual Studio. The most basic, the Empty Workflow Project, references the workflow DLLs, adds some namespace declarations, and enables the workflow debugger. All other workflow projects build on this project.

There are two sequential workflow projects. The Sequential Workflow Console Host project creates a console host for the workflow. Generally, you will use this project type when creating a simple project or for testing purposes. The Sequential Workflow Library creates a workflow but no host. Separating the workflows from the host is usually a good idea because it makes it easier to reuse workflows across multiple hosts. There are two state machine workflow projects as well that follow the sequential workflow project pattern. Finally, there is a workflow activity project type that is used to create custom activities.

If you have problems debugging workflows, it may be because your project was created from a non-workflow project that manually referenced the WF assemblies.

By the Way

If you're using Visual Studio 2005, expand the Project Types and select Workflow instead of selecting C# first in step 2.

Use the following steps to create a Sequential Workflow Console Application project now:

1. Start Visual Studio 2008. Select File, New, Project.

2. Expand the Visual C# project templates and select Workflow.

3. Select the Sequential Workflow Console Application project template.

4. Enter **FirstWorkflowProject** as the Name.

5. Enter or browse to C:\SamsWf24hrs\Hours\Hour02ASpinAroundWF for the Location.

   Your screen should now match Figure 2.1.

6. Select OK.

FIGURE 2.1
The New Project dialog.

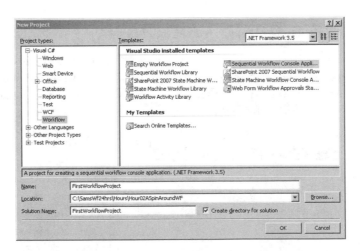

You have now created a Sequential Workflow Console Project.

> Remember to substitute your path if you are not using `C:\SamsWf24hrs\Hours\` as the root for your exercises in this book.

Building and Running a Workflow

In the next subsection you add activities to the workflow. In the immediately following seciton, you will learn to pause the host application so that you can see results printed to the console by the workflow.

Adding Activities to the Workflow

The workflow is a class, or two partial classes. One class holds the activities. The other holds the code-beside logic for these controls. By default, one file with a `.cs` extension (`Workflow1.cs`) contains the code-beside logic and another, named `.designer.cs`, holds the activities on the workflow. This structure is the same as for a form in a Windows Forms application. The activities may also be stored in XML, as will be discussed later in the "Examining the Project Files" section.

1. Right-click `Workflow1.cs` in the Solution Explorer and select View Code to open the workflow in code view. You will see some namespace declarations and a `Workflow1` class with a constructor. The constructor is the method with the same name as the class. Again, this is very similar to what you would see in the code-behind section of a form in a Windows Forms application.

2. Double-click `Workflow1.cs` in the Solution Explorer to open the workflow in design mode (see Figure 2.2). This is the `designer.cs` file being opened by the

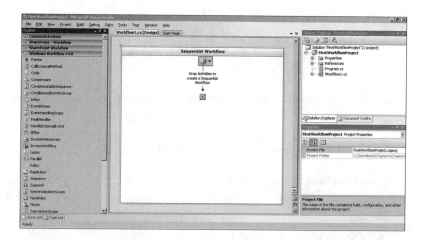

FIGURE 2.2
Workflow designer and toolbox with BAL activities.

workflow designer. I will refer to this as design mode throughout the book. The combination of the two—the `.cs` and the `designer.cs` form—represent the entire workflow class.

3. Select View, Toolbox and click the + to the left of the Windows Workflow v3.0 section to bring up the BAL activities (they are also visible in the left portion of Figure 2.2) that you will drag and drop onto the workflow and then set their properties. If the tack is not pointing down, click it to pin them. This way they will remain in place when you move your cursor away from the Toolbox.

4. The properties of the currently selected activity (or workflow if none is selected) are displayed in the Properties window, and the project files are displayed in the Solution Explorer. The Solution Explorer can be seen in the upper-right section and the Properties Window in the lower-right section of Figure 2.2.

5. Drag and drop a `Code` activity onto the workflow.

6. Click the `Code` activity and view its properties in the Property window. Click View, Properties Window, if it is not showing. The `Name`, `Description`, and `Enabled` properties are common to all activities. `Enabled` is particularly useful because it allows you to retain activities that do not execute on a workflow, which frequently comes in handy. It is equivalent to commenting out code. The `ExecuteCode` property, on the other hand, is specific to the `Code` activity. It points to a handler that executes when the `Code` activity is executed. Figure 2.3 shows the `Code` activity properties.

FIGURE 2.3
Code activity
property window.

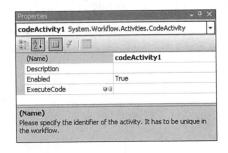

7. Double-click the `Code` activity to create an event handler, and enter the code in the next code snippet:

```
Console.WriteLine("The time is {0}",
    DateTime.Now.ToLongTimeString());
```

8. Open the workflow in design mode and drag and drop a `Delay` activity below the `Code` activity onto the workflow and set its `TimeoutDuration` property to `00:00:10`.

9. Add another `Code` activity below the `Delay` activity, double-click it to get to its handler, and add the same code to its handler that you added to the preceding code activity's handler.

Your workflow should now look like Figure 2.4. (If there are red exclamation marks, click them to see the errors, and then fix them.)

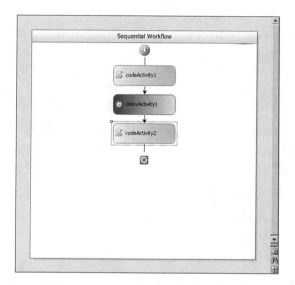

FIGURE 2.4
First workflow.

You have seen the two views of the workflow. The workflow designer is where you graphically create and view workflows. The code-beside is where you write code to support the activities on the workflow and add variables among other tasks. The workflow designer is analogous to the graphical view of a Windows Form, and the code-beside is analogous to the code-behind of a Windows Form.

Pausing the Host

Add steps to pause the host so that you can see the text printed to the console by the workflow:

1. Double-click `Program.cs` in the Solutions Explorer and insert the lines of code shown in the next code snippet below the line that has `waitHandle.WaitOne()` on it so that the content written to the console will not disappear before you can see it:

```
// Pause the display
Console.WriteLine("Press enter to continue.");
Console.Read();
```

> `Program.cs` is the *console host*. We just added a couple of lines to force the host to pause and allow us to see the text printed to the console when the workflow completes. We cover hosting in more detail in Hours 3 and 17. In this hour, we are relying on the default host outside of these minor changes and a couple of parameters we'll add shortly.

Building and Debugging the Workflow

Building and debugging a workflow solution is the same as any .NET solution with the one exception that you can insert breakpoints on workflow activities. When debugging, you can use the standard F5, F10, and F11 (start, step over, step into) keys. You can step from workflow activities into workflow code and back out to workflow activities. This is part of the developer-friendly design experience provided by WF.

You will run the workflow three times in this exercise. The first time you will run it with no debugging. The second time you will insert a breakpoint on the first Code activity and step into the code. The third time you will set the breakpoint in the code.

Let's go through the steps to build and run the workflow now:

1. Press F5 to build and run the solution (remember to wait 10 seconds for the Delay activity to complete before the second line prints).

2. You should see the results shown in Figure 2.5.

3. Double-click Workflow1 in the Solution Explorer to open the workflow in design mode.

4. Right-click the first Code activity and select Breakpoint, Insert Breakpoint from the drop-down menu.

FIGURE 2.5
First workflow results.

5. Press F5 again and notice that the workflow pauses at the breakpoint (see Figure 2.6).

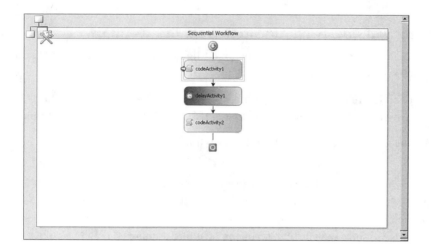

FIGURE 2.6
Workflow
stopped on
breakpoint.

6. Press F11 to step in to the Code activity's handler code.

7. Notice that you are placed in the source code that you entered. You may step though it and the workflow activities using the standard F10/F11/F5 .NET debugging keys.

8. When you're finished stepping through, select the first Code activity and remove its breakpoint by right-clicking it and selecting Breakpoint, Delete Breakpoint.

9. Double-click the second Code activity and set a standard .NET breakpoint on the first line of its handler's source code by left-clicking on the margin or pressing F9.

10. Run the workflow with F5 again and notice that it stops at the breakpoint.

11. Step through the workflow as you want.

12. When you're finished, remove the breakpoints you set on the second Code activity and in the code-beside file.

Enhancing the Workflow

In this section, we will add an IfElse activity to the workflow. The IfElse activity can be thought of as a switch statement with a break inserted in each branch to ensure that it exits after the first `true` result is returned. Ensuring the correct `IfElseBranch` executes requires that we delve into rules.

Adding and Removing Activities from the Workflow

1. Open `workflow1` in design mode and drag and drop an `IfElse` activity any-where on the workflow.

2. Drop the first `Code` activity on the workflow into the left branch of the `IfElse` activity and the second `Code` activity on the workflow into the right branch.

3. Delete the `Delay` activity from the workflow.

Click the left branch of the `IfElse` activity. It is named ifElseBranchActivity1. Each branch of an `IfElse` activity contains an `IfElseBranch` activity, which are them-selves activities. The activities inserted in `IfElse` activities are identical (with slight differences not now relevant) to `Sequence` activities. Sequence activities, like the sequential workflow you are now creating, act as containers for other activities. If you like, add a `Sequence` activity to the workflow and add other activities to it. Now delete the `Sequence` activity and other activities you added. The significance of the `IfElse` being a container for `IfElseBranch` activities that are, in turn, containers for other activities will become evident as we build workflows throughout this book.

Adding a Rule Condition

Let's go though the steps to create a Code Condition.

1. Click the first red exclamation mark in the `IfElse` activity, then click Property 'Condition' Is Not Set. You will now be into the Condition property, ready to input a rule to determine whether this `IfElseBranch` should execute.

2. In the Properties panel, click the drop-down in the Condition property and select Code Condition.

3. Click the + at the left of the Condition property, enter **CodeBasedCondition** into the Condition property, and press Enter.

   You are placed in the CodeBasedCondition handler.

4. Hard-code the Code Condition to return `true` by entering the following in the handler. (This is how WF returns a Boolean in a condition, and it represents the beginning of many uses of eventargs in WF):

```
e.Result = true;
```

Configuring the Code Activities

Complete the following steps to configure the Code activities.

1. Switch back to the workflow designer by double-clicking Workflow1.cs in the Solution Explorer.

2. Double-click the Code activity in the left branch and insert the following code (the cast is to get the activity name):

```
// Case the sender object to a codeactivity
CodeActivity ca = sender as CodeActivity;

// Print the code activity name
Console.WriteLine("{0} executed in the left branch", ca.Name);
```

3. Now it is time to update the right branch of the IfElse activity (switch back to the workflow designer again).

4. We will leave the condition blank because we want the right branch to act as an else and to always execute if the other branches (branch in this case) do not.

5. Double-click the Code activity in the right branch and replace the current code with:

```
// Case the sender object to a codeactivity
CodeActivity ca = sender as CodeActivity;

// Print the code activity name
Console.WriteLine("{0} executed in the right-hand branch", ca.Name);
```

6. Your workflow should now look like Figure 2.7. See Listing 2.1 directly following for a sample of what your code-beside should look like.

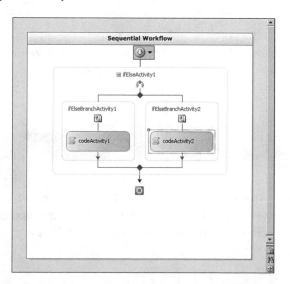

FIGURE 2.7
Enhanced work-flow.

LISTING 2.1   Enhanced Workflow Code Listing

```
namespace FirstWorkflowProject
{
    public sealed partial class Workflow1: SequentialWorkflowActivity
    {
        public Workflow1()
        {
            InitializeComponent();
        }

        private void codeActivity1_ExecuteCode(object sender, EventArgs e)
        {
            // Case the sender object to a codeactivity
            CodeActivity ca = sender as CodeActivity;

            // Print the code activity name
            Console.WriteLine("{0} executed in the left branch"
                              , ca.Name);
        }

        private void codeActivity2_ExecuteCode(object sender, EventArgs e)
        {
            // Case the sender object to a codeactivity
            CodeActivity ca = sender as CodeActivity;

            // Print the code activity name
            Console.WriteLine("{0} executed in the right branch"
                              , ca.Name);
        }

        private void CodeCondition(object sender, ConditionalEventArgs e)
        {
            e.Result = true;
        }
    }
}
```

7. Press F5 to run the workflow. The Code activity in the left branch, that is hard-coded to true, should execute and produce the results shown in Figure 2.8:

Go ahead and play around with the Code Condition if you want. You might set the true to false in the condition handler to see if the right branch executes, for instance. This represents our first entry into a workflow that features controls flow logic.

Improving Workflow Transparency

One reason for using WF is to make programs self-evident. Our current implementation, unfortunately, leaves much room for concern in this quest. All we know is that there is a decision that leads the workflow to take different paths. Let's label our activities to improve workflow comprehensibility. As with all naming schemes, many approaches exist that may, for example, prefix the descriptive names with the type of activity and so on. The purpose of this exercise is solely to show off transparency, not to define an enterprise-level naming convention.

In the next steps, you will change the labels on the workflow activities to improve transparency.

1. Select the IfElse activity and change its name to **CreditEvaluation.**

2. Select the left branch and change its name to **CreditPassed**, and then change the right branch to **CreditFailed.**

3. Rename the Code activity in the left branch **ApproveOrder** and the one in the right branch **RejectOrder.**

4. Look at the workflow to see the improvement. It now serves as a functioning flowchart.

You can now look at the workflow (as shown in Figure 2.9) and see that the purpose of the IfElse activity is to evaluate credit. You can also see which respective paths represent passing and failing credit. The process is now conveyed by looking at the workflow—as it would be if looking at a flowchart.

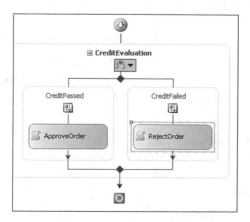

FIGURE 2.9
Workflow with descriptive names.

Passing Parameters to the Workflow

WF can receive a dictionary object as a parameter from the host when a workflow starts, and the host can access the workflow's public properties when the workflow completes; it's very reminiscent of standard method communication patterns. This is done by adding the dictionary object as an additional parameter to the `CreateWorkflow` method. We are going to use this method of communication in this section. However, this method of communication is usually not the preferred way to conduct host-workflow communication. Workflows are frequently long-running and require mid-process communication to, for example, escalate an approval request if not received on time.

Passing parameters as a dictionary object may be appropriate for workflows that do not require mid-process communication (although persistence described in Hour 3, "Learning Basic Hosting," may be a problem) and to augment other communication methods. Maybe setup data exists that must be sent to the workflow and it is most convenient to send it to the workflow at startup. Nothing precludes doing this while also using other methods for mid-process communication. Other methods of communication are covered throughout this book beginning in Hour 4, "Learning Host-Workflow Data Exchange."

By the Way

> .NET 3.5-specific methods of communication that use Windows Communication Foundation are covered in Hour 19, "Learning WF-WCF Integration."

In the steps that follow, we will now change our Code Condition to compare the value passed in from the host to a constant that will be set on the workflow. This way we can run the workflow once with an amount less than and once with an amount larger than the constant and let the Code Condition determine approval or rejection.

We need to modify the host where we will add a dictionary object and add it to the call to run the workflow instance. We need to modify the code-beside by adding a public property with the same name as the dictionary parameter to enable the exchange.

1. Open `Program.cs` and add a parameter above the line that instantiates the `workflowInstance` (starts with `WorkflowInstance instance`) with the following code:

```
// Add the parameters via a dictionary object
Dictionary<string, object> parameters = new Dictionary<string,
object>();
parameters.Add("Amount", 900);
```

2. Add the parameters to the call to the `WorkflowInstance.CreateWorkflow` method by replacing the current line that instantiates the workflow instance with the following code:

```
WorkflowInstance instance = workflowRuntime.CreateWorkflow
(typeof(FirstWorkflowProject.Workflow1),parameters);
```

3. Open `Workflow1` in code view and add a property named `Amount` below the constructor to receive the information passed to the workflow as shown:

```
private int amount;

public int Amount
{
    get { return amount; }
    set { amount = value; }
}
```

4. Add a constant below the property you just added to compare against the incoming value and to determine approval status:

```
// The approval threshold amount.
const int maxAmount = 1000;
```

5. Replace the current content (`e.Result = true;`) of the `CodeBasedCondition` handler with the code shown so that it properly evaluates the amount received from the host to the constant value in the workflow:

```
if (Amount < maxAmount)
    e.Result = true;
else
    e.Result = false;
```

6. Open the workflow in design mode, double-click the `Code` activity in the left branch, and replace the contents in its handler with the following code to reflect its approval:

```
// Case the sender object to a codeactivity
CodeActivity ca = sender as CodeActivity;

// Print the code activity name
Console.WriteLine("Approval: {0} executed in the left-hand branch",
    ca.Name);
```

7. Open the workflow in design mode, double-click the `Code` activity in the right branch, and replace the contents in its handler with the following code to reflect its rejection:

```
// Case the sender object to a codeactivity
CodeActivity ca = sender as CodeActivity;

// Print the code activity name
```

```
Console.WriteLine("Rejection: {0} executed in the right-hand branch",
    ca.Name);
```

8. Press F5 to run the workflow.

   The workflow should approve the request because the value of 900 passed in from the host is less than the 1000 constant specified in the workflow, as shown in Figure 2.10.

FIGURE 2.10
Workflow run with approval returned.

9. Change the Amount parameter in `Program.cs` to 2000 and run the workflow again, which will result in rejection.

By the Way

> You will learn to retrieve information from the workflow when covering the `WorkflowCompleted` event in Hour 3, "Learning Basic Hosting."

Using Declarative Rules

So far you have created Code Conditions to govern workflow control flow. You can also use Declarative Rule Conditions to do the same. Declarative Rules Conditions, or Declarative Rules for short, are stored as XML in `.rules` files. When creating Code Conditions, you write code inside of a handler. When creating Declarative Rules, you use the Rules Dialog editor (unless you write the XML yourself).

The fact that Declarative Rules are stored in XML is important because rules can be changed at runtime without requiring compilation, can be accessed by tools, and even stored in a database. See Hour 12, "Working with the WF `RuleSet`," for more details on rules.

Adding New Activities

Let's perform the next steps to add a third branch to the `IfElse` activity:

1. Right-click between the second `IfElse` branch (Figure 2.11) and the right border of the `IfElse` activity and select Add Branch from the drop-down.

2. Drag (move) the `Code` activity from the middle `IfElse` branch to the newly added third branch.

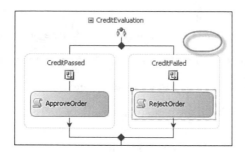

FIGURE 2.11
Add a third branch to an `IfElse` activity.

3. Rename the second branch **ApprovalRequired** and the third branch **CreditFailed**. The workflow should now appear like Figure 2.12:

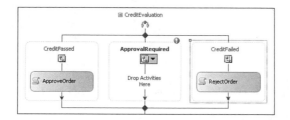

FIGURE 2.12
Workflow with `IfElse` activity with the third branch.

4. Drag and drop a (new) Code activity and insert it in the second branch.

5. Double-click the new Code activity and add the following snippet to its handler:

```
// Case the sender object to a codeactivity
CodeActivity ca = sender as CodeActivity;

// Print the code activity name
Console.WriteLine
("Additional approval required: {0} executed in the middle branch"
            , ca.Name);
```

Creating the Declarative Rule

Let's go though the next steps to create a Declarative Rule Condition.

1. Click the red exclamation mark, and then click Property 'Condition' Is Not Set. You will now be in the `Condition` property, ready to input a rule to determine whether this `IfElseBranch` should execute.

2. Click the drop-down in the `Condition` property and select Declarative Rule Condition.

3. Click the + at the left of the Condition property, enter **DeclarativeRuleCondition** in the ConditionName property, and press Enter.

4. Click the ellipses button in the ConditionName property and click the Edit button.

5. Enter **this.Amount < 2000** into the Rule Condition Editor.

6. You should have the following dialog with the expression you entered in it (see Figure 2.13):

FIGURE 2.13
Declarative Rule editor.

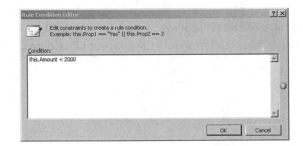

7. Click the OK button twice to save your Declarative Rule and exit both dialogs.

8. Change the Amount in the Dictionary Object in Program.cs to **1200** and run the workflow.

9. You should now see that additional approval is required because the amount is more than 1,000 and less than 2,000, as shown in Figure 2.14.

10. Double-click the .rules file in the Solution Explorer below workflow1.cs. (Expand workflow1.cs, if necessary.)

11. The Declarative Rule you entered is shown in Figure 2.15. It is based on a combination of the CodeDom (.NET code serialization technology) and XML, so it is very verbose. However, you do not need to look at this file very often. It is meant for tools to execute and analyze.

By the Way

The next logical step is to add the logic to require approval when the middle branch (approval required) is executed. This, however, requires in-flight workflow access. You will see examples of how to accomplish this when you work with more advanced host-workflow data exchange techniques, which you will do beginning with Hour 5, "Creating an Escalation Workflow."

FIGURE 2.14
Additional approval results.

```
<RuleDefinitions xmlns="http://schemas.microsoft.com/winfx/2006/xaml/workflow">
  <RuleDefinitions.Conditions>
    <RuleExpressionCondition Name="Condition1">
      <RuleExpressionCondition.Expression>
        <ns0:CodeBinaryOperatorExpression Operator="LessThan" xmlns:ns0="clr-namespace:Sy
          <ns0:CodeBinaryOperatorExpression.Left>
            <ns0:CodePropertyReferenceExpression PropertyName="Amount">
              <ns0:CodePropertyReferenceExpression.TargetObject>
                <ns0:CodeThisReferenceExpression />
              </ns0:CodePropertyReferenceExpression.TargetObject>
            </ns0:CodePropertyReferenceExpression>
          </ns0:CodeBinaryOperatorExpression.Left>
          <ns0:CodeBinaryOperatorExpression.Right>
            <ns0:CodePrimitiveExpression>
              <ns0:CodePrimitiveExpression.Value>
                <ns1:Int32 xmlns:ns1="clr-namespace:System;Assembly=mscorlib, Version=2.0
              </ns0:CodePrimitiveExpression.Value>
            </ns0:CodePrimitiveExpression>
          </ns0:CodeBinaryOperatorExpression.Right>
        </ns0:CodeBinaryOperatorExpression>
      </RuleExpressionCondition.Expression>
    </RuleExpressionCondition>
  </RuleDefinitions.Conditions>
</RuleDefinitions>
```

FIGURE 2.15
Declarative
rules (.rules
file) serialization
format.

Examining the Project Files

We used the default `Workflow1.cs` created by the sequential workflow project template. This generates what is known as a code-only workflow, which means that the controls added to the workflow are contained in a partial class with a `designer.cs` extension. These controls are loaded in the `.cs` portion of the class by a call to `InitializeComponent` in the constructor. This is exactly how a Windows Form is structured. In the next steps, you will walk through the project structure for a project that contains one code-only workflow.

1. Right-click `Workflow1.cs` in the Solution Explorer and choose View Code, which contains the code-beside logic. It is a partial class that augments the workflow and contains the code written in this lab.

2. Double-click `Workflow1.designer.cs` in the Solution Explorer to open it and click the + next to the Designer Generated Code region.
   `Workflow1.designer.cs` is also a partial class (the other half of the `Workflow1` class) that contains the activities added to the workflow. This file is the programmatic representation of the graphical display contained in the workflow designer.

3. For instance, Listing 2.2 contains the code in `Workflow1.designer.cs` that adds a `Code` activity to the workflow:

LISTING 2.2   Add a Code Activity in Code

```
private void InitializeComponent()
{
  // other code
  this.codeActivity2 = new System.Workflow.Activities.CodeActivity();
  this.codeActivity2.Name = "codeActivity2";
  this.codeActivity2.ExecuteCode +=
  new System.EventHandler(this.codeActivity2_ExecuteCode);
```

```
    // it is then added to the IfElse activity that is
    // added to the workflow
    // remmaining code
}
```

4. `Program.cs` represents the host in this example. In most cases the host will be another application because a console application isn't generally a useful place to have long running workflows.

5. As you've already seen, a `.rules` file is created when declarative rules are used, which is completely independent of the type of workflow.

If you prefer you can create the workflow via code. Whether created in code or graphically, the code and designer should remain synchronized, although this is not always the case. Therefore, be prepared to lose the ability to view your workflow if you create it programatically.

Creating a XAML + Code Workflow

The default option is to create a code-only workflow. In this section you learn to add a XAML + code workflow. This will store the workflow activities in XAML, and the code-beside remains in code. The advantage to this route is that the workflows themselves are more accessible by tools. However, there are no real compilation advantages to this option versus its code-only compatriot; both must be compiled.

Adding and Configuring Activities

The next steps walk you through creating a XAML + Code workflow.

1. Right-click FirstWorkflowProject in the Solution Explorer and choose Add, New Item.

2. Select Workflow in the left pane and select the Sequential Workflow (with code separation) item template.

3. Enter `Workflow2XOMLandCode.xoml` into the Name dialog box and click the Add button.

4. You should now have an empty workflow designer form.

5. Drag and drop a `Code` activity, `Delay` activity, and another `Code` activity onto the workflow, in that order.

6. Double-click the first `Code` activity to open its handler and enter the following:

```
Console.WriteLine("In the first code activity.");
```

7. Open Workflow2XOMLandCode in design mode. Then double-click the second Code activity to open its handler and enter the following (be careful to go back to the workflow designer for the new workflow):

```
Console.WriteLine("In the second code activity.");
```

8. Open Workflow2XOMLandCode in design mode. Change the TimeoutDuration on the Delay activity to **00:00:10** seconds.

9. Your workflow should now look like Figure 2.16:

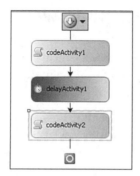

FIGURE 2.16
Workflow2XOMLa-ndCode workflow.

Examining the XAML Workflow

Let's take a look at the XAML workflow in the following steps.

1. Save the project by selecting File, Save All.

2. Open `Workflow2XOMLandCode.xoml` in the XML editor by right-clicking it, selecting Open With, XML Editor, and pressing OK. (Click Yes to dialogs that warn that files are open and request that you save, if you did not click Save, All in the previous step.)

3. The workflow is now expressed in XAML as shown:

```
<SequentialWorkflowActivity
x:Class="FirstWorkflowProject.Workflow2XOMLandCode"
x:Name="Workflow2XOMLandCode"
xmlns:x="http://schemas.microsoft.com/winfx/2006/xaml"
xmlns="http://schemas.microsoft.com/winfx/2006/xaml/workflow">
    <CodeActivity x:Name="codeActivity1"
ExecuteCode="codeActivity1_ExecuteCode" />
    <DelayActivity TimeoutDuration="00:00:10" x:Name="delayActivity1" />
    <CodeActivity x:Name="codeActivity2"
ExecuteCode="codeActivity2_ExecuteCode" />
</SequentialWorkflowActivity>
```

The file `Workflow2XOMLandCode.xoml` would be named
`Workflow2XOMLandCode.designer.cs` if this was a code-only workflow. The workflow

model is now represented in this XAML file rather than in the constructor of a
`.designer.cs` file. The `x:Class="FirstWorklfowProject.Workflow2XOMLandCode"`
points to the code-beside class that supporrs the workflow expressed in XAML.

> As explained in Hour 1, "Understanding Windows Workflow Foundation," the con-
> tents of `.xoml` files are standard XAML; `.xoml` is used so that browsers will not
> attempt to render it.

Running the XAML + Code Workflow

XAML + code workflows are compiled as if they were code-only workflows. Therefore,
the syntax to load and execute them is identical to that of a code-only workflow. The
only change in this section is that you will point the host to `Workflow2XOMLandCode`
instead of `Workflow1` in the next steps.

1. Change the host program to point to the new workflow by replacing the current line that instantiates the workflow instance (the one that starts with
   `WorkflowInstance instance =`) with the code shown next:

   ```
   WorkflowInstance instance =
       workflowRuntime.CreateWorkflow
       (typeof(FirstWorkflowProject. Workflow2XOMLandCode));
   ```

2. Run the workflow and you will see the results shown in Figure 2.17. It runs as if
   it was created entirely in code. There is no difference from an execution standpoint.

FIGURE 2.17
XOML plus code
workflow results.

Creating a XAML-Only Workflow

We will create a XAML-only version of our workflow in this task. Unlike its predeces-
sors, limitations exist to XAML-only workflows. They do not support code very well.
Therefore, they do not support `Code` activities because they do not have a code-beside
file where code can be stored.

If XAML-only workflows are limited, why use them? They can run without compilation. This enables all sorts of scenarios ranging from business analyst-friendly work-

flow designers to retrieving workflows from a database. The SharePoint Designer featured in SharePoint workflow exemplifies a business analyst-friendly designer that allows workflows to be created and run without compilation.

There are two ways to work around the fact that XAML workflows do not allow code. One is to create custom activities (described in Hours 20 to 24) that contain the custom code in ready-to-use activities. This is one of WF's major features. The other is to embed the code directly in the XAML, which is not a great option because it requires compilation.

Creating XAML-only workflows does require a few additional steps.

Modeling and Preparing the XAML-Only Workflow for Execution

In the next steps, you will now create a new workflow using the same code separation template. You will then manually modify it to be a XAML-only workflow. The main change you will make is to remove the pointer the code-beside class used in XAML plus code workflows. This class is neither needed nor allowed in XAML-only workflows. You will also configure the XAML file to not be compiled and to be copied to the bin\debug directory.

1. Right-click `FirstWorkflowProject` in the Solution Explorer and choose Add, New Item.

2. Select Workflow in the left pane and select the Sequential Workflow (with code separation) item template.

3. Enter **`Workflow2XOMLOnly.xoml`** into the Name dialog and click the Add button.

   You should now have an empty workflow designer form.

4. Add a `Delay` activity to the workflow.

5. Save the project by selecting File, Save All.

6. Open `Workflow2XOMLOnly.xoml` in the XML editor by right-clicking it, selecting Open With, XML Editor, and clicking OK. (Click Yes to dialogs that warn that files are open and request that you save, if you did not Save, All in the last step.)

7. Remove the line that points to the code-beside class `x:Class="FirstWorkflowProject. Workflow2XOMLOnly` and save the project again.

8. Select `Workflow2XOMLOnly.xoml` in Solution Explorer and change its `Copy to Output` property to Copy If Newer and its `Build Action` property to None.

9. Build the project. Make sure it builds successfully and verify that the `Workflow2XOMLOnly.xoml` file was copied to the `C:\SamsWf24hrs\Hours\Hour02ASpinAroundWF\FirstWorkflowProject\ FirstWorkflowProject\bin\Debug` directory.

Call XAML-Only Workflow from Host

You will now load the XAML workflow as an XML document in the next steps. WF will load and execute the activities on the workflow without a separate compilation step. The workflow is currently started by passing a .NET type to the WorkflowRuntime.`CreateWorkflow` method. You will create a text reader that contains the XOML workflow information and then pass it to the `CreateWorkflow` method.

1. Open `Program.cs` and replace the line of code that starts with `WorkflowInstance instance = WorkflowRuntime.CreateWorkflow` with the following two lines of code to create the XML text reader and pass it to the `CreateWorkflow` method:

    ```
    XmlTextReader xmltr = new XmlTextReader(@
    "C:\SamsWf24hrs\Hours\Hour02ASpinAroundWF\FirstWorkflowProject\FirstWorkflo
    wProject\bin\Debug \Workflow2XOMLOnly.xoml");
                WorkflowInstance instance =
    workflowRuntime.CreateWorkflow(xmltr);
    ```

2. Add the following using directive below the other using statement at the top of the file:

    ```
    using System.Xml;
    ```

3. Run the workflow. The only results you will see are the host requesting that you press any key after the delay.

This example is obviously contrived. The XAML-only workflow option is useful only in conjunction with custom activities of which there must be enough to create a workflow without code. For example, if there were `Customer`, `Credit`, and other activities, it would be possible to create a credit process workflow with the combination of BAL and these custom activities that did not require code. In this case, XAML-only workflows are attractive. As mentioned already, the SharePoint Designer uses XAML-only workflows to allow knowledge workers to create workflows without compilation, and they can create reasonably functional workflows that contain multiple levels of escalation and dynamic task assignment, among other features.

XAML-only workflows cannot receive parameters via a Dictionary Object and cannot have constructors. There are other items you should know if you're working with moderate-to-complex XAML workflows. These topics are not covered in this book. I recommend looking at this blog entry if you want to learn more about XAML-only workflows: http://blogs.msdn.com/endpoint/archive/2008/07/06/download-posted-wf-xaml-workshop.aspx.

Going forward, it is likely there will be better all-around XAML support in WF because its ability to execute without compilation and the ability for tools to access it are key to WF's vision.

Summary

This hour featured a walk through a wide range of basic WF functionality. It covered everything from project structure, to rules, to XAML-only workflows. It built on the conceptual walkthrough and installation provided in Hour 1, "Understanding Windows Workflow Foundation." You need to learn a little more about hosting, which you will do in Hour 3, "Learning Basic Hosting." After that, you are ready to build on what you learned here and create workflows that manage long-running state, approval scenarios, and escalation.

Workshop

Quiz

1. *What is the advantage of declarative rules over code-based rules?*

2. *How many types of workflows are there in WF?*

3. *What are the advantages of XAML-only workflows?*

4. *How do you debug a WF workflow?*

5. *Can code activities be used on XAML-only workflows?*

6. *Does the* `IfElse` *activity execute every branch that evaluates to* `true` *or only the first one that evaluates to* `true`*?*

7. *Passing a dictionary object as a parameter to workflows is simple. What limitations does it carry?*

Answers

1. Tooling support, and they can be changed without requiring recompilation.

2. Three: Code only, XAML + Code, and XAML only.

3. Tooling, and they can be executed without compilation. They provide for powerful options when retrieved dynamically from a database.

4. Right-click an activity and select Insert Breakpoint, or set the breakpoint in code, as would be done in any other .NET application.

5. No, they always have code to execute, and code cannot be executed on XAML-only workflows.

6. Just the first one.

7. It cannot be used to interact with workflows in-flight and is therefore not useful as the sole workflow-host interaction method for workflows that require escalation and other typical workflow actions.

HOUR 3

Learning Basic Hosting

What You'll Learn in This Hour:

- ▶ Overview of hosting
- ▶ Building a host from scratch
- ▶ Adding basic events to it
- ▶ Configuring the host to use persistence
- ▶ Adding additional events to better track the workflow life cycle
- ▶ Adding the services through configuration

WF can be run from or hosted from Windows Forms applications, Console Applications, Windows Services, or any .NET 2.0 or later app domain. WF provides a general hosting framework that can be accessed from the various applications it is hosted in. This hour describes WF's workflow hosting infrastructure and how to configure it through its use of pluggable runtime services.

You will start off building your own bare-bones host. This will help you understand what goes into inserting WF into your application. You will then add events to this host to see how your host application can listen to events that happen in your workflow. You will use the persistence runtime service to serialize your workflow to SQL Server when workflows go idle to preserve memory and improve stability. Then you will add more events that help you monitor the series of events the workflow goes through from its active state to its persisted state. Adding the persistence service will also show you how the WF host can be tailored to the needs of your application. Finally, you learn how to add persistence through an App.Config file.

The main class you will work in this hour is the WorkflowRuntime. For all intents and purposes it is the WF workflow engine. It is instantiated in a host application and runtime services are added to it. It holds the events that facilitate host-workflow interaction.

Overview of Hosting

Workflow is a part of all types of applications. Windows Forms applications, ASP.NET, Windows Services, and just about all other applications contain some sort of logic that can be supplied through a workflow. Because of this, workflows must be embeddable within all these applications. You can't, after all, tell everybody that they have to use a custom process to run workflows if you expect it to attract a mainstream adoption. .NET applications of all types run in a Windows AppDomain (a CLR application isolation unit). WF can be called from an application running in an AppDomain provided by Windows XP SP2, Windows 2003, or Windows Vista that contains the .NET Framework 3.0 or later. Therefore, WF can be embedded in any Windows application running these operating systems. It doesn't matter if the specific application is a Windows Forms, ASP.NET, Windows Service, a custom line-of-business application, or something else. The WF workflow engine can be called from any of these applications. Calling the WF workflow engine from another application is referred to as *hosting*.

Simply running from different applications is not enough to make WF practical across the many types of applications that run on Windows. It must also be able to scale up to complex server requirements and scale down to much simpler, constricted client requirements.

The hosting infrastructure in WF is supplied by the WF runtime. The WF runtime is enabled by the `WorkflowRuntime` class that is called from the host. The class is supported by three redistributable system DLLs. The capability to serve disparate hosting needs is provided by pluggable runtime services such as persistence, tracking, and transactions—that can be registered with the runtime to tune its capabilities to the needs of the host. The WF runtime executes the workflow, manages its life cycle, and acts as a broker among the host, workflow, and registered runtime services.

Figure 3.1 demonstrates an AppDomain host, which could be an ASP.NET, Windows Forms, or other type of application, that has started the WF runtime. The WF runtime is configured with four runtime services and is running three workflow instances.

Building a Host from Scratch

In this section, you will create a Console Application and manually add the hosting code yourself to create a workable host.

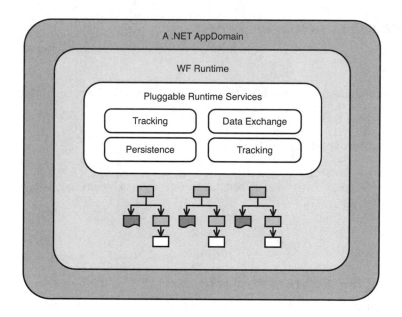

FIGURE 3.1
Workflow hosting structure.

Creating Solution and Projects

Follow the next steps to create the solution and projects.

1. Start Visual Studio 2008. Select File, New, Project.

2. Click the + to the left of Other Project Types.

3. Select the Visual Studio Solutions project template.

4. Enter **BasicHostingSolution** as the Name.

5. Enter or browse to `C:\SamsWf24hrs\Hours\Hour03BasicHosting` for the Location.

6. Click OK.

7. You should now see the BasicHostingSolution solution in the Solution Explorer. If not, click Tools, Options, expand Projects and Solutions, click the General button, and ensure that the Always Show Solution Check Box is checked, and click OK. The purpose of this step is not to show the Solution Explorer, but rather to ensure that solutions with fewer than two projects show in the Solution Explorer.

Creating the BasicHostingProject

1. Right-click BasicHostingSolution in the Solution Explorer, and select Add, New Project.

2. Expand the Visual C# project templates and select Windows.

3. Select the Console Application project template.

4. Enter **BasicHostingProject** as the Name.

5. Enter or browse to C:\SamsWf24hrs\Hours\Hour03BasicHosting\BasicHostingSolution for the Location.

6. Click OK.

Creating the WorkflowsProject

1. Right-click BasicHostingSolution in the Solution Explorer, and select Add, New Project.

2. Expand the Visual C# project templates and select Workflow.

3. Select the Sequential Workflow Library project template.

4. Enter **WorkflowsProject** as the Name.

5. Enter or browse to C:\SamsWf24hrs\Hours\Hour03BasicHosting\BasicHostingSolution for the Location.

6. Click OK.

You should have a solution with two projects, as shown in Figure 3.2.

FIGURE 3.2
Solution Explorer
with two projects.

Create a Simple Workflow

Now we will switch to the WorkflowsProject and create a workflow in the next steps that can be used throughout this hour to test the host.

1. Add a Code activity, a Delay activity, and another Code activity in that order.

2. Double-click the first Code activity and add the following code to its handler:

```
Console.WriteLine
    ("before delay: \'{0}\'", DateTime.Now.ToLongTimeString());
```

3. Go back to the workflow designer and set the Delay activity TimeoutDuration property to **00:00:05** (5 seconds).

4. Double-click the second Code activity and add the following code to its handler:

```
Console.WriteLine
    ("after delay: \'{0}\'", DateTime.Now.ToLongTimeString());
```

5. You are done creating the workflow. Build the project and fix any errors before proceeding.

By the Way

The WorkflowsProject project is not dependent on the BasicHostingProject project. Therefore, the WorkflowsProject is created first so it can be independently compiled before creating the BasicHostingProject.

Creating the Host

Now we have to turn our console host into a workflow host, which requires the following steps:

1. Referencing the three workflow DLLs—System.Workflow.Activities, System.Workflow.ComponentModel, and System.Workflow.Runtime.

2. Instantiating the WorkflowRuntime type, which for all intents and purposes is the WF runtime.

3. Instantiating the WorkflowInstance type and calling its methods to create and start a workflow instance.

4. Registering workflow completed and terminated events against the WorkflowRuntime type.

5. Ensuring that the console host remains in scope while the workflow executes. This is vital because if the console host does terminate before the workflow completes, the workflow will immediately halt execution because the workflow runs in the console host's AppDomain.

Adding the Fundamental Hosting Logic

In the next steps, you add basic hosting logic.

1. Right-click BasicHostingProject in the Solution Explorer, select Add Reference, click the .NET tab, select System.Workflow.Activities, System.Workflow.ComponentModel, and System.Workflow.Runtime, and press OK to reference the three workflow DLLs.

2. Right-click BasicHostingProject in the Solution Explorer again, select Add Reference, click the Projects tab, select WorkflowsProject, and click OK to reference the project that will hold the workflows.

3. Open `Program.cs` in the `BasicHostingProject` project and replace the current using directives with the ones shown:

   ```
   using System;
   using System.Workflow.Runtime;
   using System.Threading;
   ```

4. Instantiate the `WorkflowRuntime` inside the `Main` method (via a using `WorkflowRuntime` block so that it will be destroyed when the scope ends) as shown.

   ```
   using(WorkflowRuntime workflowRuntime = new WorkflowRuntime())
   {
   }
   ```

5. Create and start a workflow instance by adding the code shown between the brackets in the using `WorkflowRuntime` block.

   ```
   // Create the workflow instance
   WorkflowInstance instance =
       workflowRuntime.CreateWorkflow(
       typeof(WorkflowsProject.Workflow1));

   // Start the workflow instance
   instance.Start();
   ```

6. Your `Program.cs` should now look like this:

   ```
   using System;
   using System.Workflow.Runtime;
   using System.Threading;

   namespace BasicHostingProject
   {
       class Program
       {
           static void Main(string[] args)
           {
   ```

```
        using (WorkflowRuntime workflowRuntime = new WorkflowRuntime())
        {
            // Create the workflow instance
            WorkflowInstance instance =
                workflowRuntime.CreateWorkflow(
                typeof(WorkflowsProject.Workflow1));

            // Start the workflow instance
            instance.Start();
        }
    }
}
```

Pausing the Host

You have almost created a host. There is one problem, though. The host runs work-flows asynchronously. By default, the console host will terminate before running the workflow. You will block the host in the next steps, so that it will wait for the workflow to run. You will learn how to run the host synchronously in Hour 17, "Learning Advanced Hosting."

1. Insert the following line of code directly after the opening class bracket that will declare a variable used to ensure that the host remains in scope until the work-flow completes:

   ```
   static AutoResetEvent waitHandle;
   ```

2. Add the following code directly below the opening bracket of the using WorkflowRuntime block to instantiate the blocking event.

   ```
   waitHandle = new AutoResetEvent(false);
   ```

3. Now we have to tell the host at what point to wait for the blocking event (wait handle) to be set. Add the following line after the instance.Start(); line of code.

   ```
   // Position where host will wait for waithandle to be set
   waitHandle.WaitOne();
   ```

4. Because this is a console application and we may want to run it in debug mode, let's add a couple of lines to the end of the using WorkflowRuntime block (before the end bracket). This will ensure that the console messages will remain after the workflow completes (or more accurately, the AutoResetEvent is set).

   ```
   // Keep the console screen alive when workflow comnpletes
   Console.WriteLine("Press enter to continue");
   Console.Read();
   ```

5. Your main method and static variable declaration should now look like this:

```
static AutoResetEvent waitHandle;

static void Main(string[] args)
{
    using (WorkflowRuntime workflowRuntime = new WorkflowRuntime())
    {
        waitHandle = new AutoResetEvent(false);

        // Create the workflow instance
        WorkflowInstance instance =
            workflowRuntime.CreateWorkflow(
            typeof(WorkflowsProject.Workflow1));

        // Start the workflow instance
        instance.Start();

        // Position where host will wait for waithandle to be set
        waitHandle.WaitOne();

        // Keep the console screen alive when workflow comnpletes
        Console.WriteLine("Press enter to continue");
        Console.Read();
    }
}
```

Register Closed and Terminated Events with the Host

The host application interacts with and controls the WF runtime via events. There are a number of events, and you will now use two fundamental ones: completed and terminated. Other events will be covered in the "Add Monitoring Events" section later in this hour and in Hour 17, "Learning Advanced Hosting."

1. Open `Program.cs`.

2. Register the `WorkflowCompleted` event with the runtime. When the completed event is raised, you will set the wait handle event and the host will terminate, but only after the workflow is processed. To add the `WorkflowCompleted` event, move below the line that initializes `AutoResetEvent` to `false`, enter **`workflowRuntime.`**, select WorkflowCompleted from the menu, press the space-bar, enter +=, and press Tab twice.

3. You should see the following event and hander. The event is created in the Main method and the handler is created below the Main method (we will change its contents shortly):

```
workflowRuntime.WorkflowCompleted += new EventHandler
<WorkflowCompletedEventArgs>(workflowRuntime_WorkflowCompleted);
```

```
static void workflowRuntime_WorkflowCompleted
    (object sender, WorkflowCompletedEventArgs e)
{
    throw new NotImplementedException();
}
```

4. Below the `WorkflowCompleted` event registration enter **workflowRuntime**, select WorkflowTerminated from the menu, press the spacebar, enter +=, and press Tab twice.

5. Enter the following code in the `WorkflowCompleted` event handler to print workflow completed information to the console and to release the blocking event:

```
Console.WriteLine("Workflow {0} completed.",
    e.WorkflowInstance.InstanceId.ToString());

waitHandle.Set();
```

By the Way

> Public Properties and a type of property called a `DependencyProperty` (introduced in Hour 4, "Learning Host-Workflow Data Exchange") can be accessed in the `WorkflowCompleted` event as well as the workflow instance ID. The properties are stored in the `OutputParameters` collection property. The following code accesses the workflow property `MyProperty` and stores its value to a variable:
>
> `string MyProperty = (string) e.OutputParameters["MyProperty"];`

6. Enter the following code in the `WorkflowTerminated` event handler to print the workflow instance ID and the exception message to the console and to release the blocking event:

```
Console.WriteLine("Workflow {0} terminated because {1}",
    e.WorkflowInstance.InstanceId, e.Exception.Message);

waitHandle.Set();
```

7. You are done creating the host. Build the project and fix any errors before proceeding.

8. Your Main method should now look like Listing 3.1.

LISTING 3.1   Completed Host Main Method

```
static void Main(string[] args)
{
    using (WorkflowRuntime workflowRuntime = new WorkflowRuntime())
    {
        waitHandle = new AutoResetEvent(false);

        workflowRuntime.WorkflowCompleted += new
```

```
EventHandler<WorkflowCompletedEventArgs>(workflowRuntime_WorkflowCompleted);

            workflowRuntime.WorkflowTerminated += new
                EventHandler<WorkflowTerminatedEventArgs>
(workflowRuntime_WorkflowTerminated);

            // Create the workflow instance
            WorkflowInstance instance =
                workflowRuntime.CreateWorkflow(
                typeof(WorkflowsProject.Workflow1));

            // Start the workflow instance
            instance.Start();

            // Position where host will wait for waithandle to be set
            waitHandle.WaitOne();

            // Keep the console screen alive when workflow comnpletes
            Console.WriteLine("Press enter to continue");
            Console.Read();
        }
    }
```

That is it. You have now created a basic workflow host. There are many other events and runtime services that will be added to most applications. You also may want to invest in a more robust host that implements a Singleton pattern, but this host will function. You also should understand the default persistence behavior that is covered in the next section before creating a WF application.

Running the Workflow

Follow the next steps to run the workflow.

1. Right-click BasicHostingProject in the Solution Explorer and click Set as Startup Project.

2. Press F5 to run the SP project.workflow, and you should receive the results shown in Figure 3.3.

FIGURE 3.3
Workflow results.

Adding the Persistence Service

Persistence is a WF feature that stores a workflow to a specified storage medium when the workflow goes idle. A workflow will go idle when awaiting external input or for a timer to expire. Delay activities create timers, so our workflow will go idle when it executes the Delay activity. The default behavior is to leave workflows in memory when they go idle. For some scenarios, this is appropriate. As mentioned in Hour 2, "A Spin Around Windows Workflow Foundation," not all workflows run for long periods of time. Some execute in whole in one burst. There is no need for these workflows to persist because they never go idle. There are probably other scenarios that do not require persistence as well.

The default behavior, however, is not appropriate for many common workflow scenarios that feature approval-centric and other workflows that run, wait for input, run again, wait for input again, and so on before completing. The default behavior will leave all these workflows in memory during their periods of inactivity, creating scalability and reliability problems. Luckily WF does ship with an out-of-the-box (OOB) persistence service that persists idle workflows to SQL Server. The OOB persistence service is called the SqlWorkflowPersistenceService, and it is one of the pluggable runtime services mentioned earlier in the hour.

By the Way

Follow these steps to register and configure the SqlWorkflowPersistenceService:

1. Open Program.cs in the BasicHostingProject and add the variables declarations directly below the opening bracket of the using WorkflowRuntime block to configure the persistence service (they are described shortly):

```
// Persitence parameter values
bool unloadOnIdle = true;
TimeSpan reloadIntevral = new TimeSpan(0, 0, 0, 20, 0);
TimeSpan ownershipDuration = TimeSpan.MaxValue;
```

2. Add the following code to Program.cs to register the persistence service above the line of code that instantiates the workflow instance (the parameters are explained shortly):

```
// Instantiate a sql persistence service
SqlWorkflowPersistenceService sqlPersistenceService =
    new SqlWorkflowPersistenceService(connectionString,
    unloadOnIdle, ownershipDuration, reloadIntevral);
```

3. Now add the line of code shown next below the code you just added to add the persistence service to the runtime:

```
workflowRuntime.AddService(sqlPersistenceService);
```

If your connection string is different from mine, you should change it throughout this hour and the rest of the book. You will create the WFTrackingAndPersistence database a little later in this hour, and I recommend using that name for compatibility. However, if your data source is different than localhost, if your database is SQL Express and not SQL Server, or if you are not using integrated security, you will have to substitute your configuration from here on. For your reference, here is the connection string for SQL Express:

```
        static string connectionString = "Initial
Catalog=WFTrackingAndPersistence; " +
        "Data Source=localhost\\SQLEXPRESS; " +
        "Integrated Security=SSPI;";
```

4. Add the static variable below the opening class bracket to store the database connection:

```
        static string connectionString = "Initial Catalog=
WFTrackingAndPersistence;" +
        "Data Source=localhost; Integrated Security=SSPI;";
```

5. Add the following using directive to the top of the file below the existing using directives:

```
using System.Workflow.Runtime.Hosting;
```

That is it. You have now transformed the runtime from one that could only run limited workflows that would not survive a server shutdown to one that can run many workflows and free them from memory after each execution burst.

You did pass the SQL persistence service a few parameters. Let's look at them:

▶ The first holds the database connection.

▶ The second specifies that the workflow should unload, and thus persistence should take place automatically when the workflow is idled. Alternatively, you could track the idled event and persist the workflow yourself. A workflow will go idle when it is waiting either for an external event or for a timed activity to complete, such as a Delay activity.

▶ The third holds how long the runtime should hold a lock on a workflow. In this hour, we will keep it simple and set this property to the max value. This value is satisfactory for single server setups and does not account well for server crashes.

Hour 5, "Creating an Escalation Workflow," covers how to properly configure this property in server farm scenarios and to better support server crashes.

▶ The fourth determines how often the runtime will look for persisted workflows with expired timers, such as a `Delay` activity that has run its course. This property will also be looked at in more detail in Hour 5.

Adding Monitoring Events

Because you set the `UnloadOnIdle` property of the `SqlWorkflowPersistenceService` to `true`, the workflow will automatically idle and then persist each time it is waiting on external input or a timer. To see how this process works and to get a chance to work with a few more of the workflow events, let's track the process the workflow goes through from actively running to persistence.

You will register events with the WorkflowRuntime and add event handlers to track the following workflow events: idled, unloaded, persisted, and loaded. The workflow first idles, then is unloaded and persisted, and unlimitedly loaded back into memory again. Our sample workflow will go idle when it encounters the `Delay` activity and will then persist. The workflow will be reloaded when the delay expires.

You should register the events and create the handlers on the WorkflowRuntime. You will use the `workflowRuntime` variable to do so because the WorkflowRuntime has been assigned to it.

Register Additional Events and Create Handlers

In the next steps you will register additional events and create handlers for them.

1. Open `Program.cs` and move your cursor below the WorkflowTerminated event registration in the Main method.

2. Enter **`workflowRuntime.`**, select WorkflowIdled from the menu, press the spacebar, enter **`+=`**, and press Tab twice.

3. You should see the following event and hander. The event is created in the `Main` method and the handler is created outside of `Main` method (we will change its contents shortly):

```
        workflowRuntime.WorkflowIdled +=
            new
EventHandler<WorkflowEventArgs>(workflowRuntime_WorkflowIdled);

        static void workflowRuntime_WorkflowLoaded(object sender,
WorkflowEventArgs e)
        {
```

```
              throw new Exception("The method or operation is not
       implemented.");
           }
```

4. Below the `WorkflowIdled` event registration handler enter **workflowRuntime.**, select WorkflowUnloaded from the menu, press the spacebar, enter **+=**, and press Tab twice.

5. Below the `WorkflowUnloaded` event registration handler enter **workflowRuntime.**, select WorkflowPersisted from the menu, press the spacebar, enter **+=** and press Tab twice.

6. Below the `WorkflowPersisted` event registration handler enter **workflowRuntime.**, select WorkflowLoaded from the menu, press the spacebar, enter **+=** and press Tab twice.

Updating Handlers

Follow the next steps to add code to the handlers you created in the previous steps.

1. Be careful where you insert the code, because WF puts the most recently added handler on top.

2. Replace the default code in the `workflowRuntime_WorkflowIdled` handler with the following:

   ```
   Console.WriteLine("Workflow {0} idled at {1}",
       e.WorkflowInstance.InstanceId, System.DateTime.Now.ToLongTimeString());
   ```

3. Replace the default code in the `workflowRuntime_WorkflowUnloaded` handler with the following:

   ```
   Console.WriteLine("Workflow {0} unloaded at {1}",
       e.WorkflowInstance.InstanceId, System.DateTime.Now.ToLongTimeString());
   ```

4. Replace the default code in the `workflowRuntime_WorkflowPersisted` handler with the following:

   ```
   Console.WriteLine("Workflow {0} persisted at {1}",
       e.WorkflowInstance.InstanceId, System.DateTime.Now.ToLongTimeString());
   ```

5. Replace the default code in the `workflowRuntime_WorkflowLoaded` handler with the following:

   ```
   Console.WriteLine("Workflow {0} loaded at {1}",
       e.WorkflowInstance.InstanceId, System.DateTime.Now.ToLongTimeString());
   ```

6. Build and fix errors, if any.

Creating the Persistence and Tracking Databases

WF does not create a persistence or a tracking database for you when you install the product. One database can be used for both. The same tracking/persistence database can be used by different workflows. This book will use the WFTrackingAndPersistence database for all persistence and tracking exercises throughout this book. Each host specifies the connection string for these databases, so you can have multiple databases for performance, security, or other reasons if you choose to.

> The desire to avoid making SQL Server or SQL Express a hard dependency on WF is probably why persistence is not turned on by default, which seems reasonable. After all, there may be no database in some scenarios and other databases in other scenarios.

By the Way

Creating the Database and the Persistence Tables and Logic

Follow the next set of steps to create persistence and tracking databases in SQL Server.

> Per the installation requirements in Hour 1, "Understanding Windows Workflow Foundation," Sequel Server Management Studio is necessary (or at least the easiest way) to perform some of the required SQL Server tasks. Sequel Server Management Studio for express or standard SQL Server can be downloaded. This book assumes that you have Sequel Server Management Studio installed in all future directions related to SQL Server.

By the Way

1. Open Microsoft SQL Server Management Studio. Select your SQL Server and log in to the dialog.

2. Right-click Databases, select New Database, and name it **WFTrackingAndPersistence.** Then click OK at the bottom of the dialog.

3. Create a database named **WFTrackingAndPersistence** in any version of SQL Server 2000 or later. One way is to enter Create Database WFTrackingAndPersistence in the query window.

4. In the SQL Query Analyzer, select the WFTrackingAndPersistence database.

5. On the File menu, click Open, File, and then open the SQL script %WINDIR%\Microsoft.NET\Framework\v3.0\Windows Workflow Foundation\SQL\EN\SqlPersistenceService_Schema.sql. (If your language is not English, replace EN with your language code.)

6. Make sure that WFTrackingAndPersistence is open, and run the query by clicking Execute or pressing F5. This creates the persistence tables.

7. Check to ensure the `CompletedScope` and `InstanceState` tables have been added to the database.

8. On the File menu, click Open, and then open the SQL script `%WINDIR%\Microsoft.NET\Framework\v3.0\Windows Workflow Foundation\SQL\EN\SqlPersistenceService_Logic.sql`.

9. Make sure that `WFTrackingAndPersistence` is open, and run the query by clicking Execute or pressing F5. This creates the persistence stored procedures.

10. Check to ensure that about 10 stored procedures have been added to the database.

Creating the Tracking Tables and Logic

In the next steps you will add the tracking tables to the database.

1. On the File menu, click Open, `File`, and then open the SQL script `%WINDIR%\Microsoft.NET\Framework\v3.0\Windows Workflow Foundation\SQL\EN\Tracking_Schema.sql`.

2. Make sure that `WFTrackingAndPersistence` is open, and run the query by clicking Execute or pressing F5. This creates the tracking tables.

3. Check to ensure that approximately 20 tables have been added to the database.

4. On the File menu, click Open, and then open the SQL script `%WINDIR%\Microsoft.NET\Framework\v3.0\Windows Workflow Foundation\SQL\EN\Tracking_Logic.sql`.

5. Run the query by clicking Execute or pressing F5. This creates tracking the stored procedures.

6. There should now be numerous stored procedures.

Running the Workflow

1. Run the workflows and you should see the results shown in Figure 3.4.

FIGURE 3.4
Workflow result with persistence service and related events.

> You may notice the last call to persistence and think it is odd. Its purpose is to remove the workflow from the persistence store because the workflow is completed. Also note that the time between idled and reloaded may be affected by the reloading interval you specified.

2. Open `Program.cs` and set value of `unloadOnIdle` to `false`.

3. Run the workflow again; as you see, the workflow no longer unloads, persists, or reloads. It still idles, but that does not trigger the unload that previously led to the other events.

Updating the Host via Configuration

So far you added the persistence service and database connection to the host via code. It may be preferable to add one or both of these through configuration (an `App.Config file`) instead, mainly to permit change without recompilation. A workflow runtime section must be added to the `App.Config` file to configure the workflow runtime through configuration.

In the next steps you will add the persistence service and database connection to the host via configuration.

1. Add a reference to `System.Configuration` from the BasicHostingProject.

2. Create an `App.Config` file by right-clicking the project, selecting Add, New Item, selecting the Application Configuration File template, and clicking the Add button.

3. Add a configuration section that contains the internal workflow configuration instructions between the opening and closing Configuration elements in the `App.Config` file. The section name you provide here is used in the other sections of the `App.Config` file for identification purposes.

```
<configSections>
      <section name="WFR"
type="System.Workflow.Runtime.Configuration.WorkflowRuntimeSection,
      System.Workflow.Runtime, Version=3.0.00000.0, Culture=neutral,
      PublicKeyToken=31bf3856ad364e35" />
</configSections>
```

4. Add the next element between the `configSection` and `Configuration` ending elements. This element must have the same name as the section name in the previous step.

```
<WFR Name="BasicHostingExample">
</WFR>
```

5. Add a common section to store the database connection within the WFR element you just added:

```
<CommonParameters>
    <add name="ConnectionString"
        value="Initial Catalog= WFTrackingAndPersistence;
            Data Source=localhost;
            Integrated Security=SSPI;" />
</CommonParameters>
```

6. Add the Services section—that contains the SqlWorkflowPersistenceService and its parameters—within the WFR element below the element you just added:

```
<Services>
    <add
type="System.Workflow.Runtime.Hosting.SqlWorkflowPersistenceService,
        System.Workflow.Runtime, Version=3.0.00000.0,
        Culture=neutral, PublicKeyToken=31bf3856ad364e35"
        UnloadOnIdle="true"
        LoadIntervalSeconds="10"/>
</Services>
```

7. Your completed configuration file should now look like Listing 3.2.

LISTING 3.2   Workflow Configuration File

```
<?xml version="1.0" encoding="utf-8" ?>
<configuration>
  <configSections>
    <section name="WFR"
            type="System.Workflow.Runtime.Configuration.WorkflowRuntimeSection,
            System.Workflow.Runtime, Version=3.0.00000.0, Culture=neutral,
            PublicKeyToken=31bf3856ad364e35" />
  </configSections>
  <WFR Name="BasicHostingExample">
    <CommonParameters>
      <add name="ConnectionString"
                    value="Initial Catalog= WFTrackingAndPersistence;
                Data Source=localhost;
                Integrated Security=SSPI;" />
    </CommonParameters>
    <Services>
      <add type="System.Workflow.Runtime.Hosting.SqlWorkflowPersistenceService,
                System.Workflow.Runtime, Version=3.0.00000.0,
                Culture=neutral, PublicKeyToken=31bf3856ad364e35"
                UnloadOnIdle="true"
                LoadIntervalSeconds="10"/>
    </Services>
  </WFR>
</configuration>
```

8. Comment out the line of code in Program.cs that adds SqlPersistenceService to the runtime that looks like this:

`workflowRuntime.AddService(sqlPersistenceService);`. There can be only one persistence service registered with the runtime at a time, and it will conflict with the one being added through configuration now.

9. Instruct your host to use the configuration file by adding the name of your configuration element to the line that instantiates the runtime. The difference is that "WFR" is added between the two parentheses at the end of the line as shown:

```
using (WorkflowRuntime workflowRuntime = new WorkflowRuntime("WFR"))
```

10. Run the workflow and it should idle, persist, unload, and reload as it did when you ran the workflow earlier with `unloadOnIdle` set to `true`.

11. Now change `UnloadOnIdle` to `false` in the `App.Config` file and run it again. It should now idle but persist, unload, or reload, as the workflow did when it was programmatically set to `false`.

That is it. You now have a host that will persist workflows and can control persistence programmatically or through configuration. There are other services you will encounter later, but persistence is a key one. Most server and many client scenarios will call for persistence to free memory and provide durability across reboots.

Summary

You now know that the `WorkflowRuntime` class is the WF runtime or engine. You also know the basics of creating a host, registering events, and adding pluggable runtime services into the host. You have a basic idea of how persistence works and how a workflow transitions from active to persisted. Adding the persistence service offered you insight into how WF can be configured to the needs of its host. Finally, you know that runtime services can also be added through configuration files. In the previous hour you ran through a workflow and in this hour, through the runtime, or hosting a workflow. In the next hour you will learn about one more runtime service that provides for host-workflow data exchange, which is the missing component so far, because you have to move data between the host and the workflow.

Workshop

Quiz

1. *Does the host directly run workflows in a WF application?*

2. *Which class offers a handle to a workflow?*

3. *What purpose does SQL persistence serve?*

4. *What is the advantage of using a configuration file to register services?*

5. *What is the purpose for runtime services?*

6. *Can WF be persisted to any other medium than SQL Server?*

7. *Does the workflow runtime keep running when the host completes?*

Answers

1. No, it uses the WorkflowRuntime to run workflows on its behalf.

2. The `WorkflowInstance` class.

3. It saves workflows to a storage medium that both preserves memory and ensures durability across reboots.

4. The services can be changed without recompilation.

5. WF will process workflows on a range of platforms, from memory constricted clients, all the way to enterprise servers. Runtime services enable WF to scale up and down to meet these opposite requirements.

6. Yes, although the only OOB persistence service is SQL Server, the WF runtime architecture is meant to extend, and workflows can be persisted to just about any other source.

7. No, this is why you must ensure that the host continues to execute while the workflow is running.

HOUR 4

Learning Host-Workflow Data Exchange

What You'll Learn in This Hour:

- ▶ Overview of host-workflow data exchange
- ▶ Creating local service interface
- ▶ Creating an event argument payload
- ▶ Adding hosting logic to a Windows Form
- ▶ Creating a workflow with host-workflow communication activities

Host-Workflow Data Exchange

Although WF and therefore workflows run within the process space of the host, the host does not directly interact with a workflow instance. This may seem counterintuitive. After all, if the host application and workflow model are both .NET applications, why the need for an intermediary? The reason is that the WF runtime provides support services. The two main ones it provides are threading and reloading persisted workflows. When you call a workflow, the runtime accesses it for you and handles most threading details. Second, workflows sleep throughout most of their lifetime and are therefore persisted. The runtime receives the call and, if necessary, reloads the workflow and then transmits your request to it. For these reasons, and possibly others, host applications don't, or at least shouldn't, communicate directly with workflows.

Figure 4.1 illustrates the WF runtime brokering communication between hosts and workflows.

FIGURE 4.1
General host-
workflow data
exchange.

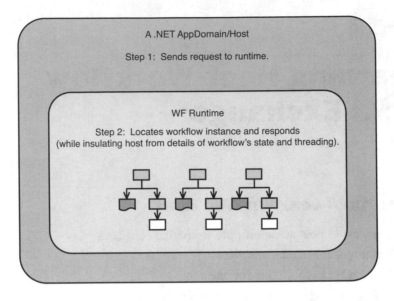

In this hour, we look at one type of host-workflow communication that is commonly referred to as external data exchange or local service. The reason is that this type of communication is conducted by a class that implements an interface that is, in turn, configured with an ExternalDataExchange attribute. There are other host-workflow communication options available in WF, including directly accessing its queuing system (discussed in Hour 22, "Creating Typed Queued and EventDriven-Enabled Activities," on which all other host-workflow communication schemes are built.

Figure 4.2 offers another view of the local service-based host-workflow data exchange. It shows the host and workflow being mediated by the local service in the

FIGURE 4.2
Local service-
based host-work-
flow data
exchange.

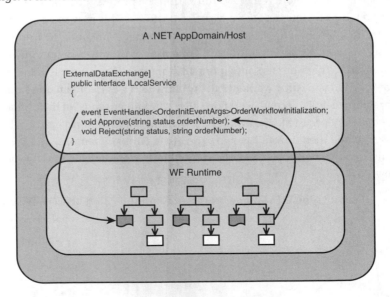

middle. The local service contains a contract with a specific set of events and methods to facilitate a particular data exchange. The host raises events to communicate with the workflow, and the workflow invokes methods to communicate with the host. These can be thought of as custom events and methods created for one particular data exchange, such as sending an order to a workflow and waiting for the workflow to announce approval or rejection. These events are in addition to the standard workflow events, such as completed and idled, that are available to all workflows.

A Windows Forms application will be used as the host because most developers are familiar with them and they are simple to use. The general concepts, however, apply to just about any other application that hosts a workflow.

There are four steps in host-workflow communication:

1. Create a local service interface that acts as a host-workflow communication contract.

2. Create a specialized payload to transmit data from the host to the workflow.

3. Create a workflow with host-workflow-communication-centric activities.

4. Implement the local service interface in the host.

A couple of other adjunct steps, such as creating the runtime host and creating dependency properties, are also covered. Some of the headings are prefixed with Step 1, Step 2, and so on to help you know which topics directly relate to implementing local service-based host-workflow communication.

> For those using the .NET 3.5, you should consider using the WCF Send and Receive activities in place of the method you learn to use in this hour. At the end of the book after using both, you can decide which method you prefer. You may also want to check the latest news at that time to see if Microsoft is indicating whether it will support both methods going forward equally, or one over the other.

By the Way

Creating the Solution and Projects

There are three projects in this solution. One will hold the Windows Forms host. Another will hold the local service interface that permits host-workflow communication. The third will hold the workflow that holds the WF local service-based communication activities. Factoring the projects out makes reuse easier.

Creating the Solution

Follow the next set of steps to create the solution.

1. Start Visual Studio 2008. Select File, New, Project.

2. Click on the plus to the left of Other Project Types.

3. Select the Visual Studio Solutions project template.

4. Enter **DataExchangeSolution** as the Name.

5. Enter or browse to
   C:\SamsWf24hrs\Hours\Hour04HostWorkflowDataExchange for the Location.

6. Click OK.

Creating the Local Service Project

Follow the next set of steps to create a local service that controls communication
between the host application and the workflow.

1. Right-click DataExchangeSolution in the Solution Explorer, and select Add,
   New Project.

2. Expand the Visual C# project templates and select Windows.

3. Select the Class Library project template.

4. Enter **LocalService** as the Name.

5. Enter or browse to
   C:\SamsWf24hrs\Hours\Hour04HostWorkflowDataExchange\DataExchangeSo
   lution for the Location.

6. Click OK.

7. Rename Class1.cs to **BasicLocalService.cs** in the Solution Explorer. (If you
   are asked to rename all references in the project to reflect the name change,
   click Yes.)

8. Right-click the LocalService project in the Solution Explorer, select Add, Class,
   and name it **LocalServiceEventArgs.cs.**

9. Add a reference to the workflow trio as well (System.Workflow.Activities,
   System.Workflow.Runtime, and System.Worfklow.Componentmodel).

Creating the Workflow Project

You add the workflow project to the solution in the next steps.

1. Right-click DataExchangeSolution in the Solution Explorer, and select Add, New Project.

2. Expand the Visual C# project templates and select Workflow.

3. Select the Sequential Workflow Library project template.

4. Enter **LocalServiceWorkflows** as the Name.

5. Enter or browse to C:\SamsWf24hrs\Hours\Hour04HostWorkflowDataExchange\DataExchangeSo lution for the Location.

6. Click OK.

7. Rename Workflow1.cs to **LocalServiceWorkflow.cs.** (Click Yes to rename all references.)

8. Add a reference to the LocalService project.

Creating the Windows Forms Project

Add the Windows Forms host project in the next steps.

1. Right-click DataExchangeSolution in the Solution Explorer, and select Add, New Project.

2. Expand the Visual C# project templates and select Windows.

3. Select the Windows Forms Application project template.

4. Enter **BasicWorkflowHost** as the Name.

5. Enter or browse to C:\SamsWf24hrs\Hours\Hour04HostWorkflowDataExchange\DataExchangeSo lution for the Location.

6. Click OK.

7. Rename Form1.cs to **BasicHostForm.cs** in the Solution Explorer. Again, click Yes to rename all references.

8. Right-click the BasicWorkflowHost project in the Solution Explorer, select Add, Add a Reference to both the LocalServiceWorkflows and the LocalService projects.

9. Add a reference to the workflow trio as well (`System.Workflow.Activities`, `System.Workflow.Runtime`, and `System.Worfklow.Componentmodel`).

10. Your Solution Explorer should now look like Figure 4.3:

Step 1: Creating the Local Service Interface

The local service interface contains the contract between the host and the workflow. The local service holds an `ExternalDataExchange` attribute, the events that will be raised against the workflow by the host, and the methods the workflow will invoke on the host. In the next steps you create a local service interface.

1. Open `BasicLocalService.cs`.

2. Replace the existing using directives with the ones shown next:

```
using System;
using System.Workflow.Activities;
using System.Workflow.Runtime;
```

3. Replace the class declaration with the following interface declaration that includes the `ExternalDataExchange` attribute. This is the attribute that tells the runtime that this interface performs host-workflow communication.

```
[ExternalDataExchange]
public interface ILocalService
{
}
```

4. Fill in the interface body with these event and method signatures:

```
void Approve(string status, string orderNumber);
void Reject(string status, string orderNumber);

event EventHandler<OrderInitEventArgs> OrderWorkflowInitialization;
```

5. The `LocalService.cs` class should look like Code Listing 4.1:

LISTING 4.1   LocalService.cs

```
using System;
using System.Workflow.Activities;
using System.Workflow.Runtime;

namespace LocalService
{
    [ExternalDataExchange]
    public interface ILocalService
    {
        void Approve(string status, string orderNumber);
        void Reject(string status, string orderNumber);

        event EventHandler<OrderInitEventArgs> OrderWorkflowInitialization;
    }
}
```

You have now created a local service interface that contains two methods for workflow-to-host communication and one event for host-to-workflow communication. The events raised on the workflow are asynchronous, and the methods from the workflow are synchronous. Communicating with the workflow asynchronously is mandated so that the WF runtime's threading and reloading services do not take place while the host is waiting for a response to its method call.

Step 2: Creating the Payload (EventArgs) Class

All local service-based event payloads are delivered by a class that is derived from `ExternalDataEventArgs`. Because WF may persist workflows, all event args payload classes (those derived from `ExternalDataEventArgs`) must be marked as serializable. The workflow instance id must be part of the payload because the WF runtime will need it to determine which workflow instance to route the event to. To ensure this the host must pass the workflow instance id in all events it raises on the workflow, and the event args class must contain the following statement in its constructor:
`: base(instanceId)`

Follow the next steps to create the `EventArgs` class.

The standard WF runtime event payloads are also derived from `ExternalDataEventArgs`. They carry event-specific payloads. For instance, the completed event contains all public workflow variables and the terminated class contains exception information.

By the Way

1. Open LocalServiceEventArgs.cs.

2. Replace the current using directives with the following:

```
using System;
using System.Workflow.Activities;
```

3. Replace the class declaration in the LocalServiceEventArgs.cs class with the following:

```
[Serializable]
public class OrderInitEventArgs : ExternalDataEventArgs
{
}
```

4. Add the following code within the OrderInitEventArgs class that defines a property to carry the order number:

```
private string orderNumber;
public string OrderNumber
{
    get { return orderNumber; }
    set { orderNumber = value; }
}
```

5. Add the constructor below the ending bracket of the OrderNumber property:

```
public OrderInitEventArgs(Guid instanceId, string number)
    : base(instanceId)
{
    orderNumber = number;
}
```

6. Your completed OrderInitEventArgs class should look like Listing 4.2.

LISTING 4.2   OrderInitEventArgs

```
using System;
using System.Workflow.Activities;

namespace LocalService
{
    [Serializable]
    public class OrderInitEventArgs : ExternalDataEventArgs
    {
        private string orderNumber;
        public string OrderNumber
        {
            get { return orderNumber; }
            set { orderNumber = value; }
        }
        public OrderInitEventArgs(Guid instanceId, string number)
            : base(instanceId)
        {
```

```
        orderNumber = number;
    }
  }
}
```

7. Right-click the `LocalService` project and select Build. Fix errors, if any.

Step 3: Creating the Workflow

Now it is time to connect the local service interface to the workflow. This is accomplished by using the `HandleExternalEvent` and `CallExternalMethod` activities. The `HandleExternalEvent` activity wraps to the events coming from the host to the workflow. The `CallExternalMethod` serves the same purpose for workflow-invoked methods on the host. These activities can be wired to any `ExternalDataExchange`-attributed interface accessible by the workflow project. This means the local service may be within the workflow project itself or in a project referenced by the workflow project. Before adding the communication activities, you will add a couple of properties as described in the next section.

Adding the `DependencyProperty` Type

The `DependencyProperty` is a .NET type that is heavily used in WF and WPF. They are essentially properties that contain a few advantages over standard .NET properties, such as data binding and event handling, which will be covered in Hour 20, "Creating Basic Custom Activities." The one advantage relevant now is that they are stored more effectively because they do not allocate memory for blank values. Dependency properties are generally strongly typed to the type they are contained in and the type of property they are. For instance, the `Customer DependencyProperty` of type string in the `Customer` class is typed to both the `Customer` type and as a `string` member. There is a shortcut to add them so it takes no longer to add them than adding a standard .NET property. They are, however, quite verbose, which can make reading them and the classes they are contained in more difficult.

Let's now create `DependencyProperty` variables that carry the approval information tracked by the workflow in the next steps:

1. Open the workflow code-beside file by right-clicking `LocalServiceWorkflow.cs` in the Solution Explorer and selecting View Code.

2. Create a DependencyProperty named OrderNo as follows:

   A. Right-click below the constructor.

   B. Select Insert Snippet.

   C. Double-click the Other choice (skip to step D if using Visual Studio 2005).

   D. Double-click the Workflow choice.

   E. Double-click the Dependency Property—Property choice.

   F. Replace the highlighted MyProperty text with **OrderNo** (leave the non-highlighted Property in the suffix) and press Tab.

   G. Press Enter to accept the string default and to leave the wizard (if the first Enter does not exit you from the wizard, press Enter again). You should see the code generated in Listing 4.3.

LISTING 4.3   OrderNo DependencyProperty

```
public static DependencyProperty OrderNoProperty =
    DependencyProperty.Register("OrderNo",
    typeof(string),
    typeof(LocalServiceWorkflow));

[DescriptionAttribute("OrderNo")]
[CategoryAttribute("OrderNo Category")]
[BrowsableAttribute(true)]
[DesignerSerializationVisibilityAttribute(DesignerSerializationVisibility.Visible
)]
    public string OrderNo
    {
        get
        {
            return
((string)(base.GetValue(LocalServiceWorkflow.OrderNoProperty)));
        }
        set
        {
            base.SetValue(LocalServiceWorkflow.OrderNoProperty, value);
        }
    }
```

3. Create another DependencyProperty named **Status** as follows:

   A. Right-click below the OrderNo DependencyProperty you just created (the entire DependencyProperty).

   B. Select Insert Snippet.

C. Double-click the Other choice.

D. Double-click the Workflow choice.

E. Double-click the Dependency Property—Property choice.

F. Replace the highlighted MyProperty text with **Status** (leave the non-highlighted Property in the suffix) and press Tab.

G. Press Enter to accept the string default and to leave the wizard. (If the first Enter does not exit you from the wizard, press Enter again.)

If you look at the generated code, you may notice that the DependencyProperty contains two types. One binds it to a class—the workflow in this case. The other tells if it is a string or double. It is by binding the property to a class that data binding and other features are enabled.

Step 3A: Creating a `HandleExternalMethod` Activity

Now back to data exchange. Let's add the `HandleExternalEvent` activities that receive the events in the next set of steps.

1. Double click on `LocalServiceWorkflow` in the solution explorer to open it in design mode.

2. Drag and drop a `HandleExternalEvent` activity onto the workflow and name it **ReceiveOrder.**

3. Click the `InterfaceType` property, then click the ellipsis, select LocalService, and then select ILocalService in the middle of the form.

If ILocalService does not show up, make sure the LocalService project is referenced and built. The easiest way is to add a new reference to it from the LocalServiceWorkflows project and build it again.

Your screen should look like Figure 4.4.

4. Click OK.

5. Click the drop-down in the `EventName` property and select the `OrderWorkflowInitialization` event.

6. Enter **OrderInvoked** in the Invoked property.

7. Enter the following code in the `OrderInvoked` handler to retrieve the `OrderNumber` from the event args.

```
// Retrieve the order number from the eventArgs
OrderNo = (e as LocalService.OrderInitEventArgs).OrderNumber;
```

8. Switch back to the workflow designer, and the ReceiveOrder activity property window should look like Figure 4.5.

FIGURE 4.4
Local Service selection dialog.

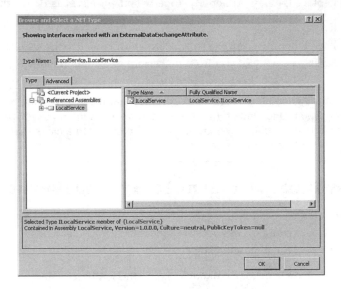

FIGURE 4.5
The ReceiveOrder activity's properties.

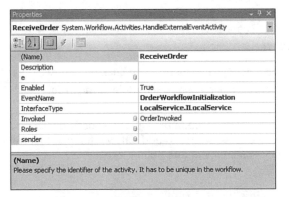

Handle External Event Activity Property Window

This activity is now wired to the OrderWorkflowInitialization event and will execute when the event is raised. In addition, the OrderInvoked method will be invoked after the event is raised and will be used to retrieve the OrderNo from the OrderInitEventArgs class.

Adding an `IfElse` Activity and Rules

In the next steps you will add an `IfElse` activity and configure its rules.

1. Drag and drop an `IfElse` activity onto the workflow below the `ReceiveOrder` activity.

2. Name the `IfElse` activity **CheckCredit,** name the left branch **IsApproved,** and name the right branch **IsRejected.**

3. Click the red exclamation mark in the left branch, then click Property 'Condition' Is Not Set. You will now be into the `Condition` property ready to input a rule to determine whether this `IfElseBranch` should execute.

4. Click the drop-down in the `Condition` property and select `Code Condition`.

5. Click the + at the left of the `Condition` property, enter **CheckOrderCondition** in the `Condition` property, and press Enter.

6. You are placed in the `CheckOrderCondition` handler.

7. Enter the following code in the `CheckOrderCondition` handler to approve orders ending in 1:

```
if (OrderNo.EndsWith("1"))
    e.Result = true;
else
    e.Result = false;
```

8. Switch back to the workflow designer, and your workflow should now look like Figure 4.6.

Adding `CallExternalMethod` Activities

Step 3B: Add the First `CallExternalMethod` Activity

This is the activity that will invoke the `Approve` method that is part of the interface and will be added to the host. From a process standpoint, it will send approval to the host. In the next steps, you add the `CallExternalMethod` activity to approve the order.

1. Drag and drop a `CallExternalMethod` activity into the left `IfElse` activity branch.

2. Click the `InterfaceType` property, then click the ellipsis, select the `LocalService`, and then select ILocalService in the middle of the form.

FIGURE 4.6
Workflow with
HandleExtern-
alEvent and
IfElse activi-
ties.

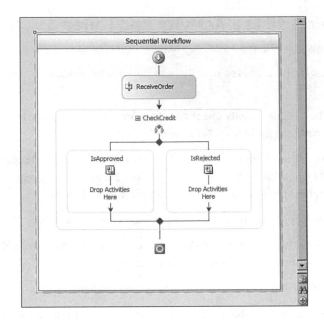

3. Click OK.

4. Click the drop-down in the MethodName property and select the Approve
   method.

5. Enter **ApproveIt** into the MethodInvoking property (called before the approve
   method is called; thus it is a good place to perform preparatory work, such as
   initializing variables).

6. Enter the following in its code handler:

   ```
   Status = "Approved";
   ```

7. Switch back to the workflow designer view.

8. Bind the OrderNo DependencyProperty to the orderNumber parameter by
   clicking the orderNumber property, then clicking its ellipsis, selecting OrderNo,
   and clicking OK.

9. Bind the Status DependencyProperty to the status parameter by clicking the
   status property, then clicking its ellipsis, selecting Status, and clicking OK.

10. Your CallExternalMethod activity property window should now look like
    Figure 4.7:

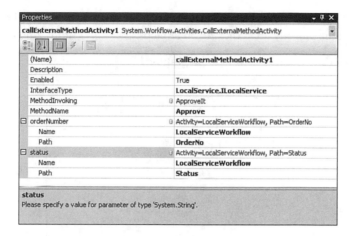

FIGURE 4.7
CallExternal
Method activity
property window.

Step 3C: Add the Second `CallExternalMethod` Activity

This is the activity that will invoke the `Reject` method that is part of the interface and will be added to the host. From a process standpoint it will send rejection to the host. In the next steps you add the `CallExternalMethod` activity that rejects the order.

1. Drag and drop a `CallExternalMethod` activity into the right `IfElse` activity branch.

2. Click the `InterfaceType` property, then click the ellipsis, select the `LocalService`, and then select ILocalService in the middle of the form.

3. Click OK.

4. Click the drop-down in the `MethodName` property and select the `Reject` method.

5. Enter **RejectIt** in the `MethodInvoking` property (called before the reject method is called; thus it is a good place to perform preparatory work, such as initializing variables).

6. Enter the following in its code handler:

   ```
   Status = "Rejected";
   ```

7. Switch back to the workflow designer view.

8. Bind the `OrderNo DependencyProperty` to the `orderNumber` parameter by clicking on the `orderNumber` property, then clicking on its ellipsis, selecting `OrderNo`, and clicking OK.

9. Bind the `Status DependencyProperty` to the `status` parameter by clicking on the `status` property, then clicking on its ellipsis, selecting Status, and clicking OK.

10. Your workflow should now look like Figure 4.8:

FIGURE 4.8
Workflow configured with `HandleExternalEvent` and `CallExternalMethod` activities.

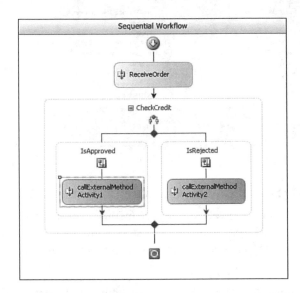

11. Build your `LocalServiceWorkflows` project and fix compilation errors, if any.

12. The code in your workflow code-beside file should look like Listing 4.4:

LISTING 4.4   `LocalServiceWorkflow` Code-Beside File

```
using System;
using System.ComponentModel;
using System.ComponentModel.Design;
using System.Collections;
using System.Drawing;
using System.Workflow.ComponentModel.Compiler;
using System.Workflow.ComponentModel.Serialization;
using System.Workflow.ComponentModel;
using System.Workflow.ComponentModel.Design;
using System.Workflow.Runtime;
using System.Workflow.Activities;
using System.Workflow.Activities.Rules;

namespace LocalServiceWorkflows
{
    public sealed partial class LocalServiceWorkflow: SequentialWorkflowActivity
    {
        public LocalServiceWorkflow()
```

```
        {
            InitializeComponent();
        }

        public static DependencyProperty OrderNoProperty =
            DependencyProperty.Register("OrderNo",
            typeof(string),
            typeof(LocalServiceWorkflow));

        [DescriptionAttribute("OrderNo")]
        [CategoryAttribute("OrderNo Category")]
        [BrowsableAttribute(true)]

[DesignerSerializationVisibilityAttribute(DesignerSerializationVisibility.Visible
)]
        public string OrderNo
        {
            get
            {
                return
((string)(base.GetValue(LocalServiceWorkflow.OrderNoProperty)));
            }
            set
            {
                base.SetValue(LocalServiceWorkflow.OrderNoProperty, value);
            }
        }

        public static DependencyProperty StatusProperty =
            DependencyProperty.Register("Status",
            typeof(string),
            typeof(LocalServiceWorkflow));

        [DescriptionAttribute("Status")]
        [CategoryAttribute("Status Category")]
        [BrowsableAttribute(true)]

[DesignerSerializationVisibilityAttribute(DesignerSerializationVisibility.Visible
)]
        public string Status
        {
            get
            {
                return
((string)(base.GetValue(LocalServiceWorkflow.StatusProperty)));
            }
            set
            {
                base.SetValue(LocalServiceWorkflow.StatusProperty, value);
            }
        }

        private void OrderInvoked(object sender, ExternalDataEventArgs e)
        {
            // Retreive the order number from the eventArgs
            OrderNo = (e as LocalService.OrderInitEventArgs).OrderNumber;
        }
```

```
private void CheckOrderCondition(object sender, ConditionalEventArgs e)
{
    if (OrderNo.EndsWith("1"))
        e.Result = true;
    else
        e.Result = false;

}

private void ApproveIt(object sender, EventArgs e)
{
    Status = "Approved";
}

private void RejectIt(object sender, EventArgs e)
{
    Status = "Rejected";
    }
  }
}
```

Creating the Windows Forms Host

You will create a Windows Forms application that implements the local service interface you created. It will create the event args payload used by the local service and raise events to the host. Likewise it will act on the methods invoked by the workflow. It will also instantiate the `WorkflowRuntime` and create and start a `WorkflowInstance` as you saw in Hour 3, "Learning Basic Hosting."

Whereas a Console Host application runs sequentially from beginning to end and then terminates, a Windows Forms application remains running until explicitly exited. The main implication of this is that you need to plan where you will instantiate the `WorkflowRuntime`. You do not want to do this each time an order is submitted. There needs to be only one WF runtime per application that will, in turn, run all the individual workflow instances.

Therefore, we are adding the runtime instantiation to the form load method, which is called only once in our application. For good measure and practice for other hosting scenarios, you first check to see if the runtime has already been instantiated. If so, you return the existing runtime. If not, you create a new runtime.

You also learn to use a new runtime service called the ExternalDataExchangeService. It is a container for one or more local services. You first add the ExternalDataExchangeService to the runtime and then add the local service you created to the ExternalDataExchangeService, as you will see shortly. We will add this service in code, but it can be added though configuration files as you did with the persistence service in Hour 3.

Adding Controls to the Form

In the next steps you add controls to the form.

1. Create the form in the `BasicHostForm.cs` designer, as shown in Figure 4.9. (Control names are conveyed in the next task.)

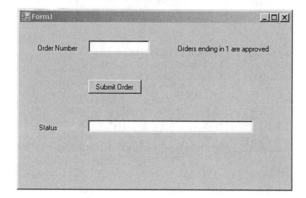

FIGURE 4.9
Basic approval form.

2. Name the text boxes **textBoxOrderNumber** and **textBoxStatus**. Name the command button **buttonSubmitOrder**. The labels can retain their default names.

Adding the WF Runtime to the Form/Host

Over the next few subsections, you add the WF runtime to the Windows Forms host.

Prepare for Runtime Hosting

You need to prepare this form to be a host. It needs to implement the local service so it can exchange data with the workflow. It also needs `WorkflowRuntime` and `WorkflowInstance` variables and the other code to host the runtime and create and run a workflow. In many ways it will be similar to the host created from scratch earlier in Hour 3.

Follow the next steps to prepare the form host for runtime hosting.

1. Open `BasicHostForm.cs` in code view.

2. Add the following using directives below the existing ones:

```
using System.Workflow.Runtime;
using System.Workflow.Activities;
```

3. Change the class signature to incorporate the local service interface as shown:

```
public partial class BasicHostForm : Form,
    LocalService.ILocalService
```

4. Add the following variable declarations below the constructor (the `UpdateDelegate` delegate will be explained shortly):

```
private WorkflowRuntime workflowRuntime;
private WorkflowInstance workflowInstance;
private delegate void UpdateDelegate();
```

Setup Method to Create `WorkflowRuntime`

In the next steps, you add a method to and begin to instantiate the WF runtime.

1. Double-click the form to create the `Form_Load` handler and populate it with the code shown in the next snippet that calls a method that either instantiates a new `WorkflowRuntime` or returns an existing `WorkflowRuntime`:

```
// Get an existing workflow runtime or create a new one
workflowRuntime = GetWorkflowRuntime(workflowRuntime);
```

2. Add the `GetWorkflowRuntime` method signature below the `Form_Load` handler. The `GetWorkflowRuntime` method creates the `WorkflowRuntime`, registers runtime events with it, and adds runtime services to it:

```
private WorkflowRuntime GetWorkflowRuntime
    (WorkflowRuntime WorkflowRuntime)
{
}
```

3. Add the logic to check whether the workflow runtime has already been instantiated inside the `GetWorkflowRuntime` method:

```
if (WorkflowRuntime == null)
    {
    }
```

4. Instantiate the runtime inside the `if` statement you just added:

```
workflowRuntime = new WorkflowRuntime();
```

Register Events and Local Service with the `WorkflowRuntime`

In the steps in this section, you register events and the local service with the WF runtime.

1. Below the code you just added, register the terminated event by entering
   `"workflowRuntime."`, then select WorkflowTerminated from the menu, press
   the spacebar, enter += and press Tab twice.

2. Add the `ExternalDataExchangeService` to the runtime below the event you
   just registered in the `GetWorkflowRuntime` method:

   ```
   // Add the local service
   ExternalDataExchangeService des = new
   ExternalDataExchangeService();
   ```

3. Add the local service to the `ExternalDataExchangeService`:

   ```
   workflowRuntime.AddService(des);
   // this implements the local service
   des.AddService(this);
   ```

Start and Return the Runtime

In this set of steps, you start the WF runtime and return it to the calling method.

1. Add code to start the runtime:

   ```
   workflowRuntime.StartRuntime();
   ```

2. Add code to return the runtime outside of the if statement scope as shown:

   ```
   return workflowRuntime;
   ```

The `GetWorkflowRuntime` method should look like Listing 4.5.

LISTING 4.5   `GetWorkflowRuntime` Hosting Method

```
private WorkflowRuntime GetWorkflowRuntime
    (WorkflowRuntime WorkflowRuntime)
{
    if (WorkflowRuntime == null)
    {
        workflowRuntime = new WorkflowRuntime();
        // Set workflow event

        workflowRuntime.WorkflowTerminated +=
          new EventHandler<WorkflowTerminatedEventArgs>
          (workflowRuntime_WorkflowTerminated);
```

```
            // Add the local service
            ExternalDataExchangeService des = new
ExternalDataExchangeService();

            workflowRuntime.AddService(des);
            // this implements the local service
            des.AddService(this);

            workflowRuntime.StartRuntime();
        }
        return workflowRuntime;
    }
```

Update the Terminated Event Handler

When you registered the terminated event, you also created an event handler for it. The reason you registered this one event is so that errors will be reported to you. There are quite a few moving parts between the workflow, local service, and host, and it is pretty easy to introduce an error that is hard to debug. Trapping this event makes it easier to know a problem exists and to identify what the problem is.

In the next step, you add code to the terminated event handler.

1. Add the following code to the workflow Runtime_WorkflowTerminated handler you generated when registering the terminated event:

```
MessageBox.Show("Workflow terminated: " + e.Exception.Message);
```

Step 4A: Creating the Workflow Instance and Raising the Initial Event

We finally go back to the host-workflow data exchange now that the host is set up.

Creating the workflow instance in the Windows Forms application is similar to doing so in a console host. Our workflow, though, differs in communication topology. You are no longer passing a dictionary object to the CreateWorkflow method. You are using local service-based communication.

Therefore, you have to raise an event to send the data to the workflow. The workflow contains a HandleExternalEvent activity as its first activity that is awaiting the event, although there will be one workflow runtime for the application. The user may create multiple workflow instances, which are created each time the user clicks the Submit button.

In the next steps, you add the logic to start the workflow instance when the Submit button is clicked.

1. Double-click the Submit button (buttonSubmitOrder) and add the following code to its handler:

```
// Create and start a workflow instance
workflowInstance = workflowRuntime.CreateWorkflow(typeof
    (LocalServiceWorkflows.LocalServiceWorkflow));

workflowInstance.Start();
```

2. Add the following code below the code you just added to create the event args payload to be delivered to the WF runtime:

```
// Pass the order number entered and raise the event specifed in
the local service
// that carries the payload defined in the order init event
argument class:
LocalService.OrderInitEventArgs eventArgs =
    new LocalService.OrderInitEventArgs
    (workflowInstance.InstanceId, textBoxOrderNumber.Text);
```

3. Raise the event to be captured by the initial HandleExternalEvent activity on the workflow and package the event args with it.

```
OrderWorkflowInitialization(null, eventArgs);
```

Step 4B: Implementing the Local Service

You need to implement the two methods and one event defined in the local service interface. The methods return either approved or rejected, which is passed to the form. Windows Forms controls, however, are not thread safe. Your workflow runs on a different thread than the Windows Form.

This book uses anonymous delegates (see MSDN or other sources if you want to learn more about anonymous delegates) to update the Windows Forms controls from the workflow threads. This is why you declared the UpdateDelegate at the top of this class. You enclose the changes to controls you want to make inside of the UpdateDelegate(). This will become clearer when you see the code for the Approve and Reject methods shortly.

Threading is covered in Hour 17, "Learning Advanced Hosting," and an option exists to run workflows on the same thread synchronously. This eliminates the need to account for cross-thread communication via delegate-based communication or other methods. I think you could make a fair argument that the synchronous threading is best suited for many UI scenarios.

1. Right before the end of the class declaration, implement the workflow event:

```
public event EventHandler<LocalService.OrderInitEventArgs>
    OrderWorkflowInitialization;
```

2. Implement the methods that each update a textbox with the order status returned from the workflow:

```
public void Approve(string status, string orderNumber)
{
    UpdateDelegate ud = delegate()
    {
        textBoxStatus.Text = "Order No: " + orderNumber + " is " +
status;
    };
    this.Invoke(ud);
}
public void Reject(string status, string orderNumber)
{
    UpdateDelegate ud = delegate()
    {
        textBoxStatus.Text = "Order No: " + orderNumber + " is " +
status;
    };
    this.Invoke(ud);
}
```

3. Build the `BasicWorkflowHost` project and fix errors, if any.

4. The code in your form class should look like Listing 4.6.

LISTING 4.6   `BasicHostForm` Windows Forms Host

```
using System;
using System.Collections.Generic;
using System.ComponentModel;
using System.Data;
using System.Drawing;
using System.Linq;
using System.Text;
using System.Windows.Forms;
using System.Workflow.Runtime;
using System.Workflow.Activities;


namespace BasicWorkflowHost
{
    public partial class BasicHostForm : Form, LocalService.ILocalService
    {
        public BasicHostForm()
        {
            InitializeComponent();
        }

        private WorkflowRuntime workflowRuntime;
```

```csharp
private WorkflowInstance workflowInstance;
private delegate void UpdateDelegate();

private void BasicHostForm_Load(object sender, EventArgs e)
{
    // Get an existing workflow runtime or create a new one
    workflowRuntime = GetWorkflowRuntime(workflowRuntime);

}

private WorkflowRuntime GetWorkflowRuntime
    (WorkflowRuntime WorkflowRuntime)
{
    if (WorkflowRuntime == null)
    {
        workflowRuntime = new WorkflowRuntime();

        workflowRuntime.WorkflowTerminated += new

EventHandler<WorkflowTerminatedEventArgs>(workflowRuntime_WorkflowTerminated);

        // Add the local service
        ExternalDataExchangeService des = new
ExternalDataExchangeService();

        workflowRuntime.AddService(des);
        // this implements the local service
        des.AddService(this);

        workflowRuntime.StartRuntime();
    }

    return workflowRuntime;

}

void workflowRuntime_WorkflowTerminated(object sender,
WorkflowTerminatedEventArgs e)
{
    MessageBox.Show("Workflow terminated: " + e.Exception.Message);
}

private void buttonSubmitOrder_Click(object sender, EventArgs e)
{
    // Create and start a workflow instance
    workflowInstance = workflowRuntime.CreateWorkflow(typeof
        (LocalServiceWorkflows.LocalServiceWorkflow));

    workflowInstance.Start();

    // Pass the order number entered and raise the event specifed in the
local service
    //  that carries the payload defined in the order init event
argument class:
    LocalService.OrderInitEventArgs eventArgs =
        new LocalService.OrderInitEventArgs
        (workflowInstance.InstanceId, textBoxOrderNumber.Text);
```

```
            OrderWorkflowInitialization(null, eventArgs);


        }

        public event EventHandler<LocalService.OrderInitEventArgs>
    OrderWorkflowInitialization;
        public void Approve(string status, string orderNumber)
        {
            UpdateDelegate ud = delegate()
            {
                textBoxStatus.Text = "Order No: " + orderNumber + " is " +
    status;
            };
            this.Invoke(ud);
        }
        public void Reject(string status, string orderNumber)
        {
            UpdateDelegate ud = delegate()
            {
                textBoxStatus.Text = "Order No: " + orderNumber + " is " +
    status;
            };
            this.Invoke(ud);
        }

    }
}
```

Building and Running the Project

The project is rather simple. Entering an order number ending in 1 will result in approval. Any other ending number will conversely result in rejection.

In the next steps, you run the project.

1. Set the BasicWorkflowHost project as the startup project.

2. Run the project, enter an order number ending in 1, and you should see results similar to Figure 4.10.

Summary

You can now create a simple workflow, build a basic host, and perform mid-flight host-workflow communication. You used local services, event args classes, HandleExternalEvent activities, and CallExternalMethod activities to conduct mid-flight host-workflow communication. You also learned about the

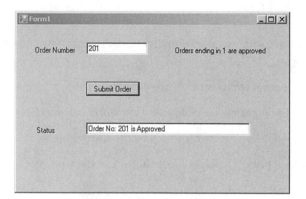

FIGURE 4.10
Approved
approval form.

DependencyProperty type and hosting the WF runtime in a Windows Forms application. In the next hour you will build on what you learned in an application that supports escalation across multiple forms.

Workshop

Quiz

1. *Why can't a .NET application communicate directly with a workflow?*

2. *Why are delegates necessary when communicating between a workflow and a Windows Forms application?*

3. *What is the purpose of a local service interface?*

4. *What are* HandleExternalEvent *activities used for?*

5. *What are* CallExternalMethod *activities used for?*

6. *Does a workflow communicate with a host synchronously or asynchronously?*

7. *Why must the local service interface payloads (the event argument classes) be marked as serializable?*

8. *How does WF know which classes can be connected to* HandleExternalEvent *and* CallExternalMethod *activities?*

Answers

1. Because the workflow runtime handles threading and workflow persistence issues for you.

2. Because Windows Forms controls are not thread safe.

3. It contains the signature for classes that perform host-workflow communication.

4. They are used to receive events raised by the host to the workflow.

5. They are used to call methods on the host from the workflow.

6. Asynchronously.

7. Because WF may need to persist the workflow; therefore, all workflow members must be serializable.

8. They are marked with `ExternalDataExchange` attributes.

HOUR 5

Creating an Escalation Workflow

What You'll Learn in This Hour:

- ► Accessing a workflow from two different forms (hosts)
- ► Retrieving workflows from the SqlWorkflowPersistence service
- ► Configuring a workflow to be tracked
- ► Configuring a workflow to be persisted in multiple hosts
- ► Using the `Listen` activity to wait for events with a timeout provision
- ► Using the `SqlTrackingQuery` type to extract tracking information
- ► Using the WorkflowMonitor SDK sample to view and track information

This application builds on an application very similar to the one you completed in the previous hour. It adds an option to require second level approval when an order amount falls between the level 1 approval threshold and the denial threshold. An escalation form is created that retrieves workflows awaiting second level approval and then allows for final approval or rejection.

The `Listen` activity is also introduced. The `Listen` activity powers the seminal workflow pattern, where the workflow awaits one or more events and times out if the events do not arrive in time.

Finally, you learn how to configure hosts to track workflows via the `SqlTrackingService`. Tracking allows running workflow information to be emitted and saved in a storage medium. You then retrieve the tracking information using the `SqlTrackingQuery` type and the WorkflowMonitor SDK sample.

From a tactical standpoint, you will modify an existing solution that is very similar to the one you ended with in the previous hour. It contains an escalation form and an order amount that is used to test approval, in contrast to using the last digit of the order number, which was done in the previous hour. Here is a summary of the steps you will perform in this hour in the order they are performed:

1. Add a new method that requests more information to the existing local service and approval form.

2. Create a new local service to support the escalation.

3. Create a new event args payload class that carries level-two approval or rejection.

4. Extend the workflow to support escalation.

5. Modify the escalation form to implement the level-two approval and rejection events and to retrieve a persisted workflow.

6. Add persistence to both hosts.

7. Add tracking to both hosts.

8. Use the `SqlTrackingQuery` type to retrieve tracking information.

9. Use the WorkflowMonitor SDK sample to graphically view tracking information.

Creating a Windows Service WF runtime host and accessing it from both forms would be a better architecture for many scenarios. This approach was not taken for simplicity's sake. An example of hosting the WF runtime in a Windows Service, however, is provided on my blog at www.reassociate.net.

Updating the Local Services

You need to add an additional method to the local service used in the previous hour that requests more information when the threshold falls in between approval and rejection. You also need to create an entirely new interface that processes the second-level approval and rejection.

Updating the Basic Local Service Interface

You need to add the method to the local services that requests additional approval in the next steps.

1. Open the Order Escalation Solution in
    `C:\SamsWf24hrs\Hour\Hour05EscalationWorkflow\Lab1\`
    `OrderEscalationSolution`.

2. Add the following code to the `BasicLocalService.cs` file below the line that contains void Reject (in the `OrderEscalationLocalServices` project).

```
void MoreInfo(string status, string orderNumber);
```

Creating the Escalation Local Service

The escalation events (second-level approval and rejection) are monitored from the same workflow but are fired by a different form, the escalation form. Therefore, a separate local service interface is created for them that will in turn be implemented in the escalation form. You do so in the next steps.

1. Add a new class to the `OrderEscalationLocalServices` project and name it **LocalServiceEscalation.cs**.

2. Replace the contents of the class file with the following:

```
using System;
using System.Collections.Generic;
using System.Text;
using System.Workflow.Runtime;
using System.Workflow.Activities;

namespace SAMS24WFBook
{
    [ExternalDataExchange]
    public interface ILocalServiceEscalation
    {
        event EventHandler<OrderLevel2EventArgs>
OrderWorkflowLevel2Approval;
        event EventHandler<OrderLevel2EventArgs>
OrderWorkflowLevel2Rejection;
    }
}
```

3. Add another class to the project named **LocalServiceEscalationEventArgs.cs** and replace its content with the following:

```
using System;
using System.Collections.Generic;
using System.Text;
using System.Workflow.Activities;

namespace SAMS24WFBook
{
    [Serializable]
    public class OrderLevel2EventArgs : ExternalDataEventArgs
    {
        private string orderApprovalStatus;
        public string OrderApprovalStatus
```

```
                        {
                            get { return orderApprovalStatus; }
                            set { orderApprovalStatus = value; }
                        }
                        public OrderLevel2EventArgs(Guid instanceId, string status)
                          : base(instanceId)
                            {
                                orderApprovalStatus = status;
                            }
                        }
                    }
```

4. Right-click the OrderEscalationLocalServices project, select Build, and fix errors, if any (do not build the entire solution yet).

Extending the Workflow

You will add the additional activities to permit additional approval to be requested and responded to. Figure 5.1 identifies the completed workflow. The highlighted section is the portion you will add in this hour.

FIGURE 5.1
Completed work-flow.

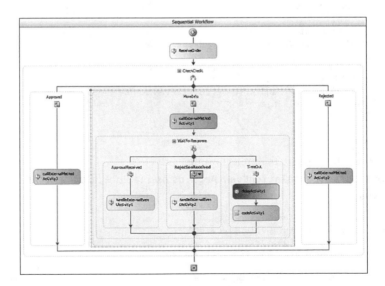

Adding the Activities

In this section, you will work with two new activities: the Listen and EventDriven activities. Listen activities underpin the seminal workflow pattern to wait for one or more events and to time out if an event is not received in time. The Listen activity, like the IfElse activity, contains one or more branches that each holds one or more activities themselves. The Listen activity and the IfElse activities look nearly identical when viewed in the workflow designer. The difference is that Listen activity branches await external input. For instance, in our sample, one branch will await approval, another rejection, and the final will time out if approval is not received in time. HandleExternalEvent activities wait for the events and a Delay activity supplies the capability to set up a timer.

Like an IfElse branch, multiple activities can also be placed in each Listen activity branch. There is, though, one restriction enforced by Listen activity branches not done so by IfElse branches. Remember that Listen activity branches are supposed to listen for an external event or wait for a timeout. To accommodate this, Listen activity branches require that the first activity placed in them be a blocking activity. Blocking activities include HandleExternalEvent and Delay activities that you have worked with, a WebServiceInput activity used with web services, and a Receive activity used with Windows Communication Foundation. The Listen activity branch activities are called EventDriven activities. EventDriven activities are not only used in Listen activities. They underpin state machine workflows as well.

You can create your own blocking activities. One way to do so is to create custom activities that derive from IEventDriven. The second way is to use WCA.exe to create strongly typed HandleExternalMethod activities (see Hour 10, "Working with EventHandlingScope and Strongly Typed Activities").

In the next steps you begin updating the workflow.

1. Open the OrderEscalationWorkflow in the workflow designer.

2. Add a third branch to the CheckCredit IfElse activity by right-clicking on the portion of the CheckCredit activity that surrounds the branches and selecting Add Branch.

3. Rename the Rejected branch **MoreInfo** (not the branch you just added).

4. Rename the new branch you just added **Rejected.**

5. Move the CallExternalMethod activity from the MoreInfo branch to the Rejected branch (this moves the activity that performs rejection into the right rejection branch).

6. The CheckCredit activity should now look like Figure 5.2.

FIGURE 5.2
CreditCheck
with unconfig-
ured MoreInfo
branch.

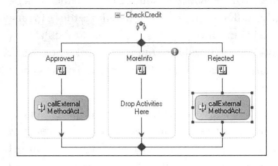

7. Add a CallExternalMethod activity to the newly added (MoreInfo) IfElse branch.

8. Now add a Listen activity below the CallExternalMethod activity in the MoreInfo branch and name it **WaitForResponse.**

9. Add a third branch to the Listen activity by right-clicking the portion of the activity that surrounds the branches and selecting Add Branch.

10. Name the left branch **ApprovalReceived** and add a HandleExternalEvent activity to it.

11. Name the middle branch **RejectionReceived** and add a HandleExternalEvent activity to it.

12. Name the right branch **TimeOut** and add a Delay and Code activity in that order. If you tried to add the Code activity first, the red exclamation mark signi-fying an error would remain because a blocking activity must be the first child.

13. The CheckCredit activity and its child WaitForResponse activity should look like Figure 5.3.

By the Way

> The Parallel activity covered in Hour 8, "Working with Parallel Activities and Correlation," and Hour 9, "Working with the Replicator and While Activities," also closely resembles the Listen activity. Many confuse it with the Listen activity and create workflows that are terribly processor intensive and at worst bring servers down. The Parallel activity runs its branches concurrently. Therefore, if a HandleExternalEvent activity exists in one branch and a Delay activity exists in another, it will keep executing both branches. Use the Parallel activity if you really want to perform two or more tasks concurrently. Use the Listen activity if you want to wait for and then act on the receipt of an event.

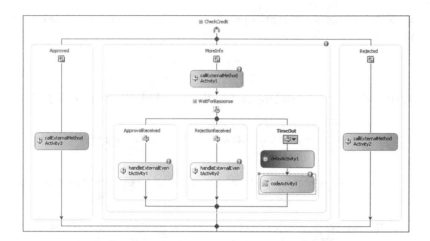

FIGURE 5.3
Workflow with
configured
CheckCredit
activity.

Configuring `CheckCredit`'s Activities

You configure the `CheckCredit` activity's child activities in this section's subsections.

Configure the `MoreInfo CallExternalMethod` Activity

Configure the `MoreInfo CallExternalMethod` activity in the next steps.

1. Click the `CallExternalMethod` activity in the `MoreInfo` branch of the `CheckCredit` activity.

2. Click the ellipsis in its `InterfaceType` property, select BasicLocalService, select ILocalService in the middle of the screen, and click OK. Be careful because there are two interfaces to select from.

3. Select the `MoreInfo` method in the `MethodName` property.

4. Enter **AdditionalApproval** in the `MethodInvoking` property, press Enter, and enter the following in its handler:

        Status = "SecondLevelApproval";

5. Switch back to the workflow designer.

6. Click the ellipsis in the `orderNumber` property and select the `OrderNumber` member to bind the `orderNumber` property to the `OrderNumber` member.

7. Click the ellipsis in the `status` property and select the Status member to bind the `status` property to the Status member.

Configure the `ApprovalReceived HandleExternalEvent` Activity

In the next steps, you configure the `ApprovalReceived HandleExternalEvent` activity.

1. Click the `HandleExternalEvent` activity in the `ApprovalReceived` branch of the `WaitForResponse` activity.

2. Click the ellipsis in its `InterfaceType` property, click the +, select BasicLocalService, select ILocalServiceEscalation in the middle of the screen, and click OK.

3. Select the `OrderWorkflowLevel2Approval` event in the `EventName` property.

4. Enter **`ApprovalLevel2Invoked`** in the Invoked property, press Enter, and enter the following in its handler:

```
MessageBox.Show("Level 2 approval for order: " + OrderNumber);
```

Configuring the `RejectionReceived HandleExternalEvent` Activity

In the next steps, you configure the `RejectionReceived HandleExternalEvent` activity.

1. Switch back to the workflow designer.

2. Click the `HandleExternalEvent` activity in the `RejectionReceived` branch of the `Listen` activity.

3. Click the ellipsis in its `InterfaceType` property, click the +, select BasicLocalService, select ILocalServiceEscalation in the middle of the screen, and click OK.

4. Select the `OrderWorkflowLevel2Rejection` event in the `EventName` property.

5. Enter **`RejectionLevel2Invoked`** in the Invoked property, press Enter, and enter the following in its handler:

```
MessageBox.Show("Level 2 approval for order: " + OrderNumber);
```

Configuring the Activities in the Timeout Branch

In the next step, you configure the activities in the Timeout branch of the Listen activity.

1. Switch back to the workflow designer.

2. Enter **00:02:00** in the Delay activity TimeoutDuration property.

3. Double-click the Code activity and enter the following in its handler:

```
MessageBox.Show("Level 2 timeout for order: " + OrderNumber);
```

Updating the Workflow Code-Beside File

In the two subsections of this section you add a dependency property and change the rules on the CheckCredit activity.

Add a DependencyProperty

In the next steps, you add a DependencyProperty named OrderAmount and initialize it when the workflow receives the order.

1. Create a new DependencyProperty named OrderAmount by right-clicking in the code-beside file below the Status dependency property, selecting Insert Snippet, double-clicking Other, and then Workflow. Select the Dependency Property—Property choice, name it **OrderAmount** (leave the Property suffix), press Tab and set its type to double, and press Enter to leave the remaining defaults.

2. Add the following code to the existing OrderInvoked handler below where the OrderNumber is initiated:

```
OrderAmount = (e as SAMS24WFBook.OrderEventArgs).OrderAmount;
```

Change the Rules on the CheckCredit Activity

In the next steps, you will now check the order amount to determine approval in the IfElse activity rather than using the last digit of the order number. Orders less than $1,000 will be approved, orders larger than or equal to $1,000 and less than $2,000 require additional approval, and orders $2,000 or larger are rejected. You will create rules for the first two possibilities in the Approved and MoreInfo branches. There is no need for a third rule. It is the else.

1. Switch to workflow designer view.

2. Click the Approved branch of the `IfElse` activity, select Code Condition from its `Condition` property drop-down, click + to the left of the `Condition` property, and overwrite the current entry in the `Condition` property with **OrderApprovedCondition.**

3. Enter the following in the handler:

```
if (OrderAmount < 1000)
    e.Result = true;
else
    e.Result = false;
```

4. Switch back to the workflow designer.

5. Click the MoreInfo branch of the `IfElse` activity, select Code Condition from its `Condition` property drop-down, click + to the left of the `Condition` property, and enter **AdditionalApprovalCondition** in the `Condition` property that appears after selecting Code Condition.

6. Enter the following in the handler:

```
if (OrderAmount < 2000)
    e.Result = true;
else
    e.Result = false;
```

7. Build the `OrderEscalationWorkflows` project and fix errors, if any.

Update the Forms (Hosts)

You update both the first level and escalation forms hosts in the subsections in this section.

Implement New Interface Members in the Escalation Form

Although the form is already created, the second-level approval and rejection events specified in the escalation interface must still be implemented. You will do so in the next steps.

1. Open the `EscalationForm` in code view.

2. Replace the existing class declaration with the following, which implements the escalation local service.

```
public partial class EscalationForm : Form,
SAMS24WFBook.ILocalServiceEscalation
```

3. Add the following event declarations at the top of the local service implementation region (which look like this: #region Local Service Implementation):

```
public event EventHandler<OrderLevel2EventArgs>
    OrderWorkflowLevel2Approval;

public event EventHandler<OrderLevel2EventArgs>
    OrderWorkflowLevel2Rejection;
```

4. In the EscalationForm designer, double-click the Approve button and add the following code to its hander:

```
// Pass the Level2Approval event to the workflow
OrderLevel2EventArgs eventArgs =
    new OrderLevel2EventArgs(workflowInstance.InstanceId,
"Approved");

OrderWorkflowLevel2Approval(null, eventArgs);
```

5. Double-click the Reject button and add the following code to its hander:

```
// Pass the Level2Rejection event to the workflow
OrderLevel2EventArgs eventArgs =
    new OrderLevel2EventArgs(workflowInstance.InstanceId,
"Rejected");

OrderWorkflowLevel2Rejection(null, eventArgs);
```

6. Build the EscalationForm project and fix errors, if any.

Implement the MoreInfo Method in the Basic Order Form

In the next steps, you implement the new additional approval request in the basic order form so that it can accept the additional approval request from the workflow. You do not need to modify the event arguments because no new events are added (or more specifically, no new event payloads are created).

1. Add the following method to the BasicOrderForm.cs file below the Reject method in the Local Service implementation region:

```
public void MoreInfo(string status, string orderNumber)
{
    UpdateDelegate ud = delegate()
    {
        textBoxStatus.Text = "Order No: " + orderNumber + " " +
status;
```

```
        };
        this.Invoke(ud);
    }
```

2. Build the `BasicOrdersForm` project and fix errors, if any.

Configure Hosts to Track and Persist

In this section, you will configure both hosts to track and persist workflows. You will learn to configure multihost persistence, which requires setting the persistence ownership to work across hosts. Tracking is a new topic that is discussed next.

Add Tracking to Basic and Escalation Forms

Tracking is a mainstay feature in business process management and workflow packages that permits running workflows to emit information that can be used to examine the execution path taken by prior workflows and to see the execution path taken so far by currently processing workflows.

The emitted tracking data is generally saved to a storage medium. WF emits the standard workflow level events you have worked with (for example, as started, completed, loaded, unloaded, and idled). It also tracks the events of each activity on the workflow. Each activity contains the following possible events that are tracked: `Canceling`, `Closed`, `Compensating`, `Executing`, `Faulting`, and `Initialized`.

You will register the out-of-the-box `SqlTrackingService` in this hour, which will provide you with workflow and activity-level tracking. Then you will use the `SqlTrackingQuery` object and the `WorkflowMonitor` SDK sample to view the persisted tracking information. These tools show that simply registering the `SqlTrackingService` provides the capability to monitor workflow execution. Additional tracking features are covered in Hour 13, "Learning to Track Workflows."

Add tracking to both workflow hosts. The `BasicOrdersForm` host takes the process from order receipt to completion if no second-level approval is required, and through waiting for second-level approval if it is required. The `EscalationForm` takes the process from waiting for second-level approval to completion.

In the next steps, you add tracking to both forms.

1. Open the `BasicOrderForm.cs` file in code view and add the following using directive:

```
using System.Workflow.Runtime.Tracking;
```

2. Add the following code to the `GetWorkflowRuntime` method above the code that adds the persistence service to the runtime:

```
// Add the sql tracking service to the runtime
SqlTrackingService sts = new SqlTrackingService(connectionString);
workflowRuntime.AddService(sts);
```

3. Build the `BasicOrdersForm` project and fix errors, if any.

4. Repeat steps 1 and 2 in the `EscalationForm.cs` file.

5. Build the `EscalationForm` project and fix errors, if any.

That is all that is necessary to add tracking in WF. As you will soon see, this adds quite a bit of transparency and auditing capability to your workflows.

Add Persistence to Both Forms

In Hour 3, "Learning Basic Hosting," you registered the SqlWorkflowPersistenceService with the host. While doing so, you set the SqlWorkflowPersistenceService parameters, which determined whether the workflow automatically unloaded when idle, specified the database connection string, specified how often the runtime should check for expired timers, and finally how long a workflow could remain locked. In Hour 3, you also set the value that determines locking to `TimeSpan.MaxValue`, which is the simplest thing to do. However, now that you are implementing more sophisticated persistence across forms, let's look closer at what this property does and how it should be set.

When the WF runtime is processing a workflow, it locks the workflow record by setting a value. Processing means while the workflow is actually executing. This does not include the time a workflow is persisted. The lock is removed each time the workflow persists. Therefore, other WorkflowRuntimes can access the workflow because it is no longer being used by that host. This default behavior is fine except when a server crash or other problem occurs that causes a workflow to be abandoned by a host during processing. In this case, the workflow remains locked for the `TimeSpan.MaxValue` default period (approximately 10,000 years).

You can override the default workflow locking behavior by setting a different ownership duration. In case a workflow execution fails, the workflow will remain locked for this period of time and not 10,000 years (or more likely, until someone goes in and manually modifies the table).

You must understand one major caveat when overriding the workflow locking behavior. If you do not set it for a long enough time period, your workflow will fail. This is because when you go to persist again, there will be no lock on the record and the WorkflowRuntime will not update it. Therefore, you must set this value to a period that is longer than your longest workflow burst. This is generally a matter of seconds (or even less). To be safe, you might want to set it at a couple of minutes or some other value that would not be reached even during abnormally slow processing.

In the next steps, you modify the period of time that the workflow remains locked for two minutes.

1. Open the `BasicOrderForm.cs` file and replace the current line of code that sets the `ownershipDuration` value with the following:

   ```
   TimeSpan ownershipDuration = new TimeSpan(0, 0, 2, 0);
   ```

2. Just to be sure, build the `BasicOrdersForm` project and fix errors, if any.

3. Open the `EscalationForm.cs` file and replace the current line of code that sets the `ownershipDuration` value with the following:

   ```
   TimeSpan ownershipDuration = new TimeSpan(0, 0, 2, 0);
   ```

4. Just to be sure, build the `EscalationForm` project and fix errors, if any.

The workflow will be owned by whichever host is running it for two minutes between persistence points. This gives each plenty of time to process a burst and allows the workflow to be accessed again in case of a crash of some type.

If you are using SQL Server 2000 and you store your tracking and persistence tables in the same database, you will spawn distributed transaction coordinator (DTC) by default, even though they are stored in the same database. The workaround for this is to use the `SharedConnectionWorkflowCommitWorkBatchService`. Using this service is not covered in this book. See MSDN or another source if this applies to you.

Retrieve Tracking Data

The `SqlTrackingQuery` class provides methods that return tracking data from the tracking database created by the SQL tracking service. We will return the tracked workflow and activity data. In this example, the retrieved information will be stored in a text box, but it could just as easily go on a report or be used for other purposes.

The WorkflowMonitor SDK application demonstrated at the end of this hour shows another example of what can be done with the standard emitted tracking data.

In the next steps, you add code to query the tracking data.

1. Open the EscalationForm and double-click the Get Tracking command button. Add the following code to its handler:

```
ShowTracking(workflowInstanceID);
```

2. Add the ShowTracking method below the Get Tracking command button handler as shown:

```
void ShowTracking(Guid instanceId)
{
}
```

3. Instantiate a StringBuilder and SqlTrackingQuery objects in the ShowTracking method as shown:

```
StringBuilder sb = new StringBuilder();

// Create a new SqlTrackingQuery object.
SqlTrackingQuery sqlTrackingQuery = new
    SqlTrackingQuery(connectionString);

// Query the SqlTrackingQuery for a specific workflow instance ID.
SqlTrackingWorkflowInstance sqlTrackingWorkflowInstance;

sqlTrackingQuery.TryGetWorkflow(instanceId, out
    sqlTrackingWorkflowInstance);
```

4. Check whether any records are returned by adding the following code (below the code you just added):

```
// Check whether there is a matching workflow with this ID.
if (sqlTrackingWorkflowInstance != null)
{
}
```

5. Add code between the brackets (from the previous step) to iterate the workflow tracking records (workflow-level events) and populate the string builder added in the previous step, as shown:

```
// Examine the workflow events.
sb.AppendLine("Workflow Events:");

foreach (WorkflowTrackingRecord workflowTrackingRecord in
    sqlTrackingWorkflowInstance.WorkflowEvents)
{
    sb.AppendLine("EventDescription : " +
        workflowTrackingRecord.TrackingWorkflowEvent +
```

```
                   "  DateTime : " + workflowTrackingRecord.EventDateTime);
            }

            sb.AppendLine("");
```

6. Add code below the code just added to iterate the activity tracking records (activity-level events) and populate the string builder as shown:

```
// Examine the activity events.
sb.AppendLine("Activity Events:");

foreach (ActivityTrackingRecord activityTrackingRecord in
  sqlTrackingWorkflowInstance.ActivityEvents)
{
    sb.AppendLine("Activity Qualified ID " +
        activityTrackingRecord.QualifiedName +
        "    StatusDescription : " +
        activityTrackingRecord.ExecutionStatus +
        "    DateTime : " + activityTrackingRecord.EventDateTime);
}
```

7. Add code below the code you just added to add the string builder text to the text box on the form as shown:

```
textBooxTrackingInfo.Text = sb.ToString();
```

8. Build the EscalationForm project and fix errors, if any.

9. The ShowTracking method should look like Listing 5.1.

LISTING 5.1   ShowTracking Method

```
void ShowTracking(Guid instanceId)
{
    StringBuilder sb = new StringBuilder();

    // Create a new SqlTrackingQuery object.
    SqlTrackingQuery sqlTrackingQuery = new
       SqlTrackingQuery(connectionString);

    // Query the SqlTrackingQuery for a specific workflow instance ID.
    SqlTrackingWorkflowInstance sqlTrackingWorkflowInstance;

    sqlTrackingQuery.TryGetWorkflow(instanceId, out
    sqlTrackingWorkflowInstance);

    // Check whether there is a matching workflow with this ID.
    if (sqlTrackingWorkflowInstance != null)
    {
        // Examine the workflow events.
        sb.AppendLine("Workflow Events:");

        foreach (WorkflowTrackingRecord workflowTrackingRecord in
```

```
                   sqlTrackingWorkflowInstance.WorkflowEvents)
            {
                sb.AppendLine("EventDescription : " +
                   workflowTrackingRecord.TrackingWorkflowEvent +
                   "  DateTime : " + workflowTrackingRecord.EventDateTime);
            }

            sb.AppendLine("");
            // Examine the activity events.
            sb.AppendLine("Activity Events:");

            foreach (ActivityTrackingRecord activityTrackingRecord in
              sqlTrackingWorkflowInstance.ActivityEvents)
            {
                sb.AppendLine("Activity Qualified ID " +
                   activityTrackingRecord.QualifiedName +
                   "    StatusDescription : " +
                   activityTrackingRecord.ExecutionStatus +
                   "    DateTime : " +
activityTrackingRecord.EventDateTime);
            }
            textBooxTrackingInfo.Text = sb.ToString();
        }
    }
```

> The SqlTrackingService is the only OOB tracking service shipped with WF. You can,
> however, create your own custom tracking services based on the
> TrackingService base class to store tracking information to a file, an Oracle
> database, or any other medium you want to. Doing so is not covered in this book.
> There are ConsoleTrackingService and FileTrackingService samples in the WF,
> WCF, and CardSpace samples. Details for accessing these samples can be found
> in Hour 1, "Understanding Windows Workflow Foundation."

Retrieve the Workflow from Persistence

The escalation form needs to be able to retrieve workflows that require second-level
approval. It will do so by extracting the workflow from the persistence store. You will
use the SqlWorkflowPersistenceService.GetAllWorkflows method to retrieve all
persisted workflows and add them to a combo box. This method returns a collection
of all persisted workflows that can be iterated through (this is described in slightly
more detail at the end of this section). The selected workflow will then be loaded into
memory, where it can be approved, rejected, and tracking information can be
retrieved.

In the next steps, you retrieve the workflow saved to the persistence store in the first
level from in the escalation form.

1. Add the following method to the top of the persistence extraction region in the
   `EscalationForm.cs` file.

   ```
   private void GetPersistedWorkflows()
   {
       comboBoxOrders.Items.Clear();
       foreach (SqlPersistenceWorkflowInstanceDescription
           sqlWid in sqlPersistenceService.GetAllWorkflows())
       {

   comboBoxOrders.Items.Add(sqlWid.WorkflowInstanceId.ToString());
       }
       comboBoxOrders.Refresh();
   }
   ```

2. Double-click the `ComboBox` on the form and add the following code to its handler to load the selected workflow back into memory:

   ```
   if (comboBoxOrders.Items.Count != 0)
   {
       workflowInstanceID = new Guid(comboBoxOrders.Text);

       // Retrieve the selected workflow from the persistence
   service
       // and load it.
       workflowInstance =
   workflowRuntime.GetWorkflow(workflowInstanceID);
       workflowInstance.Load();
   }
   ```

3. Add the following code to load the workflows into the combo box at the end of
   the `EscalationForm_Load` method:

   ```
   // Get the persisted workflows from the sql persistence service
   GetPersistedWorkflows();
   ```

4. Add the following code to load the workflows to the end of the
   `workflowRuntime_WorkflowCompleted` event handler so that the completed
   workflow is removed from the combo box:

   ```
   UpdateDelegate ud = delegate()
   {
       GetPersistedWorkflows();
   };
   this.Invoke(ud);
   ```

At this point, the workflow is loaded back into memory and ready to receive
second-level approval response. There are a couple of new items introduced:

► First, the workflows are retrieved from the persistence store by calling the
  `SqlWorkflowPersistenceService.GetAllWorkflows` method. The
  `SqlPersistenceWorkflowInstanceDescription` type is returned for

each workflow returned from the store. This type contains the `WorkflowInstanceId`, information on the next timer expiration, whether the workflow is blocked, and other information.

▶ The workflow retrieved from the combo box is loaded back into memory by calling the `WorkflowRuntime.GetWorkflow` method, and then calling the `WorkflowInstance.Load` method. This has the same effect as calling the `WorkflowRuntime.CreateWorkflow` method and then calling `WorklfowInstance.Start` method on a new workflow instance.

5. Build the `EscalationForm` project and fix errors, if any.

Running the Solution

You will run three workflows. In the first two, you examine the different persistence behaviors in workflows that do and do not require second-level approval. The third looks at tracking and shows the workflow execution using the tracking. All the workflows that contain second-level approval demonstrate the `Listen` activity and escalation support added to the workflow.

First-Level Approval or Rejection

Enter a workflow with a value less than 1,000 or larger than 2,000 and check the persistence table. You will see that the workflow did not persist because additional approval was not required.

In the next steps you run the workflow using a value that will not persist because it does not require additional approval. You will then check the persistence database to validate whether or not the workflow persisted.

1. Set the `BasicOrdersForm` project as the startup project and run the solution.

2. Enter any order number and an order amount with a value less than 1,000 and click Submit.

3. Open the `WFTrackingAndPersistence` database (in SQL Server Management Studio or through other means), select the `InstanceState` table, and choose to show all rows. The contents should be empty because nothing should have been persisted. The workflow didn't require second-level approval and therefore is not persisted while waiting for approval.

4. Exit the basic order form.

Second-Level Approval or Rejection

In the next steps, you will enter an amount that triggers persistence and verify this by checking the database. Then you will use the escalation form to provide second level approval.

1. Run the solution and enter any order number, an order amount with a value between 1,000 and 2,000 (noninclusive), and click Submit. The order form should look like Figure 5.4 (the text box should contain the message `second level approval required`).

FIGURE 5.4
Order that requires additional approval.

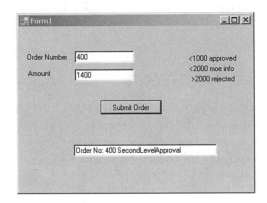

2. Now refresh the `InstanceState` table, and you should notice an entry in the table that looks similar to Figure 5.5:

FIGURE 5.5
Workflow persisted in InstanceState table.

uidInstanceID	state	status	unlocked	blocked	info	modified	ownerID	ownedUntil	nextTimer
2c4-a872d2b6ead0	<Binary data>	0	1	1		11/1/2007 10:3...	NULL	NULL	11/1/2007 10:3...
NULL	NULL	NULL	NULL	NULL	NULL	NULL	NULL	NULL	NULL

3. Exit the basic order form.

4. Set the `EscalationForm` project as the startup project.

5. Load the escalation form (shown in Figure 5.6), select the workflow from the combo box, click the Approve button, and click OK when the workflow is approved and completed dialogs appear.

6. Refresh the InstanceState table; there should no longer be any records because the workflow is completed.

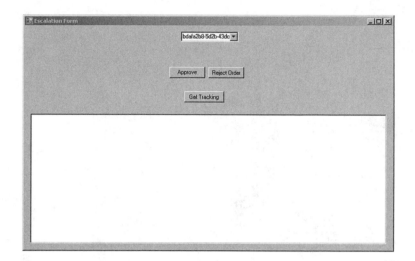

FIGURE 5.6
Workflow loaded
in escalation
form to be
approved or
rejected.

Second Level Approval and Tracking

The escalation form contains a Get Tracking button and a text box to store the tracking information. In this run of the workflow, you will view the tracking results before and after processing second-level approval. Previously, activity execution will have stopped at the `WaitForResponse` `Listen` activity. After second-level approval, the workflow executes the remaining activities. The remaining activities will take it down one of the `Listen` activity branches (for example, `Approved`, `Rejected`, `MoreInfo`).

In the next steps you will enter an amount that requires second level approval again. This time, you will utilize tracking to monitor the process.

1. Set the `BasicOrdersForm` project as the startup project and run the solution.

2. Enter any order number, and an order amount with a value between 1,000 and 2,000 (noninclusive), and click Submit.

3. Exit the basic order form.

4. Set the `EscalationForm` project as the startup project and load the escalation form.

5. Select the workflow from the combo box.

6. Click the Get Tracking button. The text box at the bottom of the form should contain the workflow and activity execution. As mentioned, the final activity event will be `WaitForResponse`, as shown in Figure 5.7.

7. Click the Approved button (and click OK on dialog buttons) and then click the Get Tracking button again. Your form should look like Figure 5.8. You will have to scroll to see all the activity events.

FIGURE 5.7
Workflow escalation form with tracking run through second-level approval.

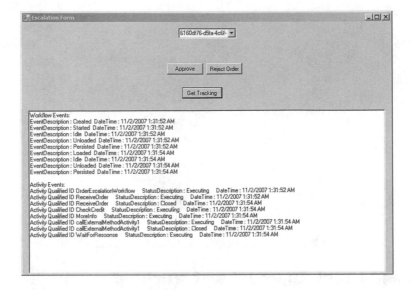

FIGURE 5.8
Workflow escalation form with tracking run through completion.

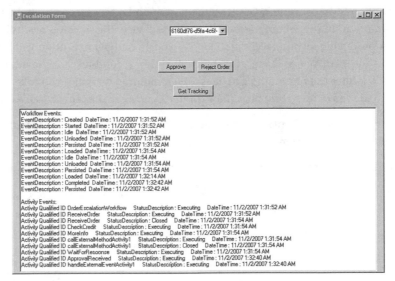

Tracking information, unlike persistence, is retained after workflow completion. Therefore, tracking provides a repository of runtime information. By default activity- and workflow-level events are tracked. Custom information, such as order number and amount, can also be tracked. The means to capture custom tracking information will be covered in Hour 13, "Learning to Track Workflows."

Capturing the execution history of workflow- and activity-level events, however, is quite powerful in itself, as you will see next.

Running the WorkflowMonitor SDK Sample

So far, you have tracked information and used queries to place the results in a text box. The WorkflowMonitor SDK sample extracts the information from running workflows and displays it in a graphical format similar to the way workflows are displayed in the workflow designer. It achieves this by rehosting the workflow designer (see the next note). Many workflow/business process management systems feature sophisticated process-monitoring capabilities that leverage business intelligence and other tools to make process data available for analysis and alerts. WF has the capability to extract the information from running processes, and the SDK sample shown in this section offers basic monitoring capabilities. These capabilities are significant though, because they alone provide the ability to monitor workflow state and to project its future execution paths. You can customize the sample because it comes with source code.

> **By the Way**
>
> Rehosting the workflow designer is not covered in this book. See Hour 1, "Understanding Windows Workflow Foundation," for designer rehosting resources if you are interested.

Downloading and Installing WorkflowMonitor

In the next steps, you download and install the WorkflowMonitor SDK sample.

1. Copy both the `BasicLocalService.dll` and `BasicLocalServiceWorkflow.dll` from `C:\SamsWf24hrs\Hour\Hour05EscalationWorkflow\Lab1\OrderEscalationS olution\BasicLocalServiceWorkflow\bin\Debug` to your sample installation directory `WF\Applications\WorkflowMonitor\CS \WorkflowMonitor\bin\Debug`.

2. If you have not already downloaded the WF sample applications, go to http:/ /msdn2.microsoft.com/en-us/library/ms741706.aspx and download and install them in any directory. My directory is `C:\WFSamples\WCF_WF_CardSpace_Orcas_Beta2_Samples\WF_Samples\Sampl es\Applications\WorkflowMonitor\CS\WorkflowMonitor\bin\Debug`, which is a manifest of following the default installation. I will assume this directory; substitute as appropriate if you use an alternative directory.

> **By the Way**
>
> You must also copy `BasicLocalService.dll` and `BasicLocalServiceWorkflow. dll` from
> `C:\SamsBook\Hour\Hour05EscalationWorkflow\Lab1\OrderEscalationSolut ion\BasicLocalServiceWorkflow\bin\Debug` to

C:\WFSamples\WCF_WF_CardSpace_Orcas_Beta2_Samples\WF_Samples\Sam-
ples\Applications\WorkflowMonitor\CS\WorkflowMonitor\bin\Debug. Yes,
you do need the local service DLL as well. Alternatively, you could copy your workflow assemblies to the GAC instead of to the workflow monitor debug directory.

3. Go to the WorkflowMonitor directory and start the WorkflowMonitor solution.

4. You may receive an error because no tracking database has been configured
   with the application. If so, ignore it because you will configure it now.

5. If the Settings form does not automatically pop up, click the Monitor menu
   choice at the top of the form and select its Options choice. You should see the
   form shown in Figure 5.9.

FIGURE 5.9
Workflow escala-
tion form with
tracking run
through comple-
tion.

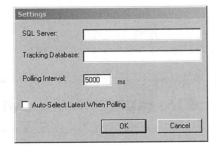

6. Enter your server name and tracking database name and click OK.

7. You will now see the escalation workflows and the WorkflowMonitor application, as shown in Figure 5.10.

FIGURE 5.10
Workflow Moni-
tor tool in action.

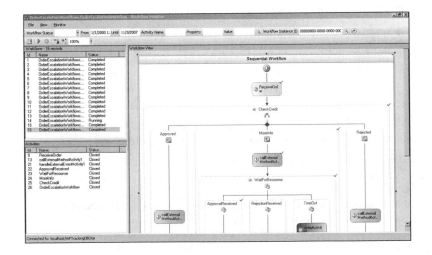

8. You can move from workflow to workflow by clicking different workflows in the upper-left pane.

9. If you want to filter only to running workflows, you can select Running from the Workflow Status drop-down and click the magnifying glass to the left of Workflow Instance ID.

The middle pane contains the workflow designer. Some activities are check marked. This signifies that they were executed. Therefore, you can observe the execution path of previously executed workflows and also the "path-to-date" for currently running workflows.

The upper-left pane lists the workflows. The lower-left pane shows the activities that have executed for the currently selected workflow. A navigation bar across the top permits the workflows displayed to be filtered by various states (such as all running workflows). Workflows can also be filtered based on workflow and activity properties, such as order amount.

In a real-world scenario, you would need to filter by values that are less than or greater than, as well as equal to, and there would be a need for and/or operators to form useful queries (such as orders over $1,000 that are on credit hold). Although this level of functionality is not offered OOB, the source code is included, and you can add this type of functionality if you need it.

Tracking is WF's main vehicle for adding runtime transparency to WF that can be combined with WF's inherent design-time transparency. The combination of design-time and runtime transparency is one of the WF's main features. WF has to be embeddable and appropriate to all types of Windows applications. Through adding the persistence and tracking services, you are seeing how it is able to mold itself to the needs of the host and fulfill its appropriate quota.

Summary

This hour saw the creation of a workflow application, demonstrated the use of tracking, extracted workflows from the persistence service, and explored the Listen activity, a seminal workflow artifact.

It is very common that people want to know why they should use WF. You have already seen the following areas where WF offers benefits:

► Runtime transparency through tracking (and designer rehosting).

► The ability to wait for events and to time out if no event arrives to support escalation scenarios (also known as asynchronous process support).

► Inherent design-time transparency through its modeling capabilities.

You will learn of many new WF features, such as Custom activities. You will also learn to enhance the escalation capabilities learned in this hour throughout the remainder of this book. However, the combination of runtime transparency, asynchronous process support, and inherent design-time transparency are solid benefits in and of themselves. You will learn about state machine workflows over the next two hours.

Workshop

Quiz

1. *What constraint does an* `EventDriven` *activity impose?*

2. *What activity composes a branch of a* `Listen` *activity?*

3. *What method is used to retrieve workflows from the SqlWorkflowPersistenceService?*

4. *Where do your workflow assemblies need to reside for the WorkflowMonitor service to use them?*

5. *What do you use the* `SqlTrackingQuery` *type for?*

6. *When are persisted workflows removed from the persistence store?*

7. *What benefit do you get by registering the SqlTrackingService?*

Answers

1. Its first child must be a blocking activity such as a `Delay` or `HandleExternalEvent` activity.

2. `EventDriven`.

3. SqlWorkflowPersistenceService.GetAllWorkflows.

4. The directory that contains the WorkflowMonitor DLL or the GAC.

5. To query workflows saved by the SqlTrackingService.

6. When the workflow completes (successfully or unsuccessfully).

7. All workflow and activity events are tracked. Through this you gain runtime transparency, which, for example, the WorkflowMonitor exploits.

PART II

State Machined Workflows and Advanced Control Flow Activities

HOUR 6

Creating Basic State Machine Workflows

What You'll Learn in This Hour:

▶ Overview of state machine workflows

▶ Summary of main state machine workflow artifacts used to build state machine workflows in WF

▶ Build a simple state machine workflow and execute it

▶ Extend the workflow to be more useful and to use more features

You build a state machine workflow in this hour in two parts. In the first part, you create a basic workflow with single-level approval support. In the second, you add second-level approval and explore state retrieval and hierarchical states, which are a couple of the capabilities unique to state machine workflows. Additional advanced features will be covered in Hour 7, "Creating Advanced State Machine Workflows."

The state machine will be connected to a Windows Form and rely on a local service for mediation. See Hour 4, "Learning Host-Workflow Data Exchange," if you need help creating and/or implementing the local service.

Explaining State Machine Workflows

State machines are a very common modeling technique—for both creating executing programs and static diagrams—built on process milestones and events. State machines are largely predicated on the notion that processes are dynamic and take many divergent paths to completion. This is why state machines are frequently associated with human-centric processes. In fact, one reason WF proclaims to offer human workflow is that it includes state machine workflow modeling. The state machine workflows in WF are similar to those offered in UML. The creators of WF saw the need to offer a state-based, event-driven workflow modeling option as well.

State machines are centered on two internal elements: states and events. The states are the business milestones or stages in the business process. In our ordering example, create, approval, distribution, and level-two approval are all states. Each state possesses one or more valid actions. The approval state, for example, contains approval and rejection actions. Structuring the process as a set of autonomous states that each contains a set of valid actions is what makes it so easy to transition to and from states throughout the process. No more effort is required to transition from the distribution state to the approval state than to follow the projected path from distribution to closed. In either case, the desired destination state must be specified. This more accurately captures the unfolding of real-world processes that, for instance, transition from create to approval to distribute, only to go back to an earlier state when last-minutes changes occur.

Figure 6.1 illustrates a generic state machine workflow. The business milestones are embodied in the states. Transitions between the milestones are identified in the lines that connect the milestones. Finally, the text represent the events that trigger the actions and potentially transitions. The states are first-class citizens. The current state is always unambiguous in a state machine workflow. This clarity carries over to the past and current valid transitions as well that are both readily extractable. This introspection capability is most powerful when the states are business milestones. This way, the current state is not only technically valuable but also contains business value.

FIGURE 6.1
Order state
machine.

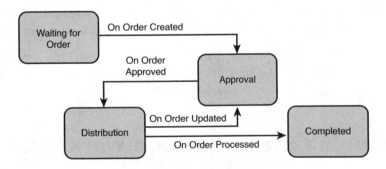

Although state machines offer many compelling features, they also own a couple of well-known limitations:

The first is that they can be hard to comprehend and implement. Although they offer a solid implementation framework for many processes, it is frequently easier to look at a process sequentially in its logical execution path than to look at a set of self-standing states connected by a collection of lines that identify all possible routes. Business people particularly find them hard to understand.

Second, whereas state machine workflows represent a rather elegant solution to transition and monitor state, they can be hard to maintain and comprehend when many states and events exist. In fact, combinational explosion is a common term used to describe this phenomenon. Imagine Figure 6.1 outfitted with exception handling and more states, as would be the case in many real-world processes. Some workarounds exist, including a concept known as hierarchical states (covered later in this hour), that alleviate this problem.

Hours 8 to 10 demonstrate activities that can be placed on sequential and state machine workflows that provide data-driven control flow and a `foreach`-like activity with parallel capabilities. These advanced control flow activities allow sequential workflows to be much more dynamic than they could traditionally be. In Hours 20 to 24, you create your own custom activities, some of which control flow. WF, therefore, offers many alternatives and augmentations to the common sequential and state machine patterns, which underlie WF's flexibility.

Investigating State Machine Workflow Components

There are six main components to a state machine workflow activity (there are others to the state machine workflow instance):

▶ The `StateMachineWorkflowActivity` encompasses the entire workflow. The `StateMachineWorkflowActivity` serves the same purpose to state machine workflows that the `SequentialWorkflowActivity` provides to sequential workflows. It is the outermost activity that all other workflow activities are placed into to compose the workflow.

▶ The `State` activity makes up half the cornerstone of the state machine workflow. The business milestones in the process, such as approval, second-level approval, and distribution, are all represented as State activities on a state machine workflow.

▶ The other half of the cornerstone of the state machine workflow, the `EventDriven` activity, holds the events in each state. For instance, both approval and rejection are events within the approval state. `EventDriven` activities in state machine workflow are nearly identical to their sequential workflow counterparts in the branches in Listen activities. (The activity contains multiple branches that require that the first activity inserted be a blocking activity, such as HandleExternalEvent or Delay.)

▶ The SetState activity updates the TargetStateName property and therefore is responsible for transitioning among states.

▶ StateInitialization activities are essentially sequence activities that permit a collection of activities (no blocking or Listen activities) to be included. These activities provide whatever preprocessing is necessary when the state is transitioned to. Sample usage scenarios include passing information to the calling program upon entering the state, checking roles, and instantiating counters.

▶ StateFinalization activities permit actions to be conducted when a state is transitioned away from. Otherwise, they are identical to StateInitialization activities.

These are the basics of state machine workflows. Next, you create one.

Creating the Project

The Windows Form and local service projects are already created. You will add a workflow project to the solution that utilizes these existing projects in the next steps.

1. Open the BasicStateMachineWorkflowSolution solution in the c:\SamsWf24hrs\Hours\Hour06StateMachineWorkflow\Lab1\BasicStateMA chineWorkflowSolution directory, right click on the solution, and select Add, and New Project.

2. Click the + to expand Visual C# Project Templates, select Workflow on the left pane, and choose the State Machine Workflow Library project template. Name the project **BasicStateMachineWorkflows.**

3. Rename Worklflow1.cs **StateMachineWorkflowBasic.cs.**

4. Add a reference to the BasicStateMachineLocalServices project.

5. Add a reference to System.Windows.Forms.

Creating the Workflow

In this section, you create the state machine workflow.

Preparatory Work

In the next steps you perform preparatory work, such as adding a reference.

1. Add a reference from `BasicStateMachineWindowsForm` to the `BasicStateMachineWorkflows` project.

2. Open `StateMachineWorkflowBasic.cs` and add the following code to initialize variables below the constructor.

```
private string orderNumber;
private double orderAmount;
const double level2OrderAmount = 1000;
```

3. Add the following using directive:

```
using System.Windows.Forms;
```

Adding `State` and `EventDriven` Activities

First, look at the workflow designer; it is different from the one used so far to create sequential workflows. It is a free-form designer that permits `State` activities to be added in any location. The states will then be connected through lines among the events contained in the states. The *x* and *y* coordinate and event connections are tracked in a `.layout` file with the same name as the workflow.

The workflow is prepopulated with one `State` activity, the initial state. Click the workflow surface (not the initial state) and look at the properties. The InitialName property is set to the name of the State that was automatically added to the workflow. This State is entered when the workflow is started. In this exercise, you add two other states. One is the completed state, a special state that signifies the end of a state machine workflow. After a state machine workflow arrives at the Completed state, it is finished. No other activities can be inserted into this state. You will also add an approval state that represents a typical state that lies between the created and completed states.

In the next steps, you will add completed and approval states to the workflow.

1. Click the `State` activity added with the workflow and set its name to **Initial**.

2. Click the workflow surface and select the drop-down in the workflow `InitialStateName` property and set it to the Initial state. (This is a workflow-level property that points to a `State` activity. It is not a property set on a `State` activity, as might be expected.)

3. Drag and drop a State activity onto the workflow to the right of the existing State activity and set its Name property to **Approval.**

4. Add another State activity below the State activity you just added and set its Name property to **Completed.**

5. Click the workflow surface and select the drop-down in the workflow CompletedStateName property and set it to the Completed state. (This again is a workflow-level property.)

6. Add an EventDriven activity into the Approval state and name it **Approved. The Approval** State should now look like Figure 6.2.

FIGURE 6.2
State machine workflow.

7. Now add another EventDriven activity to the Approval state and name it **Rejected.**

8. Add another EventDriven activity, and this time drop it in the Initial state and name it **Created.**

9. Your workflow should now look like Figure 6.3.

FIGURE 6.3
State machine workflows with states and events.

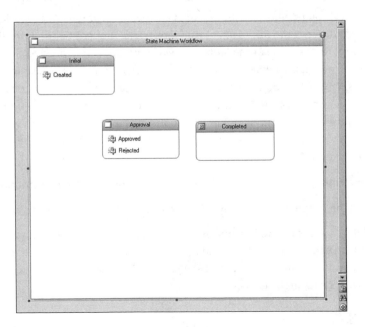

Updating the `EventDriven` Activities

Although most of the emphasis and much of the planning revolves around the states and events, specifying the logic that occurs after an event's capture is where much of the work lies. Luckily, there's not much new to you because the logic is encapsulated in an `EventDriven` activity. In sequential workflows, you worked with `EventDriven` activities when using the `Listen` activity.

The `State` activity requires that its immediate child be an `EventDriven` activity. The `EventDriven` activity requires its immediate child to be a blocking activity (for example, `Delay` or `HandleExternalEvent`). After the initial blocking activity, you may insert any other activities you can place in an `EventDriven` activity not embedded in a `State` activity with one exception. There can only be one blocking activity in the entire `EventDriven`. This is so, because state machine workflows are supposed to wait for events, act on them quickly, and then move to the next state. They are inhibited from doing this when being blocked.

Configuring the Order Initialized Event

Most of the work done in this section should be familiar because you are wiring the workflow and host together. The `SetState` activity used at the end is a simple activity where you specify the name of the next state to transition.

In the next steps, you will add child activities to the `EventDriven` activity, including a `HandleExternalEvent` activity that you associate with a local service.

1. Double-click the `Created` `EventDriven` activity. Your workflow should now look like Figure 6.4.

FIGURE 6.4
Unconfigured
`State` activity
`EventDriven`
activity.

2. Add a `HandleExternalEvent` activity to the `EventDriven` activity that appears (note the breadcrumb navigation at the top of the form if you need to return to the overall workflow form).

3. Click the HandleExternalEvent activity, click the ellipsis in its InterfaceType property, click BasicStateMachineLocalServices, and select ILocalService in the middle of the form. Your screen should now look like Figure 6.5.

FIGURE 6.5
Binding
HandleExtern-
alEvent activity
to a local service
interface.

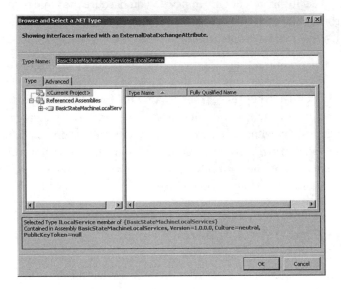

4. Click OK.

5. Click the drop-down in its EventName property and set it to the OrderWorkflowInitalization event.

6. Enter **CreatedInvoked** in the Invoked property, and then enter the following code in the handler to retrieve the order number from the event args and display a message:

```
// Retrieve the order number and amount from the eventArgs
orderNumber = (e as
BasicStateMachineLocalServices.OrderEventArgs).OrderNumber;
    orderAmount = (e as
BasicStateMachineLocalServices.OrderEventArgs).OrderAmount;

    MessageBox.Show
        ("Order number " + orderNumber + " has been created.");
```

7. In the designer, add a SetState activity directly below the HandleExternalEvent activity.

8. Click the drop-down in its TargetStateName property and set it to Approval.

9. The Created EventDriven should now look like Figure 6.6.

FIGURE 6.6
Configured
State activity
Created
EventDriven
activity.

You added a State activity, added an EventDriven activity to the State activity, and configured the EventDriven to act on an event. Then you added another child activity that transitions the workflow to another state. You may add additional logic in the EventDriven, but this covers the basic pattern to receive an event and transition to another state.

Adding a StateInitialization Activity

Each State activity can hold StateInitialization and StateFinalization activities in addition to EventDriven activities. These activities may hold any nonblocking activities (Sequence activities constrained to prohibit blocking activities). The StateInitialization and StateFinalization activities are entered when the state itself is entered and exited. The StateInitalization activity can, for example, be used to check roles at the state level rather than the event level (roles are covered in Hour 14, "Working with Roles"). User-specified tracking information can be specified here as well (user-specified tracking is covered in Hour 13, "Learning to Track Workflows"). These are a couple of sample usages. You can, however, use both initialization and finalization for any pre- or post-State activity work you see fit. Initialization and finalization activities may be inserted in any State activity other than the completed state, which may include no activities.

1. Add a StateInitialization activity to the Initial state and name it **InitalizeCreateState**. The Initial activity should look like Figure 6.7.

2. Double-click the InitalizeCreateState activity, and you should be taken to a new form with what appears to be a sequence activity that you can add other activities into.

FIGURE 6.7
Initial activity
with a
StateInitial-
ization activity
added.

3. Add a Code activity and name it **PerformInitialization**. Double-click the activity and enter the following in its handler:

```
MessageBox.Show
    ("State machine in Created state initalization.");
```

Configuring the Order Approved Event

In the steps in this section, you will configure the approved order event, which mainly entails associating a HandleExternalEvent activity with a local service interface.

1. Double-click the Approved event in the Approval State.

2. Add a HandleExternalEvent activity to the EventDriven activity.

3. Click the HandleExternalEvent activity, click the ellipsis in its InterfaceType property, click BasicStateMachineLocalServices, and select ILocalService in the middle of the form. Then click OK.

4. Click the drop-down in its EventName property and set it to the OrderWorkflowApproved event.

5. Enter **ApprovedInvoked** in the Invoked property and enter the following code in the handler to display a message:

```
        MessageBox.Show("Order number " + orderNumber + " has been
approved.");
```

6. Add a SetState activity directly below the HandleExternalEvent activity.

7. Click the drop-down in its TargetStateName property and set it to the Completed state.

8. Your completed EventDriven activity should look like Figure 6.8.

FIGURE 6.8
Configured
State activity
Approved
EventDriven
activity.

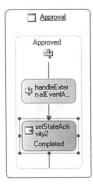

Configuring the Order Rejected Event

In this section, you will configure the `Rejected` event.

1. Double-click the `Rejected` event in the `Approval State` activity.

2. Add a `HandleExternalEvent` activity to the `EventDriven` activity.

3. Click the `HandleExternalEvent` activity, click the ellipsis in its `InterfaceType` property, click BasicStateMachineLocalServices, and select ILocalService in the middle of the form. Then Click OK.

4. Click the drop-down in its `EventName` property and set it to the `OrderWorkflowRejected` event.

5. Enter **`RejectedInvoked`** in the Invoked property and enter the following code in the handler to display a message:

   ```
           MessageBox.Show("Order number " + orderNumber + " has been
   rejected.");
   ```

6. Add a `SetState` activity directly below the `HandleExternalEvent` activity.

7. Click the drop-down in its `TargetStateName` property and set it to the `Completed` state.

The code in your workflow file to support the invoked methods should look like Listing 6.1.

LISTING 6.1   Invoked State Machine Workflow Handlers

```
        private string orderNumber;
        private double orderAmount;
        const double level2OrderAmount = 1000;

        private void CreatedInvoked(object sender, ExternalDataEventArgs e)
        {
            // Retreive the order number from the eventArgs
            orderNumber =
                (e as
BasicStateMachineLocalServices.OrderEventArgs).OrderNumber;
            orderAmount =
                (e as
BasicStateMachineLocalServices.OrderEventArgs).OrderAmount;

            MessageBox.Show("Order number " + orderNumber + " has been
created.");
        }

        private void PerformInitialization_ExecuteCode(object sender, EventArgs e)
        {
            MessageBox.Show
                ("State machine in Created state initalization.");
```

```
        }

        private void ApprovedInvoked(object sender, ExternalDataEventArgs e)
        {
            MessageBox.Show("Order number " + orderNumber + " has been
approved.");
        }

        private void RejectedInvoked(object sender, ExternalDataEventArgs e)
        {
            MessageBox.Show("Order number " + orderNumber + " has been
rejected.");
        }
```

That's it. You just created a state machine workflow. The states and events can be seen in Figure 6.9. There are also three `EventDriven` activities behind the states that contain the logic. State machine workflows in many ways are inverse sequential workflows. State machine workflows surround sequential logic with events, whereas sequential workflows surround events with sequential logic.

FIGURE 6.9
Completed basic state machine workflow.

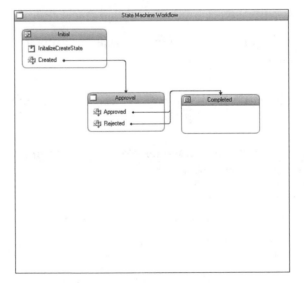

In summary, the steps to create a state machine workflow are as follows:

1. Add a `State` activity.

2. Insert an `EventDriven` activity in the `State` activity.

3. Add a `HandleExternalEvent` activity to the `EventDriven` activity, and wire it up to the local service.

4. Add a `SetState` activity and tell it what `State` to transition to.

Most of the work revolves around thinking though the states and events. We will enhance this workflow quite a bit functionally and will add many other state machine workflow features, but that's the basics.

Running the Basic Workflow

Follow the next steps to run the workflow two times, the first time approving the order and the second rejecting it.

1. Press F5 to run the project. You should see the form shown in Figure 6.10.

FIGURE 6.10
Basic workflow form.

2. Enter an order number and amount and click the Create Order button.

3. Click OK in the Order Created dialog box.

4. Click the Approve button and click OK in the Approved Order dialog box.

5. Repeat steps 3 and 4 and click the Reject button this time to reject the order.

Hierarchical States and State Introspection

Let's modify our workflow to allow second-level approval and add a distribution state so you can see how a slightly more advanced state machine looks, which involves adding more events. You will perform the following three items that rely on new concepts:

▶ Create combined, or hierarchical, states, which are designed to combat the number of events growing out of control, by allowing cross-state access. For instance, order update may be an appropriate action from multiple states, and order cancellation may be appropriate from all states.

▶ Use the `StateMachineWorkflowInstance` type to introspect a state machine workflow.

▶ Add logic within the `EventDriven` of a `State` activity to determine which state to transition to.

Figure 6.11 contains an illustration of what the enhanced workflow looks like.

FIGURE 6.11
Enhanced state machine work-flow with hierarchical states.

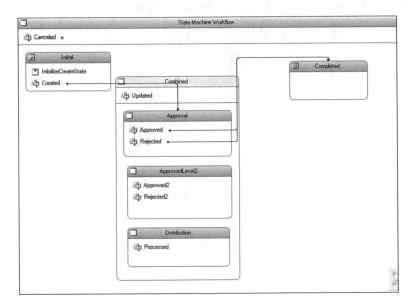

Modifying the Workflow

You will add states, configure event driven activities, and use more advanced control flow to determine the next state in this section's subsections.

Add New States and Events

In the following steps, you add the additional `State` and `EventDriven` activities to the workflow.

1. Open the `BasicStateMachineWorkflowSolution` solution in the `C:\SamsWf24hrs\Hour\Hour06StateMachineWorkflow\Lab2\BasicStateMAc hineWorkflowSolution` directory. The form and the local service have both been updated for the enhanced state machine workflow.

Add a new `State` and name it **ApprovalLevel2**.

2. Add a new State and name it **Distribution**.

3. Add a new State and name it **Combined**.

4. Add two EventDriven activities to the ApprovalLevel2 state. Name the first **Approved2** and the second **Rejected2**.

5. Add an EventDrivenActivity to the Distribution state and name it **Processed**.

6. Populate the Combined state with the other states it will share events with.

7. Drag and drop the Approval state into the Combined state.

8. Drag and drop the ApprovalLevel2 state into the Combined state.

9. Drag and drop the Distribution state into the Combined state.

10. Now add an EventDriven activity to the CombinedOrderState and name it **Updated**. This event will be valid from any state in the Combined state.

11. Add another EventDriven activity and insert it directly into the workflow. Name this event **Canceled**. This event is valid from any state on the workflow.

12. The Combined state should now look like Figure 6.12:

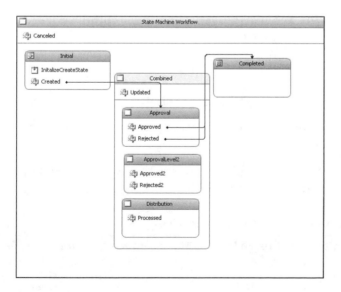

FIGURE 6.12
Combined state populated with child states.

Now the updated state machine workflow is modeled. The CombinedOrder state contains three State activities and one direct event. The events contained in its child states are exclusive to their respective states. The EventDriven that is added to the

Combined state is available to all three states. The Canceled event is available from all workflow states. This means that the valid events for any state in the Combined state are its respective states plus the Canceled and Updated events. Valid events for other states are their individual events plus the Canceled event. Although the sample uses only one level of hierarchy, no limit exists on hierarchical state nesting.

Configuring the EventDriven Activities

In the next steps, you have to configure the new HandleExternalEvent activities and add SetState activities. The local service interface and form have been updated for you.

1. Double-click the Canceled event that is located in the workflow itself.

2. Add a HandleExternalEvent activity to the EventDriven activity.

3. Click the HandleExternalEvent activity, click the ellipsis in its InterfaceType property, click BasicStateMachineLocalServices, and select ILocalService in the middle of the form. Then click OK.

4. Click the drop-down in its EventName property and set it to the OrderWorkflowCanceled event.

5. Enter **CanceledInvoked** in the Invoked property and enter the following code in the handler to display a message:

```
        MessageBox.Show("Order number " + orderNumber + " has been
canceled.");
```

6. Add a SetState activity directly below the HandleExternalEvent activity.

7. Click the drop-down in its TargetStateName property and set it to the Completed state.

8. Repeat steps 1–8 using Table 6.1 for guidance (change the message in the invoked event to reflect the event that fires):

TABLE 6.1   Event Mapping to Local Service

EventDriven Activity to Double-Click	Event Name to Select	Method Invoked	Transition To
Updated	OrderWorkflow- Updated	UpdatedInvoked	Approval
Approved2	OrderWorkflow- Approved2	Approved2Invoked	Distribution

TABLE 6.1   Event Mapping to Local Service

EventDriven Activity to Double-Click	Event Name to Select	Method Invoked	Transition To
Rejected2	OrderWorkflow-Rejected2	Rejected2Invoked	Completed
Processed	OrderWorkflow-Processed	ProcessedInvoked	Completed

Creating Advanced Control Flow from an EventDriven Activity

All previous state transitions had a one-to-one relationship with the event they are triggered from. The approved event, however, has two possible transitions. Order values less than or equal to $1,000 move to the processing state, whereas those that are larger move on to second-hand approval. This is conducted in the next steps by adding an IfElse activity after the initial HandleExternalEvent activity in the EventDriven. As previously mentioned, pretty much any activity that can be added to a Sequence activity can be added following the initial blocking activity.

1. Double-click the Approved event.

2. Add an IfElse activity below the HandleExternalEvent activity and name it **CheckOrderAmount.**

3. Name its left branch **LessThanApprovalThreshHold** and the right branch **Else.**

4. Click the drop-down in the left branch Condition property and select code condition.

5. Click the + and enter **OrderLimit** in the Condition property.

6. Enter the following code in the handler:

```
if (orderAmount <= level2OrderAmount)
   e.Result = true;
else
  e.Result = false;
```

7. Add a new SetState activity to the left branch and add the existing one to the right branch.

8. Click the drop-down in its TargetStateName property in the left branch and set it to the Distribution state.

9. Click the drop-down in its TargetStateName property in the right branch and ensure that it is set to the ApprovalLevel2 state.

10. The EventDriven should now look like Figure 6.13.

FIGURE 6.13
EventDriven
with logic deter-
mining which
state to transi-
tion to.

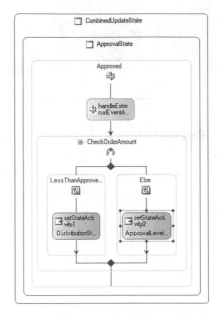

The completed, enhanced state machine workflow should look like Figure 6.14.

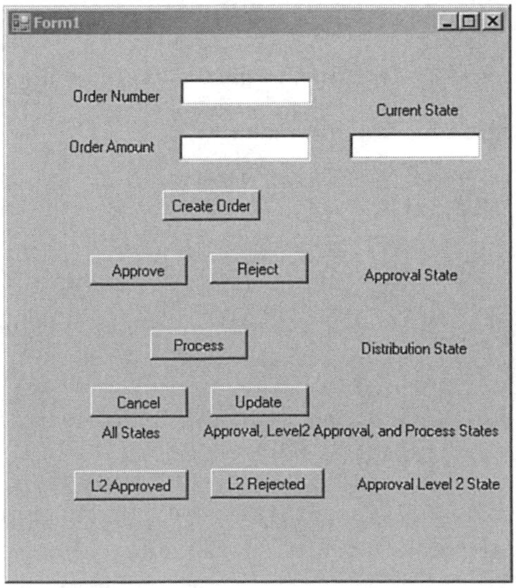

FIGURE 6.14
Completed,
enhanced state
machine work-
flow.

StateMachineWorkflowInstance and State Introspection

The StateMachineWorkflowInstance is a class that accepts the current workflow runtime and workflow instance ID as parameters and provides access to an object with a number of useful members when working with state machine workflows.

To make it easier to know which buttons are valid on the order form, the current state is displayed in the current state text box. The labels next to the buttons describe from which states they are available. This aid can be used for all states except the created state. (In the next hour you learn to dim the buttons to match the valid states. This is a temporary workaround.) The state is extracted when the workflow is idled (in the idled method), which it is, of course, when the workflow is waiting for the next button to be selected on the form.

Follow the next steps to add additional controls to the form to use the StateMachineWorkflowInstance type to track the workflows behavior.

1. Add a text box to the form and name it **textBoxCurrentState** and add a label above it named **Current State**.

2. Add the code in the next snippet to the BasicStateMachineWindowsForm.cs file to the workflowRuntime_WorkflowIdled event handler:

```
StateMachineWorkflowInstance stateMachineInstance =
    new StateMachineWorkflowInstance(workflowRuntime,
    workflowInstance.InstanceId);

UpdateDelegate ud = delegate()
{
    // Update the workflow state on the form thread
    if (stateMachineInstance.CurrentState != null)
        textBoxCurrentState.Text =
stateMachineInstance.CurrentStateName;
    else
        textBoxCurrentState.Text = "";
};
this.Invoke(ud);
```

Run the Enhanced State Machine Workflow

Follow the steps to run the enhanced state machine workflow twice, once with an amount under $1,000 and once with an amount over. The first will result in direct approval and the latter will traverse the level 2 and distribution states as well.

1. Press F5 to run the project.

You should see the form shown in Figure 6.15.

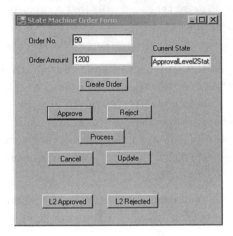

2. Enter an order amount less than $1,000 to go from approval to distribution to completed (assuming approved and not rejected is selected).

3. Enter an order amount larger than $1,000 to go from the approval state to the approval level 2 state to the distribution state and finally to the completed state.

Summary

In this hour, you created a very simple state machine workflow and then enhanced it to a more reasonable workflow and extended the features. States and EventDriven activities are key components when you create state machine workflows. The StateMachineWorkflowInstance allows for the introspection of running state machine workflows. WF's support for both sequential and state machine workflows offers a powerful combination not found in many other workflows products, which usually feature one or the other. State machine workflows (and other WF activities) allow WF to better support human-centric, dynamic workflows. More state machine workflow features will be explored in the next hour.

Workshop

Quiz

1. *What syntax is required to retrieve the current state name on a running state machine workflow?*

2. *Why are state machine workflows well suited for human-centric, dynamic workflows?*

3. *What activity transitions a state machine workflow to the next state?*

4. *What activities can be inserted into state machine* EventDriven *activities?*

5. *Why can't state machine workflow* EventDriven *activities contain multiple blocking activities?*

6. *How does WF attempt to combat workflows with a large number of common events across states?*

7. *Can events be made available across a state machine workflow?*

Answers

1. StateMachineWorkflowInstance.CurrentStateName.

2. They support processes without predetermination well because they can transition among states in any order, which is symbolic of human-centric processes.

3. The SetState activity.

4. The immediate child must be a blocking activity, and subsequent activities can be any other activity with the exception of a blocking activity.

5. Because they are designed to monitor events, which requires that they receive an event, act on it, and begin monitoring again quickly, which they cannot do if they are "stuck" in the EventDriven activity of one state.

6. Hierarchical states are container states that can hold multiple states and direct events (EventDriven activities) that are available to all child states.

7. Yes, EventDriven activities can be added to the state machine workflow, which is itself a State activity.

HOUR 7

Creating Advanced State Machine Workflows

What You'll Learn in This Hour:

▶ `StateMachineWorkflowInstance` **introspection and manipulation capabilities**

▶ **Workflow queuing to retrieve current blocking activities**

▶ **Dim and activate form controls based on workflow state and workflow queues**

This hour starts with a workflow identical to what you created in the previous hour. You will learn to use the workflow queuing system to retrieve information about what events are available at a given time. This information will then be used to control which buttons are enabled. These capabilities are important because they are one of the main factors that increases state machine workflow's ability to be monitored and introspected. You will also use additional members of the `StateMachineWorkflowInstance` type.

The new form you will create this hour will look like Figure 7.1.

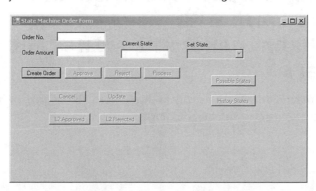

FIGURE 7.1
Order state machine.

Updating the Form and Adding Member Variables

1. Open the AdvancedStateMachineWorkflowSolution solution in the C:\SamsWf24hrs\Hour\Hour07StateMachineWorkflow\Lab1\AdvancedState MAchineWorkflowSolution directory.

2. Open the StateMachineOrderForm form in design mode.

3. Add a combo box named **comboBoxStates** to the form and add a label above it and set its Text property to **Set State**.

4. Add two command buttons. Name the first **buttonPossibleStates** and set its Text property to **Possible States**. Name the second **buttonHistoryStates** and set its Text property to **History States**.

5. Open the form in code view and add the following variable declarations to the top of the class:

```
private StateMachineWorkflowInstance stateMachineWorkflowInstance;
private delegate void UpdateDelegate();
```

6. Add the following using directives:

```
using System.Workflow.Runtime.Tracking;
using System.Workflow.ComponentModel;
using System.Collections.ObjectModel;
```

7. Add the following to the end of the form load method:

```
dimControls();
buttonCreate.Enabled = true;
```

Updating the Form Code-Behind Logic to Work with StateMachineWorkflowInstance Members

This is where the majority of the activity in this hour resides. It is where you will modify the host to interact with the workflow.

Extract "In Scope" Events

We will finally add logic to dim buttons that are not valid in the current workflow state. You will first extract the current events awaiting input and then retrieve their corollary event names. You will then compare the event names to the form buttons to see which ones should be active.

Most of the logic is similar to the work involved in determining which form controls should be dimmed or active in a UI application. The method to retrieve these events, however, calls for using WF's underlying queuing technology. So far, HandleExternalEvent activities have been used to wait for external input, and CallExternalMethod activities have been used to send data from workflow to host. These and all other communication between WF and external applications are abstractions on top of WF's queuing. The WorkflowQueueInfo and WorkflowQueue types are the two types that support WF's queuing. There are times when the best—or only—way to accomplish a WF task is through its queues. One case when queues usage is necessary is to retrieve the current blocking activity (covered later in this hour); another is in place of higher-level host-workflow data exchange abstractions, which may be the appropriate or preferred method for some programmers and some scenarios.

The UpdateControls method you create in this section dims all the buttons, extracts the current active events, and activates the corollary buttons.

1. Add a method to dim all the controls as shown, and place it in the state machine helper functions region:

```
void dimControls()
{
    buttonCreate.Enabled = false;
    buttonApprove.Enabled = false;
    buttonCancel.Enabled = false;
    buttonL2Approve.Enabled = false;
    buttonL2Reject.Enabled = false;
    buttonProcess.Enabled = false;
    buttonReject.Enabled = false;
    buttonUpdate.Enabled = false;
    buttonHistoryStates.Enabled = false;
    buttonPossibleStates.Enabled = false;
    comboBoxStates.Enabled = false;
}
```

2. Add a method signature named UpdateControls below the dimControls method as shown:

```
// Extracts the event names from the workflow queues
// for the currently active blocking activities on the
// workflow instance and matches them with the appropriate buttons
```

```
void UpdateControls()
{
}
```

3. Add the following code to the UpdateControls method to dim all the controls before beginning to selectively activate the requisite controls:

```
// dim all the controls before retreiving current ones
dimControls();
```

4. Add the following code to retrieve a collection of WorkflowQueueInfo objects:

```
// collection of in scope workflow queues. In scope means
// that if in the Approval Level 2State, the
// L2 Approved and L2 Rejected
// events will be in scope (as well as the workflow-wide canceled)
ReadOnlyCollection<WorkflowQueueInfo> wqi =
    workflowInstance.GetWorkflowQueueData();
```

5. Iterate through each WorkflowQueueInfo object in the returned WorkflowQueueInfo collection by adding the following code:

```
// iterate through each of the in scope queues and match
// them with the proper form buttons
foreach (WorkflowQueueInfo q in wqi)
{
}
```

6. Cast the WorkflowQueueInfo.QueueName property as an EventQueueName type, which contains the method name property needed. Add this code between the foreach beginning and ending brackets.

```
// Get the event name associated with the queue
EventQueueName eq = q.QueueName as EventQueueName;
```

7. After ensuring the queue is not null, compare the MethodName property of the EventQueueName type to the list of values in the switch statement to determine which buttons should be activated. Add this code following the code entered in the prior step, and again within the foreach brackets.

```
if (eq != null)
{
    switch (eq.MethodName)
    {
        case "OrderWorkflowApproved":
            buttonApprove.Enabled = true;
            break;
        case "OrderWorkflowRejected":
            buttonReject.Enabled = true;
            break;
        case "OrderWorkflowCanceled":
            buttonCancel.Enabled = true;
            break;
```

```
                    case "OrderWorkflowProcessed":
                        buttonProcess.Enabled = true;
                        break;
                    case "OrderWorkflowApproved2":
                        buttonL2Approve.Enabled = true;
                         break;
                    case "OrderWorkflowRejected2":
                        buttonL2Reject.Enabled = true;
                        break;
            }
        }
```

8. If the collection of `WorkflowQueueInfo` objects returned at the top of the method is true, activate the create button, because there are no blocking activities and therefore there is no workflow instance. If, on the other hand, it is not null, activate the helper controls. This code should be inserted *below* the closing bracket of the `foreach` statement.

```
        // if none are in scope then there is no workflow instance
        // loaded and therefore the create button should be undimmed.
        if (wqi.Count == 0)
            buttonCreate.Enabled = true;
        else
        {
            // If there is a workflow instance undim the additional
            // "nonevent" buttons
            buttonHistoryStates.Enabled = true;
            buttonPossibleStates.Enabled = true;
            comboBoxStates.Enabled = true;
        }
```

9. Build the `AdvancedWindowsForm` project and fix errors, if any.

The `UpdateControls` method should look like Listing 7.1.

LISTING 7.1   Update Controls Method with Direct Workflow Queue Access

```
// Extracts the event names from the workflow queues
// for the currently active blocking activities on the
// workflow instance and matches them with the appropriate buttons
void UpdateControls()
{

    // dim all the controls before retreiving current ones
    dimControls();

    // collection of in scope workflow queues. In scope means
    // that if in the Approval Level 2State, the
    // L2 Approved and L2 Rejected
    // events will be in scope (as well as the workflow-wide canceled)
    ReadOnlyCollection<WorkflowQueueInfo> wqi =
        workflowInstance.GetWorkflowQueueData();

    // iterate through each of the in scope queues and match
```

```
        // them with the proper form buttons
        foreach (WorkflowQueueInfo q in wqi)
        {
            // Get the event name associated with the queue
            EventQueueName eq = q.QueueName as EventQueueName;

            if (eq != null)
            {
                switch (eq.MethodName)
                {
                    case "OrderWorkflowApproved":
                        buttonApprove.Enabled = true;
                        break;
                    case "OrderWorkflowRejected":
                        buttonReject.Enabled = true;
                        break;
                    case "OrderWorkflowCanceled":
                        buttonCancel.Enabled = true;
                        break;
                    case "OrderWorkflowProcessed":
                        buttonProcess.Enabled = true;
                        break;
                    case "OrderWorkflowApproved2":
                        buttonL2Approve.Enabled = true;
                        break;
                    case "OrderWorkflowRejected2":
                        buttonL2Reject.Enabled = true;
                        break;
                }
            }
        }

        // if none are in scope then there is no workflow instance
        // loaded and therefore the create button should be undimmed.
        if (wqi.Count == 0)
            buttonCreate.Enabled = true;
        else
        {
            // If there is a workflow instance undim the additional
            // "nonevent" buttons
            buttonHistoryStates.Enabled = true;
            buttonPossibleStates.Enabled = true;
            comboBoxStates.Enabled = true;
        }
    }
```

The current queues are retrieved and the proper form controls are activated.

SetState Combo Box

We will now look through the built-in members in the
StateMachineWorkflowInstance class that interact with workflow queue info on
our behalf. The first one of these methods retrieves all the states on the state machine
workflow.

The states will be loaded when the workflow instance is created. They are retrieved from the StateMachineWorkflowInstance, thereby requiring it to be created first. A good place to do this is right after the workflow instance is started.

1. Add the following code to the buttonCreate_click handler below the line that starts the workflow instance (workflowInstance.Start). This instantiates the StateMachineWorkflowInstance and calls a method to update the comboBoxStates combo box:

```
// Initiate a state machine workflow instance
stateMachineWorkflowInstance =
    new StateMachineWorkflowInstance(
    workflowRuntime, workflowInstance.InstanceId);

// Load all the states on the state machine into a combo box.
loadStatesComboBox();
```

2. Create the loadStateComboBox method to load all workflow states via the StateMachineWorkflowInstance.States property that is iterated through and added to the combo box. Add this method to the end of the state machine helper functions region.

```
// Loads all the states in the workflow into the combo box
// where they can simply be viewed or the current state can
// be overridden
private void loadStatesComboBox()
{
    comboBoxStates.Items.Clear();

    foreach (Activity a in stateMachineWorkflowInstance.States)
    {
        comboBoxStates.Items.Add(a.Name);
    }
}
```

3. Build the AdvancedWindowsForm project and fix errors, if any.

Historical States

A collection of all states the workflow has transitioned to can be retrieved through the StateMachineWorkflowInstance.StateHistory property if and only if you are using the SqlTrackingService. This can be useful for auditing or other purposes.

1. Add the SqlTrackingService to the host by inserting the following code into the GetWorkflowRuntime method below the code where the external data exchange service is added (des.AddService(this);) as shown:

```
// Add the sql tracking service to the runtime
SqlTrackingService sts =
```

```
                new SqlTrackingService(connectionString);
            workflowRuntime.AddService(sts);
```

2. Double-click the History States button and add the following code to return a collection of the states that were previously transitioned to and display them in a message box:

```
string historyStates = "";
foreach (string s in stateMachineWorkflowInstance.StateHistory)
{
    historyStates = historyStates + s + " ";

}
MessageBox.Show(historyStates);
```

Possible State Transitions

The possible transitions can also be obtained from the StateMachineWorkflowInstance. You can use this to monitor the possible transitions during runtime.

1. Double-click the Possible States button and add the following code to return a collection of valid states to transition to and then display them in a message box:

```
        // Use the StateMachineWorkflowInstance.PossibleStateTransitions
method
        // to retrieve all states that may be transitioned to (directly or
        // indirectly) from the current state
        string possibleTransitions = "";
        foreach (string stateName in
            stateMachineWorkflowInstance.PossibleStateTransitions)
        {
            possibleTransitions = possibleTransitions + stateName + " ";

        }
        MessageBox.Show("Possible transitions: " +

stateMachineWorkflowInstance.PossibleStateTransitions.ToString());
```

2. Build the AdvancedWindowsForm project and fix errors, if any.

Override the Current State

So far you have simply introspected the state machine workflow. You can manipulate it as well using the StateMachineWorkflowInstance.SetState method. This should obviously be used sparingly, but there may be times when it is necessary to manually override the process and switch the workflow to a different state. It is consistent with the state machine autonomy premise that you can move forward and backward through the states without consequence in many scenarios.

When selecting state in the `comboBoxState` combo box (created earlier), its changed handler is called where the state is switched.

1. Add the following code to the `comboBoxState`'s on change event handler by double-clicking the `SetState` combo box to manually set a state on a state machine workflow.

```
// Sets the state machine to the new state selected in
// the combo box.
stateMachineWorkflowInstance.SetState(comboBoxStates.Text);
```

2. For readability purposes, cut and paste the methods you have created in the last few steps to the bottom of the state machine helper functions region.

Update the UI When Workflow Idles

The UI is updated when the workflow idles to reflect the state change that may occur after an event fires and the workflow then idles. This will generally happen after the workflow acts on an event, so it is a good place to update the newly available events (buttons).

1. Add the following code to the `workflowRuntime_WorkflowIdled` handler:

```
UpdateDelegate ud = delegate()
{
    if (stateMachineWorkflowInstance.CurrentState != null)
        textBoxCurrentState.Text =
            stateMachineWorkflowInstance.CurrentStateName;
    else
        textBoxCurrentState.Text = "";

    UpdateControls();
};
this.Invoke(ud);
```

Update the UI when Workflow Completes

It is also a good place to update the available buttons on a UI when the workflow completes.

1. Replace the code in the workflowRuntime_WorkflowCompleted method with the following:

```
MessageBox.Show("Workflow completed.");
UpdateDelegate ud = delegate()
{
    UpdateControls();
};
this.Invoke(ud);
```

Update the UI When Workflow Terminates

Finally, update the available buttons and UI when the workflow terminates.

1. Replace the code in the workflowRuntime_WorkflowTerminated method with the following:

```
MessageBox.Show("Workflow terminated: " + e.Exception.Message);

UpdateDelegate ud = delegate()
{
    UpdateControls();
};
this.Invoke(ud);
```

Running the Workflow

The buttons should now dim and activate as you use the form. Use the state combo box to see all workflow states and to override the current state, the PossibleStates button to see the possible transitions, and the HistoryStates to see past workflow transitions.

1. Set the AdvancedWindowsForm project as the startup project.

2. Press F5 to run the workflow.

3. Enter any order number and an amount less than 1,000 (so that second-level approval will not be required).

4. Click the Create button to create the order, then click the Approve button, and finally the Process button. The order should now be approved.

5. Enter any new order number and an amount larger than 1,000.

6. Click the Create button to create the order, then click the Approve button, the L2Approved button, and finally the Process button. The order that required second-level approval should now be approved.

7. Enter any new order number and an amount larger than 1,000.

8. When the workflow reaches the Distribution state (shown in Figure 7.2), change it to the approval state. Notice that the manual override of state

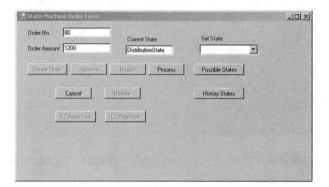

FIGURE 7.2
Distribution
state.

changes which buttons are activated, and the Current State text box also reflects the state change (shown in Figure 7.3).

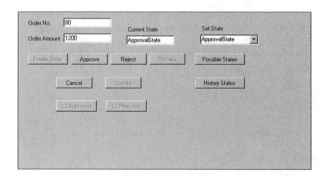

FIGURE 7.3
State machine
overridden.

9. Continue submitting orders; try the Cancel button and other buttons and overrides until you are comfortable with the form's operations.

Summary

This demonstrated WF's sate machine workflow introspection through enhanced use of the `StateMachineWorkflowInstance` type. Workflow queues—the underlying WF communication technology—were used to access information for the currently scoped events. Finally, the state machine workflow's ability to override the current state was used. The manual override of states is particularly powerful and dangerous if used incorrectly.

Workshop

Quiz

1. *What activities used throughout this book so far are abstractions on top of WF's queuing system?*

2. *How do you retrieve all workflow states?*

3. *How do you override the current state?*

4. *Do you have to have the* `SqlTrackingService` *registered with the workflow runtime to retrieve state history?*

5. *How do you return a collection of* `WorkflowQueueInfo` *objects?*

6. *What do you cast the* `WorkflowQueueInfo` *object as to retrieve the method name of the blocking activity?*

Answers

1. `HandleExternalEvent` and `CallExternalMethod`.

2. `StateMachineWorkflowInstance.States`.

3. `StateMachineWorkflowInstance.SetState`.

4. Yes.

5. `WorkflowInstance.GetWorkflowQueueData()`.

6. `EventQueueName`.

HOUR 8

Working with `Parallel` Activities and Correlation

What You'll Learn in This Hour:

▶ Using the `Parallel` activity

▶ Using the `SynchronizationScope` activity

▶ Updating the local service to use correlation to support the concurrent approval workflow

▶ Updating the approval workflow to allow concurrent approval through correlation

Many applications call for concurrent processing. This hour first shows how to use the `Parallel` activity, an activity that contains two or more child branches that run concurrently. Each branch is a `Sequence` activity. It then shows how to lock a branch of a `Parallel` activity in cases when a branch shares resources with one or more other branches. Finally, it demonstrates creating an approval workflow that requests approvals from two reviewers simultaneously. This requires not only using the `Parallel` activity but instrumenting the workflow and local service with correlation configuration parameters.

Creating the Solution and First Project

This hour contains two separate solutions. You will create the first one in the next steps and the second one later in the hour.

1. Open Visual Studio and select File, New, Project.

2. Expand other project types by clicking the +, then select Visual Studio Solutions, Blank Solution Template.

3. Name the solution **ParallelExecution** and place it in the `C:\SamsWf24hrs\Hours\Hour08ParallelAndCorrelation\Lab1\ParallelExe-cution` directory.

Create the Parallel Activity Tester Project

Create a Sequential Workflow project that will be used to test the basic operation of the Parallel activity.

1. Right-click the solution, select Add New Project, and click the + to expand Visual C# projects.

2. Choose Workflow and select the Sequential Workflow Console Application project template.

3. Name the project **ParallelTesters** and place it in the default directory.

4. Click OK.

5. Rename `Workflow1.cs` **ParallelTester.cs** in the Solution Explorer.

Creating the Workflow

In the subsections in this section, you build and run a workflow that runs in `Parallel` in both the default interleaved format and the synchronized format.

Standard Parallel Activity Execution

In the next steps, you will add a `Parallel` activity to the workflow and then add two `Code` activities to each of its branches. The `Code` activities will be instrumented and the results will be sent to the console so that you can see how the `Parallel` activity works.

1. Add a `Parallel` activity to the workflow.

2. Add two `Code` activities to each left and right branch (in any order; you will give them names shortly).

3. Your workflow should now look like Figure 8.1.

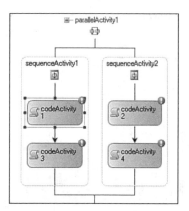

FIGURE 8.1
Parallel activity with unconfigured Code activities.

4. Now change the `Name` property of the `Code` activities in the left branch to **LeftBranch1** and **LeftBranch2**.

5. Change the `Name` property of the `Code` activities in the right branch to **RightBranch1** and **RightBranch2**.

6. Double-click the `LeftBranch1` code handler and add the following to print the current activity name, the time it begins execution, and to then pause for two seconds:

```
CodeActivity ca = sender as CodeActivity;
Console.WriteLine
    (ca + " Executed at " +
System.DateTime.Now.ToLongTimeString());
    Thread.Sleep(2000);
```

7. Repeat step 6 for each of the remaining activities.

Running the Parallel Workflow

In the next steps, you perform a couple of housecleaning items and then run and evaluate the workflow's execution.

1. Add the following code to `Program.cs` after the line that contains `waitHandle.WaitOne();` to pause the host:

```
Console.WriteLine("Press enter to continue");
Console.Read();
```

2. Add the following using directive to `ParallelTester.cs`:

```
using System.Threading;
```

3. Your workflow should now look like Figure 8.2.

FIGURE 8.2
`Parallel` activity with configured `Code` activities.

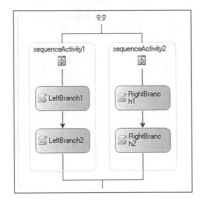

4. Run your workflow and you should receive results similar to Figure 8.3.

FIGURE 8.3
`Parallel` activity executing `Code` activities.

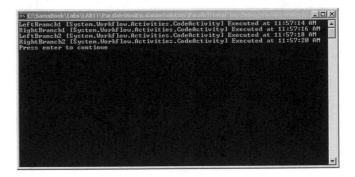

As you can see, the `Code` activities executed from left to right and then top to bottom. The activity execution is two seconds apart for each activity. A workflow instance operates on one and only one thread, so the execution is not truly parallel; each branch takes a turn. One activity in a branch executes and then onto the next activity in another branch, and when all branches are done, back to the next activity in the first branch. From a business perspective this is parallel. For example, if each branch was sending an email requesting approval, the fact that the approvals are a fraction of a second apart is not material to most business processes. If the first branch sends an email and waits for a response, and then the second branch does the same, this would be sequential business process execution. The vast majority of approval processes will run fine under WF's `Parallel` activity. For scenarios where you need true parallel execution, this is not the activity; you may need another tool or explore creating your own custom activity.

Synchronized Parallel Execution

This SynchronizationScope activity permits one or more children of a Parallel activity to execute in cases where shared resources must be locked. The SynchronizationScope activity contains a SynchronizationHandles property that can be used to associate branches that use a shared resource. Otherwise, it is essentially a Sequence activity like any other Parallel activity branch.

In the next steps, you reconfigure the Parallel activity with SynchronizationScope activity branches so that each branch executes in full before the next branch begins.

1. Add another Parallel activity to the workflow below the one you added earlier.

2. Add a SynchronizationScope activity to each parallel branch (insert them within the Sequence activities of each branch).

3. Add two Code activities within the SynchronizationScope activity in the left branch of the Parallel activity.

4. Add two Code activities within the SynchronizationScope activity in the right branch of the Parallel activity.

5. Rename the Code activities **LeftBranchSynch1**, **LeftBranchSynch2**, **RightBranchSynch1**, and **RightBranchSynch2**.

6. Your new Parallel activity should look like Figure 8.4.

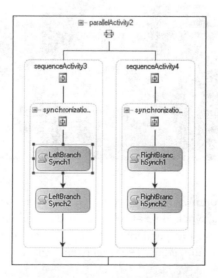

FIGURE 8.4
Parallel
activity with
Synchronizat-
ionScope
activities.

7. Double-click each of the `Code` activities in the `Parallel` activity you just added and add the following code to each handler:

```
CodeActivity ca = sender as CodeActivity;
Console.WriteLine
        (ca + " Executed at " +
System.DateTime.Now.ToLongTimeString());
        Thread.Sleep(2000);
```

8. Now add the word "same" to the `SynchronizationScope.SynchornizationHandles` property for each `SynchronizationScope` activity to specify that they should run independently, as shown in Figure 8.5.

FIGURE 8.5
The SynchronizationScope activity SynchronizationHandle setting.

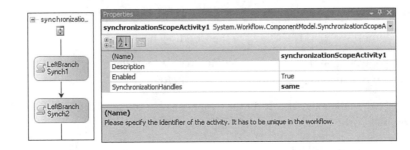

9. Click the first `Parallel` activity and set its `Enabled` property to `false` so that it will no longer execute.

10. Run the workflow and you should see the result in Figure 8.6:

FIGURE 8.6
`Parallel` activity with SynchronizationScope activities execution results.

The first branch now completes before beginning the second branch. Some branches can be equipped with a `SynchronizationScope` activity and others not. Furthermore, branches may have independent `SynchronizationHandles` property settings. It is only the branches equipped with `SynchronizationScope` activities that share the same `SynchronizationHandles` property value that executes in isolation. Other branches will execute under normal WF parallel processing. Change some of the settings if you want to see the different execution semantics.

Parallel Approval and Correlation

Approval processes in this book have so far executed in serial. Some have supported escalation, but this was still a serial process where the workflows awaited a response from each approver before proceeding. There are many approval scenarios where waiting for each approver to complete his or her review before engaging the services of another reviewer would be grossly inefficient. These scenarios require allowing multiple reviewers to be engaged in parallel.

The first step, as many of you probably guessed, is to use an activity that allows for concurrent processing, such as the `Parallel` activity. There is another area that must be supported: correlation. So far, the only correlation needed was to map the event back to the correct workflow instance. This singular level of correlation is provided for you out-of-the-box by WF. This is why the `WorkflowInstance.InstanceId` value is always passed to `EventArgs` classes in WF. But if there are concurrent approvers, how does the workflow know where to route the incoming event? It doesn't automatically; you have to configure correlation to tell it.

Following is a brief description of the three steps that must be performed to provide the additional level of correlation necessary to support concurrent processing. Each will be described in more detail when they are implemented.

1. Additional attributes must be added to the local service interface to tell it what value to correlate on and when to begin a correlation dependency between an initiating activity (for example, `CallExternalMethod`) and a receiving activity (`HandleExternalEvent`).

2. The initiating activity (`CallExternalMethod`) must be configured with a `CorrelationToken` to begin the coupling with its partner receiving activity. It must also pass information that identifies the value to be correlated on.

3. The receiving activity (`HandleExternalEvent`) likewise must be configured to follow (or be bound to) the `CorrelationToken` specified by the initiating activity.

The upcoming figure illustrates the need for correlation, where the left branch of the `Parallel` activity requests approval from Robert, and the `HandleExternalEvent` activity below responds to Robert's approval. Likewise the right branch does the same for Patricia.

Opening the Solution and Adding the Projects

You will now work with the second solution in this hour that is used to explore correlation. The form host is already created. You have to add a workflow project and a class library project to hold the workflow and the local service.

In the next steps you add the `CorrelationWorkflows` project.

1. Open the solution
   `C:\SamsWf24hrs\Hours\Hour08ParallelAndCorrelation\Lab2\CorrelationSolution.sln`.

2. Add a Sequential Workflow Library project to the solution and name it **CorrelationWorkflows**.

3. Right-click the `Workflow1.cs` file and rename it **CorrelationWorkflow.cs**.

4. Add a Class Library project to the solution and name it **LocalServices**.

5. Right-click the `Class1.cs` file and rename it **LocalService.cs**.

6. Add references to `System.Workflow.Runtime` and `System.Workflow.Activities` from the `LocalServices` project.

7. Add references to the `CorrelationWorkflows` and `LocalServices` projects from the `HostProject`. (The `HostProject` is the precreated project.)

Local Service with Correlation

Most of the code in this local service will be familiar to you. There are a few items, though, that are correlation specific. As specified earlier (this is step 1 in the overall correlation process), you will configure the local service to tell it what value to correlate on and when correlation should commence.

Perform the following steps to add correlation-related attributes to the local service.

1. Add the following namespace directives:

   ```
   using System.Workflow.Activities;
   using System.Workflow.Runtime;
   ```

2. Replace the current class declaration with the following code. The `[CorrelationParameter("approver")]` attribute you are adding to the class tells the local service that the data in the approver parameter should be used to match an outgoing request and a response. Replace the current class declaration with the following:

   ```
   [ExternalDataExchange]
   ```

```
[CorrelationParameter("approver")]
public interface IOrderCorrelationLocalService
{
}
```

3. Add the following code to the class you just added. The second line contains a standard event signature as you have seen in previous hours. The CorrelationAlias attribute maps the value in the EventArgs class to the CorrelationParameter.

```
[CorrelationAlias("approver", "e.Approver")]
event EventHandler<OrderResponseEventArgs> OrderWorkflowApprove;
```

4. Now add the following code to the event you just added. This code signifies for correlation to be initialized for each approver when the CallExternalMethod activity bound to this method executes.

```
[CorrelationInitializer]
void GetResponse(string approver);
```

You have done three things to enable correlation in the local service. First, you identified the CorrelationParameter by adding an attribute to the local service interface. Second, you mapped the value in the EventArgs class to the CorrelationParameter by adding an attribute to the event member. Third, you told WF where correlation should begin by adding an attribute to the method. You will soon configure the CallExternalMethod and HandleExternalEvent activities to use these correlation values.

The code for the interface you just created is contained in Listing 8.1:

LISTING 8.1 Local Service with Correlation

```
namespace LocalServices
{
    [ExternalDataExchange]
    [CorrelationParameter("approver")]
    public interface IOrderCorrelationLocalService
    {
        [CorrelationAlias("approver", "e.Approver")]
        event EventHandler<OrderResponseEventArgs> OrderWorkflowApprove;

        [CorrelationInitializer]
        void GetResponse(string approver);
    }
}
```

Create the Event Payload (EventArgs)

The payload itself, the EventArgs class, is no different than those created in previous hours. Although it does contain the approver that is used for correlation, it is just another class member. There are no special attributes or commands necessary.

Follow the next steps to add the EventArgs class with correlation support.

1. Right-click the LocalService project, select Add, Class, and name it **EventArgs.**

2. Add the following using directive:

   ```
   using System.Workflow.Activities;
   ```

3. Replace the class declaration in the EventArgs class with the content of Listing 8.2.

LISTING 8.2   EventArg Class with Correlation Support

```
[Serializable]
public class OrderResponseEventArgs : ExternalDataEventArgs
{
    private string approver;

    public string Approver
    {
        get { return this.approver; }
        set { this.approver = value; }
    }

    private string status;

    public string Status
    {
        get { return this.status; }
        set { this.status = value; }
    }

    public OrderResponseEventArgs(Guid instanceId,
                                  string approver,
                                  string status)
        : base(instanceId)
    {
        this.approver = approver;
        this.status = status;
    }
}
```

4. Build the LocalServices project so that it will be available to the workflow.

Concurrent Approver Workflow

You will create the workflow shown in Figure 8.7.

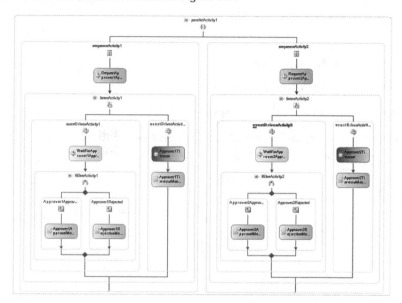

FIGURE 8.7
Concurrent approval workflow.

As you can see, it is similar to ones created in earlier hours. It allows for concurrent approval from two people instead of being limited to one. This is done by placing CallExternalMethod activities that request approval from the respective approvers at the top of the individual parallel branches. Each branch then contains its own Listen activity equipped with a HandleExternalEvent activity and a Delay activity. There is nothing new here to this point. What is new is that each CallExternalMethod activity needs to be correlated with its respective HandleExternalEvent activity. For example, the left branch of the Parallel activity requests approval from Robert and the right one from Patricia. When Patricia responds, her reply must be mapped to the HandleExternalEvent activity in the right branch, which requires configuring these activities with correlation parameters.

Preliminary Work

Perform the following preparatory steps on the CorrelationWorkflow class.

1. Enter the following variable declarations below the constructor of the workflow code-behind file in CorrelationWorkflow.cs.

```
int numOfApprovals = 0;
string approver1Status = "";
string approver2Status = "";
```

2. Add references to `System.Windows.Forms` and to the `LocalServices` project.

3. Add the following using directive:

   ```
   using System.Windows.Forms;
   ```

Add Activities for Approver 1

Follow the next steps to configure Approver 1.

1. Add a `Parallel` activity to the workflow.

2. Over the next few steps you will configure Approver 1 (the left branch of the `Parallel` activity) as shown in Figure 8.8.

FIGURE 8.8
Left-hand (Approver 1) approval activities.

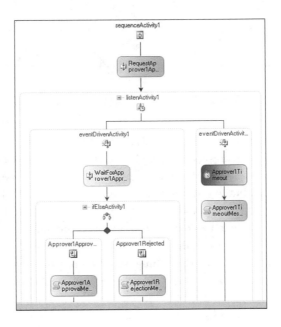

3. Add a `CallExternalMethod` activity to the left branch of the `Parallel` activity.

4. Add a `Listen` activity below the `CallExternalMethod` activity.

5. Add a `HandleExternalEvent` activity to the left branch and a `Delay` activity to the right branch of the `Listen` activity.

6. Add an `IfElse` activity below the `HandleExternalEvent` activity.

7. Add a `Code` activity to both the left and right branches of the `IfElse` activity and another one below the `Delay` activity.

Configure the `CallExternalMethod` Activity for Approver 1

Two correlation-related items must be set on the `CallExternalMethod` activity. (This is step 2 in the overall correlation process.) The first is setting its `CorrelationToken` and the `CorrelationToken`'s owner. These values are static values that are used to begin a chain between an initiating and a receiving activity. In our case, this `CallExternalMethod` activity will be bound to a `HandleExternalEvent` activity. The second is adding and populating a parameter that holds the value used to correlate on. This value is mapped to the `CorrelationParameter` in the local service you specified (`[CorrelationParameter("approver")]`). This value is dynamic and subject to change at runtime. The approver property is used for this. Some workflows may require approval from Robert and others from another person. On the other hand, this `CallExternalMethod` and `HandleExternalEvent` activity will always be bound to each other. Therefore the `CorrelationToken` binding them is determined at design time.

Follow the next steps to configure the `CallExternalMethod` for Approver 1.

1. Click the `CallExternalMethod` activity and name it **RequestApprover1Approval.**

2. Map it to the interface and method by clicking the ellipsis in the `InterfaceType` property, then select LocalServices and `IOrderCorrelationService` in the middle of the form, and click OK.

3. Select the `GetResponse` method in the `MethodName` property drop-down.

4. Enter **Approver1** in the `CorrelationToken` property and press Enter.

5. Click the + on the side of the `CorrelationToken` property, click OwnerActivityName and select `sequenceActivity1` (or substitute the proper name if this is not the name of the parent Sequence activity) from the drop-down.

6. Enter **Robert** in the approver property. (Your activity property windows should look like Figure 8.9.)

This completes the configuration for your first `CallExternalMethod` activity that requires correlation. Let's look at a couple of the additional parameters we set to support correlation:

The `CorrelationToken.OwnerActivityName` property is to provide a qualified name for the `CorrelationToken`. It can be set, in this case, to its direct parent or any other activity that precedes it in the workflow hierarchy. However, it should be set to its immediate parent because doing so is necessary in other dynamic approval scenarios we will encounter later. It is also less ambiguous to use the immediate parent.

Configure the `HandleExternalMethod` Activity for Approver 1

This is step 3 in the overall correlation process. Most of the work has now been done. All that remains is to bind this `HandleExternalEvent` activity to the proper `CallExternalMethod` activity. You do not need to specify Robert or another approver. This value is obtained from the `EventArgs` class and specifically the `[CorrelationAlias("approver", "e.Approver")]` attribute you specified in the local service.

Follow these steps to configure the `HandleExternalMethod` activity for Approver 1.

1. Click the `HandleExternalEvent` activity and name it **`WaitForApprover1Approval`**.

2. Map it to the interface and method by clicking the ellipsis in the `InterfaceType` property, select LocalServices, and `IOrderCorrelationService` in the middle of the form, and click OK.

3. Select the `OrderWorkflowApprove` event in the `EventName` property drop-down.

4. Enter **`Approver1Invoked`** in the Invoked property and the following code in its handler:

    ```
    approver1Status = (e as LocalServices.OrderResponseEventArgs).Status;
    ```

5. Click the drop-down in the `CorrelationToken` property and select Approver1. This also associates the correct `OwnerActivityName`. The completed `HandleExternalMethod` activity's Properties window should look like Figure 8.10.

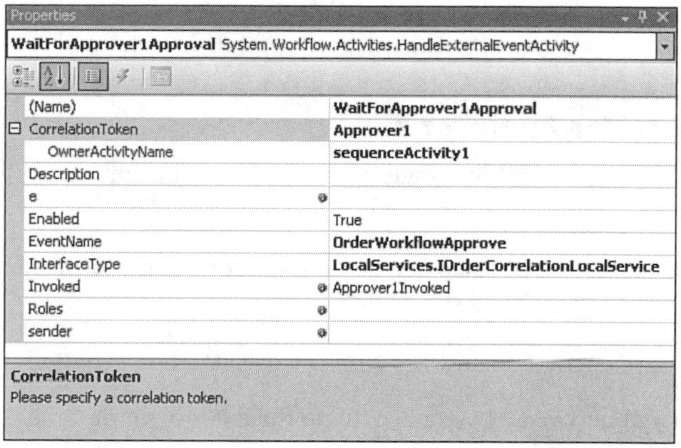

FIGURE 8.10
WaitForAppro-
ver1Approval
activity configura-
tion including cor-
relation settings.

Configure the Other Activities for Approver 1

Follow the next steps to configure the remaining activities for Approver 1.

1. Name the `Delay` activity **Approver1Timeout** and set its `TimeoutDuration` property to **00:00:30**.

2. Name the `Code` activity below the `Delay` activity **Approver1TimeoutMessage** and add the following code to its handler:

```
MessageBox.Show
        ("Timeout waiting for Approver One's response.");
```

3. Name the left branch of the `IfElse` activity **Approver1Approved** and the right branch **Approver1Rejected**.

4. Click the drop-down in the `Condition` property of the left branch of the `IfElse` activity, select Declarative Rule Condition, click the + that appears next to the `Condition` property, and enter **Approver1Rule** in the `Condition Name` property. Click the ellipsis in the `ConditionName` property, click the Edit button (to update the Approver1Rule), and enter the following in the dialog box.

```
this.approver1Status=="Approved"
```

5. Click OK twice to close both dialog boxes.

6. Name the left branch **Approver1ApprovalMessage** and add the following code to the left `Code` activity handler:

```
MessageBox.Show("Order Approved by Approver 1!");
numOfApprovals = numOfApprovals + 1;
```

7. Name the right branch **Approver1RejectionMessage** and add the following code to the right `Code` activity handler:

```
MessageBox.Show("Order Rejected by Approver 1!");
```

That's it. You have configured Approver 1; now on to Approver 2.

Add Activities for Approver 2

Perform the following steps that largely mirror configuring Approver 1 to configure Approver 2.

1. Add a `CallExternalMethod` activity to the right branch of the `Parallel` activity.

2. Add a `Listen` activity below the `CallExternalMethod` activity.

3. Add a `HandleExternalEvent` activity to the left branch and a `Delay` activity to the right branch of the Listen activity.

4. Add an `IfElse` activity below the `HandleExternalEvent` activity.

5. Add a `Code` activity to both the left and right branches of the `IfElse` activity and below the `Delay` activity.

Configure the `CallExternalMethod` Activity for Approver 2

Perform the following steps to configure the `CallExternalMethod` activity for Approver 2.

1. Click the `CallExternalMethod` activity and name it **`RequestApprover2Approval`**.

2. Map it to the interface and method by clicking the ellipsis in the `InterfaceType` property, select LocalServices and `IOrderCorrelationService` in the middle of the form, and click OK.

3. Select the `GetResponse` method in the `MethodName` property drop-down.

4. Enter **`Approver2`** in the `CorrelationToken` property and press Enter.

5. Click the + on the side of the `OwnerActivityName` property and select `sequenceActivity2` (or substitute the proper name if this is not the name of the parent Sequence activity) from the drop-down.

6. Enter **`Patricia`** in the approver property. (The activity property window should look like Figure 8.11.)

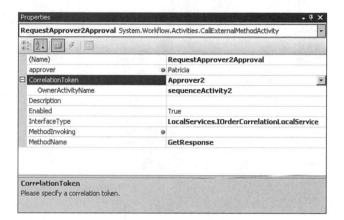

FIGURE 8.11
RequestAppro-
ver2Approval
activity configura-
tion including cor-
relation settings.

Configure the `HandleExternalMethod` Activity for Approver 2

Follow the next steps to configure the `HandleExternalMethod` activity for Approver 2.

1. Click the `HandleExternalEvent` activity and name it **`WaitForApprover2Approval`.**

2. Map it to the interface and method by clicking the ellipsis in the `InterfaceType` property, select LocalServices and `IOrderCorrelationService` in the middle of the form, and click OK.

3. Select the `OrderWorkflowApprove` event in the `EventName` property drop-down.

4. Enter **`Approver2Invoked`** in the `Invoked` property and the following code in its handler:

   ```
   approver2Status = (e as LocalServices.OrderResponseEventArgs).Status;
   ```

5. Click the drop-down in the `CorrelationToken` property and select Approver2. This also associates the correct `OwnerActivityName` (the activity property windows should look like Figure 8.12).

Configure the Other Activities for Approver 2

Follow the next steps to configure the remaining activities for Approver 2.

1. Name the `Delay` activity **`Approver2Timeout`** and set its `TimeoutDuration` property to **`00:00:30`.**

FIGURE 8.12
WaitForAppro-
ver2Approval
activity configura-
tion including cor-
relation settings.

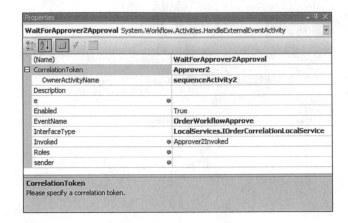

2. Name the Code activity below the `Delay` activity **Approver2TimeoutMessage** and add the following code to its handler:

```
MessageBox.Show
        ("Timeout waiting for Approver Two's response.");
```

3. Name the left branch of the `IfElse` activity **Approver2Approved** and the right branch **Approver2Rejected.**

4. Click the drop-down in the `Condition` property of the left branch of the `IfElse` activity, select Declarative Rule Condition, click the + that appears next to the `Condition` property, and enter **Approver2Rule** in the `Condition` Name property. Click the ellipsis in the `ConditionName` property, click the Edit button (to update the Approver2Rule), and enter the following in the dialog box.

```
this.approver2Status=="Approved"
```

5. Click OK twice to close both dialog boxes.

6. Name the Code activity in the left branch **Approver2ApprovalMessage** and add the following code to its handler:

```
MessageBox.Show("Order Approved by Approver 2!");
numOfApprovals = numOfApprovals + 1;
```

7. Name the Code activity in the right branch **Approver2RejectionMessage** and add the following code to its handler:

```
MessageBox.Show("Order Rejected by Approver 2!");
```

That's it. You have configured Approver 1 and 2.

Add a Total Order Validation

Now you need to check whether the order is approved or rejected. Two approvals mean the order is approved, and any other number equals rejection. This check is done by adding a rule that checks the numApprovals variable within an IfElse activity.

Perform the following steps to add total order validation.

1. Add an IfElse activity below the entire Parallel activity and name it **CheckOrderApproval.**

2. Name the left branch **OrderApproved** and the right branch **OrderRejected.**

3. Add a Code activity in each branch and name the one in the left branch **OrderApprovalMessage** and the one in the right branch **OrderRejectionMessage.**

4. Update the OrderApprovalMessage handler with the following:

   ```
   MessageBox.Show("Entire Order Approved!");
   ```

5. Update the OrderRejectionMessage handler with the following:

   ```
   MessageBox.Show("Entire Order Rejected!");
   ```

6. Click the drop-down in the Condition property of the left branch of the IfElse activity, select Declarative Rule Condition, click the + that appears next to the Condition property, enter **TotalWorkflowRule** in the ConditionName property, and click the ellipsis in the ConditionName property. Click the Edit button (to update the Approver1Rule), and enter the following in the dialog box.

   ```
   this.numOfApprovals==2
   ```

7. Click OK twice to close both dialog boxes. The CheckOrderApproval activity should look like Figure 8.13.

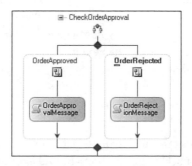

FIGURE 8.13
Total order
approval check.

Run the Workflow

Follow the next steps to run the workflow.

1. Build and run the solution.

2. Click the CreateOrder button (see Figure 8.14) to create an order and then select Approved or Rejected for each reviewer. After an order is created, the CreateOrder button will be dimmed and the approval buttons will be activated. When the entire order is approved or rejected, the CreateOrder button will be activated again.

3. Fill out the form shown in Figure 8.14.

FIGURE 8.14
Total order approval check form.

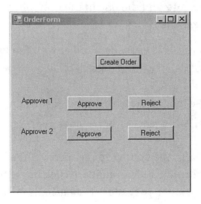

> **By the Way**
>
> Although in a real-world application, the approval and rejection would be presented to the users in an email, SharePoint task, or other means, the principles of correlation remain.

This concludes correlation. The approval scenario is useful in that it supports concurrent, correlated processing. The workflow is also very descriptive. It serves as a good flowchart of the overall process. It is very hard-coded and limited to exactly two approvers that approve in one level. The next two hours will address other activities that remedy these limitations.

Summary

This hour covered the `Parallel` activity in its default form, where it executes one activity per branch, goes back to the first branch, and executes the next activity, which provides for parallel execution at the business level. This is so even though WF is single threaded. Then `SynchronizationScope` activities were explored, which provide a way to ensure that entire branches are executed independently. The `SynchronizationScope` activity is useful when there are shared resources among the branches. Finally, you built on your experience with host-workflow data exchange by using correlation. This allows concurrent approval and other scenarios to be carried out in WF. As stated, the next two hours will build on this by showing other activities that allow the number of approvers and even the number of levels of approval to be determined at design time.

Workshop

Quiz

1. *Why is correlation needed at a high level?*

2. *If there are three branches in a* `Parallel` *activity, each with three activities, in what order will they execute?*

3. *What purpose is there for the* `SynchronizationScope` *activity?*

4. *What two elements must be updated to allow for correlation?*

5. *How is a branch in a* `Parallel` *activity transformed from standard WF parallel execution to executing in full before another branch executes?*

6. *What is the purpose of the* `OwnerActivityName` *property?*

7. *What purpose does the* `CorrelationToken` *property serve?*

8. *What are the three correlation-related items used in the local service?*

9. *What is the* `CorrelationAlias` *used for?*

Answers

1. To allow a workflow to concurrently process multiple events to the same workflow and deliver them to the correct activity.

2. The first activity in the first branch, the first activity in the second branch, the third activity in the third branch, then the second activity in the first branch, and so on.

3. To ensure that one branch executes in full (until all child activities are exhausted) before another branch executes with a matching `SynchronizationHandles` property. This is useful when shared resources are updated in independent branches.

4. The local service and workflow activities (for example, `CallExternalMethod` and `HandleExternalEvent` activities).

5. By inserting a `SynchronizationScope` activity in two or more branches of the `Parallel` activity and setting their `SynchronizationHandles` properties to the same values.

6. It points to an activity that scopes the correlation.

7. The `CorrelationToken` provides a way to bind two activities when, for instance, one initiates a request and the other responds on workflows that have multiple interactions of this type concurrently.

8. `CorrelationParameter`, `CorrelationInitializer`, and `CorrelationAlias`.

9. It maps a member in the `EventArgs` class to the `Correlation Parameter` (for example, `e.approver` to approver).

HOUR 9

Working with the Replicator and While Activities

What You'll Learn in This Hour:

▶ How to use the `Replicator` activity in sequence
▶ How to use a `Dictionary` object to pass parameters to a workflow
▶ How to use the `While` activity
▶ How to use the Replicator activity in parallel

The `Replicator` is an advanced WF activity commonly used in approval scenarios. The `Replicator` is similar to a C# foreach statement that can process *n* number of an item designated at runtime. The `Replicator` can perform work in serial or parallel, which is useful in approval scenarios where it is desired to call out for and receive multiple responses simultaneously and not wait for each approver. Another nifty feature of the `Replicator` is that its default behavior to complete when all children complete can be overridden to, say, complete when a condition is met, such as over half the votes already tallied for one side or the other. The `Replicator` is used to power almost all SharePoint workflows that come with the MOSS SDK, which are heavily document approval-centric and fairly complex.

You will use a `While` activity to perform dynamic sequential approval, which serves as a viable substitute to the `Replicator` in some scenarios.

You will use an alternative form of host-workflow communication that allows the passing of a `Dictionary` object from the host to the workflow when the workflow is created. This form of communication is similar to standard method-to-method communication.

Some of the techniques for using the `Replicator` activity in conjunction with the `CallExternalMethod` and `HandleExternalEvent` activities in this hour were learned from reading the following blog by a WF team member:

http://blogs.msdn.com/advancedworkflow/

Creating Solutions and Projects

For brevity, I omitted instructions for creating projects and solutions. See previous hours if you need help creating projects or solutions.

Follow the next steps to create the solution and projects for this hour.

1. Open the WorkflowReplicator solution in the `C:\SamsWf24hrs\Hours\Hour09ReplicatorAndWhile` directory.

2. Add a Sequential Workflow Library to the solution and name it **ReplicatorWorkflows**.

3. Rename `Workflow1.cs` to **ReplicatorWorkflow.cs**.

4. Add a reference to the `LocalServices` project.

5. Click the `ReplicatorHostForm` project and add references to the `LocalServices` and `ReplicatorWorkflows` projects.

Creating the Replicator Workflow

In this section you create and configure the `Replicator` activity.

Adding Member Variables to the Workflow

Follow the next steps to create some properties.

1. Open the `ReplicatorWorkflow` code-beside file and add the following variables below the constructor:

   ```
   ArrayList children;
   int counter = 0;
   ```

2. Right-click below the variable declarations, select Insert Snippet, double-click Other, double-click Workflow, and double-click DependencyProperty—Property

to insert a new dependency property. You should see the stub dependency property, and the text MyProperty should be highlighted.

3. Enter **NumberOfApprovers** (replacing MyProperty), press Tab and enter **int**. Press Enter to leave the wizard.

4. Repeat steps 2 and 3 to add a new dependency property named ApprovalStyle with the exception that it is a string and not an int.

5. Add the following using directive:

```
using System.Windows.Forms;
```

Placing the Activities on the Workflow

Part of the beauty of the Replicator is that workflows can use it to power complex processes with relatively few activities required. This also surfaces its limitation in that the workflows it powers are not always the most self-descriptive. The hard-coded workflows that contained one entry per parallel branch are very descriptive. Unfortunately, it is frequently inefficient to be limited to a fixed number of approvers.

Follow the next steps to add child activities to the Replicator activity.

1. Add a Replicator activity.

2. Place a Sequence activity inside the Replicator. (This is necessary because the Replicator can only hold a single activity; this is worked around by inserting a composite activity in it, which is discussed in the "ActivityExecutionContext Overview" section later in this hour.)

3. Add a CallExternalMethod activity to the Sequence activity.

4. Add a Code activity below the CallExternalMethod activity.

5. Add a HandleExternalEvent activity below the Code activity.

6. Add another Code activity below the HandleExternalEvent activity.

7. Your workflow should now look like Figure 9.1.

FIGURE 9.1
Replicator populated with unconfigured activities.

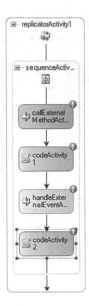

Configuring the Activities

You will configure the activities in this section.

Configuring the CallExternalMethod Activity

Follow the next steps to configure the CallExternalMethod activity.

1. Click the CallExternalMethod activity, click the ellipsis in its InterfaceType property, select IOrderCorrelationLocalService, and click OK.

2. Click the MethodName property and select GetResponse.

3. Enter **TheToken** in the CorrelaionToken property and press Enter.

4. Click the + next to the CorrelationToken property, then click the down arrow in the OwnerActivityName property and select sequenceActivity1. (It is important that you select sequenceActivity1 in the OwnerName property because of the way correlation tokens are generated in dynamic activities.)

Configure the HandleExternalEvent Activity

Follow the next steps to configure the HandleExternalEvent activity.

1. Click the HandleExternalEvent activity, click the ellipsis in its InterfaceType property, select the IOrderCorrelationLocalService, and click OK.

2. Click the EventName property and select the OrderWorkflowApprove event.

3. Click the down arrow in the CorrelationToken property and select TheToken.

Configuring the Code Activities

The first Code activity you added will spawn a message box when the approval is requested, and the second will spawn another message when approval (or rejection) is received.

Follow the next steps to configure the Code activities.

1. Double-click the first Code activity and enter the following in its handler:

```
MessageBox.Show("Approval no: " + counter.ToString() + "
requested.");
```

2. Double-click the second Code activity and enter the following in its handler:

```
MessageBox.Show("Approval no: " + counter.ToString() + "
completed.");
```

Configuring the Replicator Initialized Property

The Initialized handler constructs an array with the number of elements specified on the host form. The array, for example, will have two entries if two approvers are requested and five if five are. The array is then placed in the Replicator's ChildInitialized property. The ChildInitialized property is similar to the customer's portion of this foreach statement: foreach customer in customers. Finally, you specify that the Replicator should execute sequentially.

1. Click the Replicator activity, enter **RepInitialized** in the Initialized property, and enter the following in its handler to populate an array with the number of approvers requested on the form:

```
// Populate the data used for each instance of the Replicator's
// child instance that are created
children = new ArrayList();

for (int num = 0; num < NumberOfApprovers; num++ )
{
    children.Add("Approver" +  (num + 1));
}
```

2. Add the following code below the code you just added to place the array contents in the InitialChildData property, which is the property the Replicator will iterate through and run all instances of before terminating (unless overridden by an UntilCondition).

```
replicatorActivity1.InitialChildData = children;
```

3. Add the following code below the code you just added to set the `Replicator` to run sequentially. This means it waits for each approver before going to the next. (We will change this later.)

```
replicatorActivity1.ExecutionType = ExecutionType.Sequence;
```

4. The code in the `Initialized` handler you just created should look like this:

```
// Populate the data used for each instance of the Replicator's
// child instance that are created
children = new ArrayList();

for (int num = 0; num < NumberOfApprovers; num++)
{
    children.Add("Approver" + (num + 1));
}

replicatorActivity1.InitialChildData = children;

replicatorActivity1.ExecutionType = ExecutionType.Sequence;
```

`ActivityExecutionContext` Overview

Now it is time to configure the individual elements (the customer in the `foreach` customer in the customers example) in the `ChildInitialized` property, which, in this case, is populated with `CallExternalMethod` activities. Each one needs to be identified uniquely by labeling it with a unique correlation value. This is where we run into one of WF's intricate architectural components: `ActivityExecutionContext`, which is explained in this section. In workflows run to date, our concern has been with the activities as they are placed on the workflow. The activity can be accessed by specifying its name, such as `callExternalMethodActivity1.name`.

However, in this case, there will be one `CallExternalMethod` activity (`callExternalMethodActivity1`) that will execute multiple times, potentially even in parallel. At first thought, this implies the need for `callExternalMethodActiivty1`, `callExternalMethodActivity2`, and so on. However, this design-time hard-coding approach is exactly what we are attempting to avoid. The answer: WF can spawn individual contexts of a single activity on a workflow. This means that `callExternalMethodActivity1` will be cloned and then altered for each subsequent use. Figure 9.2 identifies spawned contexts, which may occur for children in an iterative WF activity (`While`, `Replicator`, `ConditionedActivityGroup`). Creating individual contexts are necessary for other reasons, including compensation (or specifically intra-activity compensation). It is the need to track individual contexts that precludes the `While`, `Replicator`, and other WF activities from accepting multiple children. This is worked around by insert-

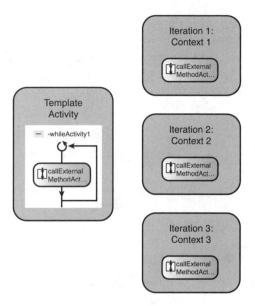

FIGURE 9.2
While activity
will
CallExternal
Method activity
spawned con-
texts.

ing a Sequence or another composite activity and then placing multiple children in it. This does frequently force an additional activity layer to be added when creating WF workflows.

Configuring the `Replicator` `ChildInitialized` **Property**

Now it is time to access our `CallExternalMethod` activities and update their approver properties that are used for correlation within the context of dynamic replicator processing.

Follow the next steps to configure the `CallExternalMethod` activities.

1. Click the `Replicator` activity, enter **RepChildInit** in the `ChildInitialized` property, and enter the following code in its handler:

```
        // Extract the "correct" CallExtnernalMethodActivity
        CallExternalMethodActivity act =
            e.Activity.GetActivityByName("callExternalMethodActivity1",
true)
            as CallExternalMethodActivity;
```

To ensure that the correct spawned context is accessed, the activity is obtained from the `e.Activity.GetActivityByName()`, which is passed the activity name and `true`. `True` states the activity should be taken from the current context, `e`, and not from the workflow root, which would always represent the static `CallExternalActivity` placed on the workflow.

2. Add the remaining code below the code you just added to the
`ChildInitialized` handler to assign the proper approver value to the
approver property of the activity retrieved from the context.

```
act.ParameterBindings["approver"].Value =
    children[counter].ToString();
counter = counter + 1;
```

That's it. You have now created a general-purpose workflow that can be passed
the number of approvers at runtime and send out requests and wait for
responses for each.

3. Build the project before creating the form.

Updating the Host Form

You have to add one method and update a dictionary object that passes the number
of reviewers to the otherwise completed form.

Adding the `ViewQueues` Method

The ViewQueues method you will create in the next steps retrieves the correlation
values from the workflows queues. This is necessary because the activity-method
name combination no longer uniquely identifies the queue.

1. Add the following method stub below the button_SubmitClick handler:

```
void ViewQueues()
{
}
```

2. Add the code to the ViewQueues method to set up the queues shown next,
which contains nothing new yet:

```
StringBuilder sb = new StringBuilder();
textBoxQueues.Text = "";
// collection of in scope workflow queues. In scope means
// that if in the Approval Level 2State, the
// L2 Approved and L2 Rejected
// events will be in scope (as well as the workflow-wide canceled)
ReadOnlyCollection<WorkflowQueueInfo> wqi =
    workflowInstance.GetWorkflowQueueData();
```

3. Create a variable that will be able to hold the returned correlation name (for
example, approver1).

```
// Name and value pair containing correlation information
CorrelationProperty[] cp;
```

4. Add the code to iterate the queues and retrieve the method name and correlation value.

```
// iterate through each of the in scope queues and match
// them with the proper form buttons
foreach (WorkflowQueueInfo q in wqi)
{
    // Get the event name associated with the queue
    EventQueueName eq = q.QueueName as EventQueueName;

    if (eq != null)
    {
        cp = eq.GetCorrelationValues();
        sb.Append(eq.MethodName);
        sb.Append("   Corr: " + cp[0].Value.ToString() + "   ");
        sb.AppendLine();                    }
}
textBoxQueues.Text = sb.ToString();
```

Passing the Number of Reviewers to the Workflow

Specifically, the number of reviewers is not part of the event-response flow; but, rather, metadata needed by the workflow to process. Therefore, this value will be passed in as a parameter to the workflow. WF can receive values in a `Dictionary` object (see Hour 2, "A Spin Around Windows Workflow Foundation") that will contain the variable name and value. WF will match the variable names to public (both dependency and standard) properties when the workflow is initialized. You will populate a dictionary object and employ a workflow constructor that can process dictionary objects.

Follow the next steps to create pass parameters from the host to the workflow.

1. Add the following code in the `buttonCreateOrder` method above the line that creates the workflow to produce a `Dictionary` object that holds the number of approvers, as shown:

```
// Add the parameters via a dictionary object
    Dictionary<string, object> parameters = new Dictionary<string,
object>();
    parameters.Add("NumberOfApprovers",
int.Parse(textBoxNumApprovers.Text));
```

2. Add the `Dictionary` object to the line of code that creates the workflow, as shown:

```
// Create and start a workflow instance
workflowInstance = workflowRuntime.CreateWorkflow
```

```
(typeof(ReplicatorWorkflows.ReplicatorWorkflow),
parameters);
```

Running the Replicator Sequentially

You will fill in the form shown in Figure 9.3.

FIGURE 9.3
Replicator
approval form.

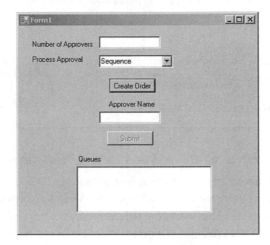

1. Enter **3** in the Number of Approvers text box and click the Create Order button. (The Process Approval combo box is not yet implemented. All approval will be sequential regardless of the value entered.)

2. Click OK in the dialog that shows approval requested of Approver1.

3. Notice that the Queues text box is filled in with the event name and first approver (correlation information), as shown in Figure 9.4.

FIGURE 9.4
Replicator
approval form
with correlation
information
filled in.

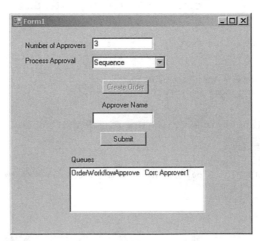

1. Enter **Approver1 and** click the Submit button. Respond to any dialogs. Then repeat for the steps for **Approver2** and **Approver3**.

2. The form should now be ready to accept a new order. Enter different numbers in the number of approvers and go through the process again.

Using the While Activity for Sequential Processing

The Replicator in sequential form is very similar to the While activity. In fact, the workflow just created could be remodeled using a While activity.

Modeling the Workflow

Follow the next steps to configure the workflow with a While activity to support sequential processing.

1. Click the Replicator activity and set its Enabled property to false.

2. Add a While activity above the Replicator activity.

3. Drag and drop the Sequence activity contained in the Replicator activity with all its children intact into the While activity.

4. The While activity should now look like Figure 9.5.

5. Click the drop-down in the Condition property of the left branch of the While activity, select Declarative Rule Condition, click the + that appears next to the Condition property, and enter **ApproversRule** in the Condition Name property. Then click the ellipsis in the ConditionName property, click the Edit button (to update the ApproversRule), and enter the following in the dialog box.

   ```
   this.counter < this.NumberOfApprovers
   ```

6. Click OK twice to close both dialog boxes.

Adding Code-Beside for the While Activity

Adding code for the While activity consists of both moving the logic from the Replicator Initialize and ChildInitialize handlers and changing the way the CallExternalActivity is retrieved from the context because of differences that arise from being accessed from a different handler.

FIGURE 9.5
Sequential
approval with
`While` activity.

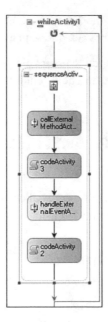

Follow the next steps throughout this section to update the workflow code to work with the `While` activity instead of the `Replicator` activity.

1. Add a `Code` activity above the `While` activity and copy the code from the `Replicator.Initialized` handler shown next. (Only the code that creates and populates the array is included. The `Replicator`-specific code is omitted.)

```
// Populate the data used for each instance of the Replicator's
// child instance that are created
children = new ArrayList();

for (int num = 0; num < NumberOfApprovers; num++)
{
    children.Add("Approver" + (num + 1));
}
```

2. Change the comments in the preceding step to reflect being used in the `While` activity.

3. Enter **CallExtMethInvoked** in the `MethodInvoking` property of the `CallExternalMethod` activity and add the following code to its handler (based off `ReplicatorChild.Initialized` handler):

```
// Extract the "correct" CallExternalMethodActivity
CallExternalMethodActivity act =
    ((CallExternalMethodActivity)sender)
    as CallExternalMethodActivity;
```

```
act.ParameterBindings["approver"].Value =
    children[counter].ToString();

counter = counter + 1;
```

The code in the `MethodInvoking` handler varies in that the
`CallExternalMethod` activity is retrieved from the sender in contrast to e. The
syntax in the `MethodInvoking` handler is now
`((CallExternalMethodActivity)sender)` in contrast to
`e.Activity.GetActivityByName("callExternalMethodActivity1", true)`
when working with the `Replicator` activity. This is a manifest of the environment available in each of the activity handlers. In the end, it shows how to get
the current activity context from e and `sender`.

4. Run the workflow and it should operate identically to the `Replicator`-powered
    solution you just ran.

Updating the `Replicator` **Workflow to Run in Parallel**

So far, we have improved on previous hours because the number of approvers is no
longer hard-coded at design time. At the same time, we have regressed because we
must process our approvals in a serial, which frequently runs counter to real-world
demands. Changing the `Replicator` to support parallel approval requires changing
its `ExecutionType` property from `Sequence` to `Parallel`. The combo box is already
on the form to pass the correct value to the `Replicator`. That is an important dis-
tinction—the `ExecutionType` property may be updated at runtime, enabling one
instance of a workflow to be processed sequentially and another instance in parallel.
This property that controls sequential or parallel operation joins the number of
approvers in being dynamic.

Adding Parallel Support to the `Replicator`

Follow the next steps to reconfigure the `Parallel` activity to process in parallel.

1. Set the enabled properties on the `Code` and `While` activities you added in the
    previous section to `false` and drag and drop the `Sequence` activity in the
    `While` activity back into the `Replicator` activity.

2. Set the enabled property on the `Replicator` activity to `true`.

3. Click the `CallExternalMethod` activity and remove the text in its `MethodInvoking` property.

4. Replace the current code that specifies that the `Replicator` should process sequentially in the `Replicator.Initalized` handler with the code shown to set the `Replicator`'s execution style at runtime to either sequential or parallel:

```
// Specify whether child instances should execute in serial or
parallel
    if (ApprovalStyle == "Parallel")
        replicatorActivity1.ExecutionType = ExecutionType.Parallel;
    else
        replicatorActivity1.ExecutionType = ExecutionType.Sequence;
```

5. Add the following code in the `buttonCreateOrder` method below the line that adds the number of approvers to the `dictionary` object, as shown:

```
parameters.Add("ApprovalStyle", comboBoxProcessingStyle.Text);
```

Running the Parallel `Replicator`

Follow the next steps to run the workflow with the newly configured `Replicator` activity.

1. Run the project, enter 3 approvers, select `Parallel` in the Process Approval combo box, and click the Create Order button (and click through all dialogs, because they are no longer useful as programmed when approving in parallel).

2. You should see all three approvers in the Queues text box as shown in Figure 9.6. This is because they are all active and awaiting response.

FIGURE 9.6
`Replicator` in parallel mode.

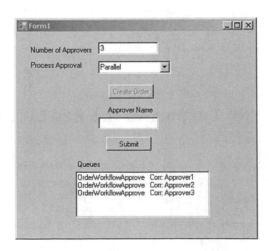

3. Enter **Approver2** and press Enter (you can enter the approvers in any order).

4. You should now see only Approver 1 and 3 in the Queues text box.

5. Enter the remaining two approvers in any order.

6. Try running the form again and selecting sequential order; the approval should be processed one-by-one, as was the case in previous examples.

You now have a `Replicator` that can support *n* number of approvers and can carry out these approvals sequentially or in parallel. One other very useful property of the `Replicator` we have not used is the `UntilCondition` property. It can override the default behavior to complete when all children are done. A particularly useful scenario is to terminate a `Replicator` when over 50% of the votes have been received as approvals or rejections, because there is no need to continue processing. We will not use this property, but it should be considered as another useful `Replicator` property that makes it more useful than a standard `While` activity at times.

Summary

This hour covered the `Replicator` activity in detail. The `Replicator` is one of the most critical activities in conducting WF approval workflows and in showing the power of activities in general in WF. The `While` activity was also used for sequential, dynamic approval. You also used an alternative overload of the `WorkflowRuntime.CreateWorkflow` method to pass a `Dictionary` object to the workflow at startup. You are now well on your way to producing real-world approval workflows with WF. In the next hour you will learn how to change workflows midflight.

Workshop

Quiz

1. *What property is used to control whether the* `Replicator` *processes in serial or parallel?*

2. *Which condition must be set to override the* `Replicator`*'s default behavior to complete when all child activities complete processing?*

3. *Why is understanding* `ActivityExecutionContext` *important when using* `While`, `Replicator`, *and other iterative activities?*

4. *Where is the collection of elements to be processed by the* Replicator *activity stored?*

5. *What event handler is used to initialize each* Replicator *activity child instance?*

6. *What is the difference between the* ChildInitialized *and* Initialized *properties?*

Answers

1. ExecutionType.

2. UntilCondition.

3. The child activities iterated over by these activities require a unique identity so that they can hold their own configurational elements.

4. InitialChildData.

5. ChildInitialized.

6. The Initialized property signifies the event handler that is invoked when the Replicator activity is initialized. The ChildInitialized property signifies the event handler that is invoked when each Replicator child activity instance is initialized.

Working with EventHandlingScope and Strongly Typed Activities

---

What You'll Learn in This Hour:

▶ Basic usage of an `EventHandlingScope` activity

▶ Using the `EventHandlingScope` and `Replicator` activity in conjunction

▶ Creation of the engine of a highly functional and dynamic approval-centric workflow

▶ Using the `wca.exe` utility to create strongly typed activities

▶ Modeling a workflow using strongly typed activities

The `EventHandlingScope` activity is a multifaceted activity that supports a default path while listening to events at the same time. The default path is supported by a `Sequence` activity that runs activities through in normal sequential progression. While the sequential path is processing, the `EventDrivenActivity`'s event handler's portion listens for and acts on events.

The capability to conduct a flow while listening to events is useful in at least a couple of scenarios. The first is to support events that may occur throughout the workflow's life cycle while it is processing, such as canceling the workflow, adding an approver, and changing approvers. The second is to allow the workflow to process events for a specific period of time—for example, if allowing orders to be shipped by FedEx, UPS, and another carrier during a one-hour time period.

Hour 5, "Creating an Escalation Workflow," introduced the `Listen` activity that permits two or more branches to be equipped with blocking activities (for example, `HandleExternalEvent` or `Delay`) as their first activities. The `EventHandlingScope` activity also permits multiple branches to be equipped with blocking activities as their first child. The difference is that the EventHandlingScope activity permits the events to reoccur, whereas the Listen activity processes one event on one branch based on the first event or expired timer it receives.

Finally, after manually binding HandleExternalEvent and CallExternalMethod activities to local service interfaces throughout this book, you will learn to create strongly typed activities already bound to interfaces, which simplifies adding them to workflows.

Learning Basic EventHandlingScope Activity Solution and Project Setup

See previous hours if you need help creating projects or solutions.

Follow the next steps to set up the solution.

1. Open the solution named EventHandlingScopeWorkflow in the C:\SamsWf24hrs\Hours\Hour10EventHandlingScope\Lab1\EventHandling ScopeWorkflow directory with a project named LocalServices and another named EventHandlingScopeHostForm.

2. Add a Sequential Workflow Library project to the solution and name it **EventHandlingScopeWorkflows.**

3. Add a reference to the LocalServices project and to System.Windows.Forms.

4. Set a reference from the EventHandlingScopeHostForm to both the LocalServices and EventHandlingScopeWorkflows projects.

Creating the Basic EventHandlingScope Workflow

In this section, you configure the EventHandlingScope activity across its different elements.

Placing the Activities on the EventHandlingScope Sequential Section

First is a brief prelude to XAML workflows because you will create them in this hour and they are one of the major pieces of the WF puzzle. Workflows can be laid out in XAML as discussed in Hour 2, "A Spin Around Windows Workflow Foundation." So far (with the exception in Hour 2), the default workflow format has been used, which lays out the workflow via code in the constructor, in a manner much like a Windows Form. In XAML workflows, the layout resides in a .XOML file (that again contains standard XAML but the extension prohibits browsers from attempting to render it). You are not specifying a XAML-only file, and so there will still be a code-beside file. The change will be limited to where the layout is specified. The reason for choosing XAML over code is that tools can operate against it much more effectively. XAML can also make looking at the logic easier and it is helpful to look at the EventHandlingScope activity in XAML to understand what it does.

In the next steps, you add an EventHandlingScope activity and add activities to its mainline element—the one that processes sequentially until completed.

1. Delete Workflows1.cs from the EventHandlingScopeWorkflows project.

2. Right-click the EventHandlingScopeWorkflows project, choose Add, New Item, choose the Sequential Workflow (with code separation) project template, and name it **EventHandlingScopeWorkflow.**

3. Add the following using directive to the workflow code-beside file:

   using System.Windows.Forms;

4. Add an EventHandlingScope activity.

5. Add a Sequence activity to the EventHandlingScope activity.

6. Add a Code activity to the Sequence activity.

7. Add a Delay activity below the Code activity.

8. Add another Code activity below the Delay activity.

9. Your workflow should now look like Figure 10.1.

Placing the Activities on the EventHandlingScope Event Handlers Section

You have completed the mainline processing element of the EventHandlingScope activity. In the next steps, you will configure its listeners that will be called on zero or more times during mainline workflow execution. This is useful because in many approval workflows it is necessary to be able to change approver midflight, and it may always be handy to cancel the workflow. Therefore, these two events are trapped in the EventHandlingScope event handling section, where they can be trapped throughout the EventHandlingScope activity's sequential execution.

FIGURE 10.1
EventHandlin-
gScope activity
in default view.

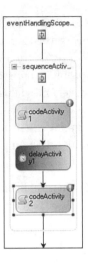

1. Right-click the EventHandlingScope activity and notice the View Event Handlers option below the standard views, which is available for most control flow
   activities.

2. Right-click the EventHandlingScope activity again and select View Event Handlers. The EventHandlingScope activity should now look like Figure 10.2.

FIGURE 10.2
EventHandlin-
gScope activity
in Event Han-
dlers view.

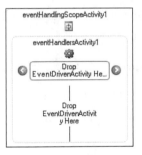

3. Place an EventDriven activity in the little rectangle (the film strip) that goes
   across the upper half of the EventHandlingScope activity and name it
   CancelWorkflow.

4. Place another EventDriven activity next to the first EventDriven in the film
   strip and name it **AddApprover.**

5. Click the CancelWorkflow EventDriven activity and drag and drop a
   HandleExternalEvent activity into the middle of the EventHandlingScope
   activity where it says Drop Activities Here.

6. Place a Code activity below the HandleExternalEvent activity.

7. Click on the AddApprover EventDriven activity and add a HandleExternalEvent activity to it.

8. Place a Code activity below this HandleExternalEvent activity as well.

9. Click either activity in the CancelWorkflow EventDriven activity, and your EventHandlingScope activity should now look like Figure 10.3.

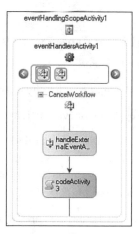

FIGURE 10.3
Partially configured EventHandlingScope activity in Event Handlers view.

Configuring the Event Handling Scope Sequential Activities

In the next steps, you configure the child activities in the EventHandlingScope activity's sequential section.

1. Right-click the EventHandlingScope activity and choose view EventHandlingScope. You should now see your two Code activities and one Delay activity that make up the standard processing (as seen in Figure 10.1).

2. Double-click the first Code activity and add the following code to its handler:

```
MessageBox.Show("The EventHandlingScope activity has started at "
            + System.DateTime.Now.ToLongTimeString());
```

3. Set the Delay activity's TimeoutDuration property to **00:00:30**.

4. Double-click the second Code activity and add the following code to its handler:

```
MessageBox.Show("The EventHandlingScope activity is completing at "
            + System.DateTime.Now.ToLongTimeString());
```

Configuring the `EventHandlingScope` Event Handling Activities

In this section, you configure the child activities in the `EventHandlingScope` activity's Event Handlers section.

Configuring the `CancelWorkflow EventDriven` Activity

In the next steps, you configure the `CancelWorkflow EventDriven` activity.

1. Right-click the `EventHandlingScope` activity and select View Event Handlers.

2. Click the `CancelWorkflow EventDriven` activity.

3. Click the `HandleExternalEvent` activity and set its `InterfaceType` property to `IEventHandlingScopeBasicLocalService` and its `EventName` property to `OrderWorkflowCancel`. (See Hour 4, "Learning Host-Workflow Data Exchange," if you need help binding activities to local services.)

4. Double-click the `Code` activity below the `HandleExternalEvent` activity and add the following code to its handler:

```
MessageBox.Show("Workflow canceled at "
        + System.DateTime.Now.ToLongTimeString());
```

Configuring the `AddApprover EventDriven` Activity

In the next steps, you configure the `AddApprover EventDriven` activity.

1. Click the `AddApprover EventDriven` activity.

2. Click the `HandleExternalEvent` activity and set its `InterfaceType` property to `IEventHandlingScopeBasicLocalService` and its `EventName` property to `OrderWorkflowAddApprover`.

3. Click the `Code` activity below the `HandleExternalEvent` activity and add the following code to its handler:

```
MessageBox.Show("Approver added at "
        + System.DateTime.Now.ToLongTimeString());
```

Running the Basic EventHandlingScope Workflow

You will now test the EventHandlingScope activity in the next steps by running a form with three buttons. The first allows you to start the workflow. The second allows you to continue to raise the cancel workflow event while the workflow is still running. The third allows you to continue to add an approver to the workflow. The workflow will run for 30 seconds after it is started, based on the Delay activity configuration.

1. Run the project and click the CreateOrder button to start the workflow. You should see the form displayed in Figure 10.4.

2. Now click the Cancel and Add Approver buttons as many times as you want before the workflow completes.

Looking at the EventHandlingScope Activity in XAML

In the next steps you view the EventHandlingScope activity's XAML representation.

1. Right-click the EventHandlingScopeWorkflow.xoml file in the Solution Explorer, select Open With, select XML editor, and click OK.

2. Listing 10.1 contains the logic for the EventHandlingScope activity. I stripped much of the details including references to the interface for brevity. As you can see, there are two main elements of the EventHandlingScope activity—one for the sequential portion and the other for the event handler's portion. Looking at

workflows and activities in XAML can be a productive way to get a picture of the activity or workflow.

LISTING 10.1   EventHandlingScopeWorkflow XAML View

```
<EventHandlingScopeActivity x:Name="eventHandlingScopeActivity1">
    <SequenceActivity x:Name="sequenceActivity1">
        <CodeActivity x:Name="codeActivity1"/>
        <DelayActivityx:Name="delayActivity1" />
        <CodeActivity x:Name="codeActivity2"/>
    </SequenceActivity>
    <EventHandlersActivity x:Name="eventHandlersActivity1">
        <EventDrivenActivity x:Name="CancelWorkflow">
            <HandleExternalEventActivity
                    x:Name="handleExternalEventActivity1"
                    EventName="OrderWorkflowCancel"/>
            <CodeActivity x:Name="codeActivity3"/>
        </EventDrivenActivity>
        <EventDrivenActivity x:Name="AddApprover">
            <HandleExternalEventActivity
                    x:Name="handleExternalEventActivity2"
                    EventName="OrderWorkflowAddAppprover"/>
            <CodeActivity x:Name="codeActivity4"/>
        </EventDrivenActivity>
    </EventHandlersActivity>
</EventHandlingScopeActivity>
```

Creating a More Advanced EventHandlingScope Workflow

By now you have much of the gist of the EventHandlingScope activity. This section combines the EventHandlingScope activity with the Replicator. The Replicator provides the capability to provision *n* number of users when the workflow begins processing and the EventHandlingScope has the ability to alter the approvers during the workflow's life cycle. This combination supplies a solid platform for many approval scenarios where flexibility is necessary throughout the process—for example, as approvers go on vacation or new approvers are required. In fact, if you look at the source code provided with the SharePoint SDK, most of the workflows are highly dependent on these two activities to allow for flexible levels of approval, flexible number and style of approval, and changes throughout their life cycle.

Setting up the Advanced EventHandlingScope Activity Solution

Follow the next steps to open and configure the WorkflowEventHandlingScopeReplicator solution.

1. Open the solution named WorkflowEventHandlingScopeReplicator in the C:\SamsWf24hrs\Hours\Hour10EventHandlingScope\Lab2\WorkflowEvent HandlingScopeReplicator directory with a project named LocalServices and another named EventHandlingScopeReplicatorForm.

2. Add a Sequential Workflow Library project to the solution and name it **EventHandlingScopeWorkflows**.

3. Add a reference to the LocalServices project and to System.Windows.Forms.

4. Delete Workflow1.cs and add a new workflow named **EventHandlingScopeReplicatorWorkflow**; specify that it uses code separation.

5. Add a reference from the EventHandlingScopeReplicatorForm project to the EventHandlingScopeWorkflows project.

Add the Activities to the Workflow

In the subsections of this section, you will configure the various EventHandlingScope activity views.

Add Activities to the Sequential View

In the next steps, you add activities to the EventHandlingScope activity's sequential view.

1. Add an EventHandlingScope activity to the workflow.

2. Add a Replicator activity to the EventHandlingScope activity.

3. Add a Sequence activity to the Replicator activity.

4. Add a CallExternalMethod activity and a HandleExternalEvent activity to the Sequence activity.

5. The overall layout of your workflow should look like Figure 10.5, although it will still have exclamation marks because it is not yet figured.

Add Activities to the Event Handlers View

In the next steps, you add activities to the EventHandlingScope activity's Event Handlers view.

1. Right-click the EventHandlingScope activity and choose its Event Handlers view.

2. Drop an EventDriven activity into its film strip and add a HandleExternalEvent activity to it.

FIGURE 10.5
EventHandlin-
gScope activity's
Sequential view.

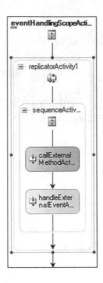

3. Drop another `EventDriven` activity into its film strip and add a
   `HandleExternalEvent` activity to it.

4. Drop a third `EventDriven` activity into its film strip and add a
   `HandleExternalEvent` activity to it.

5. Click the first `EventDriven` activity, and your `EventHandlingScope` activity
   should look like Figure 10.6.

FIGURE 10.6
EventHandlin-
gScope activity's
Event Handlers
view.

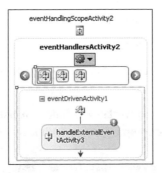

Configuring the Activities in the Sequential View

In the next steps, you configure the activities in the sequential view.

1. Right-click the `EventHandlingScope` activity and set its view to the EventHandlingScope view.

2. Click the CallExternalMethod activity; then set its InterfaceType property to the IOrderCorrelationLocalService and its MethodName property to GetResponse. (Be careful to choose the correct interface because there are two.)

3. Set its CorrelationToken property to **TheToken** and its OwnerActivityName property to sequenceActivity1.

4. Click the HandleExternalEvent activity, set its InterfaceType property to the IOrderCorrelationLocalService, and set its EventName property to OrderWorkflowApprove.

5. Set its CorrelationToken property to **TheToken**.

Configuring the Activities in the Event Handlers View

In the next steps, you configure the activities in the Event Handlers view.

1. Set the EventHandlingScope activity to its Event Handlers view.

2. Click the left-hand EventDriven activity and name it **CancelWorkflow**.

3. Click the HandleExternalEvent activity in the CancelWorkflow EventDriven activity, set its InterfaceType property to IEventHandlingScopeBasicLocalService, and set its EventName property to OrderWorkflowCancel.

4. Click the middle EventDriven activity and name it **AddApprover**.

5. Click the HandleExternalEvent activity in the AddApprover EventDriven activity, set its InterfaceType property to IEventHandlingScopeBasicLocalService, and set its EventName property to OrderWorkflowAddApprover.

6. Click the right EventDriven activity and name it **DeleteApprover**.

7. Click the HandleExternalEvent activity in the DeleteApprover EventDriven activity, set its InterfaceType property to IEventHandlingScopeBasicLocalService, and set its EventName property to OrderWorkflowDeleteApprover.

Preparatory Setup

The Approvers property you create will be an array list because this time the workflow will accept a list of approvers from the host form rather than manufacturing approvers based on a total number.

1. Add the following using directive to the workflow code-beside file:

```
using System.Windows.Forms;
```

2. Add the following variable to the top of the code-beside file class. (No constructor exists, because the workflow is expressed in XAML.)

```
int counter = 0;
```

3. Create a new DependencyProperty named OrderAmount by right-clicking in the code-beside file below the variable you just added. Select Insert Snippet, double-click Other, Workflow, select the Dependency Property, Property choice, and name it **Approvers** (leave the Property suffix). Press Tab, set its type to ArrayList, and press Enter to leave the remaining defaults.

4. Add another dependency property, name it **ApprovalStyle**, and accept all remaining defaults.

Adding Code-Beside for the Replicator Activity

In the next steps, you add the code to execute when the Replicator and its children are initialized. This is nearly identical to the code used the previous hour. The major difference is that it accepts Approvers from the form, thereby eliminating the need to combine Approver + counter to manufacture approvers.

1. Click the Replicator activity (remember to switch to the EventHandlingScope activity view if it is not shown), enter **RepInitialized** in its Initialized property, and enter the following code in its handler:

```
replicatorActivity1.InitialChildData = Approvers;
// Specify whether child instances should execute in serial or
parallel
if (ApprovalStyle == "Parallel")
    replicatorActivity1.ExecutionType = ExecutionType.Parallel;
else
    replicatorActivity1.ExecutionType = ExecutionType.Sequence;
```

2. Enter **RepChildInit** in its ChildInitialized property, and enter the following code in its handler:

```
           // Extract the "correct" CallExtnernalMethodActivity
           CallExternalMethodActivity act =
               e.Activity.GetActivityByName("callExternalMethodActivity1",
true)
               as CallExternalMethodActivity;

           act.ParameterBindings["approver"].Value =
               Approvers[counter].ToString();

           counter = counter + 1;
```

Adding Code-Beside to Update the Workflow Midflight

This is where the majority of the new code resides. You will trap the Invoked methods of each of the HandleExternalMethod activities to cancel the workflow, add an approver, or delete an approver. Approvers are added and removed from the Replicator.CurrentChildData property, which carries the replicator child data as the Replicator activity executes.

You will display a message when the workflow is canceled (cancellation is covered in Hour 16, "Working with Exceptions, Compensation, and Transactions," but you will enter code to carry out the other two choices now.

In the next steps you update the Invoked handlers of the HandleExternalEvent activities.

1. Click the HandleExternalEvent activity in the CancelWorkflow EventDriven activity (remember to switch the activity view if necessary), enter **CancelWorkflowInvoke** in its Invoked property, and enter the following code in its handler:

```
       SamsWFBook.OrderCancelEventArgs ea = e as
SamsWFBook.OrderCancelEventArgs;
       MessageBox.Show(ea.Reason.ToString());
```

2. Click the HandleExternalEvent activity in the AddApprovers EventDriven activity, enter **AddApproverInvoked** in its Invoked property, and enter the following code in its handler:

```
           this.replicatorActivity1.CurrentChildData.Add
               ((e as SamsWFBook.OrderApproverEventArgs).Approver);

           Approvers.Add((e as SamsWFBook.OrderApproverEventArgs).Approver);
```

3. Click the `HandleExternalEvent` activity in the `DeleteApprovers`
   `EventDriven` activity, enter **`DeleteApproverInvoked`** in its `Invoked` property,
   and enter the following code in its handler:

   ```
   this.replicatorActivity1.CurrentChildData.Remove
       ((e as SamsWFBook.OrderApproverEventArgs).Approver);

   Approvers.Remove((e as
   SamsWFBook.OrderApproverEventArgs).Approver);
   ```

Running the Advanced `EventHandlingScope` Workflow

The form has been changed. It allows you to enter the name of up to three approvers
and to cancel the workflow, add approvers, and to delete approvers midflight. The
workflow queues are updated each time you add or remove an approver. The new form
is shown in Figure 10.7.

FIGURE 10.7
EventHandlin-
gScope form
with cancel, add
approver, and
delete approver
options.

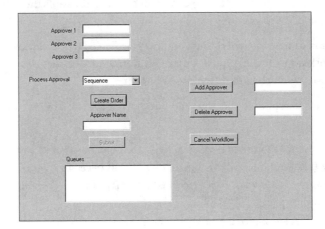

Follow the next steps to load the form, enter the values, and run the workflow.

1. Run the project and enter **Robert** in Approver 1, **Patricia** in Approver 2, and
   Matthew in Approver 3.

2. Set the form to process in parallel and click the Create Order button.

3. The Queues text box should show entries for Robert, Patricia, and Matthew.

4. Enter **New Approver** in the text box alongside the Add Approver button,
   and then click the Add Approver button.

5. The Queues text box should now contain a fourth entry for the new approver.
   You have just updated a workflow midflight, as shown in Figure 10.8.

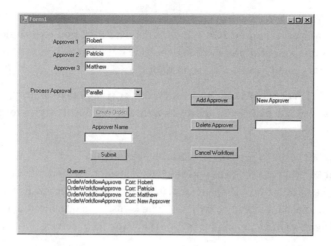

FIGURE 10.8
EventHandlin-gScope form with additional approver added at runtime.

6. Enter **Robert** in the text box alongside the Delete Approver button and then click the Delete Approver button.

7. The Queues text box should now contain only three approvers.

8. Click the Cancel Workflow button and you will be presented with a dialog box.

9. Now select the other approvers by entering a name in the Queues text box and clicking Submit. Do so for all remaining approvers in any order and then the EventHandlingScope activity and in turn the workflow will complete.

Using WCA.exe to Build the Strongly Typed Activities

The WCA.exe utility enables the creation of strongly typed communication activities (CallExternalMethod and HandleExternalEvent) that can be placed on the workflow where their properties can be set. The general advantages are that there is no need to point them to an interface and select the correct method or event. It is also more performant because the strong typing eliminates the need to use reflection to gather the type information at runtime. They can also be used to store additional information when integrating with other systems, as will be explained shortly. For communication activities that will be used frequently, strong typing is useful.

1. Shell out to a command prompt and enter the following to go to the bin directory:
   ```
   C:\SamsWf24hrs\Hours\Hour10EventHandlingScope\Lab2\WorkflowEventH
   andlingScopeReplicator\EventHandlingScopeWorkflows\bin\Debug.
   ```

2. Enter `"C:\Program Files\Microsoft SDKs\Windows\v6.0\Bin\"wca.exe` to see all options available. (On Windows Server 2003 I had to include the quotes around the path and place `wca.exe` outside the quotes as shown. Your path might vary for `WCA.exe`. If so, search for it.)

3. Enter `"C:\Program Files\Microsoft SDKs\Windows\v6.0\Bin\"wca.exe localservices.dll` to run the WCA utility on the local service for this project.

4. `IOrderCorrelationLocalService.Invoke.cs` and `IOrderCorrelationLocalService.Sink.cs` will be generated. The first contains the `CallExternalMethod` activities and the latter contains the `HandleExternalMethod` activities. (There is also an equivalent duo created for the `IEventHandlingScopeBasicLocalService` local service, which we will not use.)

5. Add a new Class Library project named **StronglyTypedActivities** to the solution and add the `IOrderCorrelationLocalService` files created above using the Project, Add Existing Item option.

6. Delete `Class1.cs`.

7. Add references to `System.Workflow.Activities`, `System.Workflow.ComponentModel`, and `System.Drawing`. Also reference the `LocalServices` project.

8. Build the project.

9. Open the `EventHandlingScopeReplicatorWorkflow` in design model and you will see that the `GetResponse` and `OrderWorkflowApprove` activities have been added under the new StronglyTypedActivities section (as shown in Figure 10.9). They are available to all projects in the current solution. In Hour 20, "Creating Basic Custom Activities," you will learn to make them available to all projects, including those outside of this solution.

Use Strongly Typed Activities on a Workflow

Because you will now add the same communication activities to multiple branches, reducing the configuration will streamline the process.

Follow the next steps to add strongly typed communication activities to the workflow.

1. Disable the `EventHandlingScope` activity.

FIGURE 10.9
`GetResponse`
and
`OrderWorkflo-`
`wApprove`
added to the
toolbox.

2. Add a `Parallel` activity at the end of the workflow and change its name to **`ParallelWithStronglyTypedActivities`**.

3. Add a `GetResponse` and an `OnWorkOrderApprove` activity, in that order, to both branches of the `Parallel` activity. The `Parallel` activity should now look like Figure 10.10.

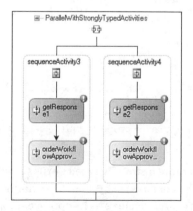

FIGURE 10.10
`Parallel` activity configured with strongly typed activities.

4. Click the `GetResponse` activity in the left branch and notice that its properties are different from those of a standard `CallExternalMethod` activity (as shown in Figure 10.11). It contains no `InterfaceType` or `MethodName` properties; they

are unnecessary because these are part of the activity, which makes the activity strongly typed.

FIGURE 10.11
Strongly typed
`GetResponse`
activity property
window.

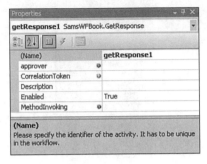

5. Enter **Branch1Token** in the GetResponse activity CorrelationToken property and then select the enclosing Sequence activity as the owner (in my case it is sequenceActivity2).

6. Enter **branch1** in the approver property.

7. Click the OrderWorkflowApprove activity in the left branch and notice its new properties (as shown in Figure 10.12).

FIGURE 10.12
Strongly typed
`OrderWorkflo-`
`wApprove` activ-
ity property
window.

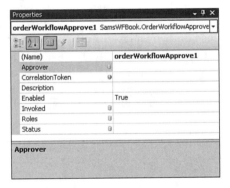

8. Enter **branch1** in its approver property and select Branch1Token in its CorrelationToken property.

9. Configure the right branch strongly typed GetResponse activity using Branch2Token as the CorrelationToken, its enclosing Sequence activity as its OwnerActivityName, and branch2 as its approver property.

10. Configure the right branch strongly typed OrderWorkflowApprove activity using Branch2Token as the CorrelationToken property and branch2 as its approver property.

11. Run the workflow, do not enter any data on the form, and click Create Order.

You should see the results shown in Figure 10.13, which represent the two queues created by the `HandleExternalEvent` activities awaiting a response.

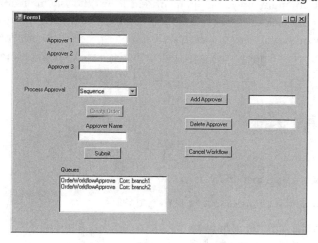

FIGURE 10.13
Running the workflow with `Parallel` activity and strongly typed activities.

12. Enter the approvers (branch1, then branch2) one at a time in the `Approver Name` text box and click Submit after each to respond to the events and complete the workflow. (This is a `Parallel` activity and not a `Listen`, so both events will be raised concurrently.)

If you like, open `IOrderCorrelationLocalService.Invokes.cs` and `IOrderCorrelationLocalService.Sinks.cs` to see the source code behind these strongly typed activities. Although used here for convenience, the extra attributes can also be used to communicate with external systems. For example, SharePoint's WF implementation features numerous task-centric activities that are strongly typed activities with attributes, such as task name, due date, and so on, that are used to interact with SharePoint tasks.

Summary

A very powerful activity was introduced in this hour: the `EventHandlingScope`. Its general usage was explored in the first section. The second section walked though how to use this activity in conjunction with the `Replicator` to create highly flexible workflows. These workflows benefit from the `Replicator`'s known abilities to configure a number of approvers when the workflow starts and to process in parallel or sequence while allowing for workflow-wide event handlers to trap and process events, such as to add an approver or cancel a workflow. A new capability of the `Replicator` to update its `Replicator.CurrentChildData` property was also used, which is changed when an event to add or delete approvers is trapped during workflow execution. Although you still have to create the distribution vehicle to reach the users—email, InfoPath forms, SharePoint tasks, or other—this workflow provides the underpinnings for many powerful approval-centric workflows. One feature you may want to add is another `Replicator` so that the number of approval levels can be specified per workflow as well. So far, all our samples process one level of approvals across all approvers. Finally, strongly typed activities were created and modeled on a workflow.

Workshop

Quiz

1. *What is the* `wca.exe` *utility used for?*

2. *What does the* `EventHandlers` *activity do?*

3. *What is the difference between a* `Listen` *activity and an* `EventHandlingScope` *activity?*

4. *What can be done with the* `Replicator.CurrentChildData` *property?*

5. *What are the two main functions of the* `EventHandlingScope` *activity?*

6. *What are the advantages of strongly typed activities?*

Answers

1. To create strongly typed activities.

2. Holds the `EventDriven` activities used to process the events processed by `EventHandlingScope` activity.

3. The `Listen` activity processes an event for its first child to fire, and then terminates. The `EventHandlingScope`, on the other hand, continues firing the event until the `EventHandlingScope` activity's sequential portion goes out of scope.

4. It can be viewed and modified at runtime to view or manipulate `Replicator` children.

5. To run its main child (essentially a `Sequence` activity) while being interruptible by one or more event handlers.

6. Streamlined modeling, faster because reflection is available, and additional attributes can be added to interaction with other systems.

PART III

Data-Driven Workflows and Rules

HOUR 11

Creating Data-Driven Workflows

What You'll Learn in This Hour:

- ▶ Overview of CAG
- ▶ Discussion of CAG and data-driven workflows
- ▶ Configuring the CAG
- ▶ Using the CAG to support a dynamic approval sample

Describing the CAG

The ConditionedActivityGroup (CAG) contains one or more lanes that each hold one or more activities, as does a Parallel activity. The CAG contains two optional condition properties. The first governs its overall execution and the second governs the individual lanes. The CAG runs until its overall condition is true (it's an UntilCondition). During this CAG's overall execution, each lane will execute, potentially more than once, while its individual condition is true. If no overall condition is set, the CAG will execute until all its child activities complete. A CAG lane with no condition executes exactly once.

The CAG is conceptually similar to a Parallel activity embedded in a While activity. Adding a condition to each branch of the Parallel activity embedded in a While activity even more closely resembles the CAG. The activities across CAG lanes will alternate processing, much as is the case with the Parallel activity (covered in Hour 8, "Working with Parallel Activities and Correlation"). See Hour 9, "Working with the Replicator and While Activities," for a description on how WF alternates activity execution across branches (Parallel activity terminology) or lanes (CAG activity terminology). This hour is focused on using the CAG's conditional capabilities to determine which lanes to execute and then executing them in their entirety.

One way to understand a CAG is to look at it its properties. Figure 11.1 contains a CAG. The figure shows the three CAG lanes (shown across the film strip at the top of the activity), and the details of one of its lanes are shown in the body of the activity. Figure 11.2 shows the overall CAG's properties, the key being its `UntilCondition`. Figure 11.3 shows the properties for one of the CAG lanes, the key being its `WhenCondition`.

FIGURE 11.1
CAG with three
lanes.

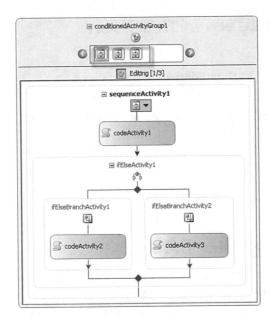

FIGURE 11.2
Overall CAG
properties.

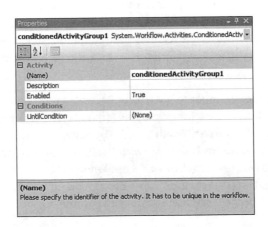

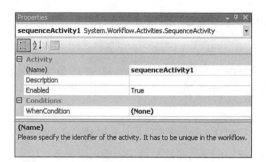

FIGURE 11.3
Individual CAG
lane properties.

This hour demonstrates using the CAG activity to permit three approvers to determine whether an order should be approved or declined. While creating this process, you will learn both basic CAG configuration and how current data values determine which CAG lanes execute.

Exploring the CAG and Data-Driven Workflows

Although the CAG is an activity that is added to a workflow (as are the IfElse and Code activities), it is also an alternative data-driven workflow approach to the better-known sequential and state machine styles. Generally, sequential workflows are recommended for deterministic processes that have a well-defined beginning and end. State machine workflows are best suited for dynamic processes that iterate through states without a guaranteed order. Data-driven workflows, on the other hand, are best suited when the data determines the process execution order. There are many pricing and promotional algorithms that may not execute a branch based on the data at the beginning of a process that will later do so when other parts of the process change the data the branch depended on. For instance, the order may not be subject to a discount until after tallying the line items.

Depending on your needs, the CAG activity may be the only activity on a sequential workflow. In this case, your child activities will be embedded in the CAG, and you will have created a data-driven workflow. In other cases, you may embed a CAG into a larger sequential or state machine workflow. In this case, only a subset of your workflow will be data driven.

CAG Approval Sample

In this section you create the workflow and run the CAG.

Creating the Project

Follow the next steps to create the project and add references.

1. Add a new Sequential Workflow Console Application project in the C:\SamsWf24hrs\Hours\Hour11CAGWorkflow directory and name it **CAGProject**.

2. Rename Workflow1.cs CAGWorkflow.cs in the Solution Explorer.

3. Add a reference to the System.Windows.Forms.

Adding Variable Declarations

Follow the next steps to add some variable. They are used to control the CAG's execution, and their use will become clear as you proceed.

1. Right-click CAGWorkflow.cs in the Solution Explorer and select View Code.

2. Add the following using directive:

```
using System.Windows.Forms;
```

3. Add the variable declarations in the next snippet below the constructor:

```
// Receive results from dialogs
DialogResult level1Dr = new DialogResult();
DialogResult level2Dr = new DialogResult();
DialogResult level3Dr = new DialogResult();

// Used to track number of approvals and rejections to
// control CAG operations, which is necessary since it
// will execute multiple times if left unchecked.
int numApprovals = 0;
int numRejections = 0;

// Used to determine which approvers are required
ArrayList approvers = new ArrayList();
```

4. Add the following code into the constructor below the call to InitializeComponent:

```
approvers.Add("Level2Approvers");
approvers.Add("Level3Approvers");
```

Add the CAG to the Workflow

Follow the next steps to add the CAG to the workflow and configure it.

1. Drag and drop a CAG activity onto the workflow.

2. Create the three CAG lanes by adding three Sequence activities to the CAG. Drag and drop three Sequence activities one at a time onto the CAG over the message that says Drop Activities Here (across the filmstrip, as shown in Figure 11.4).

FIGURE 11.4
CAG with high-lighted filmstrip.

3. Click the left activity (lane) in the CAG filmstrip. You should see the message: Drop Activities Here in the middle of the CAG. Enter **Approver1Lane** in the name property. See Figure 11.5 for an example.

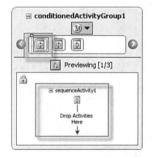

FIGURE 11.5
CAG with lane selected to change name.

4. Click the middle activity (lane) in the CAG filmstrip and change the name to **Approver2Lane.**

5. Click the right activity (lane) in the CAG filmstrip and change the name to **Approver3Lane.**

6. Click the icon next to the word Previewing in the middle of the CAG to change it from previewing mode to editing mode.

7. Your CAG should now look like Figure 11.6.

FIGURE 11.6
CAG select editing mode.

> **By the Way**
>
> If you are ever trying to add or delete activities or make other changes to a CAG and it will not accept them, make sure you are in editing and not previewing mode. If a lock icon displays in the middle of the CAG, you are in previewing mode.

Configuring the Approver1Lane of the CAG

The Approver1Lane lane is for the first approver who will always be required to approve. Therefore, this lane contains no `WhenCondition`, which means this lane will execute exactly once. You will add a `Code` activity and an `IfElse` activity to this lane. You will then add `Code` activities to both the left and right branches of the `IfElse` activity.

The first `Code` activity spawns a dialog that requests approval. The left branch of the `IfElse` activity checks whether approval is granted. The `Code` activities in the left and right branches update the approval count (left branch) or the rejection count (right branch).

Model the Approver1Lane

Follow the next steps to add child activities to the `Approver1Lane`.

1. Click the Approver1Lane in the CAG filmstrip. You should see the message "Drop Activities Here" in the middle of the CAG. See Figure 11.6 for an example.

2. Add a `Code` activity and name it **SpawnDialog1**.

3. Add an `IfElse` activity below the `Code` activity and name it **CheckApprover1Vote**. Name the left branch **Approver1Approves** and the right branch **Approver1Rejects**.

4. Add Code activities to both branches of the IfElse activity and name the one in the left branch **Approver1TallyApproval** and the one in the right branch **Approver1TallyRejection**.

Your CAG should now look like Figure 11.7.

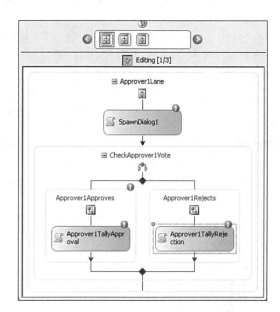

FIGURE 11.7
CAG with left lane modeled.

Add Code-Beside to the Approver1Lane

Follow the next steps to add code-beside to the activities in the Approver1Lane.

1. Double-click the SpawnDialog1 activity above the IfElse activity and enter the following in the handler to spawn an approval dialog:

```
level1Dr = MessageBox.Show
    ("Level 1 approves the order?", "", MessageBoxButtons.YesNo);
```

2. Add the following comments above the method declaration of the code condition handler you just edited:

```
//
// Level 1 section
//
```

3. Click the left branch of the IfElse activity, select Code Condition from its Condition property drop-down, click + to the left of the Condition property, enter **level1ApprovalCondition**, and press Enter.

4. Add the following code to the `level1ApprovalCondition` handler:

```
e.Result = this.level1Dr.ToString() == "Yes";
```

5. Add the following comment above the method declaration of the `Code Condition` you just updated:

```
// Selecting which branch to execute based on answer to dialog
```

6. Double-click the `Approver1TallyApproval` activity in the left branch of the `IfElse` activity and enter the following in the handler:

```
// Tallying approvals
numApprovals++;
Console.WriteLine
    ("Level 1 order approved. Approvals {0}", numApprovals);
```

7. Double-click the `Approver1TallyRejection` activity in the right branch of the `IfElse` activity and enter the following in the handler:

```
// Tallying rejections
numRejections++;
Console.WriteLine
    ("Level 1 order rejected. Rejections {0}", numRejections);
```

The code entered in this section should look like Listing 11.1.

LISTING 11.1   Level1 Section Code-Beside

```
//
// Level 1 section
//

private void SpawnDialog1_ExecuteCode(object sender, EventArgs e)
{
    level1Dr = MessageBox.Show
        ("Level 1 approves the order?", "", MessageBoxButtons.YesNo);
}


// Selecting which branch to execute based on answer to dialog
private void level1ApprovalCondition(object sender, ConditionalEventArgs e)
{
    e.Result = this.level1Dr.ToString() == "Yes";
}

private void Approver1TallyApproval_ExecuteCode(object sender, EventArgs e)
{
    // Tallying approvals
    numApprovals++;
    Console.WriteLine
        ("Level 1 order approved. Approvals {0}", numApprovals);

}
```

```
        private void Approver1TallyRejection_ExecuteCode(object sender,
EventArgs e)
        {
            // Tallying rejections
            numRejections++;
            Console.WriteLine
                ("Level 1 order rejected. Rejections {0}", numRejections);

        }
```

That concludes the Approver1Lane lane. Setting up the next two lanes or approvers is similar.

By the Way

> In a real-world scenario, the dialog box requesting a vote would not be part of the workflow. The vote would be taken in a UI application and the results sent back to the workflow. A CallExternalMethod activity would send a request to a Windows Forms, email, or other client. A response would then be submitted from the client. A HandleExternalEvent activity would capture this response. This hour uses dialog boxes in place of a more elaborate process to focus on the CAG and not the actual communication wiring method used.

Configuring the Approver2Lane of the CAG

A second approver may or may not be necessary. Therefore the Approver2Lane lane (which holds the second approver) contains a WhenCondition.

Placing a condition on a CAG lane also triggers another change in the way the CAG behaves. Lanes with no conditions execute exactly once, whereas lanes with conditions execute 0 or more times. The CAG's capability to reexecute lanes is part of its power. You must, however, be aware of it, so that you do not continually request approval from approver2, for instance, in this case.

The next two bullets describe how to ensure approver2 will be requested to approve only when the process calls for approval from approver2 and that this request will happen only once:

▶ Check the approvers ArrayList defined earlier to see if it contains an entry for Level2Approvers. This is populated once and does not change throughout the process.

▶ To ensure approval is requested once and only once, a couple of variables will be used. The first tallies approvals, and the second rejections. The second approver should not be requested unless the sum of these two variables equals 1, because approval is performed in order. One of these variables will be updated after each approver tallies a vote. Setting the condition to execute only when the sum of these variables is 1 ensures that the Approver2Lane lane does not execute until after the first Approver1Lane lane completes, and that it does not continue to request a vote over and over.

Modeling the Approver2Lane

Follow the next steps to add child activities to the Approver2Lane.

1. Click the Approver2Lane in the CAG filmstrip.

2. Add a Code activity and name it **SpawnDialog2**.

3. Add an IfElse activity below the Code activity and name it **CheckApprover2Vote**. Name the left branch **Approver2Approves** and the right branch **Approver2Rejects**.

4. Add Code activities to both branches of the IfElse activity and name the one in the left branch **Approver2TallyApproval** and the one in the right branch **Approver2TallyRejection**.

Adding Code-Beside to the Approver2Lane

Follow the next steps to add code-beside to the activities in the Approver2Lane.

1. Now you'll set a condition that will determine when and if this lane executes. Click the middle Approver2Lane lane in the filmstrip, select Code Condition from its WhenCondition property drop-down, click + to the left of the Condition property, enter **Approver2LaneCondition**, and press Enter.

2. Add the following code to the Approver2LaneCondition handler (this is the when condition that evaluates whether the Approver2LaneCondition lane should execute):

```
e.Result = approvers.Contains("Level2Approvers")
    && numApprovals + numRejections == 1;
```

3. Add the following comments above the method declaration of the code condition handler you just edited:

```
//
// Level 2 section
//

// Is level 2 approval required?
```

4. Double-click the SpawnDialog2 activity above the IfElse activity and enter the following in the handler:

```
level2Dr = MessageBox.Show
    ("Level 2 approves the order?", "", MessageBoxButtons.YesNo);
```

5. Add a Code Condition named **level2ApprovalCondition** to the left branch of the IfElse activity.

6. Add the following code to the level2ApprovalCondition handler:

```
e.Result = this.level2Dr.ToString() == "Yes";
```

7. Double-click the Approver2TallyApproval activity in the left branch of the IfElse activity and enter the following in the handler:

```
// Tallying approvals
numApprovals++;
Console.WriteLine("Level 2 order approved. Approvals {0}", numApprovals);
```

8. Double-click the Approver2TallyRejection activity in the right branch of the IfElse activity and enter the following in the handler:

```
// Tallying rejections
numRejections++;
Console.WriteLine("Level 2 order rejected. Rejections {0}",
numRejections);
```

That's it for the Approver2Lane lane.

Running the Workflow with Two Lanes

The CAG is now functional. It will request both level 1 and level 2 votes. There is no level 3 yet.

Follow the next steps to add a Code activity to tally the results and run the workflow.

1. Add a Code activity below the CAG activity named **DisplayResults** that will print success if there are two approvals and rejection if there are fewer than two.

2. Double-click the Code activity and add the following code to its handler:

```
Console.WriteLine();
if (numApprovals == 2)
    Console.WriteLine("Order is Approved!");
else
    Console.WriteLine("Order is rejected!");
```

3. Click the Approver3Lane in the CAG filmstrip and set its Enabled property to false.

4. Run the workflow, and you should see similar results to Figure 11.8. Remember to pause the host if you run the workflow with debugging by adding a Console.Read statement.

FIGURE 11.8
CAG results with
two operational
lanes.

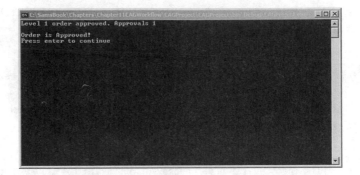

Configuring the Approver3Lane of the CAG

This lane mirrors the second lane in that it contains a WhenCondition. However, the condition will evaluate to true only if the first two voters split, creating the need for a tie breaker. This demonstrates how the CAG can be used for additional approval levels and for other items that change mid-process.

You'll now set up the third lane, which is nearly identical to the second.

Modeling the Approver3Lane

Follow the next steps to add child activities to the Approver3Lane.

1. Click the Approver3Lane in the CAG filmstrip and set its enabled property to true.

2. Add a Code activity and name it **SpawnDialog3**.

3. Add an IfElse activity below the Code activity and name it **CheckApprover3Vote**. Name the left branch **Approve3Approves** and the right branch **Approver3Rejects**.

4. Add Code activities to both branches of the IfElse activity and name the one in the left branch **Approver3TallyApproval** and the one in the right branch **Approver3TallyRejection**.

Add Code-Beside to the Approver3Lane

Follow the next steps to add code-beside to the activities in the Approver3Lane.

1. Now you'll set a condition that will determine when and if this lane executes. Click the Approver3Lane lane in the filmstrip, select Code Condition from its WhenCondition property drop-down, click + to the left of the Condition property, enter **Approver3LaneCondition**, and press Enter.

2. Add the following code to the `Approver3LaneCondition` handler to ensure that this lane executes only if there is a tie:

```
e.Result = approvers.Contains("Level3Approvers")
        && numApprovals == 1 && numRejections == 1;
```

3. Add the following comments above the method declaration of the code condition handler you just edited:

```
//
// Level 3 section
//

// Is level 3 approval required?
```

4. Double-click the `SpawnDialog3` activity above the `IfElse` activity and enter the following in the handler:

```
level3Dr = MessageBox.Show
    ("Level 3 approves the order?", "", MessageBoxButtons.YesNo);
```

5. Add a Code Condition rule named **level3ApprovalCondition** to the left branch of the `IfElse` activity.

6. Add the following code to the `level3ApprovalCondition` handler:

```
e.Result = this.level3Dr.ToString() == "Yes";
```

7. Double-click the `Approver3TallyApproval` activity in the left branch of the `IfElse` activity and enter the following in the handler:

```
// Tallying approvals
numApprovals++;
Console.WriteLine("Level 3 order approved. Approvals {0}", numApprovals);
```

8. Double-click the `Approver3TallyRejection` activity in the right branch of the `IfElse` activity and enter the following in the handler:

```
// Tallying rejections
numRejections++;
Console.WriteLine("Level 3 order rejected. Rejections {0}",
numRejections);
```

That's it for the Approver3Lane lane.

Run the Workflow with Three Lanes

The CAG is now complete. It will request both level 1 and level 2 votes. In case of a tie, it will request the third tiebreaker vote. If the first two votes result in two approvals or rejections, no third vote occurs.

Follow the next steps to run the workflow and see the new processing logic with the third lane.

1. Run the workflow, approve at level 1, and approve at level 2. The workflow should complete without requesting level 3 approval.

2. Run the workflow again, approve level 1, and reject at level 2. You should now be requested to perform a level 3 approval. The final approval will match your level 3 choice—it is the tiebreaker.

3. If you like, remove level3Approvers from the approvers ArrayList and you will not be prompted for level 3 approval.

That's it for the three lane CAG.

> The CAG also has an UntilCondition property. The CAG will terminate when this property is no longer true. This property is useful in many scenarios and can be set at runtime to provide a way to terminate after half of the votes are affirmative or negative, for instance.

Summary

In this hour, you experimented with the CAG activity. The CAG activity represents WF's third workflow authoring style, known as data driven. In this hour's example, three lanes were each covered by a different WhenCondition variant. The overall CAG did not have an UntilCondition in this example. The CAG is generally considered WF's most dynamic and flexible workflow style and is well suited for workflows that are data driven. It is also useful when embedded in the other workflows that call for its functionality as part of a larger workflow. It is not as transparent as the other two styles of workflow, because the contents in its lanes are hard to see, so its use should be limited to scenarios that call for it.

Workshop

Quiz

1. *Does the CAG run items sequentially or in parallel?*

2. *What two places can conditions be applied to in a CAG?*

3. *By default, will the CAG run a lane that has a* when *condition one or more times?*

4. *What scenarios is the CAG best suited for?*

5. *Exactly what order does the CAG run its child activities in?*

6. *Can each CAG lane contain multiple activities?*

7. *When will the CAG complete if there is no condition on the entire CAG?*

Answers

1. In parallel.

2. To the entire CAG and to each lane.

3. Multiple times.

4. Dynamic and data driven.

5. It runs them "largely" parallel across lanes in an iterative fashion, but the precise order cannot be guaranteed.

6. Not directly but a composite activity, such as a Sequence activity, can be added and multiple activities can be added to it.

7. When all child activities have completed execution, which occurs when all of the CAG's lanes WhenConditions evaluate to false.

Working with the WF RuleSet

What You'll Learn in This Hour:

▶ **WF rule overview**

▶ `RuleSet` **creation through the** `Policy` **activity**

▶ `RuleSet` **dependency calculations**

▶ **Calling methods from rules and dependency attributes**

▶ **External RuleSet application**

▶ **Configuring a workflow to access an external** `RuleSet`

So far we have looked at executing single rules that are bound to an activity. The structure of a common rule is this: `if (ItemQuantity < 0) CancelOrder();`. This matches the way rules are used in traditional code. We will now look at The WF RuleSet, another form of rules much more closely aligned with rules engines. Rule sets in general differ from traditional rules in two ways:

▶ In addition to providing evaluational criteria, they provide the corresponding action. In the preceding example, a `Rule` in a `RuleSet` will contain both the `if (ItemQuantity < 0)` and the `CancelOrder();` action.

▶ They frequently contain a number of interrelated rules (a set) that process in conjunction to perform a function such as calculating a price or a promotional amount. If you looked into the source code of a promotional or pricing calculation, for example, you are likely to find many `if`, `else`, `while`, `switch`, and other statements that churn in tandem to return an answer.

In WF, a `RuleSet` is always stored in a `.rules` file. Declarative Rule Conditions are also stored in `.rules` files. The only WF rules not stored in `.rules` files are Code

Conditions. The two main advantages to storing rules in .rules files are that they are more accessible to tools and they can be loaded and/or changed at runtime.

In this hour you learn to create a WF RuleSet. Then you will learn to call methods from a Rule within a RuleSet. You will use the External RuleSet Toolkit that permits .rules files to be stored, versioned, and accessed at runtime from a SQL database. Finally, you will learn to trace RuleSet execution using standard .NET tracing.

Creating the RuleSet

This section begins with an overview of RuleSet terminology and then takes you through creating a RuleSet.

RuleSet Terminology and Project Ruleset

As previously stated, a RuleSet contains one or more rules. Each RuleSet rule contains the following attributes:

- ▶ A Name property that provides the rule with a name.

- ▶ A Condition property that holds the evaluation criteria (for example, if (itemqty > 0)).

- ▶ A Then Actions property that holds the actions performed if the Condition evaluates to true.

- ▶ An optional Else Actions property that holds the actions performed if the rule Condition evaluates to false.

- ▶ An optional Priority property that can override the order that individual rule executes in.

- ▶ A Reevaluate property that determines whether the rule should be automatically reevaluated if a value it depends on is changed by another rule (this is referred to as forward or full chaining in rules-engine speak and is described shortly).

- ▶ RuleWrite and RuleRead attributes that can be added to Rule methods to explicitly state dependencies on a WF rule when WF is incapable of inferring them itself.

You will create a RuleSet in this hour that has three rules: DiscountPercent, TotalOrderAmount, and YearlySales. These rules are all dependent on each other. Table 12.1 shows each rule, its evaluational criteria, and its execution semantics.

TABLE 12.1 Sample Rules

Rule Name	Rule	Priority/Reevaluate	Dependency
DiscountPercent	If this.subtotal > 2000 Then this.discount = 0.05	2/Always	None
TotalOrderAmount	If this.discount > 0 Then this.total = (1 - this.discount) * this.subtotal Else this.total = this.subtotal	1/Always	DiscountPercent
YearlySales	If this.total != 0 Then this.totalYear Sales = this.originaTotal YearSales + this.total	3/Always	TotalOrderAmount

A WF RuleSet is processed through a forward (or full) chaining rules engine, which means it can reprocess dependent rules. The neat part is that WF can do much of this automatically via clever CODEDOM programming (a .NET serialization capability), in contrast to forcing the developer to attribute the dependencies. For example, the yearly sales must be updated with the current order amount, but the discount must be factored in or else yearly sales will be erroneously inflated. The next steps demonstrate how WF executes the sample RuleSet.

1. Evaluate the Condition property on the YearlySales rule because it contains the highest Priority. It evaluates to false.

2. Evaluate the Condition on the DiscountPercent rule because it contains the second highest Priority. It evaluates to true, so the ThenActions updates the discount attribute.

3. Evaluate the Condition on the TotalOrderAmount rule because it is next and it is dependent on the discount changed in the prior rule. It evaluates to true, so execute its ThenActions.

4. Reevaluate the YearlySales rule because it depends on the total attribute contained in the preceding rule.

Creating the Project

1. Create a new blank solution (Other Project Types, Visual Studio Solutions) named **RulesetSolution** in the C:\SamsWf24hrs\Hours\Hour12Rules directory.

2. Add a Sequential Workflow Console Application project named **RulesetProject** to the solution.

3. Open Program.cs and add the following code below the WaitHandle.WaitOne(); line to pause the host:

   ```
   Console.WriteLine("Press enter to continue");
   Console.Read();
   ```

4. Rename Workflow1.cs to **RulesetWorkflow.cs** in the Solution Explorer.

5. Add the following member variables to the RulesetWorkflow code-behind file below the constructor:

   ```
   double discountThreshold = 2000.00;
   double subtotal = 3000.00;
   double total = 0.00;
   double discount = 0.00;
   double totalYearlySales = 0.00;
   double originalTotalYearlySales = 5000.00;
   ```

Creating the RuleSet via the Policy Activity

The workflow will be sparse. It consists of a Policy activity that contains a RuleSetReference property that a RuleSet is bound to. Therefore a RuleSet, through the Policy activity, can be modeled into workflows.

1. Drag and drop a Policy activity onto the workflow.

2. Click its RuleSetReference property and click the ellipsis.

   You should see the Select Rule Set dialog shown in Figure 12.1.

3. Click the New button to add a new RuleSet.

Adding the DiscountPercent Rule

1. Click the Add Rule button to add the first rule (a rule within the RuleSet).

   You should see the Rule Set Editor dialog as shown in Figure 12.2.

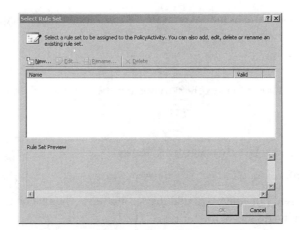

FIGURE 12.1
Select Rule Set
dialog.

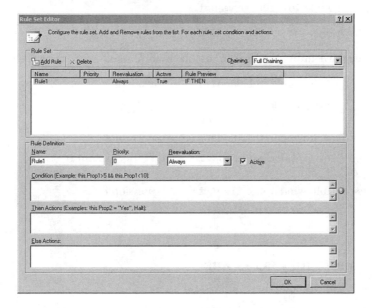

FIGURE 12.2
Rule Set Editor
dialog.

2. Name the rule `DiscountPercent`.

3. Set its priority to 2.

4. Leave the default Reevaluation (set at Always) and make sure the Active check
   box is checked.

5. Enter the following in the Condition expression box:

```
this.subtotal > 2000
```

6. Enter the following in the ThenActions expression box (this action occurs if the rule is true):

```
this.discount = 0.05
```

7. Leave the ElseActions expression box empty. (Don't click OK yet.)

Adding the TotalOrderAmount Rule

In the next steps, you add the TotalOrderAmount rule.

1. Click the Add Rule button to add the second rule. (The first one will be displayed in the middle of the form.)

2. Name the rule TotalOrderAmount.

3. Set its Priority to 1.

4. Leave the default Reevaluation as Always and make sure Active is checked.

5. Enter the following in the Condition expression box:

```
this.discount > 0
```

6. Enter the following in the ThenActions expression box:

```
this.total = (1 - this.discount) * this.subtotal
```

7. Enter the following in the ElseActions expression box:

```
this.total = this.subtotal
```

Adding the YearlySales Rule

In the next steps, you add the YearlySales rule.

1. Click the Add Rule button to add the third rule. (The second rule will be displayed in the middle of the form.)

2. Name the rule YearlySales.

3. Set its Priority to 3.

4. Leave the default Reevaluation as Always and make sure Active is checked.

5. Enter the following in the Condition expression box:

```
this.total != 0
```

6. Enter the following in the `ThenActions` expression box:

```
this.totalYearlySales = this.originalTotalYearlySales + this.total
```

7. Leave the `ElseActions` expression box empty.

8. Your Rule Set Editor dialog with completed rules should now look like Figure 12.3.

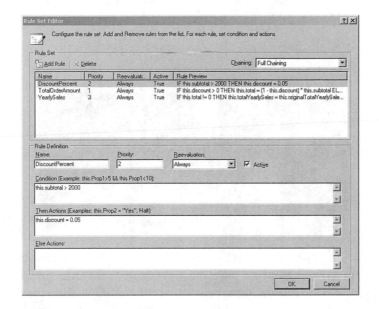

FIGURE 12.3
Rule Set Editor dialog with completed rules.

9. Click the OK button.

10. You should now be returned to the Select RuleSet form where the rule set you just added should be displayed.

11. Make sure your newly added `RuleSet` is highlighted and click the Rename button.

12. Chang the rule set name to **MyRuleSetDeclarative** in the Rename RuleSet dialog.

13. Click the OK button twice to leave both dialogs.

Running the Workflow

Follow the next steps to add a `Code` activity to print the results to the console and run the workflow.

1. Drag and drop a Code activity onto the workflow below the Policy activity to display the results.

2. Double-click the Code activity and enter the following in its handler:

```
Console.WriteLine("Subtotal {0}", subtotal);
Console.WriteLine("Total {0}", total);
Console.WriteLine("Discount {0}", discount);
Console.WriteLine("Total Yearly Sales {0}", totalYearlySales);
Console.WriteLine("Original Total Yearly Sales {0}",
        originalTotalYearlySales);
```

3. Press F5 to run the workflow and you should receive the results shown in Figure 12.4.

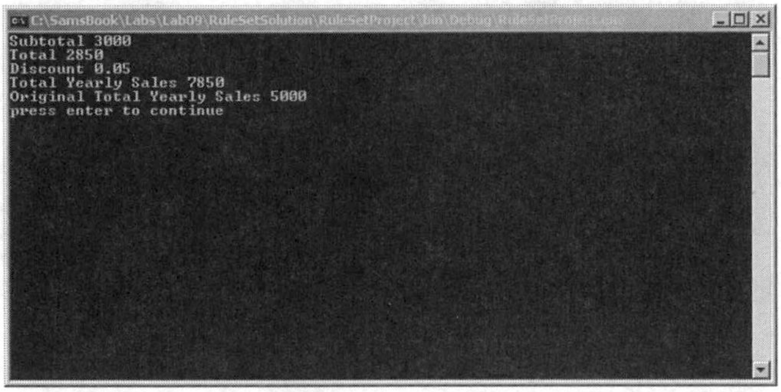

FIGURE 12.4
RuleSet execution results.

The key is that the TotalYearlySales is 7,850, which reflects the discounted total order amount. WF automatically infers the dependency of the total in the YearlySales and TotalOrderAmount rules. In a simple sample with three rules this is not a great help; however, in many more complex pricing, promotional, and trading rules that contain 10s, 100s, or even 1,000s of rules, this automated dependency processing can be immensely useful. In the upcoming section that shows how to call methods from a rule, you will see what happens when dependencies are not observed.

Monitoring the RuleSet

It is important that you understand exactly how rules in a WF RuleSet are processed. Because although it is useful, the automated reevaluation could be disastrous if it calculated differently than you expected. Both WF tracking and standard .NET tracing can be used to trace RuleSet execution.

Tracking provides the Rule Name and Condition evaluation result. Tracing, depending on the level of detail requested, first enumerates the evaluation and then the execution. It provides Rule Names, then and else condition effects (described shortly), the rules that executed, and the conditional evaluation results for the executed rules.

This exercise covers tracing. RuleSet tracking is covered in Hour 13, "Learning to Track Workflows."

Adding RuleSet Tracing

An application configuration file must be added and the level of tracing specified to determine what RuleSet information will be traced.

Follow the next steps to configure the workflow to be traced.

1. Add an App.config file by right-clicking the project, choosing Add, New Item, selecting the Application Configuration File template.

2. Click the Add button. (Leave the default App.Config name.)

3. Insert the following snippet between the Configuration opening and closing elements to specify the maximum tracing information be collected:

```
<system.diagnostics>
    <switches>
        <add name="System.Workflow.Activities.Rules" value="All" />
    </switches>
</system.diagnostics>
```

4. Your App.config file should look like Listing 12.1.

LISTING 12.1   **App.Config File Configured to Trace**

```
<?xml version="1.0" encoding="utf-8" ?>
<configuration>
  <system.diagnostics>
      <switches>
          <add name="System.Workflow.Activities.Rules" value="All" />
      </switches>
  </system.diagnostics>
</configuration>
```

Evaluating Pre-Execution Results

Follow the next steps to run the workflow and evaluate the results.

1. Press F5 to run the workflow; you should see RuleSet evaluation results in the Output Window following all the loading statements (Click View, Output if

your Output Window is not shown). The content is described immediately following its display.

```
        Verbose: 0 : Rule Set "MyRuleSet": Rule "YearlySales" Condition
dependency:
            "this/total/"
        Verbose: 0 : Rule Set "MyRuleSet": Rule "YearlySales" THEN side-
effect:
            "this/totalYearlySales/"
        Verbose: 0 : Rule Set "MyRuleSet": Rule "DiscountPercent" Condition
dependency:
            "this/discountThreshold/"
        Verbose: 0 : Rule Set "MyRuleSet": Rule "DiscountPercent" Condition
dependency:
            "this/subtotal/"
        Verbose: 0 : Rule Set "MyRuleSet": Rule "DiscountPercent" THEN
side-effect:
            "this/discount/"
        Verbose: 0 : Rule Set "MyRuleSet": Rule "TotalOrderAmount"
Condition dependency:
            "this/discount/"
        Verbose: 0 : Rule Set "MyRuleSet": Rule "TotalOrderAmount" THEN
side-effect:
            "this/total/"
        Verbose: 0 : Rule Set "MyRuleSet": Rule "TotalOrderAmount" ELSE
side-effect:
            "this/total/"
        Verbose: 0 : Rule Set "MyRuleSet":Rule "DiscountPercent" THEN
actions trigger
            rule "TotalOrderAmount"
        Verbose: 0 : Rule Set "MyRuleSet":Rule "TotalOrderAmount" THEN
actions trigger
            rule "YearlySales"
        Verbose: 0 : Rule Set "MyRuleSet": Rule "TotalOrderAmount" ELSE
actions trigger
            rule "YearlySales"
```

The pre-execution evaluation data contains the following (this is WF's plan for executing the `RuleSet` before it actually does so):

▶ The trace level, which is `Verbose` in our case. (Try setting it to different levels to see how it affects the trace output, if you want.)

▶ Each rule's conditional dependency, the data attribute evaluated in the condition.

▶ Each rule's THEN side effect, the data updated by the `Then` action.

▶ Each rule's ELSE side effect, the data updated by the `Then` action.

▶ The rules triggered by each rule are shown. For example, the `DiscountPercent` rule triggers the `TotalOrderAmount` rule because a change in the discount necessitates adjusting the order amount.

The System.Workflow.Activtities.Rules and workflow instance information was omitted for clarity.

Evaluating Post-Execution Results

The post-execution results are immediately below their pre-execution counterparts next (their content is described immediately following):

```
Rule Set "MyRuleSet": Executing
Rule Set "MyRuleSet": Evaluating condition on rule "YearlySales".
Rule Set "MyRuleSet": Rule "YearlySales" condition evaluated to False.
Rule Set "MyRuleSet": Evaluating condition on rule "DiscountPercent".
Rule Set "MyRuleSet": Rule "DiscountPercent" condition evaluated to True.
Rule Set "MyRuleSet": Evaluating THEN actions for rule "DiscountPercent".
Rule Set "MyRuleSet": Evaluating condition on rule "TotalOrderAmount".
Rule Set "MyRuleSet": Rule "TotalOrderAmount" condition evaluated to True.
Rule Set "MyRuleSet": Evaluating THEN actions for rule "TotalOrderAmount".
Rule Set "MyRuleSet": Rule "TotalOrderAmount" side effects enable rule
"YearlySales" reevaluation.
Rule Set "MyRuleSet": Evaluating condition on rule "YearlySales".
Rule Set "MyRuleSet": Rule "YearlySales" condition evaluated to True.
Rule Set "MyRuleSet": InstanceId Evaluating THEN actions for rule "YearlySales".
```

The execution results data contains the following:

- ▶ A row that states that execution has begun.

- ▶ The condition of the first rule is evaluated.

- ▶ The results of the first rule are output (false in our case).

- ▶ Any rules that evaluate to true trigger their respective Then actions, as would be expected. Likewise, Else actions are triggered when rules evaluate to false.

- ▶ The most interesting result (which is boldface in the preceding code) takes place when the TotalOrderAmount rule's Then/Else action executes: it triggers reevaluation of the Yearly Sales rule. We already know this, but it is interesting to see WF's implementation.

The data before RuleSet in each line was omitted for clarity.

Calling Methods from Rules

You can call methods from the rules in a RuleSet. We will now replace Then and Else actions in the TotalOrderAmount rule to use a method to update the values instead of doing so declaratively. This requires that we attribute the method, because

WF will no longer be able to automatically infer the dependency of the total attribute that is used to calculate yearly sales.

1. Add the following method to your workflow code-beside file below the handler that displays the results:

   ```
   private void UpdateTotal()
   {
       this.total = (1 - this.discount) * this.subtotal;
   }
   ```

2. Click the Policy activity, click the + next to the RuleSetReference property, and click the ellipsis in the RuleSet Definition property.

3. Click the TotalOrderAmount rule and replace the contents in the Then Actions and the Else Actions sections with a call to UpdateTotal().

4. Your TotalOrderAmount rule should now look like Figure 12.5.

5. Run the workflow and you should see the results shown in Figure 12.6 wherein the Total Yearly Sales is 0.

This does not match earlier processing. The reason is that the YearlySales rule is not invoked because the Total field is now updated inside a method and WF cannot automatically detect this. WF only detects members manipulated in the method signature. Those updated in the body must be explicitly noted, as shown next.

FIGURE 12.5
Calling a method from a RuleSet.

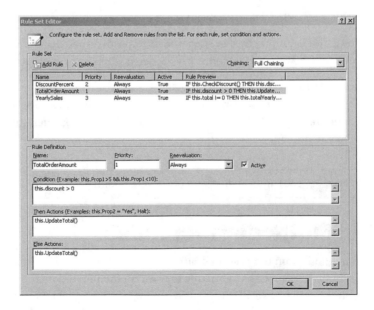

FIGURE 12.6
RuleSet processing results with undetected dependency.

Attributing Methods to Detect Dependency

In the next subsection you attribute a method called from an action and in the following you do so for a method called from a condition. In both cases, the reason for doing so is to explicitly state dependency.

Attributing a Method Called from an Action

Follow the next steps to attribute the UpdateTotal method to explicitly state dependencies from a method from a Rule action.

1. Add the following attributes above the UpdateTotal method that inform the RuleSet that the total field is written to and the discount field is read from:

    ```
    [RuleWrite("total")]
    [RuleRead("discount")]
    ```

2. The method should now look like this:

    ```
    [RuleWrite("total")]
    [RuleRead("discount")]
    private void UpdateTotal()
    {
        this.total = (1 - this.discount) * this.subtotal;
    }
    ```

3. Run the workflow and you should see results that match the original declarative results.

If a dependent value is updated in a method that is called from a method that was called by a rule, use the RuleInvoke attribute to denote indirect dependencies because of method calls.

Attributing a Method Called from a Condition

So far you have called a method from a `Rule` action, which performs a write or an update. You can also call methods from a `Rule` condition. These methods can be attributed to reflect which values are read inside of them so they will reevaluate.

Follow the next steps to attribute the `UpdateTotal` method to explicitly state dependencies from a method from a `Rule` condition.

1. Add the following attributed method to your workflow code-beside file, below the previous method.

   ```
   [RuleRead("subtotal")]
   [RuleRead("discountThreshold")]
   private bool CheckDiscount()
   {
       return this.subtotal > this.discountThreshold;
   }
   ```

2. Now you must edit the `DiscountPercent` rule to use this method.

3. Edit the `RuleSet` and select the `DiscountPercent` rule.

4. Replace the contents in the `Condition` property with the call to `CheckDiscount()`. (It will automatically insert `this.` before the method name when you save.)

   Your `RuleSet` (and specifically the `DiscountPercent` rule) should now look like Figure 12.7.

FIGURE 12.7
RuleSet processing results with undetected dependency.

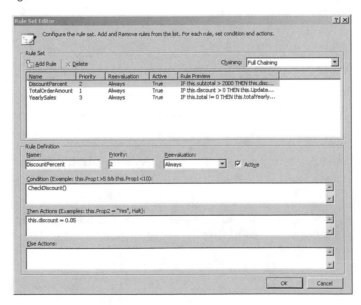

5. Run the workflow again and you should get the correct results with all values updated as expected. The dependent values in the methods are detected and the rules reevaluate accordingly.

Using the External RuleSet Application

By default, a RuleSet is stored in a .rules file and is bound to one workflow (as a resource). In this exercise you will download an application that permits a RuleSet to be stored and versioned in a database. The RuleSet is then loaded and executed at runtime. The RuleSets are maintained from a Windows application that is part of the External RuleSet Toolkit. The dialogs used to maintain a RuleSet are available via an API, making a RuleSet available to any .NET 2.0 or later application. The External RuleSet Toolkit is not part of WF, but rather a community application developed by a Microsoft Program Manager. In addition to being useful, the External RuleSet application exemplifies the type of tooling being built around the WF's XML Serialized formats:—whether XAML or .rules. It also shows how to create custom runtime services and to call the rules dialogs from a .NET app.

The next lists contains the items you will perform to download and use the External RuleSet application.

1. Download the External RuleSet application.

2. Use the demo workflow included with it.

3. Store the RuleSet you created earlier in the External RuleSet application.

4. Configure a new workflow to access the RuleSet stored in the External RuleSet application.

Downloading the External RuleSet Application

Perform the next steps to download and install the External RuleSet application.

1. Create a directory to hold the application, such as ExternalRuleSet.

2. Download the External RuleSet application from http://wf.netfx3.com/files/folders/rules_samples/entry309.aspx.

3. Run the self-extracting .exe file and browse to the directory you just created.

4. View the Setup.cmd file and change the database settings if necessary. The default setting is to localhost\SQLExpress. To use it with SQL Server and localhost, delete the \SQLExpress reference in the file.

5. The command calls a SQL script that creates a database named rules, which holds the RuleSet information.

Running the Sample Workflow

To ensure that the External RuleSet application is functioning and to see how it works, run the sample workflow solution included with the External RuleSet application. This workflow executes a RuleSet even though it does not contain a policy activity. It achieves this through a custom activity that mediates communication between the database and the .rules file. The custom activity binds to a .rules file in a database rather than in the current workflow.

Follow the next steps to run the sample workflow that comes with the External Rule-Set application.

1. Open the RuleSetToolkitUsageSample solution by navigating to the C:\ExternalRuleSet\RuleSetToolkitUsageSample directory and clicking the RuleSetToolkitUsageSample.sln file.

2. Pause the host by adding the requisite code to Program.cs, as you did earlier in the hour.

3. Press F5 to run the sample; you should see the results shown in Figure 12.8 in the command window. (If not, verify that the External RuleSet application was installed properly.)

FIGURE 12.8
Sample External RuleSet application processing results.

4. The custom (Policy) activity on the workflow is configured as shown in Figure 12.9.

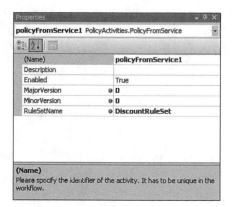

FIGURE 12.9
Custom Policy
activity configu-
ration.

5. The `DiscountRuleSet` is the name of a `RuleSet` stored in the rules database by the External RuleSet application.

6. If the different versions of the `RuleSet` are stored in the External RuleSet application, the specific version can be specified in the `MajorVersion` and `MinorVersion` properties. If they are both set to 0, the latest version will always be retrieved.

Uploading Rules to the External Database

Follow the next steps to upload the `RuleSet` created earlier in this hour to the External RuleSet application. This way these rules can be edited outside of the workflow they were created with, versioned, and changed at runtime.

1. Open the `ExternalRuleSetToolkit` solution by navigating to the `C:\ExternalRuleSet` directory and clicking the `ExternalRuleSetToolkit.sln` file.

2. Make sure the `RuleSetTool` project is set as the startup project and then run the project.

3. You should see the RuleSet Browser dialog with `DiscountRuleSet` RuleSet included with the sample application already loaded, as shown in Figure 12.10.

4. Click Data, Import, browse to the `RulesetWorkflow.rules` file in the `C:\SamsWf24hrs\Hour\Hour12Rules\RulesetSolution\RulesetProject` directory and select the file. This is the project with the `Policy` activity and `RuleSet` you created in an earlier exercise.

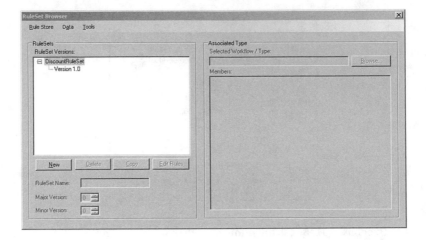

5. The MyRuleSet RuleSet will be displayed in the RuleSet Selector dialog. The
    dialog allows for selection when there are multiple RuleSets stored in a work-
    flow, which is not the case with our sample. Your screen should now look like
    Figure 12.11.

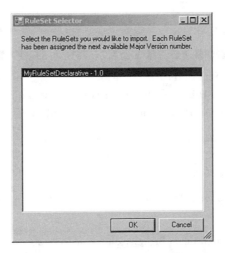

6. Click OK and the MyRuleSetDeclarative RuleSet is now added to the list of
    RuleSets in the RuleSet Browser form, as shown in Figure 12.12.

7. Version 1.0 of the MyRuleSetDeclarative RuleSet should be selected.

8. Select Rule Store, Save to upload the MyRuleSetDeclarative RuleSet to the
    rules database.

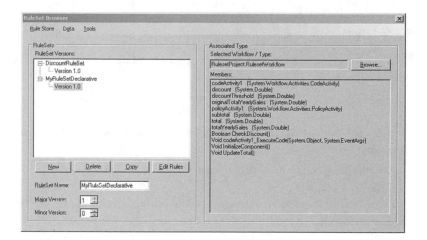

FIGURE 12.12
RuleSet
Browser with
sample workflow
loaded.

Adding the Custom Policy Activity to the Toolbox

To make the custom `Policy` activity available to all workflows, follow the next steps to add it to the toolbox.

1. Go back to the `RulesetProject` project you created earlier and open the workflow in design mode.

2. Right-click the Toolbox, select Choose Items. (This may take a while.)

3. Select the Activities tab.

4. Browse to the `PolicyActivities.dll` file in the `C:\ExternalRuleSet\PolicyActivities\bin\Debug` directory.

5. Ensure that the `PolicyFromService` activity is selected in the Choose Toolbox Items dialog and click OK.

6. You should now see the `PolicyFromService` activity on the Toolbox.

Preparing the Workflow to Use External Rules

Follow the next steps to add another workflow project to your `RulesetSolution` solution. You will configure this workflow to use the `PolicyFromService` activity.

1. Right-click the `RuleSetSolution` in the Solution Explorer, choose Add, New Item, select Project, select the `Sequential Workflow Console` application template, and name it `RuleSetExternalWorkflowsTester`.

2. Reference the `C:\ExternalRuleSet\PolicyActivities\bin\Debug\ PolicyActivities.dll` and

```
C:\ExternalRuleSet\PolicyActivities\bin\Debug\RuleSetService.dll
```
projects, which are needed to execute the `PolicyFromService` activity.

3. Add the following statement to the using statement declaration section at the top of `Program.cs`.

```
using RuleSetServices;
```

4. Add the following statement above the line that starts the workflow instance to `Program.cs`.

```
workflowRuntime.AddService(new RuleSetService());
```

5. Add an `App.config` file by right-clicking the project, choosing Add New Item, and selecting the `Application Configuration File` template.

6. Click the OK button. (Leave the default `App.Config` name.)

7. Insert the following snippet between the `Configuration` opening and closing elements to specify your connection string (substitute for your settings as appropriate):

```
<connectionStrings>
    <add name="RuleSetStoreConnectionString"
connectionString="Initial
        Catalog=Rules;Data Source=localhost;Integrated Security=SSPI;"
        providerName="System.Data.SqlClient"/>
</connectionStrings>
```

Configuring the Workflow to Use External Rules

Follow the next steps to add a `PolicyFromService` activity to the workflow. As with the standard `Policy` activity, the `PolicyFromService` binds a workflow to a `RuleSet`, but does so to one stored in the `Ruleset` database in contrast to a `.rules` file stored with the workflow.

1. Drag and drop a `PolicyFromService` activity onto the workflow. This is the custom activity you added to the Toolbox a couple of steps ago.

2. Click the `PolicyFromService` activity and set its `RuleSetName` (not the activity name) property to **MyRuleSetDeclarative** to configure it to use the `RuleSet` you added to the External Rule application.

3. Add the member variables used by the `RuleSet` to the workflow code-beside file below the constructor, as shown:

```
double discountThreshold = 2000.00;
double subtotal = 3000.00;
double total = 0.00;
double discount = 0.00;
```

```
double totalYearlySales = 0.00;
double originalTotalYearlySales = 5000.00;
```

4. Add the custom methods used by the RuleSet below the member variables as shown (your rules are stored in the external application, but not your custom methods):

```
[RuleWrite("total")]
[RuleRead("discount")]
private void UpdateTotal()
{
    this.total = (1 - this.discount) * this.subtotal;
}

[RuleRead("subtotal")]
[RuleRead("discountThreshold")]
private bool CheckDiscount()
{
    return this.subtotal > this.discountThreshold;
}
```

Running the Workflow with External Rules

Add a Code activity to display rule processing results and run the workflow.

1. Drag and drop a Code activity below the PolicyFromService activity onto the workflow and add the following to its handler:

```
Console.WriteLine("Workflow name {0}", this.Name);
Console.WriteLine("Subtotal {0}", subtotal);
Console.WriteLine("Total {0}", total);
Console.WriteLine("Discount {0}", discount);
Console.WriteLine("Total Yearly Sales {0}", totalYearlySales);
Console.WriteLine("Original Total Yearly Sales {0}",
        originalTotalYearlySales);
```

2. Add code to Program.cs to pause the host.

3. Press F5 to run the workflow, and you should receive the results shown in Figure 12.13. (If you choose F5, remember to pause the host with a Console.Read() statement.)

FIGURE 12.13
Custom workflow
processed from
RuleSet loaded
from the Exter-
nal Ruleset
application.

Summary

This hour demonstrated WF's RuleSet capabilities, which are a collection of interrelated rules. WF's automatic dependency processing was covered. You learned to monitor the execution of rules. Then the ability to call methods and custom attribute
them when the automated dependency checking no longer suffices was covered.
Finally, the External RuleSet application was demonstrated, which shows how to centrally manage and operate RuleSets. In addition it previews WF's XML capability to
work in conjunction with XML tools and rehosting the rules designers.

Workshop

Quiz

1. *What WF activity is used to bind a RuleSet to a workflow?*

2. *What is the difference between a RuleSet and a traditional code-based rule?*

3. *What advantage do rules stored in .rules files offer?*

4. *Does WF provide forward-chaining support?*

5. *Can WF detect interrule dependencies within a RuleSet?*

6. *How are rule dependencies within method bodies handled?*

7. *What is the structure of a rule in a RuleSet?*

Answers

1. `Policy.`

2. A `RuleSet` contains multiple rules and corollary actions to perform updates.

3. They can be changed at runtime using Dynamic Update, and tooling can be constructed, such as the External RuleSet application to centrally store, manage, and load them at runtime.

4. Yes.

5. Yes, in some cases. It will detect them in declarative rules and within method signatures.

6. By attributing the methods with `RuleRead` and `RuleWrite` attributes.

7. `Condition, ThenAction, ElseAction.`

PART IV

Intermediate and Advanced Features

HOUR 13

Learning to Track Workflows

What You'll Learn in this Hour:

- ▶ Tracking architecture
- ▶ How to create TrackingProfiles with the `TrackingProfileDesigner`
- ▶ How to manually modify TrackingProfiles and update them to the tracking database
- ▶ How to extract and query workflow and activity properties
- ▶ How to create and query user tracking records

Tracking underpins WF's runtime transparency. Tracking's runtime transparency capabilities also play a major role in WF's capability to offer agility. Dynamic Update discussed in the next hour, graphical workflow construction, and XAML workflows (which do not require compilation) all aid agility. Although useful, these features can wreak havoc without a control mechanism. Through Tracking, these workflows can be logged, audited, and versioned, which enables agile, governable processes. This hour covers Tracking, and the next hour shows you how Tracking teams with Dynamic Update to allow constantly changing applications.

Tracking was looked at in Hour 5, "Creating an Escalation Workflow." As you saw, registering the out-of-the-box (OOB) `SqlTrackingService` with the WF runtime extracts workflow information and saves it to a SQL database, where it can be monitored, analyzed, and used for other purposes. You populated a text box with all workflow and activity events. Then you used the `WorkflowMonitor` SDK application that graphically displays previously executed and the already executed activities on active workflows. The `WorkflowMonitor` application highlighted the runtime transparency Tracking offers.

This hour first begins with an overview of the WF Tracking architecture and a description of business activity monitoring (BAM). The main emphasis of this hour is using the `TrackingProfileDesigner` SDK sample to create a custom `TrackingProfile`. Custom `TrackingProfiles` are used to control what information is tracked. You will use the tool to create `TrackingProfiles` that both limit and enrich what data is tracked. Limiting generally involves tracking only selected events, such as closed and executing. Enrichment involves including workflow and activity properties, such as order number and order amount. You will also learn to manually modify the `TrackingProfiles` the tool produces and to update them to the tracking database via a Windows Forms app. This is useful because, like most tools, there are scenarios where the `TrackingProfileDesigner` will get you part way, but not all the way, to a solution. Then you will learn to create and query `UserTrackingRecords`. `UserTrackingRecords` are similar to the `WorkflowTrackingRecords` and `ActivityTrackingRecords` you worked with in Hour 5. They are generated through custom code and `RuleSets`. Finally, you will learn another form of filtering using predicates to determine what data is tracked.

If you are wondering why you would ever want to limit or enrich the information tracked, following are three reasons:

▶ There is a performance cost associated with emitting all workflow, activity, and user events. Therefore, it may be worthwhile limiting the activities and events tracked to those you need. For instance, you only need to track the executing and closed events to use the `WorkflowMonitor` SDK sample. Tracking the unload/reload/persistence cycle may be unnecessary overhead if you want to use only the `WorkflowMonitor`.

▶ You may want to include contextual information, such as purchase order and amount.

▶ You may want to include a customized tracking service in one or more workflows that, for instance, listen for aborted events. You could then email or take other actions. You can register multiple tracking services with one workflow, so you could register an aborted tracking service with all workflows.

Tracking Architecture

Let's take a look at how Tracking works. The WF runtime evaluates running workflows to determine which information has been selected for tracking. Records that match the criteria are sent to the host. The host is then responsible for storing the information. The reason records are evaluated by the runtime is to avoid incurring unnecessary overhead when sending data to the host that it does not want. The host can persist to any medium it chooses, although the only OOB implementation uses SQL Server. Figure 13.1 illustrates the WF Tracking architecture.

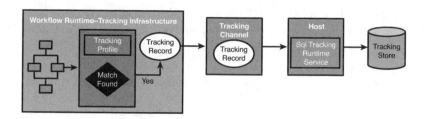

FIGURE 13.1
Tracking archi-
tecture.

▶ `TrackingProfiles` (the text above the diamond) are used to specify what information should be tracked.

▶ Matching `TrackingRecords` are sent over a `TrackingChannel` to the host.

▶ The `TrackingService` registered with the host then stores the received `TrackingRecord` to the storage medium specified by the `TrackingService`. (If multiple `TrackingServices` are registered, each may have its own profile that dictates what events are routed to it.)

You can store information to Oracle, MySQL, file systems, and other destinations by creating a custom `TrackingService`. Creating a custom `TrackingService` is not covered in this book. If you are interested in learning how to create custom `TrackingServices` to persist tracking information to an alternative medium, you can look at the `ConsoleTrackingServiceSample` and `FileTrackingService` SDK samples.

Tracking and Business Activity Monitoring

Static models are useful. For many reasons, binding execution to models is frequently more useful. You can also use the same models, or permutations thereof, for analytical and reporting needs. For one, this helps create one version of the truth, because both the executable process and reports are produced from the same information source. In fact, many business process management systems feature sophisticated process monitoring capabilities that combine running process information with business intelligence and other tools to provide real-time business reporting, query capabilities, and alerts. Business Process Management (BPM) products generally refer to this feature as BAM, and in other parlors they are referred to as digital dashboards.

BAM consists of three parts: extraction, persistence, and reporting. The first two parts are covered very well by WF Tracking, where its extensibility makes it shine. WF is not a major player in the third. The `SqlTrackingQuery` and the `WorkflowMonitor` SDK application are not full-fledged reporting and analytics tools, like the ones found in BAM products. As a platform, WF must ensure that rich BAM reporting tools can be built on it—which it does with excellent extraction and solid persistence capabilities—but leaves the actual rich reporting steps to others to build on top of it.

`TrackingProfileDesigner` SDK Sample

The `TrackingProfileDesigner` tool simplifies creating `TrackingProfiles`. You click an activity or the workflow and specify which events and properties you want to track.

Functional `TrackingProfiles` can be created using the `TrackingProfileDesigner`. The `TrackingProfiles` it produces can also be analyzed to understand the inner workings of `TrackingProfiles`. They can also be modified to produce a workable solution when the `TrackingProfileDesigner` comes close but cannot quite meet your objective (a common pattern with many graphical tools).

Throughout this section, you will create various custom `TrackingProfiles` in the `TrackingProfileDesigner` tool. Using the `TrackingProfileDesigner` requires loading the `TrackingProfileDesigner` SDK application itself. Then you tell the application which workflow you want to track. The last step is to save the `TrackingProfile` to the tracking database. The workflow will now be associated with the `TrackingProfile` you created. The information tracked for this workflow will be determined by the `TrackingProfile` you created.

You will create two `TrackingProfiles` in this section. In the first, you specify which workflow and activity events are to be tracked. In the second, you incorporate order number and other workflow properties, and you apply conditions to what is tracked.

Reviewing the `TrackingSolution`

Before creating a custom `TrackingProfile`, follow the next steps to take a look at the solution that will be used to support our effort this hour:

1. Open the `TrackingWorkflow` in the `TrackingWorkflows` project in design mode. Then click the `codeActivityUserData` activity and set its `Enabled` property to `false`.

2. Open the `TrackingSolution` in the `C:\SamsWf24hrs\Hours\Hour13Tracking\TrackingSolution` directory.

3. Open `TrackingForm.cs` in the `TrackingHostForm` project. It serves a dual role as the host for the tracking workflow that will be used in this hour. It also holds the text box where tracking information can be displayed.

4. The `TrackingLocalServices` project holds the local service for host-workflow communication.

5. `Form1.cs` in the `TrackingProfileForm` project is used to manually update `TrackingProfiles` to the tracking database.

6. The `TrackingWorkflows` project holds the tracked workflow. It contains specific activities that force persistence, and it creates `UserTrackingRecords`.

7. Run the project (make sure the `TrackingHostForm` is set as the startup project), enter any order number, any order amount, and click Submit Order.

8. Wait until the workflow completion dialog is spawned, and then click OK. (It will take a little while because the workflow contains a `Delay` activity.)

9. Click the Get Tracking button and you should see results similar to Figure 13.2. This is what is tracked by the default `TrackingProfile`. You get this by registering the `SqlTrackingService` with the runtime.

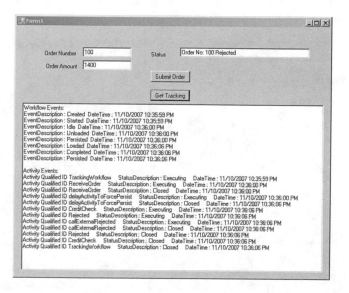

FIGURE 13.2
Tracking results using default tracking profile.

The key is that all workflow events, all activities, and all activity events are tracked. User events (which produce `UserTrackingRecords`) are tracked as well, but are not shown because we have not produced any yet. We add user events later in this hour.

Opening the `TrackingProfileDesigner` and Loading a Workflow

Follow the next steps to open the `TrackingProfileDesigner` and use it to graphically create a custom `TrackingProfile`.

1. Open the `TrackingProfileDesigner` by double-clicking the `TrackingProfileDesigner.sln` file in your sample installation directory `WF\Applications\TrackingProfileDesigner\CS`.

2. Open the `App.Config` file and change the `ConnectionString` value to point to your server and tracking database. If you followed the book default, the database is named `WFTrackingAndPersistence`.

By the Way

See Hour 1, "Understanding Windows Workflow Foundation," for more details on setting up connection strings and using other databases such as SQL Express.

3. Make sure the `TrackingProfileDesigner` project is set as the startup project, and then start the project.

4. You should now see the `Workflow Tracking Profile Designer` form shown in Figure 13.3.

FIGURE 13.3
Workflow Tracking Profile Designer form.

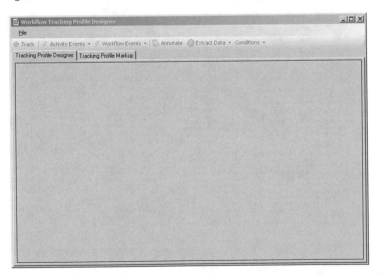

5. Click File, Open, Workflow from File, and select the `TrackingWorkflows.dll` file from the `C:\SamsWf24hrs\Hours\Hour13Tracking\TrackingSolution\TrackingWorkflows\bin\Debug` directory to load the workflow to work with.

6. The Workflow Tracking Profile Designer form should now look like Figure 13.4.

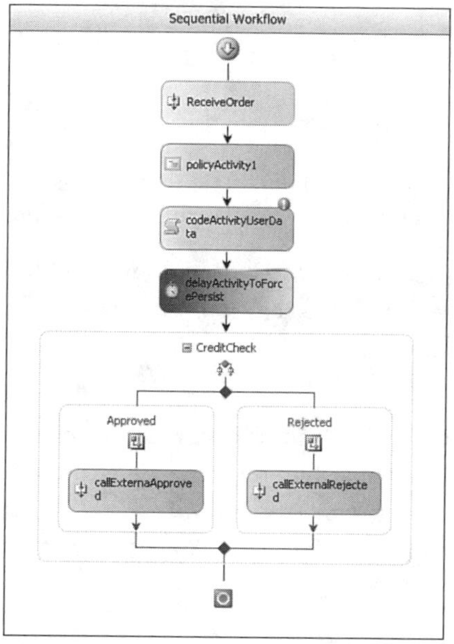

FIGURE 13.4
Workflow Tracking Profile Designer form with a Workflow.

Tracking Workflow Level Events

At the workflow level, you can track the workflow life cycle events. These events include Created, Started, Loaded, Suspended, and Aborted. These are the same events the host uses to interact with the workflow. We will track the workflow Executing and Completed events at the workflow activity level. It may seem hard to keep straight, but workflows are activities. Therefore, the only events we are interested in capturing at the workflow level are Exception, Terminated, and Aborted. We want this to be a light profile and are therefore omitting Loaded, Unloaded, and other workflow life cycle events.

1. Click the workflow away from any activity on the Workflow Tracking Profile Designer form.

2. You should see two buttons under the File menu choice on the Workflow Tracking Profile Designer form. The first button should have a large green plus sign followed by Tracking Workflow. The second button should have a lightning mark and read Workflow Events. This means that you are at the workflow level. See Figure 13.5 for an example.

3. Click the Workflow Events drop-down and select the Exception event.

FIGURE 13.5
Workflow Track-
ing Profile
Designer form
workflow level
event tracking.

4. Click the Workflow Events drop-down and select the Terminated event.

5. Click the Workflow Events drop-down again and select the Aborted event. You are now tracking the workflow `Exception`, `Terminated`, and `Aborted` events.

6. Click the Tracking Profile Markup button under the Workflow Events button, and you should see that the `Exception`, `Terminated`, and `Aborted` events are being tracked, as shown in Figure 13.6.

Now you can be thankful for the `TrackingProfileDesigner` tool. Without it, you would have to manually produce the XML or create it through the CodeDom, which is used to generate code in the .NET Framework. Neither is that intuitive. The nice thing is that because the tool generates the XML, you can modify the XML as needed and learn it over time.

FIGURE 13.6
Workflow Track-
ingProfile section
containing the
selected events.

```
<WorkflowTrackingLocation>
  <TrackingWorkflowEvents>
    <TrackingWorkflowEvent>Exception</TrackingWorkflowEvent>
    <TrackingWorkflowEvent>Terminated</TrackingWorkflowEvent>
    <TrackingWorkflowEvent>Aborted</TrackingWorkflowEvent>
  </TrackingWorkflowEvents>
</WorkflowTrackingLocation>
```

Tracking Activity Level Executed and Completed Events

Tracking at the activity level in the `TrackingProfileDesigner` is done at the type level. For instance, clicking the `ReceiveOrder` activity and specifying tracking information applies to all `HandleExternalEvent` activities on the workflow. Specifying all activities or a single activity by name cannot be accomplished with the `TrackingProfileDesigner` (although both can be done by manually modifying the `TrackingProfile` or using the CodeDom). You can use the Match Derived Types to include activities derived from the specified activity, as discussed in the Annotate and Match Derived Types Options section.

Tracking `HandleExternalEvent` Activities

Follow the next steps to configure the `HandleExternalEvent` activities to be tracked.

1. Click the Tracking Profile Designer button to return to graphical view.

2. You need to switch from workflow tracking to the activity tracking. To do this, click the `ReceiveOrder` activity at the top of the workflow.

3. You should see a button with a large green plus sign and the text Track Handle-ExternalEventActivity.

4. Click the Track HandleExternalEventActivity button to specify that you want to track this type of activity.

5. You should now see new menu choices to the right of the button you just clicked; also, the `ReceiveOrder` activity contains a thumbtack and an exclamation mark, as shown in Figure 13.7.

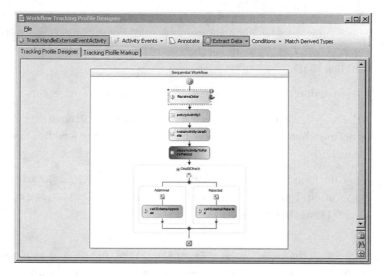

FIGURE 13.7
TrackingProfile
ReceiveOrder
Activity Event
menu.

6. Click the Activity Events drop-down and select the `Executing` event.

7. Click the Activity Events drop-down again and select the `Closed` event. You are now tracking when `HandleExternalEvent` activities on the workflow are in the executing and closed states. The `ReceiveOrder` activity should no longer have an exclamation mark, because you have specified events. The thumbtack, however, should remain.

8. Click the Tracking Profile Markup button under the Track HandleExternalEventActivity button, and you should see the `Executing` and `Closed` events as shown in Figure 13.8.

```
<ExecutionStatusEvents>
    <ExecutionStatus>Executing</ExecutionStatus>
    <ExecutionStatus>Closed</ExecutionStatus>
</ExecutionStatusEvents>
```

FIGURE 13.8
Activity Tracking-
Profile section
containing
selected events.

Tracking `CallExternalMethod` Activities

Follow the next steps to configure the `CallExternalMethod` activities to be tracked.

1. Click the Tracking Profile Designer button to return to graphical view.

2. Click one of the `CallExternalMethod` (blue) activities near the bottom of the workflow.

3. You should now see a button with a large green plus sign and the text Track CallExternalMethodActivity.

4. Click the Track CallExternalMethodActivity button to specify that you want to track this type of activity.

5. You should now see new menu choices to the right of the button you just clicked, and both `CallExternalMethod` activities contain a thumbtack and an exclamation mark.

6. Click the Activity Events drop-down and select the `Executing` event.

7. Click the Activity Events drop-down again and select the `Closed` event. You are now tracking when `CallExternalMethod` activities on the workflow are in the executing and closed states.

8. Click the Tracking Profile Markup button under the Track HandleExternalEventActivity button. You should see a new set of `Executing` and `Closed` events for the `CallExternalMethod` activities.

You are now tracking the workflow level `Exception`, `Terminated`, and `Aborted` events. You are also tracking the `Executing` and `Completed` events for all `HandleExternalEvent` and `CallExternalMethod` activities.

> If you wanted to track the workflow `Executing` and `Completing` events, you would click the workflow surface away from an activity. Then click the Track TrackingWorkflow button. This gives you the standard activity menu. You could then select the `Executing` and `Completed` events from the Activity Event menu. Using this method, you are accessing the workflow as an activity. You will access the workflow as an activity when you specify workflow properties a little later in the Access Properties in Tracking section.

Uploading and Examining the Profile and Running the Workflow

You have created a valid `TrackingProfile`, and you must upload it to the tracking database before the `SqlTrackingService` will use it. The "Examine How Profile Works" section discusses how the `SqlTrackingService` locates `TrackingProfiles`.

Uploading Profile to Database and Running Workflow

Follow the next steps to upload the TrackingProfile you created to a database and run the workflow.

1. Click the File in the menu in the upper-left corner of the form. Then choose Save, Profile to SQL Tracking Database. Click OK.

2. If you are requested to enter a profile number, enter a number one larger in the third digit than the Current Profile Version Number, as shown in Figure 13.9.

FIGURE 13.9
Profile Update Version form.

3. Run the TrackingHostForm again, enter any order number, any order amount, and click Submit Order.

4. Wait for the workflow to finish and click the Get Tracking button.

5. You should now see the results shown in Figure 13.10. (No workflow events are shown because none of our tracked workflow events occurred).

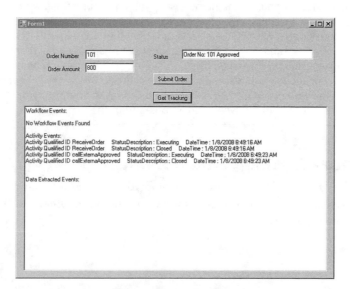

FIGURE 13.10
Tracking results filtered to show selected workflow and activity events.

Examining How Profiles are Processed

You now have a custom `TrackingProfile` assigned to the `TrackingSolution` workflow. You can see how this works by examining the tables in the tracking database (`WFTrackingAndPersistence`).

Follow the next steps to look at the `TrackingProfile` tables and see how the runtime selects the proper `TrackingProfile`.

1. This workflow is now associated with the `TrackingProfile` you just created. To see how, open your tracking database and look at the `TrackingProfile` table. It contains a record for your workflow with a non-null TrackingProfileXml field, which contains your custom profile. It is the same markup you saw when clicking the Tracking Profile Markup button. See Figure 13.11.

2. Open the `DefaultTrackingProfile` table as well and examine its one record. Until you created the custom `TrackingProfile`, this profile had been applied to all tracked workflows. It still applies to all workflows other than the `TrackingSolution` one that is now bound to a custom `TrackingProfile`. If you wanted to change the default tracking behavior, you would change its entry here, and all current and future workflows that use the default profile would adhere to its new configuration.

	11	1.0.0	19	NULL	1/7/2008 8:25:4...
▶	12	1.0.1	19	<?xml version="...	1/8/2008 6:39:4...

FIGURE 13.11
Tracking Profile record entry.

By the Way

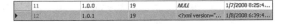

If you add, remove, or change the name of activities on your workflow and rebuild without versioning the assembly, Tracking will no longer function. The reason is that the SqlTrackingService uses a couple of tables that contain one record for each activity on a workflow. The tables are constructed on initial build and are not updated during rebuilds. Reversioning your assembly will fix this problem. Alternatively, if you choose, you can also modify the Activity and `ActivityInstance` tables. This has worked for me but is not supported by Microsoft. If you choose this route, you can obtain the type used in tables from the `Type` table.

Additional Tracking Functionality

In this section, you learn to access workflow properties such as order number. You also learn to restrict which information is shown by adding conditions, such as only showing approved orders.

Accessing Properties in Tracking

Although it's useful to know event enumerations at the workflow and activity level, it's frequently helpful to see order number, amount, and other properties as well. These properties can be used to augment the tracking information for operational needs. They can also be used for analytical purposes and by BAM tools.

Follow the next steps to track Status and other properties on the workflow.

1. Close the TrackingProfileDesigner form.

2. Run the Tracking Profile Designer project again and select File, Open, Workflow from File, and load the TrackingWorkflows again.

3. Click the Track TrackingWorkflow button. You are now at the workflow level and will utilize activity tracking against it. You could, for instance, specify that the Closed and Activity events be tracked at the workflow level here. We will track properties here instead.

4. Click the Extract Data drop-down, select TrackingWorkflow, and then select Status from the menu of members, as shown in Figure 13.12.

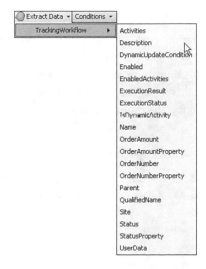

FIGURE 13.12
Tracking profile specifying extracted values.

5. Click the Extract Data button, select TrackingWorkflow, and then select OrderAmount.

6. Click the Extract Data button again, select TrackingWorkflow, and select OrderNumber.

7. Notice the exclamation mark in the upper-right corner of the workflow. This is because you need to select an event in which to access the selected tracking data.

8. Select the Activity Events button and then select the Closed event. The exclamation marks should disappear. This means that you will access all the values you selected when the workflow is closed (or completed).

9. Click the Tracking Profile Markup button under the Track TrackingWorkflow button, and you should see that the Closed activity event is selected. In addition, you'll see an Extracts element that contains all the extracted values, as shown in Figure 13.13:

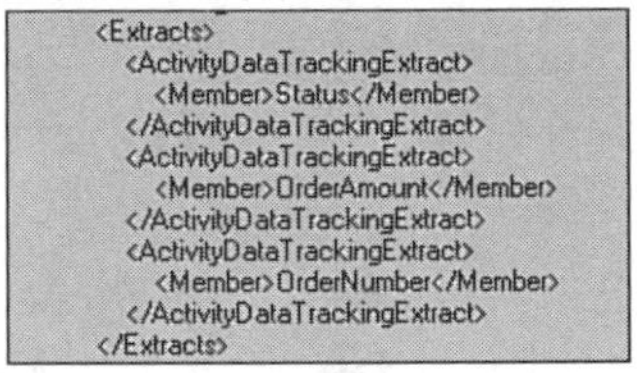

FIGURE 13.13
Tracking profile
specifying
extracted values.

```
<Extracts>
    <ActivityDataTrackingExtract>
        <Member>Status</Member>
    </ActivityDataTrackingExtract>
    <ActivityDataTrackingExtract>
        <Member>OrderAmount</Member>
    </ActivityDataTrackingExtract>
    <ActivityDataTrackingExtract>
        <Member>OrderNumber</Member>
    </ActivityDataTrackingExtract>
</Extracts>
```

Applying Conditions

Follow the next steps to filter the profile to show only approved orders. Filtering can be useful, if you want only very large or otherwise sensitive orders tracked and potentially sent to an alerting mechanism or analytical system. Filtering can also be useful to lessen the load. Later in this hour, you will learn to apply less than and larger conditions by manually modifying the profile, because you can only select = and != using the tool.

1. Click the Tracking Profile Designer button to switch back to design view.

2. Select Conditions, Add New Condition, click the Select member drop-down and select Status; leave the == default, enter **Approved** in the text box. See Figure 13.14 for an example.

FIGURE 13.14
Tracking filtered
to approved
orders.

3. Click Save.

4. You will now see a `Conditions` element in your `TrackingProfile`, as shown in Figure 13.15.

```
<Conditions>
  <ActivityTrackingCondition>
    <Operator>Equals</Operator>
    <Member>Status</Member>
    <Value>Approved</Value>
  </ActivityTrackingCondition>
</Conditions>
```

FIGURE 13.15
Tracking Profile with Conditions element that filters what data is emitted.

By the Way

Click a `CallExternalMethod` activity on the workflow surface, and click the Track CallExternalMethod activity button. Note that you can also Extract Data (access the properties) of the activity type. Any property native to `CallExternalMethod` activity can be tracked here. If you created a custom activity (Hours 20–21) with the properties you are interested in, they could be tracked here. Click the Track CallExternalMethod activity button again to remove `CallExternalMethod` activities from the `TrackingProfile`.

Saving the Profile and Running the Workflow

Follow the next steps to create both approved and nonapproved orders to see how the emitted tracking data differs between the two.

1. Click the File option in the menu in the upper-left corner of the Tracking Profile Designer form. Then choose Save, Profile to SQL Tracking Database.

2. Click OK. If you are requested to enter a profile number, enter a number one larger in the third digit than the Current Profile Version number.

3. Run the `TrackingSolution` again. Enter any order number, enter **800** for the order amount, and click the Submit Order button.

4. After the order is rejected, click OK in the Workflow Completed dialog. Also, when you click Get Tracking, it generates an error.

5. This time you should see that only the activity `Closed` event and the three extracted properties were selected as shown in Figure 13.16.

6. Enter any new order number, enter **1500** for the order amount, and click the `Submit Order` button. (You can overwrite the current values.)

7. After the order is approved, click OK in the Workflow Completed dialog and click the Get Tracking button.

FIGURE 13.16
Tracking results
with extracted
values.

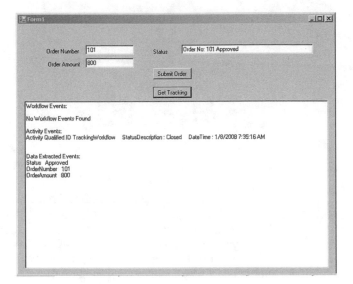

8. You should get the message No tracking events located and an Extracted
    Events header. The order is now rejected because it no longer conforms to the
    TrackingProfile.

Manually Updating Tracking Profile and UserTrackingRecords

There are times when the TrackingProfileDesigner alone is not sufficient. Maybe
you want to specify conditional criteria that uses less than or larger than—for
instance, orders > 2000. WF stores certain tracking information in
UserTrackingRecords. This information consists of custom information that can be
specified in the otherwise opaque Code activity, or in a custom activity. The Policy
activity (which holds RuleSets) is also tracked at the user level. Hence the reason for
the Policy activity on the workflow. The rules data will begin to show after we specify that UserTrackingRecords display. The TrackingProfileDesigner does not
support adding user tracking criteria to tracking profiles. This section will demonstrate the following:

▶ Inject tracking data into the workflow (`UserTrackingRecords`)

▶ How to update custom `TrackingProfiles` to the tracking database

▶ How to manually modify `TrackingProfiles`

Adding User Tracking Data

Follow the next steps to track data in the `Code` activity's handler.

1. Click the `codeActivityUserData` and set its `Enabled` property to `true`.

2. Double-click the `codeActivityUserData` activity on the TrackingWorkflow workflow and add the following to its handler:

```
CodeActivity ca = sender as CodeActivity;
this.TrackData(ca.Name + " is executing line 1.");
this.TrackData(ca.Name + " is executing line 2.");
```

Using this method, you may emit any information you want to Tracking. User tracking data is frequently specified inside `Code` activities to specify what function the otherwise opaque activity performs. It is also used by the `Policy` activity to emit rules data. Finally, it is frequently used in custom activities.

Retrieving and Saving the `TrackingProfile` to a File

Follow the next steps to retrieve the profile you created and manually modify it to include user tracking events.

1. Close the `TrackingProfileDesigner` application if it is running.

2. Run the `TrackingProfileDesigner` application.

3. Select File, Open, and From SQL Tracking Database.

4. Click the TrackingWorkflows.TrackingWorkflow choice in the Choose a Workflow step of the Load Workflow and Profile from Store form.

5. Click the last version of the profile in Choose a Profile section of the form (as shown in Figure 13.17).

6. Click OK, and click OK in the dialog. Browse to the `TrackingWorkflows.DLL` and select it if you receive a message that the assembly cannot be found.

7. The workflow and `TrackingProfile` are now both loaded into the `TrackingProfileDesigner`.

8. Select File, Save, and Profile as File.

FIGURE 13.17
Retrieve a
`Tracking`
`Profile` with
the Tacking
Profile Designer
tool.

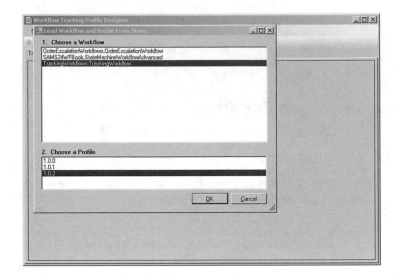

9. Select the `C:\SamsWf24hrs\Hours\Hour13Tracking` directory and name the
file **StartingDesignerProfile.xml**.

Manually Modifying and Uploading a Tracking Profile

Tracking profiles can be created using the CodeDom, or they can be hand rolled in
XML, as you have seen when observing the output created by the Tracking Profile
Designer tool. However, both of those methods are a bit complex. In this section, you
will "mash up" a new profile based on the one you saved to a file and the default
profile. You will insert the default profile's `UserTrackPoint` (the element in the
`TrackingProfile` that retrieves `UserTrackingRecords`) element into the profile you
just saved to a file. This way you will enable your custom profile to track
`UserTrackPoints`.

Manually Modifying a `TrackingProfile`

Follow the next steps to manually modify the `TrackingProfile`.

1. Open the `StartingDesignerProfile.xml` file you just created.

2. Open the `DefaultTrackingProfile` table in the tracking database, copy the
contents of the TrackingProfileXml field, and paste the content into Notepad. If
more than one record exists, copy the data from the last record.

3. Page down near the end of the Notepad document, and you should see a `UserTrackPoint` element.

4. Copy the `UserTrackPoint` element and its children, and then insert it into the `StartingDesignerProfile.xml` file you created between the `ActivityTrackPoint` and `TrackPoints` ending elements, as shown in Figure 13.18.

```
    </ActivityTrackPoint>
  <UserTrackPoint>
      <MatchingLocations>
          <UserTrackingLocation>
              <Activity>
                  <Type>System.Workflow.ComponentModel.Activity, System.Workflow.ComponentMod
                  <MatchDerivedTypes>true</MatchDerivedTypes>
              </Activity>
              <Argument>
                  <Type>System.Object, mscorlib, Version=2.0.0.0, Culture=neutral, PublicKey
                  <MatchDerivedTypes>true</MatchDerivedTypes>
              </Argument>
          </UserTrackingLocation>
      </MatchingLocations>
  </UserTrackPoint>
    </TrackPoints>
```

FIGURE 13.18
Mashed up tracking profile.

5. Save the updated file.

6. You now have to get this updated profile into the `TrackingProfile` table. You could manually update the proper record in the `TrackingProfile` table; however, we will use a stored procedure named UpdateProfile in the tracking database instead. This way you can automate the update and use it in cases when the profile is hand-coded or augmented via the CodeDom or XML.

Uploading the Modified Tracking Profile

Follow the next steps to upload the manually modified `TrackingProfile` to the database.

1. There is another form in this project named `UpdateTrackingProfile`. It permits a profile to be pasted into a text box, a profile number to be entered, and it then updates the ProfileTable (via the `UpdateProfile` stored procedure) with this information.

2. The code to call the `UpdateProfile` proc is provided by Microsoft in the SqlDataMaintenance WF SDK sample. See the `InsertTrackingProfile` method of the `TrackingHostForm.cs` file, if you are interested in its content. The only parts of this code that are specific to a given workflow are the `typFullName.SqlValue` and `assemblyFullName.SqlValue` properties that must be set to the tracked workflow type. I modified the code to accept these two values as parameters.

3. Set the `TrackingProfileForm` project (in the `TrackingSolution`) as the startup project and run it.

4. Look in the `TrackingProfile` table to see the last profile for our `TrackingWorkflows` project. It should be 1.0.2, but check yours to make sure.

5. Enter a profile number one greater than the current (1.0.3 in my case), paste the contents of the `StartingDesignerProfile.xml` file into the text box and click Submit. See Figure 13.19 for an example:

FIGURE 13.19
Tracking Profile Upload form.

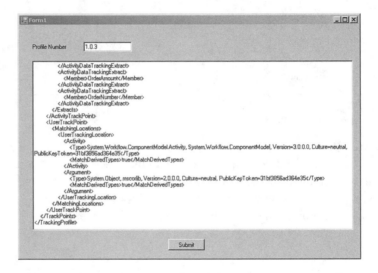

6. Close the `TrackingProfileForm` project.

Uncommenting the `UserTrackingRecords` Query Code

There is code in the `ShowTracking` method in `TrackingForm.cs` that displays `UserTrackingRecords`. The code to access the `UserTrackingRecords` is identical in structure to the code that accesses the `ActivityTrackingRecords` and `WorkflowTrackingRecords`, with one exception. The rules data is stored as properties of the `UserTrackingRecord.UserData` type returned from the query. Therefore, you must test whether the type returned is `RuleActionTrackingEvent`. If so, you access the `ConditionName` and `RuleName` properties of the returned value. Look at the source if you want more details.

Follow the next steps to uncomment the `UserTrackingRecords` Query Code and then run the workflow

1. Open `TrackingForm.cs` and search for `"#if false"` to access the code that searches for `UserTrackingRecords`.

2. Remove the `#if false` and its corresponding `#endif` entries located about 20 lines below.

3. Run the `WorkflowTracking` solution. Enter any order number, enter **800** for the order amount, and click the Submit Order button.

4. Click the Get Tracking button. Scroll to the bottom of the tracking text box to see the UserEvents section, and you should see the results shown in Figure 13.20.

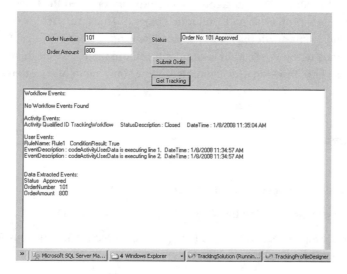

FIGURE 13.20
Tracking results using "mashed" Tracking Profile.

Your "mashed-up" TrackingProfile now shows the Code activity and rule `UserTrackingRecords`. This is in addition to the extracted properties and workflow activity `Closed` event previously specified in the `TrackingProfile` from last section.

Annotate and Match Derived Types Options

You may have noticed the Annotate and Match Derived Types buttons on the `TrackingProfileDesigner` form menu. Annotate permits you to inject custom text into tracking at the specified location. Match Derived Types will, as the name says, match all derived types. If you look at the `DefaultTrackingProfile`, you will see that `MatchDerivedTypes` is true. The activity is set to the base WF activity. This how the `DefaultTrackingProfile` is able to include all activities on any workflow without knowing what they are in advance and enumerating them all.

Summary

Tracking is a very broad, intricate, and important component of workflow. We started in this hour reviewing WF's Tracking architecture and where Tracking fits in the workflow world. Then you used the `TrackingProfileDesigner` to create various `TrackingProfiles` that both limited and enriched the data provided by the `DefaultTrackingProfile`. You created a mashup and updated the tracking database with the new profile. There is still much more to Tracking, such as programmatically creating profiles with the CodeDom and creating custom `TrackingServices`. You should look to the WF SDK for examples if you are interested. In the next hour, you will learn how Tracking and Dynamic Update combine to allow interesting new applications.

Workshop

Quiz

1. *What is the purpose of creating a custom* `TrackingProfile`*?*

2. *What purpose does the* `DefaultTrackingProfile` *serve?*

3. *After the* `SqlTrackingService` *is registered with a host, how does it apply a* `TrackingProfile` *to a workflow?*

4. *Why would you create a custom* `TrackingService`*?*

5. *What are the three kinds of tracking records?*

6. *What purposes do* `UserTrackingRecords` *serve?*

7. *What is* `MatchDerivedTypes` *used for?*

8. *How are workflow and activity properties tracked?*

9. *What are reasons to limit the tracking data collected?*

Answers

1. To limit and enrich the standard data tracked with the `DefaultTrackingProfile`.

2. It is the `TrackingProfile` applied to all workflows that do not have a custom `TrackingProfile`.

3. It first looks in the `TrackingProfile` database for a record that matches the current workflow type and has a non-null TrackingProfileXml field. If multiple `TrackingProfile` versions exist for a workflow, it uses the latest one by default. If no records for the current workflow are found, the `DefaultTrackingProfile` is used.

4. To store tracking information to a different storage medium than SQL Server.

5. `WorkflowTrackingRecords`, `UserTrackingRecords`, and `ActivityTrackingRecords`.

6. They track `Policy` activity execution (`RuleSets`) and allow custom information to be injected using the `TrackData` method from `Code` and custom activities.

7. To match activities derived from the activity the derived type element is associated with.

8. Via the Extracts element.

9. It is expensive to emit all data for all workflow, activity, and user events. Also, you want a `TrackingProfile` that only tracks aborted, exceptions, and other events that can be applied to multiple workflows. Finally, the data may be private and therefore security may dictate limiting the tracking data collected.

Working with Roles

What You'll Learn in This Hour:

- ▶ Overview of roles
- ▶ Setting up ASP.NET role provider
- ▶ Modify the host and local service to support roles
- ▶ Modify the workflow to support roles

This hour covers roles, which are used to validate external access to workflows.

Explaining Roles

Workflows wait for other systems to raise events and, in turn, workflows respond. Some workflows may support processes that take days, weeks, or even years. During the time they await response from external systems, the workflow must be able to ensure that the systems contacting it are authorized to do so. WF's `HandleExternalEvent` and other event-receiving (`WebServiceInput` and `ReceiveActivity`) activities contain a `Roles` property that when used ensures only authorized systems can access WF workflows.

Valid roles—those authorized to interact with the workflow—must be placed in the `WorkflowRoleCollection` collection. The `WorkflowRoleCollection` then must be bound to the `Roles` property of a WF event-receiving activity. If an external system attempts to access the workflow without credentials contained in one of the valid roles, the workflow will not allow the external system access.

Two types of roles can be placed into the `WorkflowRoleCollection`: ASPNET and Active Directory. ASPNET roles are supported through the `WebWorkflowRole` type, and Active Directory roles are supported through the `ActiveDirectoryRole` type.

Both role types must be populated with a role, such as `Level1Approver`, and then placed in the `WorkflowRoleCollection` collection. Their implementations are similar.

> The ASPNET role provider can be used by nonweb applications. It simply accesses a SQL Server database of names and roles.

Only the `WebWorkflowRole` type is covered in this hour. As mentioned, the `ActiveDirectoryRole` implementation is similar, so most of the `WebWorkflowRole` information covered in this hour is relevant to implementing the `ActiveDirectoryRole` type as well.

Implementing roles in WF involves three steps:

1. Populating the `EventArgs` class with an identity property.

2. Configuring the event-receiving activities.

3. Instantiating the `WorkflowRoleCollection` collection and populating it with `WebWorkflowRole` types in the workflow code-beside.

You should also write code to handle the exception WF raises if an invalid identity is passed. We will catch this in the host aborted event in this hour, where all workflow uncaught exceptions wind up. You will learn other exception handling options in Hour 16, "Working with Exceptions, Compensation, and Transactions."

Before actually implementing roles, you need to know a couple of housekeeping items. The first is a brief description of the solution used. The second is instructions to set up an ASPNET role provider.

Describing the Role Solution

The OrderEscalationSolution in the `C:\SamsWf24hrs\Hours\Hour14Roles\OrderEscalationSolutionCompeteWRoles` directory contains a workflow project, a Windows Forms host, a local service, and a Windows Forms project named `UserAndRoleManagement` that can be used to add users and roles to the ASPNET membership database.

Setting up an ASP.NET Role Provider

First, check to see if you have the ASPNET role provider installed. If not, you need to install it. Then you add the roles and users used to process roles.

Ensuring ASP.NET Role Provider Installation

1. Open the `OrderEscalationSolution` in the
   `C:\SamsWf24hrs\Hours\Hour14Roles\OrderEscalationSolutionCompete`
   `WRoles` directory.

2. Click on View, Server Explorer, Data Connections, and look for the ASPNET database.

3. If you see the ASPNET database, skip to the "Adding Roles and Users" section.

4. Go to your .NET Framework directory. For instance,
   `C:\WINDOWS\Microsoft.NET\Framework\v2.0.50727`. If you have a different
   directory or version of the framework, substitute them as required.

5. Double-click the `ASPNET_REGSQL.exe` file.

6. Click Next on the Welcome to ASP.NET SQL Server Setup Wizard shown in
   Figure 14.1.

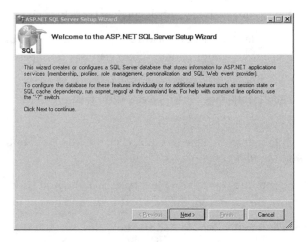

FIGURE 14.1
ASPNET Role
membership
setup form.

7. Choose the Configure SQL Server for Application Services option on the Select a
   Setup Option form. Click Next.

8. Enter your server name (for example, `localhost`), choose your authentication
   scheme, and select the <default> choice in the Database drop-down on the
   Select a Server and Database form (Figure 14.2). Click Next.

9. Click Next on the Confirm Your Settings form and click Finish on The Database
   Has Been Created or Modified screen.

You now have an ASP.NET role provider setup.

FIGURE 14.2
ASP.NET Role
membership
select server and
database form.

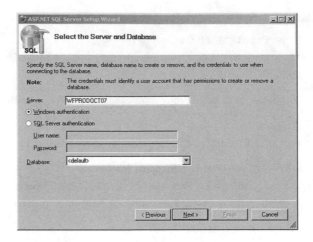

Adding Roles and Users

Follow the next steps to prepare for processing, in which you will add two roles: Level1Role and Level2Role. Then you will add two users to each role.

1. Right-click the OrderEscalationWorkflows project and select Unload Project. (This project is not yet complete and will prevent you from performing the task in the next step.)

2. Set the UserAndRoleManagement project as the startup project and then run the project.

3. Enter **Level1Role** into the Role text box, click the Add Roles button, and accept the confirmation dialog.

4. Enter **Robert** into the Users to Add text box, click the Add Users to Role button (do not remove the data from the Role text box), and accept the confirmation.

5. Enter **Patricia** into the Users to Add text box, click the Add Users to Role button (do not remove the data from the Role text box), and accept the confirmation.

6. Enter **Level2Role** in the Role text box, click the Add Roles button, and accept the confirmation dialog.

7. Enter **Brian** into the Users to Add text box, click the Add Users to Role button (do not remove the data from the Role text box), and accept the confirmation.

8. Enter **Janet** into the Users to Add text box, click the Add Users to Role button (do not remove the data from the Role text box), and accept the confirmation.

9. Exit the form.

Updating the Host

The host form named `OrderEscalationForm` that you use to work with roles contains a `Leve1User` and a `Lever2User` (as shown in Figure 14.3). The `Level1User` is input along with the order and validated when the order is received. `Level2User` will be used in the Add Level2Role Support section.

FIGURE 14.3
OrderEscalation Form used for role processing.

Follow the next steps to update the `EventArgs` class to support roles.

1. The only programmatic change made to the host for role processing is to add the identity to the `EventArgs` passed to the workflow. Uncomment the following line of code in the `buttonSubmitOrder_Click` handler:

```
eventArgs.Identity = securityIdentifier;
```

> **By the Way**
>
> In a production system, the credentials of the logged in user would be used. To facilitate working with roles across multiple users, the host form creates Windows identities. The `securityIdentifer` variable in the preceding code snippet is just that—a manufactured Windows identity. I used the code from the WF WebWorkflow-Role SDK sample to produce this identity. The steps to produce the identity are not covered because they are used solely to enable demo or testing and are not relevant to a production system. See the additional code in the

buttonSubmitOrder_Click handler if you are interested in how to programmatically create a Windows identity.

Updating the Workflow

The workflow you will use is shown in Figure 14.4. It receives an order and approves
or rejects it. The MoreInfoNeeded branch is not used yet and is therefore not enabled.
It will be used in the Add Level2Role support section. The condition on the
Rejection branch is also temporarily set to true to make it act as an else. The
rejection branch must catch all orders that are not approved until Level2Role support is added.

FIGURE 14.4
Role workflow
with the MoreIn-
foNeeded branch
not enabled.

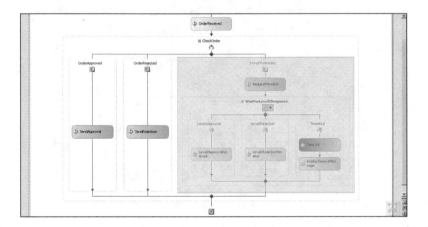

Updating Member Variables

Follow the next steps to add member variables.

1. Right-click the OrderEscalationWorkflows project and select Reload Project.

2. Add the following code below the OrderAmount DependencyProperty:

   ```
   // Collection that valid workflow roles will be stored in
           public WorkflowRoleCollection ValidRoles =
               new WorkflowRoleCollection();

           // Workflow roles where valid roles are stored
           WebWorkflowRole Role1;
           WebWorkflowRole Role2;
   ```

Updating the Workflow Model

The main topic of interest here is binding the Roles property of the OrderReceived activity to the ValidRoles (WorkflowRoleCollection) variable. The OrderReceived activity will no longer process events unless the identities contained in the EventArgs payload are members of the roles contained in the ValidRoles collection.

Follow the next steps to add handlers to the workflow and the HandleExternalEventActivity in which to evaluate the roles.

1. Click the workflow designer away from any activity and enter **OnWorkflowInitialized** in the Initialized property to create a workflow initialized handler. Then press Enter.

2. Click the OrderReceived activity, click its Roles property, and click the Ellipsis. Now click the Bind to an Existing Member tab, select ValidRoles, and click OK.

3. Enter **OrderReceivedInvoked** in the Invoked property and press Enter to create the handler.

Our workflow model now validates roles on its one HandleExternalEvent activity.

Updating the Code-Beside—Step 1

The two new role-related items covered in this section are the following:

▶ In the OnWorkflowInitialized handler, you add the valid WebWorkflowRoles to the ValidRoles collection.

▶ Retrieve the identity from OrderReceivedInvoked handler to make it available to the workflow.

Follow the next steps to add code to the handlers you just created:

1. Add the following code to the OnWorkflowInitialized workflow initialized handler to initialize the roles and update the valid roles when the workflow is created.

```
            // Initializing the two WebWorkflowRole varaibles to the
            // two valid approvers. These roles must exist in the role
provider
            // which is ASPNET in our case
            Role1 = new WebWorkflowRole("Level1Role");
            Role2 = new WebWorkflowRole("Level2Role");

            // Because both roles can create the initial order, they are
            // both added to the ValidRoles collection because both roles
            // may initiate the order.
```

```
ValidRoles.Add(Role1);
ValidRoles.Add(Role2);
```

2. Now when the host raises the event and starts the workflow, the OrderReceived activity executes. At this time we can extract the identity contained in the EventArgs. Then we display the identity in a message box to show it has been received. Add the following code to the OrderReceivedInvoked handler:

```
// Extracting identity from EventArgs
string user =
        (e as
OrderEscalationLocalService.OrderEscInitEventArgs).Identity;

        OrderNumber =
                (e as
OrderEscalationLocalService.OrderEscInitEventArgs).OrderNumber;
        OrderAmount =
                (e as
OrderEscalationLocalService.OrderEscInitEventArgs).OrderAmount;

        MessageBox.Show
                ("Order number: " + OrderNumber + " received for " + user);
```

Running the Solution with Level 1 Support

1. Set the OrderEscalationFormHost project as the startup project and run it.

2. Enter any order number and amount. Enter **Patricia** as the user.

3. The workflow should return approved if you entered an amount less than 1,000; otherwise, it returns rejected.

4. Now enter any order number and amount again. This time enter **John** as the user. You should see the dialog shown in Figure 14.5. The workflow threw

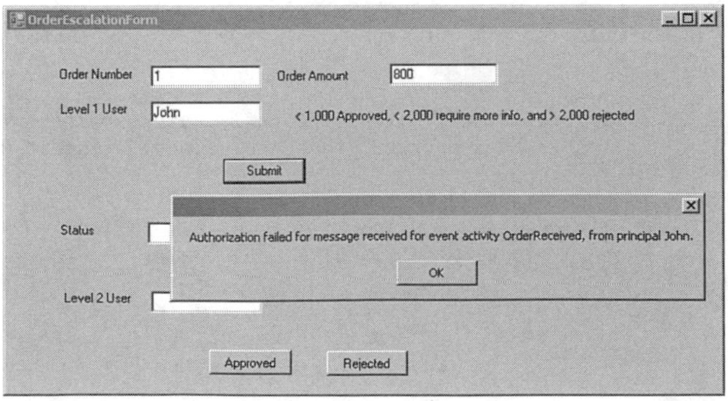

FIGURE 14.5
Role exception
dialog.

an exception. Because we do not have any exception handling in the workflow, our host `Terminated` event caught the exception and displayed the dialog.

Adding Level2Role Support

When the workflow requires additional information, only users in the Level2Role role must either approve or reject the order. We will now need to make the MoreInfoNeeded branch of the workflow functional, which requires the following:

- ▶ Setting the `MoreInfoNeeded Enabled` property to `true`

- ▶ Binding the `Roles` property of the `Level2ApprovalReceived` and `Level2RejectionReceived` activities to the `ValidRoles` variable

- ▶ Changing the `OrderRejected Condition` property's handler

- ▶ Removing the Level1Role from the ValidRoles collection

Adding Level2Role Support to the Workflow

Follow the next steps to add Level2Role support to the workflow activities.

1. Click the `MoreInfoNeeded` activity, the third branch of the `CheckOrder` activity, and set its `Enabled` property to `true`.

2. Click the `Level2ApprovalReceived` activity and bind its `Role` property to the `ValidRoles` variable.

3. Click the `Level2RejectionReceived` activity and bind its `Role` property to the `ValidRoles` variable.

Adding Level2Role Support to the Code-Beside

Follow the next steps to add Level2Role support to the workflow code-beside.

1. Replace the code in the `RejectedCondition` method that always sets `e.Result` to `true` with the following, which sets it to `true` if the `OrderAmount > 2000`.

```
e.Result = OrderAmount > 2000;
```

2. Add the following code to the `SendMoreInfoInvoking` method to remove Role1 from the `ValidRoles` collection.

```
ValidRoles.Remove(Role1);
```

Running the Solution with Level 2 Support

Follow the next steps to run the application, and when you enter an amount between 1000 and 2000, level 2 approval should be requested.

1. Run the OrderEscalationFormHost project.

2. Enter any order number and an amount of **1200**. Enter **Patricia** as the user. Click OK on the dialog.

3. The OrderEscalationForm should show that second-level approval is required, as shown in Figure 14.6.

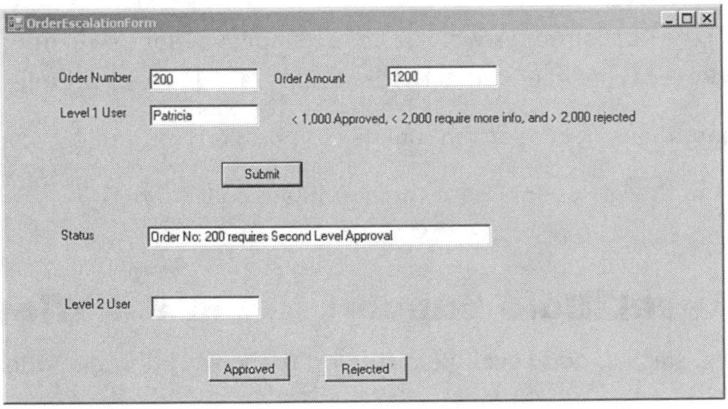

FIGURE 14.6
Second level approval is required.

4. Enter **Brian** as the Level 2 User and click Approved. The workflow should flash a Level 2 Approved dialog. Click OK.

5. Enter any order number and an amount of **1200**. Enter **Patricia** as the user. Click OK on the dialog.

6. The OrderEscalationForm should show that second-level approval is required.

7. Enter **Brian** as the Level 2 User and click Approved. The workflow should flash a Level 2 Approved dialog. Click OK.

8. Now make sure to start at the top and submit an order; then approve or reject it. If you click Approved again without first submitting the order, you will get an exception when raising the event to the host.

9. Enter any order number and an amount of **1200**. Enter **Patricia** as the user. Click OK on the dialog.

10. The OrderEscalationForm should show that second-level approval is required.

11. Enter **Sarah** as the Level 2 User and click Approved. The workflow should flash an `Authorization failed for...` message.

That's it for roles in WF.

Summary

Roles were covered this hour. Event-receiving activities can authenticate external systems raising events on workflows via roles. WF ships with OOB Roles support for both Active Directory and the general purpose ASPNET role provider.

Workshop

Quiz

1. *What are roles used for in WF?*

2. *What type of role providers does WF support OOB?*

3. *What are the three role-related types in WF?*

4. *How do you add valid* `WebWorkflowRoles`?

5. *What three things must be done to add role authorization to WF?*

Answers

1. To ensure that those attempting to access workflows are authorized to do so.

2. Active Directory and ASPNET.

3. `WorkflowRoleCollection`, `WebWorkflowRole`, and `ActiveDirectoryRole`.

4. Instantiate the `WebWorkflowRoles` and add them to a `WorkflowRoleCollection` typed variable.

5. Populate the `EventArgs.Identity` property with the user, add authorized roles to the `WorkflowRoleCollection` in the code-behind, and bind the `WorkflowRoleCollection` typed variable to the event-receiving activity.

HOUR 15

Working with Dynamic Update

What You'll Learn in This Hour:

▶ Dynamic Update overview
▶ Dynamic Update from inside
▶ Dynamic Update from outside
▶ Dynamic Update and rules
▶ Workflow change application

This hour covers Dynamic Update, one of the intriguing features in WF. It permits running workflows to be changed by adding and removing activities. The changes are unique to the workflow instance they are applied to, which permits per order, invoice, or other business transaction customization. Increased flexibility is one of WF's goals. One way to provide this is to permit already running workflows to be changed. Midprocess change alone, however, is not good enough in many cases. It can lead to chaos. That's why it is important for the midprocess change to be supported by tracking. With the two coupled, it is possible that new types of versioning and deployments can be supported that are less rigid than compiled code but that still supply solid versioning support.

Furthermore, WF provides a couple of other features that increase Dynamic Update's plausibility. The first is that WF provides a `DynamicUpdateCondition` property that can restrict at which points of a process, if any, Dynamic Update is allowed.

Second, the WF validation architecture permits midprocess changes to be validated. In fact, the same validation performed on activities at design time is carried out at runtime when Dynamic Update is applied. The WF validation architecture is covered in Hour 24, "Creating Control Flow Activities Session 2." The fact that validation is abstracted and therefore equally employable at runtime and design time demonstrates that changing workflows at runtime is central to the WF model and not an afterthought.

Dynamic Update works on both sequential and state machine workflows. It is especially synergistic with state machine workflows because of the autonomous design of states. This state machine design makes it easier to add or remove a step (state) without adversely affecting the process. One scenario that works well on state machine workflows is to add a hold state to a workflow or series of workflows when, for instance, quality problems are discovered.

> If you are interested in looking further into how Dynamic Update can be used with state machine workflows, the `OrderingStateMachine` SDK example provides a good example of adding a state through Dynamic Update. This hour will not cover using Dynamic Update with state machine workflows.

The next section of this hour covers applying Dynamic Update to add and remove activities from running workflows. The following section covers using Dynamic Update to change workflow rules. Finally, a sample application that creatively employs Dynamic Update is explored at a high level.

Applying Dynamic Update: Outside and Inside

You can apply Dynamic Update in two ways: from outside the workflow and from within the workflow. Applying from outside requires a way to communicate, as well as knowledge of the current step of the running workflow instance, whereas applying from within requires design-time knowledge of where (not necessarily what) the changes are to be applied. Both methods are similar, although additional steps and logistics are involved when applying from outside.

The general dynamic update practice is straightforward. First, a copy of the workflow instance to be changed is copied to a clone for manipulation. After the changes are made, the original workflow is overwritten by the clone, thereby updating a running workflow instance. Two types combine to enable Dynamic Update:

▶ First, the `WorkflowChanges` type contains a `TransientWorkflow` property that serves as a workspace to hold proposed changes. The `TransientWorkflow` property is a composite activity collection that represents the cloned workflow instance. The `TransientWorkflow` property serves as the framework to add activities to, remove activities from, and change rules on.

▶ The WorkflowChanges type contains a Validate method that validates the proposed changes and a Condition property that controls when and if Dynamic Update can be applied to a workflow. As previously mentioned, this Validate method plays a major role in WF's ability to support performing running workflow change with fidelity.

▶ The second type, the WorkflowInstance, contains helper methods to retrieve a workflow instance, and it requests that the cloned copy replace the workflow instance. It also holds the specific Dynamic Update rules for the given workflow model.

Let's now add a Delay activity to a workflow from both the inside and the outside.

Applying Dynamic Update from the Inside

Tracking and a call to query the tracking service was added to the host to make it easier to show the changes made by Dynamic Update.

Follow the next steps to apply Dynamic Update from the inside.

1. Open the DynamicUpdateFromInside solution in the
   C:\SamsWf24hrs\Hours\Hour15DynamicUpdate\DynamicUpdateFromInside
   directory.

2. Open InsideWorkflow shown in Figure 15.1.

3. Double-click the codeActivityWDynamicUpdate activity and enter the code shown in Listing 15.1 in its handler (which is explained directly following).

LISTING 15.1   Dynamic Update From Inside

```
    Console.WriteLine
        ("Printed from Code activity before Dynamic Update Code activity
at {0}",
        DateTime.Now.TimeOfDay);

    // use WorkflowChanges class to author dynamic change and pass
    // it a reference to the current Workflow Instance
    WorkflowChanges workflowTochange = new WorkflowChanges(this);

    // Create a new Delay, initialized to 2 seconds
    DelayActivity delayOrder = new DelayActivity();
    delayOrder.Name = "delayOrder";
    delayOrder.TimeoutDuration = new TimeSpan(0, 0, 2);

    // Insert the Delay Activity to the TransientWorkflow collection
```

```
    // (the workspace) between the two Code Activities
    workflowTochange.TransientWorkflow.Activities.Insert(1, delayOrder);

    // Replace the original Workflow Instance with the clone
      this.ApplyWorkflowChanges(workflowTochange);
```

FIGURE 15.1
DynamicUpdat-
eFromInside
workflow.

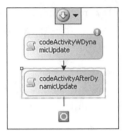

Adding a `Delay` activity dynamically took four steps:

1. Pass a workflow definition to the `WorkflowChanges` type. After changes are made, the updated `WorkflowChanges` type will replace the current workflow definition.

2. The `Delay` activity is programmatically created.

3. The `Delay` activity is added to the `WorkflowChanges.TransientWorkflow` property that contains a modifiable clone of the current workflow. Both the activity to add and its index position on the workflow are passed to the `WorkflowChanges.TransientWorkflow.Activities.Insert` method.

4. The changes are applied to the workflow instance. Validation is performed when `WorkflowInstance.Applychanges` is called, and it will throw an exception if validation fails.

This encapsulates the basic steps to perform dynamic updates from within a workflow. The `WorkflowChanges.TransientWorkflow.Activities.Insert` method, which permitted us to specify the position of the `Delay` activity, was used. There are also Add, Remove, Count and other members that facilitate managing the workflow clone or `TransientWorkflow` collection. No change method exists because activities *cannot* be changed. To change an activity you must delete the activity that requires change, create a new activity that includes the change, and then update the workflow with the new activity.

Running the `DynamicUpdateFromInside` Workflow

Follow the next steps to run the workflow.

1. Run the workflow, and you should see the results shown in Figure 15.2.

FIGURE 15.2
Dynamic Update
Workflow from
inside results
one.

2. You can tell that the `Delay` activity was added because the time difference between the start of the first and second `Code` activities matches the `Delay` activity `TimeoutDuration` property. You can also tell because the `delayOrder` (the name of the `Delay` activity) is included in the tracking query returned. The tracking database has an `AddedActivity` and a `RemovedActivity` table that is populated by Dynamic Update. It theoretically allows for per instance change to be performed with visibility, although this is just an SDK sample that is probably not enterprise-ready.

3. Now you can override Dynamic Update. Click the workflow designer away from any activity.

4. Click the `DynamicUpdateCondition` property, click its drop-down, select Code Condition, enter **DynamicCondition**, and press Enter. Then enter the following in its handler:

```
e.Result = false;
```

5. You get an exception because Dynamic Update is no longer allowed on this workflow.

By the
~~Way~~

> Why the need for Dynamic Update from the inside? One scenario is that some WF hosts are closed (for example, the SharePoint workflow host) and the only way to perform Dynamic Update would be from the inside. In these cases, custom activities (see Hours 20–24) could be embedded in the workflow that communicates with external programs that send the update instructions.

You have run the workflow with Dynamic Update where you saw a `Delay` activity added to a running workflow. Then you changed the Dynamic Update rule to prohibit Dynamic Update, and the change was no longer allowed. The combination of tracking support, conditional evaluation, and activity validation (see Hour 24, "Creating Control Flow Activities Session 2") incorporated in Dynamic Update makes Dynamic Update very intriguing. Whereas XAML-only workflows can be run without compilation, Dynamic Update takes it a step further and permits change while in-flight on a per-instance basis. With Dynamic Update you can update a single workflow or selected workflow instances. Changing the XAML directly affects all workflows that run from that point.

In the "Applying Dynamic Update from the Outside Unplanned" section, you will conduct an unplanned change from the host. You will not implement a planned change from the host, but how to do so is discussed.

Applying Dynamic Update from the Outside Unplanned

You will now work with a similar workflow. This time, though, you will change from the host (the outside). Scenarios where changing from the host may be useful range from changing one or more in-flight workflows because of new requirements that may range from putting the workflows on hold because of a product defect to meeting new design requirements. Another possibility is changing all workflows from the host when they are started to allow changes to be implemented this way until next time you redeploy the workflow with the changes embedded.

This time, because the changes are from the outside and are unplanned, they are performed when the workflow idles. This will lessen the chance of race conditions, in contrast to simply placing the request on the queue while the workflow is running without consideration to what it is doing. (Workflow queues are covered in Hour 21, "Creating Queued Activities," and Hour 22, "Creating Typed Queued and `EventDriven`-Enabled Activities.")

1. Open the DynamicUpdateFromOutside solution in the
   `C:\SamsWf24hrs\Hours\Hour15DynamicUpdate\DynamicUpdateFromOutside`
   directory.

2. Open the `OutsideWorkflow` shown in Figure 15.3.

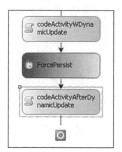

FIGURE 15.3
DynamicUpd-
ateFromOutside
workflow.

3. Now open `Program.cs` and add the code shown in Listing 15.2 to the
   `OnWorkflowIdled` handler, which is explained afterward.

LISTING 15.2   Dynamic Update From Outside Unplanned

```
if (wasChanged)
    return; wasChanged = true;

// Instantiate a Workflow Instance
WorkflowInstance workflowInstance = e.WorkflowInstance;

// Static definition of the WF (replacing this when the change
// is conducted from within.
Activity clonedWorkflow =
    workflowInstance.GetWorkflowDefinition();

// use WorkflowChanges class to author dynamic change
WorkflowChanges workflowChanges =
    new WorkflowChanges(clonedWorkflow);

Console.WriteLine("  Host is adding a new Delay Activity");

// Create a new Delay, initialized to 2 seconds
DelayActivity delayOrder = new DelayActivity();
delayOrder.Name = "delayOrder";
delayOrder.TimeoutDuration = new TimeSpan(0, 0, 2);

// Add the Approval Activity to the collection
workflowChanges.TransientWorkflow.Activities.Add(delayOrder);

// apply transient changes to instance
workflowInstance.ApplyWorkflowChanges(workflowChanges);
```

First, the variable wasChanged is checked to test whether the update has previously been performed. The OnWorkflowIdled event may be called many times in most real-world workflows, and the Delay activity should be added only once.

Second, it requires an extra step to get the workflow from the host. The WorkflowInstance.GetWorkflowDefintion method returns a clone of the workflow instance. You can't just refer to the workflow as you can from inside the workflow. This copy is then passed to the WorkflowChanges type. The rest of the code is identical to when performing Dynamic Update from the inside.

Running the DynamicUpdateFromOutside Unplanned

Follow the next steps to run the DynamicUpdateFromOutside unplanned.

1. Run the workflow, and you should see the results shown in Figure 15.4.

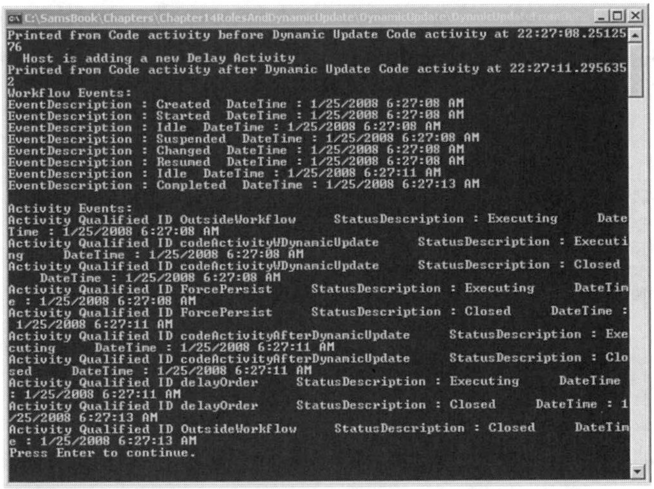

FIGURE 15.4
Dynamic Update
Workflow from
outside
unplanned.

2. This time the delayOrder activity is executed after the codeActivityAfterDynamicUpdate because that's the way the WF scheduler works. You will learn about scheduling and queuing in the custom activity hours (20–24).

Explaining Dynamic Update from the Outside Planned

If you know your process is spontaneous and workflow instances will frequently require change, another approach is to pause the workflow with a Suspend activity at a point of the workflow that you know will (is likely to) require change at design time. Then catch the Suspended event. The advantage is that you know ahead of time where to make the change—if not what change to make—and you don't have to attempt to capture the workflow at an idle state at the point of the workflow in which you want to make the change. You know that it is stopped, and you know exactly where it is stopped. This method of (know where but not what) Dynamic Update can be useful for processes that contain parts that vary widely across workflows. For instance, maybe the credit-hold process is unique across orders because of all the human intervention, and a template is built for each order that can be changed as needed. In this situation, you may even carve out a section of the workflow after the Suspend activity and place stub activities that you will later change.

There is no example for this because it is so similar to the previous section. The main difference is placing the code in the suspended event handler rather than the idled.

Updating Rules Dynamically

It is important that rules be changeable at runtime because they are frequently the least deterministic element or processes. For instance, an order will go on credit-hold if it exceeds the credit limit. The actual credit limit, who to request approval from, and how many levels to escalate within are all determined by rules. These rules tend to change frequently.

WF RuleSets and declarative rule conditions can both be modified at runtime. The RuleDefinitions type contains a RuleSets property that holds a collection of RuleSets in the workflow and the Conditions property that holds a collection of workflow declarative rule conditions. The RuleDefinitionsProperty is a dependency property known by the workflow. Modifying the rules therefore requires accessing one or both of these properties during Dynamic Update, and then applying the changes to update the current workflow instance with the new values.

You can update the RuleSets and Conditions properties through CodeDom expressions or by updating the .rules file that holds their serialized representation. Updating the CodeDom permits programmatic rules change from the host. The .rules files can be updated directly or via a user interface that updates the .rules files. In a scenario that calls for workflows that continually update rules throughout the workflow life cycle, you could allow the .rules file to be updated from an external application. The host could then check the .rules file at each persistence point and update any changes.

All parts of the rules and corresponding actions can be changed regardless of which change method is selected. For example, all aspects of the rule (OrderValue < 1000

Then OrderPriority = 1) can be changed, including changing OrderValue to OrderValue + Tax or OrderValue to InvoiceAmount. The changes implemented in our examples will be limited to changing the literal values (1000 and 1 in the preceding example) because complex CodeDom programming is not within the scope of this book. However, changing the literal values offers a glimpse into changing other parts of the rule expressions. The ability to change the entire rule without recompilation is clearly a powerful feature that is not easily done in compiled software.

By the Way

Code conditions can be applied to IfElse, While, and other activities, just as declarative rule conditions can. Code conditions, however, are not captured by the Conditions property and are therefore not changeable at runtime. This again exemplifies that XML representations both (XAML and .rules) are better supported by WF tools in some areas.

The rest of this section provides a sample of changing a RuleSet and Conditions property via the CodeDom and changing a RuleSet property through a .rules file. The workflow shown in Figure 15.5 will be used for all three changes, although the SetPriorityPolicy activity is enabled only when changing the RuleSet rule.

FIGURE 15.5
Dynamic Update rules.

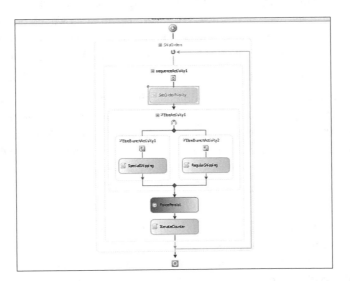

By the Way

A custom Policy activity as covered in Hour 12, "Working with the WF RuleSet," may be more appropriate to update rules at runtime. For XAML-only workflows, you can simply load the .rules file at runtime if it is sufficient to make the changes when starting the workflow. This allows business users to change the rules until the workflow begins. The rules cannot be modified after the workflow starts processing, however, which may not be sufficient, especially for some long-running workflows. The scope of the intended change is also important when deciding which approach to use. Dynamic Update can be applied to one or a select group of workflows. XAML and custom `Policy` activities generally apply to all future workflows. The custom `Policy` activity may also apply to currently processing workflows, depending on its implementation.

Selecting Which Version to Run

Follow the next steps to add code to allow which Dynamic Update scenario to run:

1. Open the DynamicUpdateRules solution in the `C:\SamsWf24hrs\Hours\Hour15DynamicUpdate\DynamicUpdateRules` directory.

2. Open `Program.cs` and add the following code below the opening bracket of the `using (WorkflowRuntime...` line of code. This code allows for choosing which of the Dynamic Update scenarios to execute. It is necessary because only one host is being used for all three types of Dynamic Update that will be processed in this section.

```
Console.WriteLine("Enter 1 and press Enter for rule condition,");
Console.Write("2 for RuleSet rule,");
Console.Write("3 for .rules file: ");
selection = Console.ReadLine();
Console.WriteLine("Choice {0} selected.", selection);
Console.WriteLine();
```

Changing Declarative Rule Conditions with Dynamic Update

Now you will employ Dynamic Update to change the rule condition on the left branch of the `IfElse` activity. The initial value of the rule condition of the left branch is `this.orderPriority == 1`. The `OrderPriority` is passed in from the host as 2. Thus, the conditional will evaluate to `false` and regular shipping will be received. When the workflow reaches the `Delay` activity, it will persist. The host's idled handler will be called, where the left branch rule condition will be set to `"orderPriority <= 2"`. The rule will therefore evaluate to `true` on the next iteration and receive special shipping.

The `IfElse` activity will execute two times, because it is embedded in a `While` activity with the following code condition: `Counter < 2`.

Follow these steps to change a rule with Dynamic Update.

1. Add the code below the following comment in the `Progam.cs Main` method: Add Dynamic Update Selection Code here. This code passes in the property parameters to run scenario 1 (change rule condition via CodeDom).

```
            // Dynamically changing rule condition via CodeDom
            if (selection == "1")
            {
                Console.WriteLine(
                    "Orders with OrderPriority equal to 1 get special
shipping. ");
                Console.WriteLine("(The initial OrderPriority value = 2)."
                    , orderPriority);
                Console.WriteLine();

                parameters.Add("OrderPriority", orderPriority);
            }
```

2. Add the following code to the `OnWorkflowIdled` method. The code you enter over the next few steps will execute when the host idled event is triggered and you select option 1.

```
            // Change the rule condition on the left-hand branch of the IfEsle
activity
            // from orderPriority == 1 to orderPriority <= 2.
            if (selection == "1" & !wasChanged)
            {
            }
```

3. Add the following code within the `If {}` brackets you entered in the preceding step. The code begins implementing Dynamic Update and is so far no different from what you have done earlier when using Dynamic Update to change the workflow activities and not the rules.

```
            wasChanged = true;
            Console.WriteLine("Dynamically changing Rule Condition from
Priority = 1 to priority  <= 2");

            // Retrieving a workflow instance and cloning it
            WorkflowInstance workflowInstance = e.WorkflowInstance;

            // Dynamic update of order rule
            WorkflowChanges workflowchanges =
                new WorkflowChanges(workflowInstance.GetWorkflowDefinition());

            CompositeActivity workflowActivityToChange =
                workflowchanges.TransientWorkflow;
```

4. Now we begin with the code specific to changing rules. Add the following code below the code you added in the preceding step. It retrieves the `RuleDefinitionsProperty` dependency property from the workflow being changed. The `RuleDefinitionsProperty` holds both the `RuleSets` and `Conditions` properties.

```
            RuleDefinitions ruleDefinitions =
                (RuleDefinitions)workflowActivityToChange.GetValue
                (RuleDefinitions.RuleDefinitionsProperty);
```

5. Enter the following code below the code you just added to access the Conditions property of the RuleDefinitions property. This will provide you with a collection of all rule conditions in the workflow.

```
        RuleConditionCollection ruleConditions =
ruleDefinitions.Conditions;
```

6. Enter the following code below the code you just added to select the BranchCondition rule condition from the collection of rule conditions and instantiate it as a RuleExpressionCondition. BranchCondition is the name of the rule condition in the left branch of the IfElse activity.

```
        RuleExpressionCondition conditionBranchCondition =
            (RuleExpressionCondition)ruleConditions["BranchCondition"];
```

7. Enter the following code below the code you just added to change the rule condition via the CodeDom. The conditionBranchCondition instantiated in the previous step is now instantiated as a CodeBinaryOperatorExpression. You have now entered the CodeDom, where the expression will be changed.

```
        CodeBinaryOperatorExpression expression
            = conditionBranchCondition.Expression as
CodeBinaryOperatorExpression;
```

8. Enter the following code below the code you just added to change the operator of the BranchCondition rule to less than or equal and the value compared to 2. When it is complete, you will have changed the BranchCondition rule condition from orderPriority == 1 to orderPriority <= 2. You can't see it, but the expression is changed, just as if you entered the second expression yourself.

```
        expression.Operator = CodeBinaryOperatorType.LessThanOrEqual;
        expression.Right = new CodePrimitiveExpression(2);
```

9. Enter the following code below the code you just added to update the changes to the running workflow instance.

```
        workflowInstance.ApplyWorkflowChanges(workflowchanges);
```

10. Run the workflow, enter 1 when prompted, and you should receive the results shown in Figure 15.6. The key is that regular shipping is received on the first iteration and special shipping on the second (the counter is 0-based, so the actual iteration values are 0 and 1).

Be careful when using Dynamic Update to change rules because neither tracking nor tracing shows that a rule has been changed. Both tracking and tracing still

By the Way

work, but the information they display does not tell you that a rule has been changed. This is problematic because changing rules can—and frequently should—alter workflow behavior. This may cause confusion and challenge auditability. For instance, why in a workflow that specifies `orderReult == 1`, does an order with a value of 2 receive special shipping?

Dynamic rules changes call for clear tracking that shows the rule was changed and what it was changed to. The tracking should also show when the outcome was changed because of Dynamic Update rule changes. There is a `Diff` method of the `RuleDefinitions` type that shows the differences between the original rules and the changed rules that could be used to show the differences. You could employ this from the place that Dynamic Update take place. It would still, however, be up to you to get the information to tracking and build other infrastructures. Some of these features may be reserved for Microsoft Rules Engine and BPM products.

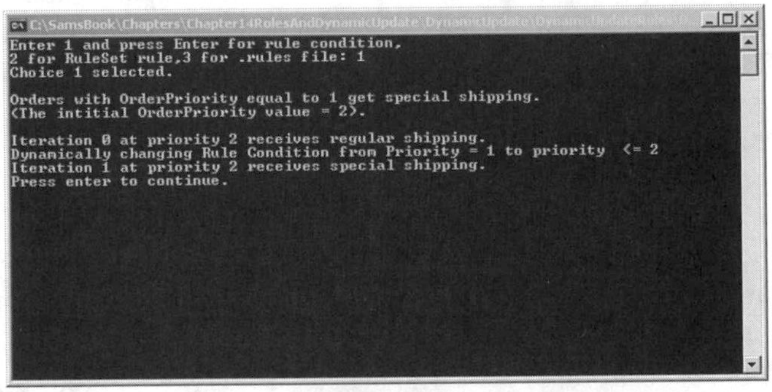

FIGURE 15.6
Results of running workflow with rule condition dynamically changed in second iteration.

Changing a `RuleSet` Rule via the CodeDom

You can also change all elements of `RuleSet` rules. In this scenario, you will enable the `Policy` activity that sets the `orderPriority` to 1 for orders larger than 100,000 and to 2 for those that are less than 100,000. The `OrderAmount` is set to 50,000 and passed from the host to the workflow. Therefore, the first run sets the `orderPriority` to 2. The `BranchCondition` rule retains its default value (`orderPrioroty == 1`), causing the workflow to select the right branch of the `IfElse` activity and to supply regular shipping. When the workflow persists, the idled handler changes the `RuleSet` rule to set the priority to 1 for orders with an `orderAmount > 25,000`. This then produces special shipping on the second iteration.

1. If it is not already enabled, in the Workflow Designer, enable the `SetOrderPriority` activity.

2. Add the code shown in Listing 15.3 to the `Program.cs Main` method below the ending bracket of the `if (selection == "1")` if statement. This passes the proper parameters to run scenario 2 (change `RuleSet` rule via CodeDom).

LISTING 15.3   Changing a Rule in a `.rules` File with Dynamic Update

```
// Dynamically changing RuleSet rule condition via CodeDom
if (selection == "2")
{
    Console.WriteLine(
        "The OrderPriority is set to 1 for Orders>100,000. This earns them
special shipping.");
        Console.Write("(The intitial OrderAmount value = $50,000)."
            , orderPriority);
        Console.WriteLine();

        parameters.Add("OrderAmount", orderAmount);
}
```

3. Add the following code to the end of the `OnWorkflowIdled` method. It is explained directly following.

```
// If selection = 2, change RuleSet rule condition
if (selection == "2" & !wasChanged)
{
    wasChanged = true;
    Console.WriteLine("Dynamically changing hard-coded order amount
threshold in RuleSet to 25000");

    // Retrieving a workflow isntance and cloning it
    WorkflowInstance workflowInstance = e.WorkflowInstance;

    // Dynamic update of order rule
    WorkflowChanges workflowchanges =
        new
WorkflowChanges(workflowInstance.GetWorkflowDefinition());

    CompositeActivity workflowActivityToChange =
        workflowchanges.TransientWorkflow;

    RuleDefinitions ruleDefinitions =
(RuleDefinitions)workflowActivityToChange.GetValue(RuleDefinitions.RuleDefi
nitionsProperty);

    RuleSet ruleSet =
ruleDefinitions.RuleSets["CalculateOrderPriority"];

    foreach (Rule rule in ruleSet.Rules)
    {
        if (rule.Name == "SetPriority")
        {
            RuleExpressionCondition condition =
                rule.Condition as RuleExpressionCondition;

            CodeBinaryOperatorExpression expression
                = condition.Expression as
CodeBinaryOperatorExpression;

            //Resetting the hard-coded order amount threshold
            expression.Right = new CodePrimitiveExpression(25000);
        }
    }
    workflowInstance.ApplyWorkflowChanges(workflowchanges);
}
```

The code is identical to the code that changed the rule condition with three exceptions. First, the `ruleDefinitions.RuleSets` property is accessed instead of `ruleDefinitions.Conditions` property, because we are accessing `RuleSet` rules and not rule conditions. Second, the `SetPriority` rule is selected by iterating the rule in the `ruleDefinitions.RuleSets` collection. Finally, after the `SetPriority` rule is located, the CodeDom is used to change the condition from `OrderAmount > 100000` to `OrderAmount > 25000`.

4. Run the workflow, enter **2** when prompted, and you should receive the results shown in Figure 15.7. The key again is that regular shipping is received on the first iteration and special shipping on the second. In this case, the `BranchCondition` rule condition remains `orderPriority == 1`. It is the `SetPriority RuleSet` rule that changes the value of the `orderPriority` from 2 to 1, which causes the "standard" `BranchCondition` rule evaluation to change from `false` to `true`.

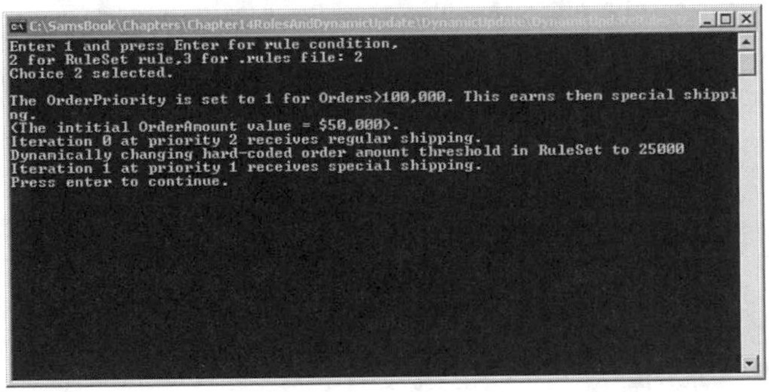

FIGURE 15.7 Results of running workflow with a `RuleSet` rule dynamically changed in second iteration.

By the Way

Other `RuleSet` and rule attributes, such as whether the rule is active and whether the `RuleSet` supports forward chaining, can also be updated via the `Rule` and `RuleSet` types.

Change `RuleSet` Rule via `.rules` File

So far you have changed the `RuleSet` and `Conditions` properties via the CodeDom and then passed them to the `WorkflowChanges` object. A viable alternative approach is to change the `.rules` file that contains the serialized `RuleSet` and `Conditions`. From there, you can update the `RuleSet` or `Conditions` properties with the updated `.rules` file that contains the new values. This method can be used to support directly updating the `.rules` file to implement ad hoc changes or to fix bugs, for instance. As you saw in Hour 12, the RuleSet Dialog Editor can be rehosted. Using the RuleSet Dialog Editor or your own custom one, the .rules file could be edited by business users throughout the workflow life cycle. This may be appropriate for some long-running workflows that could then update the rules at each persistence point. Let's begin.

Follow the next steps to change a rule in a .rules file.

1. Disable the SetOrderPriority activity.

2. Add the following code to the Program.cs Main method below the ending bracket of the if (selection == "2") if statement. This passes the proper parameters to run scenario 3 (change RuleSet rule via .rules file).

```
// Dynamically chnage RuleSet rule condition via .rules file
if (selection == "3")
{
    Console.WriteLine("The OrderPriority is set to 1 for Orders >
100k which earns them special shipping.");
    Console.Write("(The intitial OrderAmount value = $50,000).",
orderPriority);
    Console.WriteLine();

    parameters.Add("OrderAmount", orderAmount);
}
```

3. Add the following code to the end of the OnWorkflowIdled method. It is explained directly following:

```
// Update RuleSet rule via .rules file
if (selection == "3" & !wasChanged)
{
    wasChanged = true;

    Console.WriteLine("Dynamically changing hard-coded order amount
threshold in RuleSet to 25000");

    // Retrieving a workflow isntance and cloning it
    WorkflowInstance workflowInstance = e.WorkflowInstance;

    // Next two lines serialize external rules into a type
    WorkflowMarkupSerializer serializer =
        new WorkflowMarkupSerializer();
    XmlTextReader reader =
        new
XmlTextReader(@"\SamsWf24hrs\Hours\Hour15DynamicUpdate\DynamicUpdateRules\D
ynamicUpdateRules\ManuallyUpdateRulesFile.rules");

    WorkflowChanges workflowchanges =
        new
WorkflowChanges(workflowInstance.GetWorkflowDefinition());

    CompositeActivity workflowActivityToChange =
        workflowchanges.TransientWorkflow;

    // Get ruleDefinitions from exteranl rule
```

```
                    RuleDefinitions ruleDefinitions =
        serializer.Deserialize(reader) as RuleDefinitions;

                    // Replace the current rules value DependencyProperty with
        the value
                    // from the external rules.

        workflowActivityToChange.SetValue(RuleDefinitions.RuleDefinitionsProperty,
        ruleDefinitions);

                    workflowInstance.ApplyWorkflowChanges(workflowchanges);
                    }
```

There are two changes. A new `WorkflowMarkupSerializer` type is instantiated. The `WorkflowMarkupSerializer` type can serialize and deserialize XAML and `.rules` files (see the next note). In this case, it is used to deserialize the `.rules` file (convert it to a .NET type). The deserialized `.rules` file is then passed to an `XmlTextReader` type on the next line. The line of code shown next uses the `WorkflowMarkupSerializer` to deserialize the reader that contains the `.rules` file.

```
            // Get ruleDefinitions from exteranl rule
            RuleDefinitions ruleDefinitions = serializer.Deserialize(reader)
    as RuleDefinitions;
```

The rules in the `RuleDefinitions` property are now those contained in the `.rules` file (which presumably contains changes). When updating rules via the CodeDom, the initial `RuleDefinitions` was obtained from the `RuleDefinitionsProperty` dependency property.

```
        RuleDefinitions ruleDefinitions =
            (RuleDefinitions)workflowActivityToChange.GetValue
            (RuleDefinitions.RuleDefinitionsProperty);
```

Finally, you update the `DependencyProperty` that holds the `RuleDefinitions` property as shown:

```
workflowActivityToChange.SetValue(RuleDefinitions.RuleDefinitionsProperty,
ruleDefinitions);
```

1. Browse to the `ManuallyUpdateRulesFile.rules` file in the `C:\SamsBook\Hours\Hour15DynamicUpdate\DynamicUpdate\DynamicUpdate Rules\DynamicUpdateRules` directory and open the file with Notepad.

2. Search for 100000 and change the 100000 to `25000`. Then save the file.

3. Run the workflow, enter **3** when prompted, and you should receive the results shown in Figure 15.8. The key again is that regular shipping is received on the first iteration and special shipping on the second. In this case, lowering the order threshold from 100,000 to 25,000 is done by changing the `.rules` file.

FIGURE 15.8
Results of running workflow with a `RuleSet` rule dynamically updated from a `.rules` file in second iteration.

Dynamic Update: Exploring Workflow Changes Sample

One of the WF developers at Microsoft created a sample application named Workflow Changes that adds visibility to Dynamic Update and integrates it with tracking in a similar manner to the WorkflowMonitor SDK sample demonstrated in Hour 5, "Creating an Escalation Workflow." It demonstrates the kinds of applications that can be constructed by developers or that may be added by Microsoft and/or third parties using WF as a platform. The application itself does not appear ready for production use. It is shown again because of how well it expresses key WF potential application. There is no code in this section. If you want to learn more, you can follow a link to the application, which includes source code, at the end of this section.

The ability to update workflows midprocess is very powerful. However, our Dynamic Update implementation to date has lost a good deal of two of WF's key features: design-time transparency and graphical construction. Runtime transparency has been maintained via tracking; however, even then the tracking display used leaves room for improvement.

The Workflow Changes application allows you to graphically modify running workflows using the same workflow designer used to create workflows in Visual Studio.

Your changes are thereby reflected in the designer as you make them. The Workflow Changes application extends the design-time experience and transparency to run-time change. Let's take a look at the Workflow Change application.

Figure 15.9 shows the main form. From this form you can select to view currently running or previously executed workflows. You can double-click one of the currently running workflows to bring it up in detail view. The difference (as shown in Figure 15.10) is that a menu appears across the top, where you can suspend, resume, terminate, or change the workflow. An activity toolbox and property windows also show up in a right pane, though they are not yet active.

FIGURE 15.9
Workflow Change application main form.

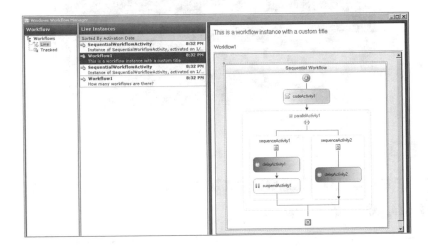

FIGURE 15.10
Workflow Change application detail form.

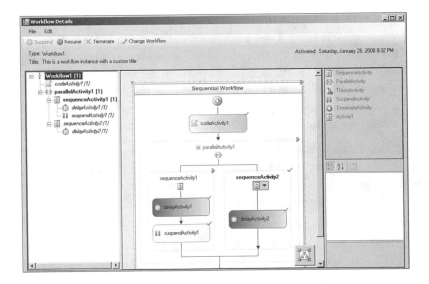

After you select Change Workflow, the activity toolbox and property window are activated. What does this mean? You can add activities to this workflow instance from
the toolbox as you normally do in Visual Studio. As shown in Figure 15.11, a
Parallel activity was added, and a Suspend activity was placed in each branch.

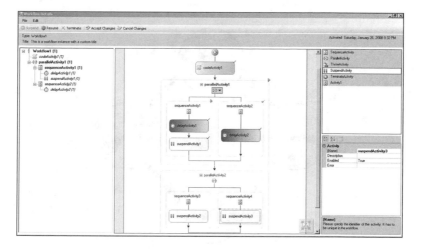

FIGURE 15.11
The Workflow
Change applica-
tion is used to
add activities to
a running work-
flow instance.

Now click the Accept Changes button, and all the Dynamic Update logic is handled
behind the scenes. From the user standpoint, locate a workflow, add new activities,
and apply the changes. You can even run the workflow from the UI by clicking the
Resume button, which, as shown in the left pane of Figure 15.11, executes the
remaining activities. Finally, you can view the results in tracking (not shown) so that
the changes made to each workflow can be identified.

Some of you may have noticed that the activity toolbox contained only a subset of
the standard WF activities. There was also a custom activity named Activity1.
When rehosting the designer, you choose which activities to display and in many
cases it is likely that many custom activities exist, such as Customer and Order,
that allow business analysts to create simple workflows. Designer rehosting is
not covered in this book. The workflow designer, though, is a Windows Control
that can be hosted in a .NET 2.0 and later application. See the DesignerHosting
SDK sample or the "Windows Workflow Foundation: Everything About Re-Hosting
the Workflow Designer" article for more information on designer rehosting. The
article comes with a comprehensive sample application that permits compilation,
rules rehosting, and contains all WF OOB activities. In Hour 17, "Learning
Advanced Hosting," you will learn about the WF workflow loading methodology
that can be used to process a workflow created in Visio or another modeling tool,
which offers an alternative to designer rehosting.

The Workflow Change application shows how a combination of WF features—Dynamic Update, designer rehosting, tracking, abstracted validation, general workflow designer transparency—combine to add efficiencies to the software development, run, modify, and deployment processes, as shown in Figure 15.12.

FIGURE 15.12
Software development process enabled by Workflow Change application.

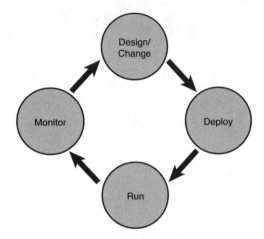

The concept of the Workflow Changes application is useful to permit business analysts and other nondevelopers to create simple workflows. It is also useful to developers as part of the general development process. The business analysts would have limited activities that allow for simpler, confined workflow creation. The developers would, on the other hand, have a richer set of activities and capabilities.

Here is the URL to the Workflow Change application if you want to learn more: http://wf.netfx3.com/files/folders/sample_applications/entry4074.aspx.

Summary

Dynamic Update is useful to change one, selected, all future, and other permutations of workflow instances at runtime or even thereafter. When adding and removing activities, the changes are reflected in tracking, which serves as an interesting versioning mechanism. When rules are changed, they are not reflected in tracking, which is unfortunate. It may, however, fall in the realm of a server product and not a workflow/rules platform to provide this functionality. Dynamic Update is fairly hard to use, and XAML-only workflows overlap in some areas. It will be interesting to see where Dynamic Update goes in future versions.

Workshop

Quiz

1. *What is the purpose of Dynamic Update?*

2. *What changes can be made with Dynamic Update?*

3. *What are the two types used in Dynamic Update?*

4. *What is the function of the* `WorkflowChanges` *type?*

5. *What is the function of the* `WorkflowInstance` *type in relation to Dynamic Update?*

6. *What are the three steps to implementing Dynamic Update?*

7. *What are the main differences between applying Dynamic Update from the inside and the outside?*

8. *What is the difference between performing Dynamic Update from the outside planned and unplanned?*

9. *What steps must be performed to update a declarative rule condition that are not necessary when using Dynamic Update and not updating rules?*

Answers

1. To change selected workflows at runtime.

2. Activities can be added and deleted and RuleSet rules and declarative rule conditions can be changed.

3. `WorkflowChanges` and `WorkflowInstance`.

4. Through its `TransientWorkflow` property, the `WorkflowChanges` type holds a cloned copy of the workflow that can be updated and then used to replace the current workflow instance.

5. The `WorkflowInstance.ApplyWorkflowChanges` method replaces the currently running workflow with the changed workflow.

6. Pass a workflow definition to the `WorkflowChanges` type, make changes to the `WorkflowChanges.TransientWorkflow` property, and then apply the changes via the `WorkflowInstance.ApplyWorkflowChanges` method.

7. The original workflow to be modified is retrieved through the `WorkflowInstance.GetWorkflowDefintion` method instead of (this) and you

have to find a "safe" point to perform the changes, such as when the workflow is idled.

8. When performing Dynamic Update from the outside planned, you know where on the workflow it may be changed and can therefore suspend it. You can make the changes safely and securely because you know where the workflow is and that it is and will remain stopped. Performing it unplanned requires you to attempt to inject your changes at a persistence point if possible or through workflow queues. Making the changes unplanned makes it difficult to ensure the workflow is in the state you want it to be in at the time of change.

9. Instantiate a `RuleDefinitions` type with the `RuleDefinitionsProperty` dependency property. Instantiate the `RuleDefinitions.Conditions` typed variable. Make the changes to the `RuleDefinitions.Conditions` typed variable via the CodeDom.

HOUR 16

Working with Exceptions, Compensation, and Transactions

What You'll Learn in This Hour:

- ▶ WF exception (fault) handling
- ▶ Compensation
- ▶ Cancellation
- ▶ Transactions

WF applications need to trap and handle errors and ensure transactional integrity, as do all applications. The error handling and transaction support is very similar to standard .NET exception handling and transaction support. WF also features support for two new error handling-centric concepts not found in standard .NET: compensation and cancellation.

WF error handling is associated with WF composite activities, which are activities that can hold child activities, such as the `Parallel`, `IfElse`, `ConditionedActivityGroup`, and `SequentialWorkflow` activity. Each of the different types of WF error handling and transactional support are described next.

The WF `FaultHandlers` (plural) activity is used in conjunction with the `FaultHandler` (singular) and `Throw` activities to trap and handle errors. The combination of these activities provides the same capabilities found in try-catch blocks.

`CancellationHandlers` allow code to execute when an executing activity needs to be terminated early. Early termination may be needed because an exception occurred or simply because the business process calls for it to exit early.

CompensationHandlers allow code to be associated with selected activities that are triggered later to perform corrective action. If a CRM system is updated with an order and then the same order is added to an ERP system, compensation may be used to remove the order from the CRM system if the order cannot be added to the ERP system. The CompensatableSequence activity allows compensation handlers to be associated with it.

Transactions are implemented via the TransactionScope activity. Any activities in the same TransactionScope activity are placed in the same transaction. Therefore they either all complete or all roll back.

Each of the preceding topics has its own section, with examples in the following sections of this hour.

Creating the Project

You will specify that the workflow be created in XAML to make viewing the handlers you create more evident. Be sure to select the workflow with code separation when adding the workflow in step 5.

Follow the next steps to create the project.

1. Create a new Sequential Workflow Console Application project, name it **ExceptionsCompensationAndTransactions**, and place it in the C:\SamsWf24hrs\Hours\Hour16ExceptionsAndCompensation directory.

2. Click OK.

3. Delete Workflow1.cs.

4. Right-click the ExceptionsCompensationAndTransactions, select Add, and then New Item.

5. Select Workflow in the left pane, select Sequential Workflow (with code separation), name it **ExceptionWorkflow**, and click OK.

6. Pause the host (see Hour 3, "Learning Basic Hosting").

Basic Exception Handling

WF relies on FaultHandlers, FaultHandler, and Throw activities to catch and react to errors (exceptions). The activities combine to supply very similar functionality to a standard .NET try-catch block. WF uses the term FaultHandler in contrast to exception handler because WF executes the handlers asynchronously, the ramifications of which are beyond the scope of this book. The terms *exception handler* and *fault handler* will be used interchangeably. WF exceptions can be captured from most specific to most general, and they bubble up just like standard .NET exceptions can when using try-catch blocks.

In this section, the workflow will catch and handle an exception. In the next section, an `IfElse` activity will also be configured to catch and handle errors. Catching selected errors and bubbling up exceptions will be demonstrated when working with the `IfElse` activity.

StateMachineWorkflows do not have workflow-level exception handling. Microsoft's reasoning is that this would break the canonical WF state machine rule that a state machine workflow is never in two states concurrently. The current state would represent one state and the exception handler another. When using state machine workflows, it is imperative to register the terminated workflow event and catch unhandled errors in it. Workflows are terminated when an exception is not handled and the terminated event can be used to identify the error. See Hour 3 for an example of how to use the terminated event.

Modeling the `ExceptionWorkflow`

The workflow will contain one `Code` activity that will throw an exception.

1. Open `Program.cs` and replace the current line that instantiates the workflow instance with the following:

   ```
   WorkflowInstance instance = workflowRuntime.CreateWorkflow
   ```

   `(typeof(ExceptionsCompensationAndTransactions.ExceptionWorkflow));`

2. Open the `ExceptionWorkflow` in design mode.

3. Add a `Code` activity to the workflow, double-click it, and add the following code to its handler:

   ```
   Console.WriteLine("In the Code activity before throwing
   exception.");
           throw new Exception("Exception thrown");
   ```

Adding a Workflow-Level `FaultHandlers` Activity

FaultHandlers are supported through an activity that looks very much like a Condi-tionedActivityGroup (CAG) activity. The FaultHandler activities going across the filmstrip are the exception to be captured (for example, `System.Exception`, `System.DivideByZeroException`). Each type of exception in the filmstrip then may have one or more activities associated with it to handle the error.

Follow the next steps to add fault handling to the workflow.

1. Right-click the workflow designer and select View Fault Handlers from the menu shown in Figure 16.1.

FIGURE 16.1
Workflow menu
with View Fault
Handlers choice.

2. You should now be in fault handler view, as shown in Figure 16.2.

FIGURE 16.2
Workflow level
fault handler
view.

3. Add a `FaultHandler` activity into the filmstrip, where it requests activities to be placed here, as shown in Figure 16.3.

FIGURE 16.3
`FaultHandler`
activity added.

4. Click the `FaultHandler` activity you just added, click its `FaultType` property, and click the ellipsis.

5. You should now be in Browse; select a .NET type as shown in Figure 16.4.

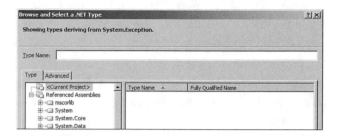

FIGURE 16.4
.NET Type selec-
tor dialog.

6. Click the + next to mscorlib and then click System, as shown in Figure 16.5.

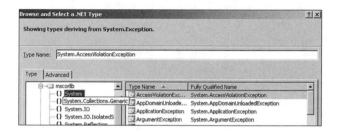

FIGURE 16.5
Selecting a type
of exception for
the fault handler
to catch.

7. In the middle pane, scroll down and select Exception, as shown in Figure 16.6.

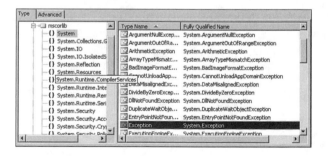

FIGURE 16.6
System.Exception
selected.

8. Click OK.

The FaultHandler.Fault property is updated when the error is captured by WF. Therefore, it is not configurable like the FaultType property is. You will see how to access it when handling the exception in the next section.

Any workflow-level or unhandled exceptions of any type that bubble up are caught in the exception handler you just created. You will learn to capture more specific exceptions and to use the Throw activity to bubble up an exception shortly.

Handling the Exception

Now that the exception is caught (by the FaultHandler in the filmstrip), it is time to create a handler and add some activities to it. The FaultHandler body is very similar to a Sequence activity and can have just about any combination of child activities added to it.

The FaultHandlerActivity.Fault property is retrieved in the Code activity. The workflow updates the Fault property when the workflow throws an exception and the FaultHandler captures it.

Follow the next steps to add exception handling logic to the FaultHandler activity.

1. Add a Code activity to the FaultHandler activity in the middle section of the FaultHandlers activity (Figure 16.7).

FIGURE 16.7
Code activity
added to
FaultHandler.

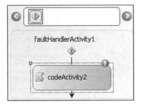

2. Double-click the Code activity to add a handler, and add the following code in its handler.

```
// Retrieve the Exception object for the current fault.
Exception ex = faultHandlerActivity1.Fault;
// Display the exception error message.
Console.WriteLine("The workflow captured this exception:"
    + ex.Message);
// Display the exception stack trace.
Console.WriteLine("Here is the stack trace:"
    + ex.StackTrace);
```

The exception message and StackTrace are displayed on the console in this example. In a real-world example, the error would most likely be logged and other provisions taken.

To return to the standard workflow view, right-click the workflow away from any activities and select View SequentialWorkflow.

Configuring Visual Studio Debugger to Not Trap CLR Exceptions

Follow the next steps to ensure that the Visual Studio debugger does not trap the exception before WF can handle it. If the Visual Studio debugger does trap it, the workflow will terminate because of an unhandled exception, and the exception will not be captured. You will need to change this setting each time Visual Studio is started.

1. Click the Debug menu choice from the Visual Studio menu.

2. Select Exceptions.

3. Remove the check mark from the Common Language Runtime Exceptions row and User-unhandled column (Figure 16.8).

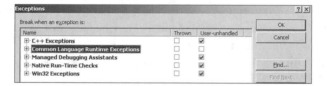

FIGURE 16.8
Prevent the debugger from trapping exceptions.

4. Click OK.

5. Press F5 to run the workflow and you should see that the exception was captured and its message and StackTrace were printed to the console (Figure 16.9).

FIGURE 16.9
ExceptionWorkflow results.

The activities included in the handler sections are updated to the SQL Tracking tables along with the standard execution path activities. The activities processed

By the Way

> in the handlers can be viewed in the WorkflowMonitor application (Hour 5, "Creating an Escalation Workflow") by clicking the arrow on the composite activity that has the arrow and selecting the handler of interest. This allows stepping through the handler activity execution in addition to the standard workflow execution.

Hierarchical Exception Handling and the Throw Activity

A workflow is a tree of activities. On that tree, most composite activities can have fault handlers associated with them. However, it is up to you as the workflow author to decide where to capture and handle errors. Sometimes you may want to capture and handle the errors in the composite activity in which they are raised. At other times, you may want to capture the error and pass it on to be handled by a higher-level activity or the workflow itself. As with .NET, WF exceptions will bubble up until they are handled, and even when handled they may be rethrown so that they still bubble up. As previously mentioned, you can place multiple `FaultHandler` activities in a `FaultHandlers` activity to capture exceptions from most specific to most broad.

In the exercise portion of this section, you will add an `IfElse` activity and equip it with exception handling. You will then raise an exception from one of the `IfElse` activity's children. Finally, you will catch and handle the error in the `IfElse` first and then in the workflow.

Updating the Exception Workflow

Follow the next steps to see an error bubble up from a child activity to the workflow.

1. Open the ExceptionWorkflow in design mode.

2. Add an `IfElse` activity below the `Code` activity.

3. Drag the `Code` activity that produces the exception into the left branch of the `IfElse` activity. Double-click it and replace the current code in its handler with the following code to produce a divide-by-zero error.

   ```
   Console.WriteLine("In the Code activity before throwing
   exception.");
           int x = 4;
           int y = 0;
           int z = x / y;
   ```

4. Add a new `Code` activity to the right branch.

5. Double-click the new Code activity in the right branch and add the following code to its handler:

```
Console.WriteLine("No exception thrown.");
```

6. Click the left branch of the IfElse activity, select Code Condition from its Condition property drop-down, click the + to the left of the Condition property, enter **LeftHandBranchCondition**, and press Enter.

7. Add the following code to the LeftHandBranchCondition handler:

```
e.Result = true;
```

8. Even though the exception occurs in the IfElse activity, it bubbles up and is handled by the workflow-level exception handler. This occurs because no error handling is configured at the IfElse activity level.

9. Press F5 to run the workflow, and you should see the results shown in Figure 16.10:

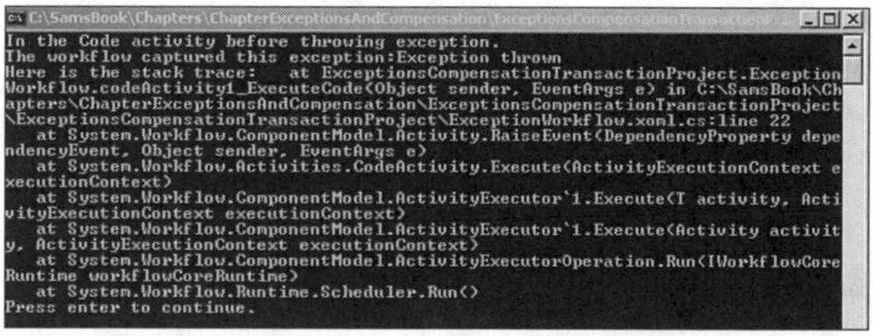

FIGURE 16.10
IfElse activity exception handled by workflow results.

Catching Exceptions in the IfElse Activity

Follow the next steps to configure the IfElse activity to capture exceptions. It will then capture the exception raised by its child. The error will no longer bubble up to the workflow-level handler. You will also specify a more narrow type of exception to be caught. Only divided by 0 errors will be captured, rather than the generic System.Exception.

1. Right-click the IfElse activity in the upper-right corner away from the branches (Figure 16.11). (The branches have fault handlers as well, so be careful to not select a branch.) Then select View Fault Handlers.

2. Add a FaultHandler to the filmstrip of the FaultHandlers activity.

FIGURE 16.11
Select the han-
dlers from
IfElse, not the
IfElse branch.

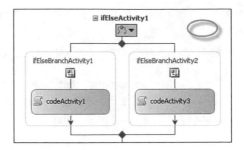

3. Click the `FaultHandler` activity you just added.

4. Click the ellipsis in its `FaultType` property.

5. Expand mscorlib, select System, and then select the DivideByZeroException in the middle pane (Figure 16.12).

FIGURE 16.12
Capturing divide-
by-0 exceptions.

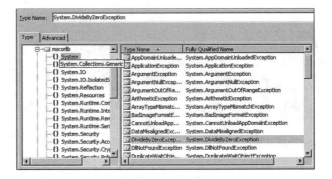

> To return to the standard `IfElse` activity view, right-click the `IfElse` activity and select View IfElse Activity.

Handling Exceptions in the `IfElse` Activity

Follow the next steps to handle the error as well as to capture it in the `IfElse` activity.

1. Add a `Code` activity to the `FaultHandler` activity in the middle section of the `FaultHandlers` activity.

2. Double-click the Code activity and add the following code:

```
// Retrieve the fault from the HandleFault activity
// in the IfElse activity.
Exception ex = faultHandlerActivity2.Fault;
```

```
            // Display message to the console from IfElse.
            Console.WriteLine("The IfElse activity captured this
exception:"
                + ex.Message);
```

The exception should now be caught by the IfElse activity handler. It should no longer bubble up to the workflow-level handler.

3. Press F5 to run the workflow, and you should see the results shown in Figure 16.13.

FIGURE 16.13
Divide-by-zero error captured by the IfElse activity handler.

> To return to the standard IfElse activity view, right-click the IfElse activity and select View IfElse Activity.

Use the Throw Activity

The Throw activity is equivalent to the C# throw statement. It is used to create an exception. It is commonly used inside of handlers to rethrow an exception captured by a lower-level handler, just as the throw statement is used in C# try-catch blocks. You will replace the Code activity that produces the divide-by-0 error with a Throw activity.

1. Set the Enabled property of the Code activity located in the left branch to False.

2. Add a Throw activity to the left branch above the Code activity you just disabled.

3. Click the ellipsis in its FaultType property.

4. Expand mscorlib, select System, and then scroll down and select Exception in the middle pane.

   The exception should now revert to being caught by the workflow because the IfElse handler is looking for divide-by-zero errors and not System.Exception errors, which are now produced by the Throw activity.

5. Press F5 to run the workflow, and you should see results shown in Figure 16.14.

Reconfiguring the Throw Activity

Follow the next steps to reconfigure the Throw activity to raise a divide-by-zero exception.

FIGURE 16.14
Workflow handler catches exception.

1. Click the Throw activity and then click the ellipsis in its FaultType property.

2. Expand mscorlib, select System, and then select the DivideByZeroException in the middle pane.

   The exception should now be caught by the IfElse activity because the Throw activity raises a divide-by-zero exception and the IfElse handler looks for a divided-by-zero exception.

3. Press F5 to run the workflow, and you should see the results shown in Figure 16.15.

FIGURE 16.15
Throw activity set to System.Exception handled by workflow results.

Activity Handlers Elements and Views

A WF composite activity's default execution, exception handling, and other handlers are all child elements of a single activity. The next code segment is a stripped version of the ExceptionWorkflow's IfElse activity's XAML representation (namespaces and other unnecessary attributes are removed for readability). If you look, you will see that the IfElse activity has three children. The first two are its branches, and the third is the FaultHandlers activity you just added to and configured on it. If the activity was configured with a cancellation handler, there would be a CancellationHandler child element as well. If you like, open the ExceptionWorkflow XAML file in an XML editor or Notepad (see Hour 2, "A Spin Around Windows Workflow Foundation," for help opening a XAML file in an XML editor), and you will see that the ExceptionWorkflow has two immediate children, the IfElse activity and the workflow-level exception handler.

WF executes the standard child activities when the workflow is in normal execution mode and the appropriate handler when it is faulting or canceling.

You will work more with the different handlers and the activity execution semantics in Hour 23, "Creating Control Flow Activities Session 1," and Hour 24, "Creating Control Flow Activities Session 2."

```
<IfElseActivity x:Name="ifElseActivity1">
    <IfElseBranchActivity x:Name="ifElseBranchActivity1">
        <IfElseBranchActivity.Condition>
            <CodeCondition Condition="LeftHandBranchCondition" />
        </IfElseBranchActivity.Condition>
        <CodeActivity x:Name="codeActivity1"/>
        <ThrowActivity x:Name="throwActivity1" />
    </IfElseBranchActivity>
    <IfElseBranchActivity x:Name="ifElseBranchActivity2">
        <CodeActivity x:Name="codeActivity3" />
    </IfElseBranchActivity>
    <FaultHandlersActivity x:Name="faultHandlersActivity2">
        <FaultHandlerActivity x:Name="faultHandlerActivity2" >
            <CodeActivity x:Name="codeActivity4"/>
        </FaultHandlerActivity>
    </FaultHandlersActivity>
</IfElseActivity>
```

Cancellation Handlers

Cancellation occurs in WF in many cases. For instance, parallel staffing requests may be submitted; when an acceptable staffing response is received, the other requests will no longer be needed. WF supports this scenario via cancellation. This early termination could easily be modeled with a `Parallel` or CAG activity. The CAG activity `UntilCondition` event provides automated early cancellation, which can occur when the CAG's `UntilCondition` becomes true and it still has currently executing children. Cancellation is necessary because WF will not allow a composite activity to complete that has currently executing children (see Hour 23).

It is mandatory that the children be canceled in some cases, and a faulting activity will perform this task on its children (see Hour 23 and 24). Cancellation handlers, on the other hand, can be optionally applied to perform cleanup before an activity is canceled.

Performing Preliminary Setup

Follow the next steps to add the CancellationWorkflow.

1. Right-click the ExceptionsCompensationAndTransactions and select Add, New Item.

2. Select Workflow in the left pane, select Sequential Workflow (with code separation), name it **CancellationWorkflow**, and click OK.

3. Set the host to point to the CancellationWorkflow.

Modeling the CancellationWorkflow

To test cancellation, follow the next steps to create a workflow with a `Parallel` activity. Place a `Delay` activity in one branch and a `Throw` activity in another. The `Throw` activity will then send the `Parallel` activity into a faulting state. The faulting parallel activity will then cancel its currently executing child activity, the branch with the `Delay` activity.

1. Open the `Cancellation` workflow in design mode.

2. Add a `Parallel` activity.

3. Add a `Delay` activity to the left branch and a `Throw` activity to the right branch.

4. Set the `Delay` activity's `TimeoutDuration` to `00:00:30`.

5. Set the `Throw` activity's `FaultType` to `System.Exception`.

Adding the Cancellation Handler

The cancellation will take place automatically when the `Parallel` activity enters the faulting state. As mentioned previously, though, an optional cancellation handler can be applied to perform cleanup or other work. Also note that the cancellation handler is placed on the `Parallel` activity branch that holds the `Delay` activity, because it is being canceled.

Follow the next steps to add a cancellation handler.

1. Right-click the left `Parallel` activity branch (not the `Parallel` activity itself, but the branch).

2. Select the View Cancel Handler option to switch to cancellation handler view (Figure 16.16).

3. Add a `Code` activity to the `CancellationHandler`, double-click it, and add the following code to its handler:

```
Console.WriteLine("I am the cancellation handler for the delay
branch.");
```

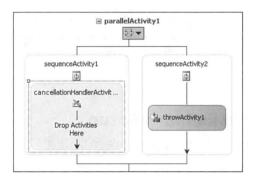

FIGURE 16.16
Cancellation
handler menu
option.

The workflow will run. The exception will be thrown and then the branch containing the `Delay` activity will be canceled. This will invoke the cancellation handler on the `Delay` activity branch.

4. Press F5 to run the workflow, and you should see the results shown in Figure 16.17.

FIGURE 16.17
Cancellation
workflow results.

Compensation Overview

The purpose of compensation is to allow already completed work to be corrected (or compensated for). This means that only units of work that have successfully completed are eligible for compensation.

Let's look at an example. An order must be updated by two systems: a CRM system and an accounting system. It is first placed in the order system. When successfully updated, it is placed in the accounting system. If the accounting system will not accept the order, the order entry system must be compensated. The compensation route is taken because the order may be reviewed by a person before being rejected from the accounting system, which prohibits placing both updates in a transaction and locking resources for an unspecified period of time.

Compensation handlers may be applied to `CompensatableSequence` activities. In the preceding example, the activities that update the CRM system would be placed in a `CompensatableSequence` activity. The accounting process may throw an exception when it cannot be updated. Depending on the structure of the workflow, the CRM compensation may be triggered via default compensation when the exception is thrown, or may be explicitly specified. Both compensation invocation methods will be demonstrated.

Performing Preliminary Setup

Follow the next steps to add a CompensationWorkflow.

1. Right-click the ExceptionsCompensationAndTransactions and select Add, New Item.

2. Select Workflow in the left pane, select Sequential Workflow (with code separation), name it **CompensationWorkflow**, and click OK.

3. Set the host to point to the CompensationWorkflow.

Registering the SQL Persistence Service

The CompensatableSequence activity calls the persistence service registered with WF (SqlWorkflowPersistenceService or other) when it completes successfully. This provides a known state to compensate from if compensation is applied later.

Follow the next steps to register the SqlWorkflowPersistenceService. A persistence service must be registered to use compensation and transactions.

1. Open Program.cs and add a static variable below the opening class bracket to store the database connection:

```
    static string connectionString = "Initial Catalog=
WFTrackingAndPersistence;" +
    "Data Source=localhost; Integrated Security=SSPI;";
```

2. Add variable declarations directly below the opening bracket of the using statement to configure the persistence service:

```
    // Persistence parameter values
    bool unloadOnIdle = true;
    TimeSpan reloadIntevral = new TimeSpan(0, 0, 0, 20, 0);
    TimeSpan ownershipDuration = TimeSpan.MaxValue;
```

3. Add the following code to register the persistence service above the line of code that instantiates the workflow instance:

```
        // Instantiate a sql persistence service
        SqlWorkflowPersistenceService sqlPersistenceService =
```

```
new SqlWorkflowPersistenceService(connectionString,
unloadOnIdle, ownershipDuration, reloadIntevral);
```

4. Now add the persistence service to the runtime by adding the following code below the code you just added:

```
workflowRuntime.AddService(sqlPersistenceService);
```

Modeling the CompensationWorkflow

You will add the CompensatableSequence activity and place a Code activity in it that mimics creating the order. Then you will add a Throw activity outside of the CompensatableSequence activity that simulates the accounting system raising an exception because of the order.

Follow the next steps to model the CompensationWorfklow.

1. Add a CompensatableSequence activity.

2. Add a Code activity to the CompensatableSequence activity, double-click it, and add the following to its handler:

```
Console.WriteLine("I update the CRM system with an order.");
```

3. Add a Throw activity below the CompensatableSequence activity and set its FaultType to System.Exception. It is important to add the Throw activity below the CompensatableSequence activity, for reasons demonstrated shortly.

Adding the Compensation Handler

Follow the next steps to add a compensation handler to the CompensatableSequence activity. The SequentialWorkflow (activity) will then enter the faulting state. This will lead to the SequentialWorkflow invoking the compensation handlers of its child activities. The child compensation handlers are called when a parent activity enters the faulting state and does not handle the exception (or rethrows it).

1. Right-click the CompensatableSequence activity and notice the View Compensation Handler option available to the CompensatableSequence activity (Figure 16.18).

2. Right-click the CompensatableSequence activity and select View Compensation Handler to switch to the compensation handler view (Figure 16.19).

FIGURE 16.18
Compensation
handler option
is available to
the Compensat-
ableSequence
activity.

FIGURE 16.19
Compensation
handler.

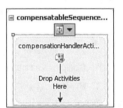

3. Add Code activity to the compensation handler, double-click it, and add the following code to its handler:

```
Console.WriteLine("I compensate an order.");
```

4. The CompensatableSequence activity compensation handler will be invoked by its SequentialWorkflow parent when the Throw activity places the workflow into a faulting state.

5. Press F5 to run the workflow, and you should see the text from the compensation handler sent to the console (Figure 16.20).

FIGURE 16.20
Compensation
handler.

Adding a `FaultHandlers` Activity to the Workflow and Rerunning the Workflow

Follow the next steps to add fault handling to the CompensationWorkflow. The compensation handler will no longer be called because the exception raised by the `Throw` activity is now captured and handled. Catching the exception also eliminates the `System.Exception` message being sent to the console that occurred in the prior compensation examples, which resulted from the unhandled exception.

1. Right-click the workflow away from any activity and select View Fault Handlers.

2. Add a `FaultHandler` activity and set its type to `System.Exception`.

3. Add a `Code` activity to the `FaultHandler` activity, double-click it, and add the following code to its handler:

```
Console.WriteLine("I am the workflow-level fault handler.");
```

   The workflow handles the error, so the compensation handler on the workflow's child activity is no longer invoked.

4. Press F5 to run the workflow, and you should see that the compensation handler is no longer invoked (Figure 16.21).

FIGURE 16.21
Compensation handler is no longer invoked because of workflow-level exception handling.

Adding a `Compensate` Activity to the Fault Handler

Follow the next steps to apply explicit compensation invocation by specifying which `CompensatableSequence` activity to invoke in the workflow exception handler. The `Compensate` activity allows explicit `CompensatableSequence` activity invocation and for exceptions to be handled without eliminating compensation from continuing.

1. Right-click the workflow away from any activity and select View Fault Handlers.

2. Add a `Compensate` activity to the `HandleFault` activity below the `Code` activity.

3. Set its `TargetActivityName` property to `compensatableSequenceActivity1`.

The workflow handles the error; however, because the Compensate activity points to a CompensatableSequence activity, it is still invoked.

4. Press F5 to run the workflow, and now both the fault handler and compensation handler execute (Figure 16.22).

Moving the Throw Activity into the CompensatableSequence Activity

Compensation can be applied only to activities that successfully completed. To demonstrate this, you will move the Throw activity into the CompensatableSequence activity below the Code activity. Because this prevents the CompensatableSequence from successful completion, its compensation handler is not invoked. This is so even though the exception handler explicitly invokes the CompensatableSequence handler.

Follow the next steps to move the Throw activity into the CompensatableSequence activity and prevent compensation from being invoked.

1. Move the Throw activity on the workflow into the CompensatableSequence activity below the Code activity.

2. Press F5 to run the workflow, and only the fault handler executes. The CompensatableSequence activity did not successfully complete, and therefore compensation is not triggered (Figure 16.23).

Transactions

Transactions maintain integrity by ensuring that a unit of work, such as a database update, completes in full or is rolled back. There are two ways to implement transactions in WF. The first uses the `TransactionScope` composite activity as a transactional boundary. Any activities included in a `TransactionScope` activity are enrolled in a standard .NET `System.Transactions.Transaction` transaction. This leverages all the benefits of a `System.Transactions.Transaction` transaction—such as the less-expensive local transaction when possible, and automatically promoting the transaction to a distributed transaction when necessary. See MSDN or another resource for more information on the `System.Transactions` namespace.

The second transactional method uses the `WorkflowEnvironment` type. You are in charge of updating a `WorkflowEnvironment.WorkBatch` property with the transactional work and implementing an `IPendingWork` interface. This is a lower-level way of performing transactions in WF and is not covered in this book.

The `TransactionScope` activity persists within the same transaction as the `TransactionScope` child activities. This ensures that the updates from activities in the `TransactionScope` activity and the child activities remain synchronized.

Under the hood, WF transactions are processed by a runtime service, which makes their behavior changeable to a degree. The DefaultWorkflowTransactionService is used by default (see Hour 17, "Learning Advanced Hosting"). The SharedConnection-WorkflowTransactionService can be used to avoid promoting transactions to distributed transactions when the tracking and persistence services both use the same SQL Server 2000 database. SQL Server 2005 and 2008 will not promote to a distributed transaction if both services use the same database, even when the DefaultWorkflow-TransactionService is used. Even if your application shares the same connection as the tracking and persistence service, transactions will be promoted to distributed transactions when updating application data (regardless of which out-of-the-box transaction service is used). The only way around this is to create a custom transaction service, which is also not covered in this book.

In this section, you will add a `Code` activity that updates a database to a `TransactionScope` activity. Then you will add a `Throw` activity below the `Code` activity to the same `TransactionScope` activity to halt the database from updating.

Performing Preliminary Setup

Follow the next steps to create the TransactionWorkflow.

1. Right-click ExceptionsCompensationAndTransactions in Solution Explorer and select Add, New Item.

2. Select Workflow in the left pane, select Sequential Workflow (with code separation), name it **TransactionWorkflow**, and click OK.

3. Set the host to post to the TransactionWorkflow.

4. Open the TransactionWorkflow (not the host) in code view and add the following using directive:

   ```
   using System.Data.SqlClient;
   ```

Model and Configure the TransactionWorkflow

The TransactionScope activity TransactionOptions property allows the transaction IsolationLevel and TimeoutDuration to be set. You will leave these set to their default values—Serializable and 30 seconds. Look for more details on these properties at MSDN or another source. The TransactionScope activity has no handlers. It either completes or fails. The TransactionScope activity's parent activity is the place to put exception and cancellation handlers, as needed.

Follow the next steps to model and configure the TransactionWorkflow.

1. Open the TransactionWorkflow in design mode.

2. Add a TransactionScope activity.

3. Add Code activity to the TransactionScope activity.

4. Double-click the Code activity and add the following code to its handler:

   ```
   string connectString =
       "Initial Catalog=TestTransaction;Data
   Source=localhost;Integrated Security=SSPI;";
       using (SqlConnection testConn = new
   SqlConnection(connectString))
       {
           SqlCommand cmd = testConn.CreateCommand();
           cmd.CommandText = "Insert Into TransactionTester (Data)
   Values ('DataToInsert')";
           testConn.Open();
           cmd.ExecuteNonQuery();
       }
   ```

5. Add a Throw activity below the Code activity (inside the TransactionScope activity) and set its type to System.Exception.

6. Add a Code activity below the TransactionScope activity.

7. Double-click the Code activity and add the following code to its handler:

```
Console.WriteLine("I made it past the TransactionScope.");
```

Running the SQL Script to Create the TestTransaction Database

There is a SQL script that will create a TestTransaction database. The database will have one table. The following directions show how to run the script in Microsoft SQL Server Management Studio.

Follow the next steps to run the SQL script to create the TestTransaction database.

1. Open Microsoft SQL Server Management Studio. Select your SQL Server and log in to the database.

2. Click File, Open, File, and then open the SQL script
`C:\SamsWf24hrs\Hours\Hour16ExceptionsAndCompensation\`
`SQL\CreateTestTransactionDatabase.sql`.

3. Click Execute or press F5 to run the query.

4. Verify that the `TestTransaction` database was created and that it has a Trans-actionTester table.

Running the Workflow

Follow the next steps to first run the workflow with the Throw activity disabled. The database should be updated. Then you will Enable the Throw activity and run it again. This time the database should not be updated.

1. Click the Throw activity and set its Enabled property to `false`.

2. Press F5 to run the workflow.

3. The Code activity following the TransactionScope activity should execute. The record should be added to the table and the message in the Code activity should be displayed (Figure 16.24).

4. Check the database to ensure the record was added.

5. Click the Throw activity and set its Enabled property to `true`.

FIGURE 16.24
Transaction
Scope activity
executes suc-
cessfully
because the
Throw activity is
not enabled.

6. Press F5 to run the workflow.

7. The Code activity should not execute. A new record should not be added to the table and an exception message should be displayed (Figure 16.25).

FIGURE 16.25
Transaction
Scope activity
does not exe-
cute success-
fully because the
Throw activity is
enabled.

8. Check the database to ensure that the record was not added.

CompensatableTransactionScope Activity

There is a CompensatableTransactionScope activity that allows transactions to be encapsulated, as does the CompensatableSequence activity. The CompensatableTransactionScope also allows a compensation handler to be applied to it so that error correction can be invoked after the fact. This activity is useful if the transaction completes successfully, but a downstream error requires that it be corrected or reversed. It can no longer be rolled back, so compensation must now be performed.

Summary

Three different handlers and transactions were covered in this hour. Let's review each with an emphasis on when they are appropriate.

Transactions are appropriate when it is plausible to lock a database while the transaction processes. They require you to have complete control of all the resources. The transaction then guarantees complete success or rolls everything back.

A `Cancellation` handler is designed for a very specific case. Activities are canceled only when the parent activity needs to close while one or more of its children are executing. This need may arise because of an exception or the need for early termination. This is why the cancellation example featured a `Parallel` activity with a `Delay` activity in one branch and a `Throw` activity in the other. When the `Throw` activity threw an exception, it caused its parent activity to fault, which then cancels or closes its currently executing child activities. The handler allows cleanup before the child activity is closed. Cancellation handlers are not mainstream error correction, but rather designed for a specific WF need.

Compensation and fault handlers are similar. Both allow error corrections to commence when an exception occurs. Nothing is automatically undone. The error correction performed is up to the author, whether choosing to send a retraction email or create a reversing database entry. The differences are that compensation can be called for only activities that have completed successfully, and the rules used by WF to invoke the compensation handlers are different from those for invoking fault handlers. It is up to you to choose the invocation scheme that works better for a given error.

Workshop

Quiz

1. *What is the purpose of a* `Throw` *activity?*

2. *What activity should encapsulate a call to a database update to ensure it updates in full or rolls back?*

3. *What is compensation used for?*

4. *What is the* `FaultHandler` *activity used for?*

5. *How do you ensure that exceptions are captured from most specific to least specific?*

6. *What is* `Cancellation` *used for?*

7. *What happens to activities placed in a* `TransactionScope` *activity?*

8. *If a divided-by-zero exception occurs in a branch of a* `Parallel` *activity, and the* `Parallel` *activity catches* `System.Exception` *and the workflow catches* `System.DivideByZeroException`, *will the* `Parallel` *activity or workflow catch the exception?*

Answers

1. The Throw activity is equivalent to the C# throw statement. It is used to create an exception. It is commonly used inside of handles to rethrow an exception captured by a lower-level handler.

2. TransactionScope activity.

3. The purpose of compensation is to allow already completed work to be corrected (or compensated for). This means that only units of work that have successfully completed are eligible for compensation.

4. To catch a specific type of exception.

5. Add most specific FaultHandler activities to FaultHandlers activity from left to right.

6. Used by currently executing child activities to perform cleanup when a parent activity needs to close while they are still executing.

7. They are enrolled in the same System.Transactions.Transaction transaction.

8. The Parallel activity.

HOUR 17

Learning Advanced Hosting

What You'll Learn in This Hour:

► **Workflow events**
► **Runtime services**
► **ManualWorkflowSchedulerService and threading**
► `InvokeWorkflow` **activity**
► **Host retention with the** `InvokeWorkflow` **activity**
► `InvokeWorkflow` **activity synchronous augmentation**

WF is not a server product. The `WorkflowRuntime` type can be hosted in any .NET 2.0 or later Windows application. Host applications communicate with the `WorkflowRuntime` through a set of events it exposes. The `WorkflowRuntime`'s capabilities are defined via pluggable runtime services. The pluggable runtime services are managed through a set of `WorkflowRuntime` methods. There is also a `WorkflowInstance` type that operates on a one-to-one basis with a workflow instance. It is, however, primarily a helper object that works through the workflow runtime.

Hour 3, "Learning Basic Hosting," briefly discussed the `WorkflowRuntime` and `WorkflowInstance` types. Hour 3 and other hours also covered selected runtime services and events as they became relevant. This hour summarizes all the runtime events and services. It then covers selected individual runtime events and services that have not yet been covered (or have been sparsely covered) in more detail. Threading and synchronous workflow loading are covered in a ManualWorkflowSchedulerService example.

The hour concludes by going through a new activity, the `InvokeWorkflow` activity, which allows a workflow to be called from another workflow. This activity is covered in this hour because its asynchronous operation creates many hosting considerations. Some of these considerations include keeping the host alive until the called workflow completes and ways to call workflows synchronously. Examples are shown that allow synchronous-like operation with the `InvokeWorkflow` activity and that keep the host alive.

Exploring `WorkflowRuntime` Events

All the workflow events—for example, `Started`, `Loaded`, `Unloaded`—are summarized in the following list. Then a sample application is used that illustrates the workflow instance life cycle as the instance transitions among events. The application also allows the user to manually execute the `Suspended`, `Resumed`, `Aborted`, `Terminateed`, `WorkflowCreated`, and `Started` events to see the effect of these events. Many of WF's workflow events have already been covered throughout the book and especially in Hour 3, where the `Persist`, `Load`, and `Unload` events were covered.

- ▶ **`ServicesExceptionNotHandled`**—Occurs when a runtime service registered with the `WorkflowRuntime` raises an unhandled exception.

- ▶ **`Started`**—Occurs when the workflow runtime is started.

- ▶ **`Stopped`**—Occurs when the workflow runtime is stopped.

- ▶ **`WorkflowAborted`**—Occurs when a workflow instance is aborted. The `WorkflowInstance.Abort` method may be called from the host. Aborting a workflow discards all work since the last persistence (save) point. The workflow instance is still active when it is returned to the persistence point.

- ▶ **`WorkflowCompleted`**—Occurs when a workflow instance successfully completes.

- ▶ **`WorkflowCreated`**—Occurs when a workflow instance has been created—more precisely, when `WorkflowInstance.CreateWorkflow` is called, which occurs before the workflow is actually started. The `Initialized` method, called when the workflow is created, is generally used to perform preparatory work, such as to set up a custom queue for any activity (see Hour 21, "Creating Queued Activities," and Hour 22, "Creating Typed Queued and `EventDriven`-Enabled Activities."

- ▶ **`WorkflowIdled`**—As seen in Hour 3, the workflow idled event is triggered when the workflow has to wait before continuing to process, because the next activities in its path are blocking activities, such as HandleExternalEvent and Delay.

▶ **WorkflowLoaded**—Occurs when the workflow instance is loaded back into memory by the persistence service and before the workflow begins reexecuting.

▶ **WorkflowResumed**—Occurs when execution of a workflow instance is resumed following a suspension. It is also called when dynamic update is performed before the workflow begins reexecuting.

▶ **WorkflowStarted**—Occurs when a WorkflowInstance.Start method is called to start workflow execution.

▶ **WorkflowSuspended**—Occurs when the WorkflowInstance.Suspend method is called, when the Suspend activity is executed, and when the workflow runtime suspends the workflow during dynamic update. The workflow will remain suspended until the WorkflowInstance.Resume method is called, unless it is suspended by the runtime during dynamic update, wherein the workflow is resumed during the update process.

▶ **WorkflowTerminated**—Occurs when the WorkflowInstance.Terminate method is called, when the Terminate activity is executed, and when an unhandled exception occurs on a workflow. Unlike aborted workflows, terminated workflows are complete and cannot be restarted.

▶ **WorkflowUnloaded**—Occurs when a workflow goes idle and the unload method is called from the idled event handler. Alternatively, workflows are unloaded when a workflow reaches an idle state and a persistence service is configured to unload workflows in an idle state registered with the host.

> The ServicesExceptionNotHandled, Started, and Stopped events operate on the workflow runtime. All other events are handled by the workflow runtime but are specific to a workflow instance. These workflow instance-level events are mediated by the runtime so it can ensure that the workflow is interacted with on the correct thread and that the workflow is ready to receive the event.

By the Way

Workflow Events Sample Application

A Windows Forms application and a workflow are used in this section to demonstrate workflow events. The workflow event handlers update the form display so that the workflows event transition can be followed. There are also buttons that permit you to manually Suspend, Resume, Abort, Terminate, Create, and Start a workflow.

Because you have already registered events and created event handlers, you will not do that again here. Running the application is the exercise. Figures 17.1 and 17.2 show the form and workflow that will be used.

FIGURE 17.1
Form used to demonstrate events.

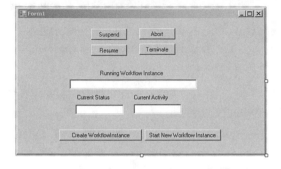

FIGURE 17.2
Workflow used to demonstrate events.

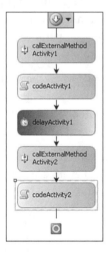

The workflow (Figure 17.2) is structured to send messages to the Windows Form that contain the name of the currently executing activity. The `CallExternalMethod` activities both send the current activity to the form. The `Delay` activity causes the workflow to unload during its brief timeout duration. The code activities both sleep for a couple of seconds to give you a chance to interact with the form buttons while the workflow remains on a given activity.

Running the `AdvancedHostingForms` Project

You will run the workflow four times in this section. The first time, you run it through its standard course. Then you will abort, suspend, and terminate the workflow.

Running the Workflow in Its Normal Course

Follow the next steps to run the workflow in its normal course.

1. Open the `EventHandlerSolution.sln` in the
   `C:\SamsWf24hrs\Hours\Hour17AdvancedHosting\EventHandlerSolution`
   directory.

2. Press F5 to run the application.

3. Click the CreateWorkflowInstance button. The status changes to Created, and
   the workflow instance ID text box is populated (Figure 17.3). The workflow is
   created but not yet started. In this state, workflow queues are updated (see
   Hours 21 and 22) and other preparatory work takes place.

FIGURE 17.3
Workflow in created state.

4. Click the StartNewWorkflowInstance button. The workflow is now started (or
   running). See Figure 17.4.

FIGURE 17.4
Workflow running.

5. The workflow will run through the activities. It will be unloaded when the
   `Delay` activity is reached. It will then reload after the `Delay` activity expires and
   execute the remaining activities until it completes (Figure 17.5).

FIGURE 17.5
Workflow in completed state.

The Current Activity text box on the form is populated with Before Delay, Probably
Delay, or After Delay. The Before Delay and After Delay messages are sent from

By the Way

> the `CallExternalMethod` activities before and after the `Delay` activity. The `Delay` activity cannot communicate with the form, so it is assumed that when the workflow is in the unloaded state it is in the `Delay` activity (thus, Probably Delay).

Suspending and Resuming the Workflow

Follow the next steps to suspend and resume the workflow.

1. Click the CreateWorkflowInstance button and then click the StartNewWorkflowInstance button. Click the Suspend button and the workflow will transition (it may take a few seconds) to the suspended state.

2. Click the Resume button and the workflow will complete.

Aborting the Workflow

Abort returns the workflow to its last persistence state. Therefore its only valid execution point is when executing the activities that follow the `Delay` activity. The `Delay` will cause the workflow to unload.

Follow the next steps to abort the workflow.

1. Click the CreateWorkflowInstance button and then click the StartNewWorkflowInstance button.

2. Wait until the workflow is executing the activities that follow the `Delay` activity and click the Abort button. The activities that follow the `Delay` activity will execute again. The abort caused the workflow execution to go back to the persistence point. The workflow then completes.

> The SQL workflow persistence service is registered with the runtime, and its `UnloadOnIdle` property is set to `true`. If this were not the case, the workflow would not automatically restart after the `Delay` activity expired.

Terminating the Workflow

Follow the next steps to terminate the workflow.

1. Click the CreateWorkflowInstance button and then click the StartNewWorkflowInstance button.

2. At any point, click the Terminate button and the workflow is terminated. Termination results in workflow completion, unlike abort, which goes back to the last persistence point.

Runtime Services

WF has to run pretty much anywhere Windows runs. This means that it has to run on client PCs with limited resources, on fault-tolerant server applications, and at many points between these two extremes. The large footprint it must support also produces unpredictability. It cannot assume that SQL Server, or any database for that matter, will be available to persist, which is most likely the case in many client scenarios. The need, then, is to create a workflow runtime that can be absorbed into various computing environments.

A large part of the solution is runtime services. Runtime services can be registered with the runtime to change the runtime. For instance, registering the persistence service with the WF runtime changes the WF runtime behavior to save workflows to a storage medium when they idle. The default persistence service saves workflows to SQL Server. You can, however, create your own persistence service that stores the workflows to XML files or to an Oracle database. The first is a good solution in many client scenarios, the latter in environments where Oracle is used.

The workflow runtime can run with no persistence service. It can run with the default SQL Persistence service. Or it can run with a custom persistence service. The end result is a runtime capable of supporting just about any persistence requirements. The persistence, tracking, and ExternalDataExchangeService services have been used extensively throughout the book to change the capabilities of the underlying runtime.

Other runtime services exist as well. Some control how WF schedules workflow instance, or WF's threading. Others determine how WF loads a workflow model into memory. You can create your own runtime services as well. One common use case for a custom runtime service is to create a common library (a type provider) that can then be accessed by workflow instances.

All WF runtime services inherit from the base `WorkflowRuntimeService` base class that provides general runtime service capabilities applicable to any runtime service. On top of the `WorkflowRuntimeService` is a class specific to one type of runtime service. For instance, the TrackingService provides functionality needed by all tracking services, and the `WorkflowLoaderService` is the base class for all loading services. The `SqlTrackingService` can be used as is to store tracking data in SQL Server.

The DefaultWorkflowLoaderService (described shortly) loads workflows into memory. The SqlTrackingService is sealed, and the DefaultWorkflowLoaderService is not.

Therefore, in most cases, if you were to create a custom tracking service, you would derive the TrackingService base class. If you want to create a custom workflow loading service, you can derive from either the base WorkflowLoaderService or the DefaultWorkflowLoaderService, depending on which one your requirements align with better.

As stated before, if you are interested in creating custom runtime services, see the tracking and persistence samples in the SDK.

Some runtime services are loaded by default. The DefaultWorkflowSchedulerService, for instance, is loaded by the runtime if no other scheduler service is registered. So, this service has been with us on all the workflows we've run, even though it has not been explicitly registered. Other runtime services, such as the tracking service, allow for multiple entry registration. Table 17.1 contains a listing and a few details on each of the runtime services.

TABLE 17.1   WF Runtime Services

Type	OOB Implementation(s)	Multiple	Description
Scheduling	DefaultWorkflowScheduler and ManualWorkflowScheduler	No	Determines whether workflow instances are called synchronously or asynchronously
Transactions	DefaultTransactionService and SharedWorkflow TransactionService	No	Determines whether tracking and persistence do or do not spawn a DTC
Tracking	SqlTrackingService	Yes	Permits some or all running workflow data to be captured and archived
Persistence	SqlWorkflowPersistence	Yes	Stores running workflow data: reliability and memory management

TABLE 17.1 WF Runtime Services

Type	OOB Implementation(s)	Multiple	Description
Data Exchange	ExternalDataExchange	Yes	Permits host/workflow data exchange
Workflow Loading	WorkflowLoaderService	No	Creates an in-memory activity tree for processing
Low Level Exchange	WorkflowQueuingService	N/A	Provides conduit to WF underlying communication scheme
Custom	N/A	Yes	Your runtime services

Let's first look at the out-of-the-box (OOB) runtime services offered by WF that have not been previously used (or used only sporadically).

Loading Service

The DefaultWorkflowLoaderService loads workflows, and it is employed by default. Therefore, unless you create your own workflow loading service, no action on your part is required. Your hosts will load and run workflows. However, just about everything in WF is extensible, including the way it loads a workflow to process. The default loading service can load either a .NET type or a XAML workflow (and a `.rules` file).

The `WorkflowLoaderService` (the base loading service class) can accept either a .NET type or an XML text reader. If you derive your own custom loader from the `WorkflowLoaderService` type, you can serialize any XML document and run it in WF. One of the benefits of XAML (or any XML) workflows is that they can be stored in a database. A custom loader could be created to retrieve the XAML workflow directly from a database. Another excellent reason for a custom loader is to directly load Visio diagrams into WF. Visio diagrams can be saved to XML, so the job of the custom loader would be to deserialize the Visio XML format into an object that WF could load. WF does this for XAML. For other XAML formats, you must create the object graph. See my blog at www.reassociates.net for an example that loads Visio diagrams from a database into WF where they are executed.

Workflow Queuing Service

All host-workflow communication operates on top of WF's internal workflow queues. All high level WF communication, including `ExternalDataExchangeService`, web services, and Windows Communication Foundation, is built on the `WorkflowQueuingService`. The WF queuing service is implemented by .NET delegates and is not a message queuing system (MSMQ). The low-level queuing was used briefly when you worked with state machine workflows and will be used more in Hours 22 and 23.

Scheduling (Threading) Services

WF ships with two scheduling services: the `DefaultWorkflowSchedulerService` and the `ManualWorkflowSchedulerService`. Both queue workflow instances and process them when a thread is made available. The biggest difference is that the default scheduling service runs workflows asynchronously, whereas the manual scheduling service runs them synchronously.

The default scheduling service uses CLR threadpool threads to run workflow instances on. Depending on the server configuration, about five runtime instances can be loaded and executing at any given time. This means actively running workflow instances. Persisted workflows do not count. You can control the number by setting its `MaxSimultaneousWorkflows` property.

By the Way

> Even if you have thousands of long-running workflows, it is unlikely that a large number of them will receive an external event or have a timer expire at the exact same time. Only during their execution bursts do workflows take a thread (assuming you have a persistence service registered). You can also have multiple WF runtime servers and multiple back-end persistence servers for scalability and durability reasons.

The `ManualWorkflowSchedulerService` runs workflows synchronously. In this case, a processing workflow blocks the host during the workflow's execution burst. The thread is returned to the host as soon as the workflow unloads, suspends, terminates, or otherwise completes. The host cannot run any more workflows until the workflow unloads from memory. This manual scheduling service is generally considered the correct choice when hosting the WF runtime in IIS because IIS has its own thread reuse mechanisms and it has very few spare threads. For these reasons, this service is sometimes used synonymously with using WF in ASP.NET (see Hour 18, "Working with Web Services and ASP.NET Hosting").

When using your Windows Forms application to host workflows in earlier chapters, you employed anonymous delegates to communicate across the workflow and the host thread. The Windows Forms application needed to host only one application at a time. It executed quickly enough that blocking would not adversely affect the UI. It actually would be preferable if it blocked, because it would prevent the user from trying to activate another event while the current one is processing. Therefore, employing the manual scheduling service from your Windows Forms host may have been preferable.

If you used a Windows Service application to host the WF runtime that fronted multiple Windows Forms hosts, the default scheduling would seem more logical because there would be a benefit to simultaneously process multiple workflows instances from different Windows Forms hosts.

Using the manual scheduling service will be demonstrated next.

All runtime services can be added via configuration. See Hour 3 for an example of general steps involved. The `SqlWorkflowPersistenceService` is used, but most of the steps to create a config file and how to access it are identical across all services. Then see MSDN for the precise details on the service you want to add via configuration.

Building the Scheduling Service Project

A workflow console project will be used to demonstrate the differences between the `DefaultWorkflowSchedulerService` and the `ManualWorkflowSchedulerService`. The console host will run three workflows. A variable in the host will determine which scheduling service is used. When running the application, you will see that each workflow executes in serial when the manual scheduling service is used and in parallel when the default scheduling service is used.

Ironically, a `Delay` activity is not used to cause the workflows to pause to make the workflows take longer to run and therefore make it easier to spot when they start and end. The `Delay` activity causes the workflow to unload, and they then appear to execute in parallel even when the manual scheduling service is used because of the short execution bursts (as will be demonstrated in this section).

A console application exists that will run three workflows.

Modeling and Configuring the Workflow

Follow these steps to model and configure the workflow.

1. Create a new Sequential Workflow Console Application project named **SchedulingServiceProject** and place it in the `C:\SamsWf24hrs\Hours\Hour17AdvancedHosting` directory.

2. Add two `Code` activities to the workflow.

3. Double-click the first Code activity and add the following code to its handler:

```
string instanceId = this.WorkflowInstanceId.ToString();
Console.WriteLine
    ("Workflow " + instanceId + " is in the first Code
activity at " +
DateTime.Now.TimeOfDay);
Thread.Sleep(5000);
```

4. Right-click Thread and select Resolve, using System.Threading.

5. Double-click the second Code activity and add the following code to its handler:

```
string instanceId = this.WorkflowInstanceId.ToString();
Console.WriteLine
    ("Workflow " + instanceId + " is in the second Code
activity at "
    + DateTime.Now.TimeOfDay);

Thread.Sleep(5000);
```

Updating the Host to Run Three Workflows

Follow the next steps to update the host to run three workflow instances.

1. Open Program.cs.

2. Add the following code to create a static variable (below the class's opening bracket).

```
static bool RunManual = false;
```

3. Replace the code that creates and starts the workflow instance with the following that starts three workflow instances.

```
WorkflowInstance instance1 =
workflowRuntime.CreateWorkflow(typeof(SchedulingServiceProject.Workflow1));
    instance1.Start();

WorkflowInstance instance2 =
workflowRuntime.CreateWorkflow(typeof(SchedulingServiceProject.Workflow1));
    instance2.Start();

WorkflowInstance instance3 =
workflowRuntime.CreateWorkflow(typeof(SchedulingServiceProject.Workflow1));
    instance3.Start();
```

4. Add the following code to pause the host (below the waitHandle.WaitOne(); line of code).

```
Console.WriteLine("Press Enter to continue.");
Console.Read();
```

Running the Workflow with the DefaultWorkflowSchedulerService

The DefaultWorkflowSchedulerService will be used because it is the default scheduling service and no other was specified. Each workflow's first Code activity will start at almost the same time, and the workflows will complete at near the same time as well, because all workflows run in parallel.

Follow the next steps to run the three workflow instances in parallel.

1. Press F5 to run the application.

2. You will see results similar to Figure 17.6 as the workflows run in interleaved fashion.

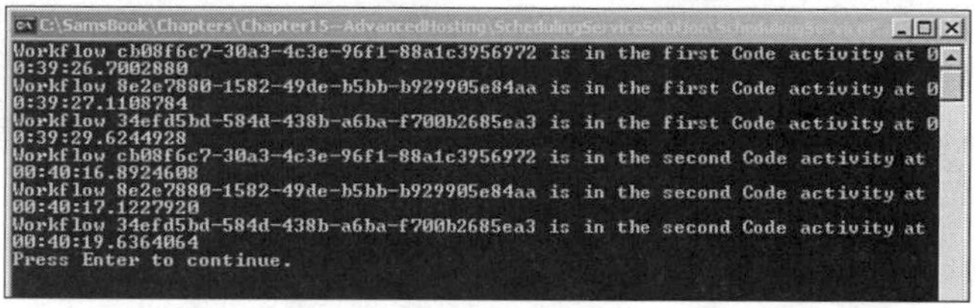

FIGURE 17.6
Parallel workflow execution.

Updating the Host to Use the ManualWorkflowSchedulerService

After switching to the ManualWorkflowSchedulerService, the first workflow will run until completion, then the second will run all the way through, and finally, the third will do the same. When instantiating the manual scheduler service, you will tell it to automatically reload when timers expire. The ManualWorkflowSchedulerService. RunWorkflow method must be used to run workflows under the manual scheduler service after the starting the workflow. The WorkflowRuntime.GetAllServices method will also be used to return the registered runtime services.

Follow the next steps to configure the host to run the workflows sequentially.

1. Open Program.cs.

2. Change RunManual to true.

3. Add the following code to the top of the Using block to instantiate the manual scheduling service.

```
ManualWorkflowSchedulerService manualScheduler =
    new ManualWorkflowSchedulerService(true);
```

4. Add the following code below the code you just added to load the manual scheduling service if RunManual is true:

```
        if (RunManual)
            workflowRuntime.AddService(manualScheduler);
```

5. Replace the code that creates and starts the workflow instances with the following that includes the extra step required by the manual scheduling service to run the workflow:

```
        WorkflowInstance instance1 =
workflowRuntime.CreateWorkflow(typeof(SchedulingServiceProject.Workflow1));
        instance1.Start();
        if (RunManual)
            manualScheduler.RunWorkflow(instance1.InstanceId);

        WorkflowInstance instance2 =
workflowRuntime.CreateWorkflow(typeof(SchedulingServiceProject.Workflow1));
        instance2.Start();
        if (RunManual)
            manualScheduler.RunWorkflow(instance2.InstanceId);

        WorkflowInstance instance3 =
workflowRuntime.CreateWorkflow(typeof(SchedulingServiceProject.Workflow1));
        instance3.Start();
        if (RunManual)
            manualScheduler.RunWorkflow(instance3.InstanceId);
```

6. Add the following code below the code that creates and starts the workflows that use the `WorkflowRuntime.GetAllServices` method to display all the services registered with the runtime.

```
        Console.WriteLine();
        Console.WriteLine("Registered Services");

        // Retrieve registered runtime servies.
        ReadOnlyCollection<object> services =
            workflowRuntime.GetAllServices(typeof(object));
        for (int i = 0; i < services.Count; i++)
        {
            Console.WriteLine(services[i].ToString());
        }
```

7. Right-click `ReadOnlyCollection`, select Resolve, using System.Collections.ObjectModel.

Running the Workflow with the ManualWorkflowSchedulerService

Follow the next steps to run the workflows in serial and see which runtime services are registered.

1. Press F5 to run the application.

2. You will see results similar to Figure 17.7 as the workflows run in serial.

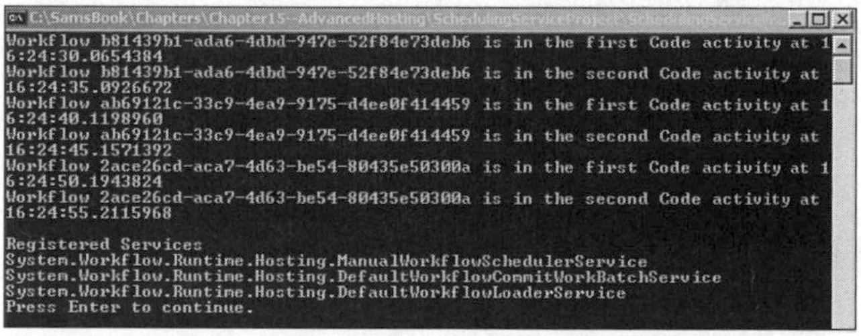

FIGURE 17.7
Serial workflow
execution.

As you can see, the default scheduler and default loader services are registered in addition to the manual scheduler service. The first two are registered by default.

Modifying the Workflow to Use Delay Activities

The Thread.Sleep statements in the Code activities do not trigger WF's unload and persist events. Therefore, they produce workflows that block for long periods of time within an activity. Follow the next steps to remove the Thread.Sleep statements from the Code activities and insert a Delay activity between the Code activities. The workflow—even though still using the manual scheduling service—will appear to run in parallel, because control is returned to the host each time the Delay activity begins and the workflow unloads.

1. Add the following static variable below the RunManual declaration:

```
        static string connectionString = "Initial Catalog=
WFTrackingAndPersistence;" +
            "Data Source=localhost; Integrated Security=SSPI;";
```

2. Add the following code to instantiate and register the persistence service at the beginning of the Using block:

```
            // Persistence parameter values
            bool unloadOnIdle = true;
            TimeSpan reloadIntevral = new TimeSpan(0, 0, 0, 20, 0);
            TimeSpan ownershipDuration = TimeSpan.MaxValue;

            // Instantiate a sql persistence service
            SqlWorkflowPersistenceService sqlPersistenceService =
                new SqlWorkflowPersistenceService(connectionString,
                unloadOnIdle, ownershipDuration, reloadIntevral);

            workflowRuntime.AddService(sqlPersistenceService);
```

3. Remove the Thread.Sleep lines of code from both Code activity handlers.

4. Add a `Delay` activity between the two `Code` (see Figure 17.8) activities and set its timeout duration to **00:00:10**.

5. Run the workflow and (as shown in Figure 17.9) it should appear to run in parallel even though the manual scheduling service is used. The SqlWorkflowPersistenceService should also be listed as one of the services.

InvokeWorkflow Activity

The `InvokeWorkflow` allows the current workflow to call another workflow in the current project or a referenced assembly. Configuring the activity itself is trivial; simply point it to a workflow in the current project or a referenced assembly. The issue, however, is that it calls the workflow asynchronously, and it is up to you to keep the host running while the invoked workflow executes, unless your scenario calls for fire-and-forget. If not, the host will prematurely complete and the called workflow will be aborted before completing. Most of the effort involved with using the `InvokeWorkflow` activity revolves around understanding the hosting implications. The next exercise will show how to use the `InvokeWorkflow` activity in fire-and-forget mode and then check that all workflows have finished executing before the host expires, thereby terminating any running workflows.

You will go through three exercises with the InvokeWorkflow activity. The first uses a standard host, and the host expires before the called workflow completes. The second shows one way to configure the host to ensure that it remains active until all workflows started by it complete. The third method emulates a synchronous call and passes parameters between the workflows. The third method requires quite a bit of code to achieve a synchronous call.

A third-party activity exists that allows workflows to be called synchronously. The third-party activity can be found at www.masteringbiztalk.com/blogs/jon/PermaLink,guid,33cfb35c-aca7-4a5e-8b35-ff983b0b83e4.aspx. This activity is not covered here, but is recommended if you need to perform synchronous calls. You will configure synchronous calls the hard way in this hour, so you will have that to fall back on.

InvokeWorkflow **Project: Host Prematurely Exits**

In the next subsection you create a workflow that runs and prematurely exits and in the following subsection you run the workflow in this configuration.

Create Simple Workflow with InvokeWorkflow **Activity**

Follow the next steps to create CallingWorkflow, which will call an already created CalledWorkflow using an InvokeWorkflow activity. The CalledWorkflow contains two Code activities that display identifying messages, and each has Thread.Sleep(30000) statements.

1. Open the InvokeWorkflowSolution solution in C:\SamsWf24hrs\Hours\Hour17AdvancedHosting\InvokeWorkflowSolution.

2. Right-click the project and select Add, Sequential Workflow.

3. Name the workflow **CallingWorkflow** and click Add.

4. Add a Code activity, double-click it, and add the following code to its handler:

```
        Console.WriteLine("Calling Workflow " +
this.WorkflowInstanceId.ToString() +
            " is executing in code activity 1");
```

5. Add another Code activity below the Code activity, double-click the new Code activity, and add the following code to its handler:

```
        Console.WriteLine("Calling Workflow " +
this.WorkflowInstanceId.ToString() +
            " is executing in code activity 2");
```

6. Add an InvokeWorkflow activity between the two Code activities.

7. Click the ellipsis in its TargetWorkflowProperty, select CalledWorkflow, and click OK.

8. Your workflow should now look like Figure 17.10, with the CalledWorkflow visible in the `InvokeWorkflow` activity.

FIGURE 17.10
Modeled Called-Workflow.

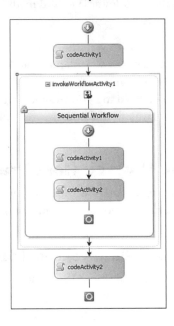

The `InvokeWorkflow` activity should show the called workflow. However, my experience is that it sometimes shows the workflow and at other times instructs to compile to see the called workflow. If it shows that the workflow is bound in the `InvokeWorkflow` activity `TargetWorkflow` parameter, it is probably okay.

Running the Fire-and-Forget Configuration

When running the workflow, the host will expire as soon as the calling workflow completes. It will not wait for the called workflow because it's invoked asynchronously. Both the calling and called workflows share the same host and workflow runtime. It is up to you, the host author, to ensure the host remains in scope until both workflows complete. To the workflow runtime, both workflows are the same. Again, it is up to you to add logic to the host to make sure it remains in scope as long as it needs to run the workflows spawned from it.

Follow the next step to run the workflow.

1. Press F5 to run the workflow and you will get results similar to Figure 17.11. (Even if you wait a couple of minutes, the second Code activity in the Called workflow will not execute.)

FIGURE 17.11
Host prematurely
completes.

InvokeWorkflow Project: Host Waits

Luckily, a pretty easy solution exists. The WorkflowRuntime provides a
GetLoadedWorkflows method that returns all loaded workflows. Checking that there
are 0 workflows in both the completed and terminated event handlers ensures there
are no active workflows. You may also want to insert the check for active workflow in
the persisted handler, but that depends on your implementation.

Follow the next steps to configure the host to wait until the called workflow completes.

1. Add the following code to the end of the WorkflowCompleted handler:

```
            Console.WriteLine("Workflow completed: " +
e.WorkflowInstance.InstanceId.ToString());
            if
(e.WorkflowInstance.WorkflowRuntime.GetLoadedWorkflows().Count == 0)
                waitHandle.Set();
```

2. Add the following code to the end of the WorkflowTerminated handler:

```
            if
(e.WorkflowInstance.WorkflowRuntime.GetLoadedWorkflows().Count == 0)
                waitHandle.Set();
```

3. Run the workflow again, and both the calling and called workflows should run
until completion (Figure 17.12):

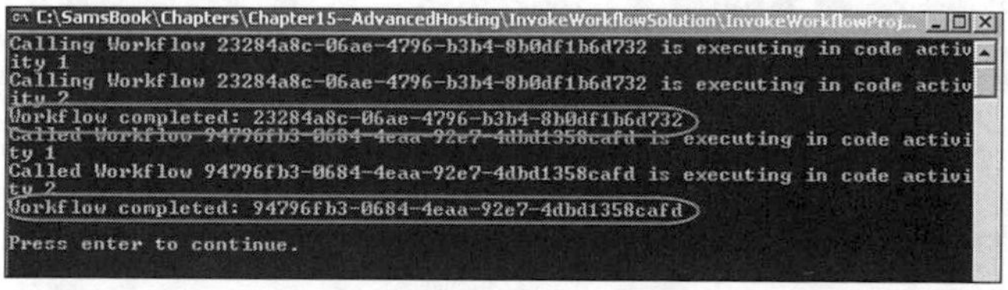

FIGURE 17.12
Host completes
both workflows
before exiting.

InvokeWorkflow Project: Synchronous Calls and Parameters

This option supports performing a synchronous-like call between the workflows. The
InvokeWorkflow activity is still used to call the workflow, and it still does so asynchronously. A HandleExternalEvent activity is added below the InvokeWorkflow
activity that waits for the called workflow to send completion notification. This mimics a synchronous call because the calling workflow does not move beyond the

HandleExternalEvent activity until the called workflow triggers the event when it is ready. Calling the workflow synchronously may also eliminate the need to check that all workflows are complete in the workflow runtime completed handler, if the CallExternalMethod activity performing the notification is the last activity in the called workflow.

Parameters are passed from the InvokeWorkflow to public properties on the called workflow. The CallingWorkflow can receive data back via the HandleExternalEvent activity as it waits for response from the CalledWorkflow.

Creating the Local Service Project

Follow the next steps to add a local service class that carries the status from the called to the calling workflow. It also includes the calling workflow instance ID for reasons described shortly.

1. Add a new Class Library project to the solution and name it **InvokeWorkflowLocalServices**.

2. Rename Class1.cs to **IInvokeWorkflowLocalService.cs** in the Solution Explorer. (If you are asked to rename all references in the project to reflect the name change, click Yes.)

3. Right-click the LocalService project in the Solution Explorer, select Add, Class, and name it **CompletedWorkflowEventArgs.cs**.

4. Add a reference to the workflow trio as well (System.Workflow.Activities, System.Workflow.Runtime and System.Workflow.ComponentModel).

Creating the Local Service Interface

Follow the next steps to code the local service.

1. Open IInvokeWorkflowLocalService.cs.

2. Replace the entire file contents with the following:

```
using System;
using System.Collections.Generic;
using System.Linq;
using System.Text;
using System.Workflow.Activities;

namespace InvokeWorkflowLocalServices
{
    [ExternalDataExchange]
    public interface IInvokeWorkflowLocalService
    {
```

```
        void CommunicateWorkflowStatus(Guid callingWorkflowInstancedId,
string
workflowStatus);
        event EventHandler<CompletedWorkflowEventArgs> WorkflowCompleted;
    }
}
```

Creating the `EventArgs` Class

Follow the next steps to code the `EventArgs` class.

1. Open `CompletedWorkflowEventArgs.cs` and replace the entire file contents with the following:

```csharp
using System;
using System.Collections.Generic;
using System.Linq;
using System.Text;
using System.Workflow.Activities;

namespace InvokeWorkflowLocalServices
{
    [Serializable]
    public class CompletedWorkflowEventArgs : ExternalDataEventArgs
    {
        private string workflowStatus;
        public string WorkflowStatus
        {
            get { return workflowStatus; }
            set { workflowStatus = value; }
        }

        // Instance Id is the calling workflow instance id
        public CompletedWorkflowEventArgs(Guid instanceId, string
workflowStatus)
            : base(instanceId)
        {
            this.workflowStatus = workflowStatus;
        }
    }
}
```

2. Right-click the `InvokeWorkflowLocalServices` project and select Build. Fix errors, if any.

Adding Parameters to the `InvokeWorkflow` Activity

The following steps are required to pass parameters using the `InvokeWorkflow` activity:

1. Create a dependency property in the `CalledWorkflow` named `CallingWorkflowInstanceId`. Public properties and dependency properties in the called workflow are available as parameters to the invoke workflow activity.

2. Create the `CallingWorkflowInstanceId` field in the calling workflow. This is the value that will be bound to the invoke workflow activity parameter and then passed to the called workflow.

3. Store the `WorkflowInstanceId` to the `CallingWorkflowInstanceId` field in the `InvokeWorkflow` activity `Invoked` handler.

Behind the scenes you are using `WorkflowParameterBinding`. You used it previously when passing parameters via dictionary object from the host. These public properties and dependency properties are accessed by way of the `InvokeWorkflow` activity rather than through a dictionary object.

1. Open `CalledWorkflow` and switch to the code view.

2. Right-click below the class opening bracket, select Insert Snippet, double-click Other, double-click Workflow, and double-click DependencyProperty—Property to insert a new dependency property. You should see the stub dependency property, and the text MyProperty should be highlighted.

3. Replace the highlighted MyProperty text with **CallingWorkflowInstanceId**, press Tab, and set its type to Guid. Then press Enter to exit the wizard.

4. Open `CallingWorkflow` and click the `InvokeWorkflow` activity. Its Properties window should now contain a `CallingWorkflowInstanceId` property as shown in Figure 17.13. (If it does not show, build the `InvokeWorkflowProject`.)

FIGURE 17.13
Invoke workflow activity now has `Calling Workflow InstanceId` property.

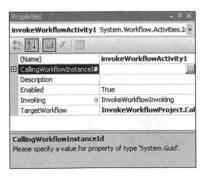

5. Click the ellipsis in the CallingWorkflowInstanceId property of the InvokeWorkflow activity. Select the Bind to New Member tab. Enter **CallingWorkflowInstanceId** as the name, and choose Field. Then click OK.

6. Enter **InvokeWorkflowInvoking** in the InvokeWorkflow activity's Invoking property. Then press Enter and enter the following code in the handler:

```
CallingWorkflowInstanceId = this.WorkflowInstanceId;
```

Updating the Calling and Called Workflows

Follow the next steps to add activities to the calling and called workflows.

1. Add a HandleExternalEvent activity to the CallingWorkflow below the InvokeWorkflow activity.

2. Add a CallExternalMethod activity to the end of the CalledWorkflow.

Configuring the CallExternalMethod Activity

Follow the next steps to configure the CallExternalMethod activity.

1. Open the CalledWorkflow in design mode.

2. Add a project reference from the InvokeWorkflowProject to the InvokeWorkflowLocalServices project.

3. Click the CallExternalMethod activity's InterfaceType property, select the IInvokeLocalService interface, and click OK.

4. Select the CommunicateWorkflowStatus method from the MethodName drop-down.

5. Click the ellipsis in the CallingWorkflowInstanceId property of the CallExternalMethod activity. Select the CallingWorkflowInstanceId property and click OK.

6. Enter **Completed** in the workflowStatus property.

Configuring the HandleExternalEvent Activity

Follow the next steps to configure the HandleExternalEvent activity.

1. Open the CallingWorkflow in design mode.

2. Click the HandleExternalEvent activity's InterfaceType property, select the IInvokeLocalService interface, and click OK.

3. Select the `WorkflowCompleted` event from the `EventName` property.

4. Build the entire solution.

5. Your updated workflows should now look like Figures 17.14 and 17.15.

FIGURE 17.14
Calling workflow
now blocks and
waits.

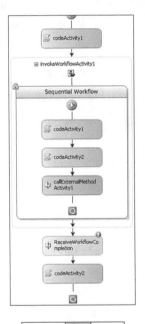

FIGURE 17.15
Called workflow
sends notifica-
tion.

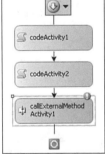

Now `CallingWorkflow` calls `CalledWorkflow` via `InvokeWorkflow` activity. Then `CallingWorkflow` completes synchronous call when it is ready by raising an event on `CallingWorkflow` via its `CallExternalMethod` activity.

Implement the Interface

The one major difference with this interface is that it is called from a different work-flow than it raises an event on. It is called from the `CalledWorkflow` and raises an event on the CallingWorkflow. This is why the WorkflowInstanceId was passed as a parameter in the InvokeWorkflow activity when the calling workflow invoked the called workflow. It is this passed instance ID that is now used when raising the event on the calling workflow.

Follow the next steps to create and code the local service.

1. Add a new class to the InvokeWorkflowProject and name it **InvokeWorkflowLocalService.cs.**

2. Replace the entire class contents with the following:

```
using System;
using System.Collections.Generic;
using System.Linq;
using System.Text;
using InvokeWorkflowLocalServices;

namespace InvokeWorkflowProject
{
    class InvokeWorkflowLocalService : IInvokeWorkflowLocalService
    {
        public event EventHandler<CompletedWorkflowEventArgs>
WorkflowCompleted;

        // The called workflow calls this method via a CallExternalMethod
activity.
        public void CommunicateWorkflowStatus(Guid
callingWorkflowInstanceId, string
workflowStatus)
        {
            // An event is now passed to the calling workflow to signify
completion
            // the called workflow.
            CompletedWorkflowEventArgs eventArgs =
                new CompletedWorkflowEventArgs
                (callingWorkflowInstanceId, workflowStatus);

            WorkflowCompleted(null, eventArgs);

        }

        }
    }
```

Registering the ExternalDataExchange Service with the Host

Follow the next steps to register the ExternalDataExchangeService with the host and run the workflow.

1. Add the following code to Program.cs in the InvokeWorkflowProject at the top of the using block to register the external data exchange service with the host.

```
                    InvokeWorkflowLocalService iwls = new
            InvokeWorkflowLocalService();
                    ExternalDataExchangeService eds = new
            ExternalDataExchangeService();
                    workflowRuntime.AddService(eds);
                    eds.AddService(iwls);
```

2. Right-click InvokeWorkflowLocalServices, select Resolve, and choose using InvokeWorkflowProject.

3. Press F5 to run the workflow, and you should receive results similar to Figure 17.16. Both workflows now end nearly simultaneously at the end of processing.

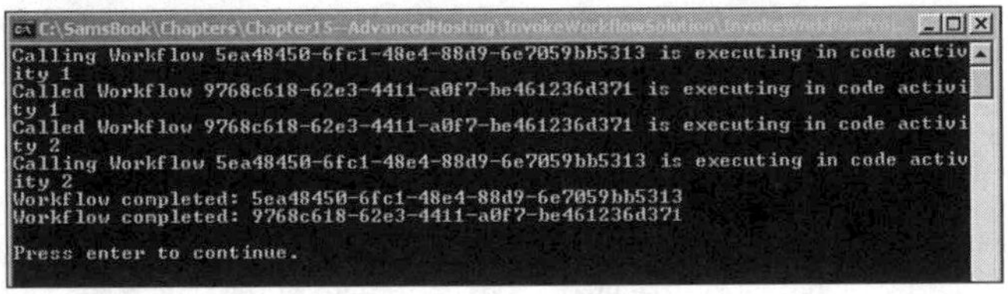

FIGURE 17.16
Invoke workflow activity augmented with CallExternal Method and HandleExtern alEvent activities.

Summary

A wide range of topics were covered in this hour. It started with the workflow event and then discussed workflow services. The threading differences between the manual and default scheduling services were shown, and the synchronous nature of the manual scheduler service was pointed out as a potential benefit in some UI scenarios. The InvokeWorkflow activity was covered in fire-and-forget mode and then in a mode in which the host waited for all workflows to complete before expiring. Finally, a synchronous-like experience was created by augmenting the InvokeWorkflow activity with CallExternalMethod and HandleExternalEvent activities. In the same step, parameters were passed from the calling to the called workflow and back.

Workshop

Quiz

1. *What is the purpose of the* ManualWorkflowSchedulerService?

2. *What is the purpose of the* WorkflowLoaderService?

3. *What is the major limitation of the* InvokeWorkflow *activity?*

4. *What is one of the major items you must provide a solution for when using the* InvokeWorkflow *activity?*

5. *What does the* Abort *event do?*

6. *Can terminated workflows be restarted?*

7. *What event should be used to indefinitely stop a workflow from executing that allows it to be restarted?*

8. *What does the* DefaultWorkflowSchedulerService *use to run workflows?*

9. *How can a WF host run thousands of workflows if the CLR threadpool on a given computer dedicates 5 or so threads to it?*

10. *What is the general purpose for runtime services?*

11. *What is the purpose of the* WorkflowQueuingService?

Answers

1. It runs workflows synchronously and is therefore frequently employed when IIS is the host.

2. The WorkflowRuntime delegates loading the workflow to be executed to it.

3. It can only call workflows asynchronously.

4. Keeping the calling workflow blocked while awaiting the response.

5. It returns the workflow to its last persistence state (like an undo in a word processor).

6. No. Terminated workflows are unsuccessfully completed.

7. The Suspend event.

8. The CLR threadpool.

9. At any given time, most workflows are persisted and therefore do not require any CLR threadpool threads.

10. To allow the WF runtime to add additional features necessary for a given application or host.

11. It is the underlying communication infrastructure for WF. Even when local services and other higher-level abstractions are used, under the hood it is the WorkflowQueuingService that is moving data into and out of WF.

HOUR 18

Working with Web Services and ASP.NET Hosting

What You'll Learn in This Hour:

▶ Exposing a workflow as a web service using the `WebServiceInput` and `WebServiceOutput` activities

▶ Calling a web service from a workflow using the `InvokeWebService` activity

▶ Returning SOAP faults via the `WebServiceFault` activity

▶ A description of how workflows are published as web services

▶ A description of the `WebServiceProxy` property

▶ Hosting WF in an ASP.NET application

The first part of this hour walks you through the creation of two workflows. The first is exposed as a web service. The second is capable of calling a web service from a workflow. The second workflow then calls the first to bring it all together. The workflow published as a web service receives a customer ID and then returns approved or rejected. The calling workflow uses an `InvokeWebService` activity to call the published workflow. It passes the customer ID in the call and receives the results.

The next part of this hour shows you how to use SOAP faults on the service provider and the service consumer.

The third part of this hour discusses the files that are generated when publishing a workflow as a web service. You also learn how to customize communication between the client and the service to add security and other needed components in web service communication.

The fourth and final part of this hour covers hosting WF, or the `WorkflowRuntime`, in an ASP.NET application.

Creating the Solution and Projects

See Hour 2, "A Spin Around Windows Workflow Foundation," if you need help creating solutions or projects.

1. Create a new blank solution in the `C:\SamsWf24hrs\Hours\Hour18WorkingwithWebServicesandAspNet` directory and name it `WebServiceWorkflows`.

2. Add a Sequential Workflow Library project to the solution and name it `PublishedWorkflows`.

3. Rename `Workflow1.cs` to `PublishedWorkflow.cs`.

4. Add a Sequential Workflow Console Application project to the solution and name it `CallWebServices`.

5. Rename `Workflow1.cs` to `CallWebService.cs`.

Creating a Workflow and Publishing It as a Web Service

This section contains a brief summary of what is required to create and publish a workflow as a web service. The activities mentioned will be described shortly. Publishing a workflow as a web service requires using a `WebServiceInput` activity that is bound to the web service proxy that receives the call from the calling web service. If the web service call is synchronous, there will be a `WebServiceOutput` activity as well that returns the results to the calling web service. The final two steps are to create an interface that serves as a contract for both the `WebServiceInput` and `WebServiceOutput` activities. Finally, you must publish the workflow as a web service.

Let's now walk through the steps to create and publish a workflow as a web service.

Creating Dependency Properties

Follow the next steps to create the dependency properties that will hold the `CustomerId` passed to the web service and the `CustomerStatus` returned from the web service.

1. Open the PublishedWorkflow in code view.

2. Right-click below the constructor, select Insert Snippet, double-click Other, double-click Workflow, double-click DependencyProperty—Property, name it **CustomerId**, and press Enter to accept the remaining defaults.

3. Right-click below CustomerId DependencyProperty, select Insert Snippet, double-click Other, double-click Workflow, double-click DependencyProperty—Property, name it **CustomerStatus**, and press Enter to accept the remaining defaults.

Modeling and Publishing the Workflow

Follow the next steps to model and publish the workflow as a web service. The workflow will receive the call from the web service through the WebServiceInput activity, evaluate the CustomerId, and return approved or rejected depending on which CustomerId is received.

1. Open the PublishedWorkflow in design mode.

2. Add a WebServiceInput activity to the workflow.

3. Add an IfElse activity below the WebServiceInput activity, name it **CheckApprovalStatus**, name the left branch **Approved**, and the right branch **Rejected**.

4. Place a Code activity in each branch of the IfElse activity.

5. Add a WebServiceOutput activity below the IfElse activity. The modeled and unconfigured workflow should look like Figure 18.1.

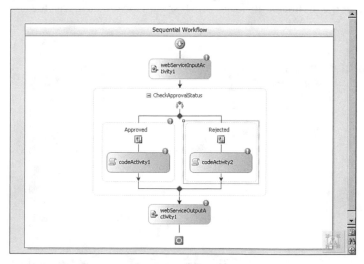

FIGURE 18.1
Modeled and unconfigured PublishedWork-flow.

Creating the Interface to Produce the WSDL

Follow the next steps to create a standard .NET interface, not a WF-specific local service. The interface will contain the method name exposed by the WebServiceInput activity, the value received as a parameter by the `WebServiceInput` activity, and the value returned by the `WebServiceOutput` activity. The value returned is expressed as an out parameter.

1. Right-click the PublishedWorkflow project and select Add, New Item; choose Interface, and name it `ICustomers`.

2. Add the following code to the interface that signifies CustomerId will be sent to the PublishedWorkflow web service, and the CustomerStatus will be returned from the PublishedWorkflow web service.

   ```
   void CheckCustomer(string CustomerId, out string CustomerStatus);
   ```

Configure the `WebServiceInput` Activity

The `WebServiceInput` activity exposes the workflow as a web service. It receives the method and parameter information from the interface you just created. In addition to configuring method and parameter related information, the `IsActivating` property and the `InputReceived` properties must also be set.

Follow the next steps to configure the `WebServiceInput` activity.

1. Click the `WebServiceInput` activity, click the ellipsis in its `InterfaceType` property, click the + next to Current Project, and select the `ICustomers` interface in the middle of the form, which should look like Figure 18.2.

FIGURE 18.2
`WebServiceIn-put` activity interface selection form.

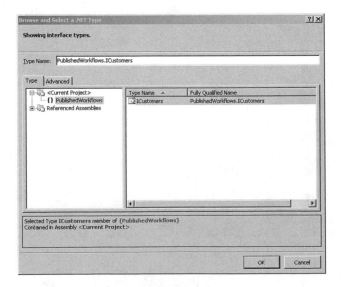

2. Click OK.

3. Click the drop-down in the MethodName property and choose the CheckCus-tomer method.

4. Click the ellipsis in the CustomerId property of the WebServiceInput activity and select the CustomerId property from the list of variables in the dialog. This binds the workflow property value to the activity property.

5. Click the InputReceived property (that points to a handler that is executed when the CheckCustomer method of the web service is called), enter **WebServiceExecuting**, press Enter, and then enter the following code in the handler to write to the event log the time the CheckCustomer method is invoked:

```
System.Diagnostics.EventLog.WriteEntry("PublisedWorkflow",
    "CheckCustomer method invoked at" + DateTime.Now);
```

6. Click the drop-down in the IsActivating property and select True. This tells WF that this WebServiceInput activity starts a new workflow instance. There may be WebServiceInput activities on the workflow that receive information mid-process and therefore do not trigger a new workflow instance.

7. The property window for your WebServiceInput activity should now look like Figure 18.3.

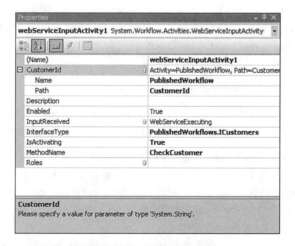

FIGURE 18.3
WebServiceIn-put activity con-figured property window.

Configuring the IfElse Activity

Follow the next steps to configure the IfElse activity and its child activities.

1. Click the Approved branch of the IfElse activity. Then click its Condition prop-erty, select Declarative Rule Condition, click the + that appears next to the

Condition property, and enter **ApprovedCustomerRule** in the `ConditionName` property. Click the ellipsis in the `ConditionName` property, click the Edit button (to update the `ApprovedCustomerRule`), and enter the following in the dialog box.

```
CustomerId=="000001"
```

2. Click OK twice to exit the dialogs.

3. Double-click the `Code` activity in the Approved branch and enter the following in its handler:

```
CustomerStatus = "Approved";
```

4. Double-click the `Code` activity in the Rejected branch and enter the following in its handler:

```
CustomerStatus = "Rejected";
```

Configuring the `WebServiceOutput` Activity

The `WebServiceOutput` activity is mandatory for all incoming, synchronous web service calls. Its purpose is to return results for the `WebServiceInput` activity that it is bound to.

If you look at the workflow, you will see a red exclamation mark on the `WebServiceInput` activity, even though all necessary properties it exposes have been set. This is so because it has yet to be bound to a `WebServiceOutput` activity, and because this is a synchronous web service (per the interface), being bound is mandatory.

Follow the next steps to configure the `WebServiceOutput` activity.

1. Click the `WebServiceOutput` activity, select the drop-down in its `InputActivityName` property, and select webServiceInputActivity1.

2. Click the `SendingOutput` property (which points to a handler that is executed when the GetCustomer method of the web service responds), enter **WebServiceReturning**, press Enter, and then enter the following code in the handler to write to the event log the time that the CheckCustomer method is returning results to the consumer:

```
System.Diagnostics.EventLog.WriteEntry("PublishedWorkflow",
    "CheckCustomer method returning results at" + DateTime.Now);
```

3. Click the ellipsis in the `CustomerStatus` property of the `WebServiceOutput` activity and select the `CustomerStatus` from the list of variables. Then click OK.

4. The property window for your `WebServiceOutput` activity should now look like Figure 18.4.

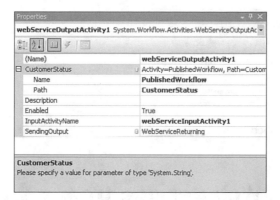

FIGURE 18.4
`WebService-`
`Output` activity
configured prop-
erty window.

Publishing the Workflow as a Web Service

Follow the next steps to publish the workflow as a web service.

1. Right-click the `PublishWorkflow` project and select Publish as Web Service, as shown in Figure 18.5.

FIGURE 18.5
The Publish as
Web Service
choice.

2. You should see a dialog that says the workflow has been successfully published. If so, click OK. Otherwise, look at any error messages and try to resolve the problem.

3. You should now see a `PublishedWorkflows_WebService` project in your solution that contains the files shown in Figure 18.6.

The files are described in the "Exploring Generated Project and Cookie Usage" section later in the hour.

Calling a Web Service from a Workflow

You are going to create a workflow and configure it to call a web service. It will call the workflow you just published as a web service. The workhorse in this section is the `InvokeWebService` activity that sets off the standard .NET Web Reference wizard that creates a proxy the client can use to call the remote web service.

Creating Dependency Properties

Follow the next steps to create the `CustomerId` and `CustomerStatus` dependency properties. The client workflow sets the `CustomerId` property, passes it to the service, and receives the `CustomerStatus` property back from the service.

1. Open the `CallWebService` code-beside file.

2. Right-click below the constructor, select Insert Snippet, double-click Other, double-click Workflow, double-click DependencyProperty—Property, name it **CustomerId**, and press Enter to accept the remaining defaults.

3. Right-click below CustomerId DependencyProperty, select Insert Snippet, double-click Other, double-click Workflow, double-click DependencyProperty—Property, name it **CustomerStatus**, and press Enter to accept the remaining defaults.

Modeling the Workflow

Follow the next steps to place an `InvokeWebService` activity and a `Code` activity on the workflow. Because of the way the web reference wizard works, you will also partially configure the `InvokeWebService` activity.

1. Open the CallWebService workflow in design mode.

2. Add an InvokeWebService activity, and you will see the standard .NET Add a Web Reference dialog shown in Figure 18.7.

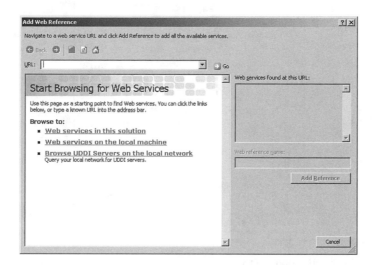

FIGURE 18.7
.NET Web Service reference dialog.

3. Click the web service in this solution link in the middle of the form.

4. Click the PublishedWorkflows.PublishedWorkflow link.

5. Click the AddReference button (leave the default localhost web reference name) and ignore the namespace warning if you receive one.

6. Add a Code activity below the InvokeWebService activity.

7. Your workflow should now look like Figure 18.8.

Finishing Configuring the InvokeWebService Activity

Follow the next steps to complete configuring the InvokeWebService activity.

1. In the invokeWebServiceActivity1, click the drop-down in the MethodName property and select the CheckCustomer method.

2. Click the ellipsis in the ReturnValue property of the InvokeWebService activity and select the CustomerStatus property. Then click OK.

3. Enter 000001 into the CustomerId property to hard-code this value to the property.

FIGURE 18.8
Workflow that
calls a web
service.

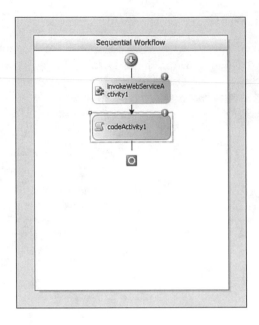

4. Double click the Code activity and add the following to its handler:

```
Console.WriteLine("The customer is " + CustomerStatus);
```

Running the Basic Workflow Solution

Follow the next steps to pause the host and run the workflow.

1. Modify `Program.cs` in the `CallWebServices` project to pause the host. If you need help, see Hour 3, "Learning Basic Hosting."

2. Set the `CallWebServices` project as the startup project, and press F5 to run the solution. The customer will be approved, as shown in Figure 18.9.

FIGURE 18.9
Web service
results with
approval
granted.

3. Enter a different value in the `CustomerId` property and run the solution. This time the customer will be rejected.

Additional Workflow Topics

You learned the very basics of invoking a web service from a workflow and publishing a workflow as a web service in the previous section. In this section you will learn about some of the more advanced topics: SOAP faults, web service publisher generated files, and using the WebServiceProxy object. SOAP faults will be covered in a hands-on lab typical of this book. The other two topics will be summarized only, with the intent of pointing you in the right direction. This balance was chosen because although the latter two are advanced topics, being aware of them is important because they are frequently important parts of real-world applications.

Working with SOAP Faults

You will modify the PublishedWorkflow to check for CustomerIds with a length of 0. When a CustomerId with a length of 0 is found, a SOAP fault will be sent to the calling workflow. To enable this, a new IfElse activity named CheckForFaults is added to the workflow and the existing CheckApprovalStatus is added to the left branch of the new CheckForFaults IfElse activity. A SOAP fault is thrown if the length of the CustomerId is 0.

The WebServiceFault activity does not throw an exception in the workflow that it occurs in. It sends an exception to the calling workflow. Therefore, a workflow will continue executing in its normal sequential path after processing a WebServiceFault activity. You should use a Throw activity to throw an exception if you want internal WF exception handling to be triggered.

The calling workflow must catch the exception and handle it. Therefore, the workflow published as a web service throws a fault, and the fault is returned to the client workflow as a SOAP exception. Finally, the client workflow must catch and handle the exception.

Modeling the Web Service Workflow to Include SOAP Faults

Follow the next steps to reconfigure the workflow to process SOAP faults.

1. Add an IfElse activity to the PublishedWorkflow above the current CheckApprovalStatus IfElse activity and name it CheckForFaults.

2. Drag and drop the existing CheckApprovalStatus IfElse activity into the left branch of the CheckForFaults IfElse activity you just placed on the workflow.

3. Drag and drop the `WebServiceOutput` activity already on the workflow and place it in the left branch of the `CheckForFaults` `IfElse` activity below the `CheckApprovalStatus` `IfElse` activity.

4. Add a `WebServiceFaultActivity` to the right branch of the `CheckForFaults` `IfElse` activity.

5. Add a `Code` activity below the `WebServiceFault` activity and add the following code to its handler (which, a bit counterintuitively, will be executed even though it follows the `WebServiceFaultActivity`):

```
System.Diagnostics.EventLog.WriteEntry("PublishedWorkflow",
    "After SOAP Fault " + DateTime.Now);
```

6. Your workflow should now look like Figure 18.10:

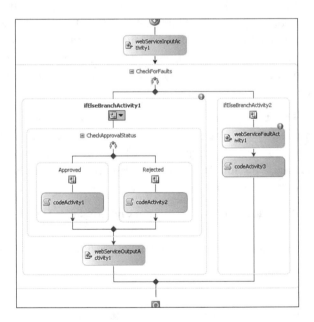

FIGURE 18.10
PublishedWorkflow with fault handling `IfElse` activity added.

In the first version of the workflow, there was one `WebServiceInput` activity and one `WebServiceOutput` activity. They were a singular pair that always completed with execution of the `WebServiceOutput` activity (barring an exception). Now things are a bit more complex because the `WebServiceFault` activity is also a valid partner to the `WebServiceInput` activity. When a `WebServiceInput` activity is partnered with both a `WebServiceOutput` activity and a `WebServiceFault` activity, it is up to you to model the workflow so that exactly one will execute on a given workflow instance.

If processing works, the results must be returned to the calling workflow via the `WebServiceOutput` activity. If processing does not work, they must be returned via the `WebServiceFault` activity. That is why we placed one of these activities in the left branch of the `CheckForFaults` `IfElse` activity and the other in the right branch.

Configuring the `WebServiceFault` Activity

The `WebServiceFault` activity contains two primary properties: `InputActivityName` and `Fault`. The first is the `WebServiceInput` activity it partners with. The second is a variable of type exception. The last property, `SendingFault`, is an optional handler you can use to log or perform other tasks when the `WebServiceFault` activity executes.

Follow the next steps to configure the `WebServiceFault` activity.

1. Go to the code-beside file of the `PublishedWorkflow` and enter the following code below the constructor to create a variable of type exception:

   ```
   public Exception ex = new Exception();
   ```

2. Click the ellipsis in the `Fault` property of the `WebServiceFault` activity and select the ex property. Then click OK.

3. Click the drop-down in the `InputActivityName` property and choose the `webServiceInputActivity1` property.

Configuring the Condition

Follow the next steps to configure the `NullCustomerRule`.

1. Click the drop-down in the `Condition` property of the left branch of the `IfElse` activity, select Declarative Rule Condition, click the + that appears next to the Condition property, and enter **NullCustomerRule** in the `ConditionName` property. Click the ellipsis in the `ConditionName` property, click the Edit button (to update the `NullCustomerRule`), and enter the following in the dialog box:

   ```
   this.CustomerId.Trim().Length != 0
   ```

2. Click OK to close all open dialogs.

Receiving the SOAP Fault in the Client Workflow

No additional soap fault activities need to be added to the client workflow. It simply must be able to receive and handle a SOAP fault. Remember to switch to the client workflow. Follow the next steps to configure the client workflow to receive a SOAP fault.

1. Go to the code-beside file of the `CallWebService` workflow and enter the following code below the constructor to create a variable of type exception:

   ```
   public Exception ex = new Exception();
   ```

2. Right-click the `CallWebService` workflow away from any activity and select View Fault Handlers.

3. Add a `FaultHandler` activity to the filmstrip near the top of the `FaultHandlers` activity.

4. Set its `FaultType` to `SOAPException` by clicking the ellipsis, selecting System.Web.Services, SOAPException, and clicking OK.

5. Add a `Code` activity to the `FaultHandler` and add the following to its handler:

   ```
   Console.WriteLine("Workflow faulted");
   ```

See Hour 16, "Working with Exceptions, Compensation, and Transactions," for instructions on extracting more information from the exception.

Running the SOAP Fault Workflow Solution

Follow the next steps to run the solution with the newly configured SOAP fault-enabled workflow.

1. Right-click the workflow and select View SequentialWorkflow.

2. Click the `InvokeWebService` activity, enter **000001** in the `CustomerId` property, and run the solution. Approved should be returned, as it was when you ran the workflow previously.

3. Delete the content in the `CustomerId` property and run the solution. This time you will see the fault message you just entered in the console window (Figure 18.11).

FIGURE 18.11
Returned fault
message.

Exploring Generated Project and Cookie Usage

The Publish as Web Service Wizard created an ASP .NET Web Service project, which can be published as a website to your chosen version of IIS. First, you learn about cookie usage, and then each of the project files are summarized (as seen earlier in Figure 18.6).

Cookie Usage

WF workflows exposed as web services may run for long periods of time and therefore persist, as is the case with any workflow. The runtime needs the workflow instance ID to reinstate a workflow. Therefore, the client must store and forward the workflow instance ID. By default, this is achieved through the use of client-side cookies that hold the workflow instance ID. The WorkflowWebHostingModule (referenced in the Web.config file) module routes the workflow instance ID between the client cookie and the workflow web service. If client cookies are not permitted, you must use custom SOAP or HTTP handlers to add a key to the SOAP header to exchange the workflow instance ID, which is not covered in this book.

Web.config File

The Web.config file contains two sections related to WF. The first is contained in the WorkflowRuntime section, where the ManualWorkflowSchedulerService and Default-WorkflowCommitWorkBatchService runtime services are added. The first sets the threading operations to better fit the IIS host that runs workflows published as web services (described in Hour 17, "Learning Advanced Hosting"). The second controls transactions. The second relevant section contains a reference to the aforementioned WorkflowWebHostingModule module.

ASMX File

As with a typical .NET web service, this file contains a reference to the web service class.

DLL File

WF activities have the capability to produce source code as part of the activity programming model (which is briefly discussed in Hour 20, "Creating Basic Custom Activities"). The WebServiceOutput activity takes advantage of this capability to produce a proxy object. Unlike most proxy generators on .NET, however, there is only a DLL produced; there is no source code.

One problem with the generated code is that it embeds http://tempuri.org as the namespace. This is a problem because of the lack of source code. Fortunately, at least two workarounds exist. The first is to create your own proxy class that derives from WorkflowWebService, which communicates between the workflow and the web service and starts the runtime. The second involves changing the Registry to not delete the source and then manually modifying the namespace. Although neither of these topics is covered in this book, some resources follow.

The following link is to a blog entry that contains the source code to build a web service workflow proxy that derives from WorkflowWebService. Looking at it offers the added bonus of showing you what happens under the hood when you publish a workflow via the Publish as Web Service Wizard.

www.request-response.com/blog/PermaLink,guid,21c95c2c-63d7-44f6-8357-1be0ecb6f264.aspx

The next link contains directions to change the Registry and manually change the proxy source code.

http://blogs.msdn.com/pandrew/archive/2006/10/25/extending-the-wf-publish-as-web-service-or-get-rid-of-tempura-org.aspx

Exploring the WebServiceInvokeActivity.WebServiceProxy Property

Our client workflow is connected to the workflow web service through a web reference. It communicates via HTTP and does not perform any type of authentication. If you do need to perform authentication, set the URL dynamically, encrypt the transmitted data, access Web Service Enhancements 3.0, or perform any of a number of other functions, you can use the WebServiceInvokeActivity.WebServiceProxy property. We will not completely perform any of these tasks but I will show how to access the WebServiceProxy property.

You can access the WebServiceProxy property from the Invoking property of the InvokeWebService activity. You cast the InvokeWebServiceEventArgs.WebServiceProxy passed into the handler to the web reference name plus the workflow (localhost.PublishedWorkflow_WebService in this case).

Follow the next steps to explore the WebServiceProxy property.

1. Enter **InvokeWebServiceInvoking** in the Invoking property, and enter the following code in the handler to generate the URL at runtime:

   ```
   (e.WebServiceProxy as localhost.PublishedWorkflow_WebService).Url =
   "http://mydoman.com/workflowwebservice.asmx";
   ```

2. Enter a period (.) before the .URL to see the many items available to you from the WebServiceProxy. All these properties are available to you when communicating to a web service.

Again, the `WebServiceProxy` property will be essential to you in many real-world applications. This concludes its brief coverage here.

Learning ASP.NET Hosting

You can also call a workflow from an ASP.NET application. The workflow then provides the "logic" on behalf of the ASP.NET application. IIS is a stateless server architected to provide high scalability. It also manages resources, including threads, stringently. Therefore, in most cases you should use the `ManualWorkflowSchedulerService`, as described earlier in this hour (and in detail in Hour 17, "Learning Advanced Hosting") to run workflows synchronously on the same thread used by the ASP.NET application.

Although ASP.NET applications are stateless, the `WorkflowRuntime` should be started only once during the ASP.NET application's lifecycle to avoid the hit that would be incurred if was instantiated on each page request. Therefore, you will load it in the `Gloabal.asax` page.

This section covers running a workflow (or more specifically, hosting the `WorkflowRuntime`) in an ASP.NET application. This is different than calling a workflow published as a web service. Doing the latter involves calling a web service. Therefore, the rules for calling a workflow published as a web service from an ASP.NET application are largely the same as calling any other web service from an ASP.NET application.

> Most of the underlying logic used to host a workflow in ASP.NET is explained in previous hours that cover hosting. See Hour 3, "Learning Basic Hosting" for an introduction to hosting and Hour 17 for more advanced coverage, including details on the scheduling service used in this section to run workflows in ASP.NET.

Opening the Existing Solution and Creating the ASP.NET Project

In this section you open an existing solution that already has a workflow. The workflow checks whether the order amount that you will pass in from the host form you will create is less than 100. If so, the order is approved; otherwise it is rejected. The workflow has two properties, `OrderAmount` and `OrderStatus`. The first, the `OrderAmount`, is sent from the host web form you create to the workflow in a

Dictionary object. It is then evaluated by the workflow. The second, the
OrderStatus is updated by the workflow to either approved or rejected, subject to the
workflow's evaluation. The workflow completed handler implemented by the host
retrieves the OrderStatus. The result is displayed on the web form you create.

Follow the next steps to open the solution and add the ASP.NET project.

1. Open the AspNetHostingSolution in the
   C:\SamsWf24hrs\Hours\Hour18WorkingwithWebServicesandAspNet\AspNet
   HostingSolution directory.

2. Add an ASP.NET Web Application project, which can be found by expanding
   C# and Web. Name the project **AspWfRuntimeHost.**

3. Add a reference from the AspWfRuntimeHost project to the workflow trio:
   System.Workflow.Activities, System.Workflow.ComponentModel, and
   System.Workflow.Runtime. Then add a reference to the
   AspNetHostedWorkflowProject.

Instantiating the `WorkflowRuntime`

The WorkflowRuntime is instantiated and configured in the Global.asax OnStart
handler. The instantiated WorkflowRuntime is stored to an application level variable
so that it can be accessed throughout the ASP.NET application. The
WorkflowRuntime is also configured to use the ManualWorkflowSchedulerService.

Follow the next steps to instantiate the WorkflowRuntime in the Global.asax file.

1. Right-click the AspWfRuntimeHost in Solution Explorer and select Add, New
   Item, Web, Global Application Class, and click Add.

2. Open the Global.asax file in code view and add the following using directives:

   ```
   using System.Workflow.Runtime;
   using System.Workflow.Runtime.Hosting;
   ```

3. Enter the following code in the Application_Start handler to start the
   WorkflowRuntime and to store it to an application variable:

   ```
   WorkflowRuntime workflowRuntime = new WorkflowRuntime();
   Application["WorkflowRuntime"] = workflowRuntime;
   ```

4. Enter the following code to configure the WorkflowRuntime to use the
   ManualWorkflowSchedulerService and to configure the service to restart

when timers expire (Delay activities), and to create an application level variable to hold the scheduler service:

```
ManualWorkflowSchedulerService manualScheduler =
    new ManualWorkflowSchedulerService(true);
Application["ManualScheduler"] = manualScheduler;
workflowRuntime.AddService(manualScheduler);
workflowRuntime.StartRuntime();
```

5. The completed Application_Start handler should look like Listing 18.1.

LISTING 18.1 **WorkflowRuntime** Started in **Application_Start** Handler

```
WorkflowRuntime workflowRuntime = new WorkflowRuntime();
Application["WorkflowRuntime"] = workflowRuntime;

ManualWorkflowSchedulerService manualScheduler =
    new ManualWorkflowSchedulerService(true);
Application["ManualScheduler"] = manualScheduler;
workflowRuntime.AddService(manualScheduler);
workflowRuntime.StartRuntime();
```

6. Add the code shown to the Application_End handler to stop the WorkflowRuntime.

```
WorkflowRuntime workflowRuntime;
workflowRuntime = Application["WorkflowRuntime"]
    as WorkflowRuntime;
workflowRuntime.StopRuntime();
```

Creating the ASP.NET Web Form

Follow the next steps to create the ASP.NET form that will start the workflow instance.

1. Open Default.aspx in design view by right-clicking it in the Solution Explorer and selecting View Designer.

2. Add two TextBox controls and a Button to the form. Then enter **Order amount:** to the left of the first textbox and **Order status:** to the left of the second. Your form should now look like Figure 18.12.

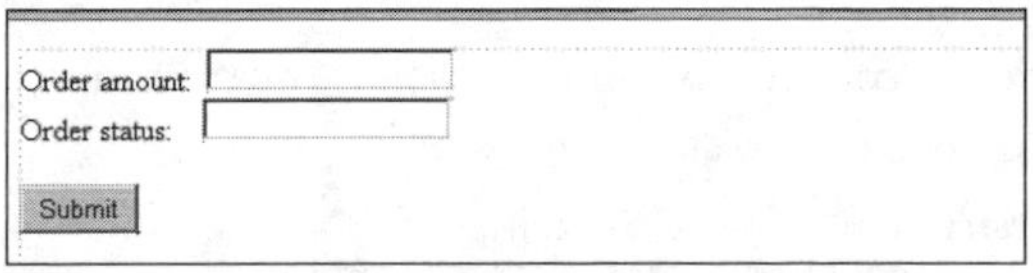

FIGURE 18.12
Web form.

3. Set the ID property of the first TextBox to **TextBoxOrderAmount** and the second to **TextBoxOrderStatus.** Change the property of the Button to **Submit.**

Starting the Workflow Instance

Follow the next steps to configure the SubmitButton handler to start a WorkflowInstance and to send data to it in a Dictionary object. The main differences compared to hosting in a Windows Forms or Console application as you have done throughout this book are that the WF runtime and scheduling services are retrieved from the application variables you created, and the RunWorkflow method is called to start the workflow because the manual scheduling service is used.

1. Double-click the Submit button to create a handler for it. First add the following using directives:

```
using System.Workflow.Runtime;
using System.Workflow.Runtime.Hosting;
using System.Collections.Generic;
```

2. Add the following code the Submit_Click handler you just created to create and populate a Dictionary object with the order amount:

```
Dictionary<string, object> parameters =
    new Dictionary<string,object>();
parameters.Add("OrderAmount",
    double.Parse(TextBoxOrderAmount.Text.ToString()));
```

3. Add the following code to retrieve the WF runtime and manual scheduler from the application variables you created. Then it instantiates both the WF runtime and manual scheduler.

```
WorkflowRuntime workflowRuntime =
    Application["WorkflowRuntime"] as WorkflowRuntime;
ManualWorkflowSchedulerService manualScheduler =
    Application["ManualScheduler"] as
ManualWorkflowSchedulerService;
```

4. Add the following code to register the completed event handler with the runtime:

```
workflowRuntime.WorkflowCompleted +=
    new EventHandler<WorkflowCompletedEventArgs>
        (workflowRuntime_WorkflowCompleted);
```

5. Add the following code to instantiate a WorkflowInstance, pass it the Dictionary object, and to start the instance:

```
WorkflowInstance instance =
    workflowRuntime.CreateWorkflow(
    typeof(AspNetHostedWorkflowProject.Workflow1), parameters);
instance.Start();
```

6. Now add code to run the workflow via the scheduler services `RunWorkflow` method. This step is necessary because the manual scheduling service is being used.

```
manualScheduler.RunWorkflow(instance.InstanceId);
```

7. Add the workflow completed event handler below the `Submit` button handler. It will populate the order status text box with the order approval status returned from the workflow:

```
void workflowRuntime_WorkflowCompleted
    (object sender, WorkflowCompletedEventArgs e)
{
    TextBoxOrderStatus.Text =
        e.OutputParameters["OrderStatus"].ToString();
}
```

8. The code to start the workflow instance from an ASP.NET application should look like Listing 18.2.

LISTING 18.2 `WorkflowInstance` Started in ASP.NET Application

```
protected void Submit_Click(object sender, EventArgs e)
{
    Dictionary<string, object> parameters =
        new Dictionary<string, object>();
    parameters.Add("OrderAmount",
        double.Parse(TextBoxOrderAmount.Text.ToString()));

    WorkflowRuntime workflowRuntime =
        Application["WorkflowRuntime"] as WorkflowRuntime;
    ManualWorkflowSchedulerService manualScheduler =
        Application["ManualScheduler"] as
ManualWorkflowSchedulerService;

    workflowRuntime.WorkflowCompleted +=
        new EventHandler<WorkflowCompletedEventArgs>
        (workflowRuntime_WorkflowCompleted);

    WorkflowInstance instance =
        workflowRuntime.CreateWorkflow(
        typeof(AspNetHostedWorkflowProject.Workflow1), parameters);
    instance.Start();

    manualScheduler.RunWorkflow(instance.InstanceId);
}

void workflowRuntime_WorkflowCompleted
    (object sender, WorkflowCompletedEventArgs e)
{
    TextBoxOrderStatus.Text =
        e.OutputParameters["OrderStatus"].ToString();
}
```

Running the ASP.Net Hosted Workflow

Follow the next steps to run the workflow and see the results returned to the form.

1. Set the `AspWfRuntimeHost` project as the startup project.

2. Press F5 to run the workflow and answer yes to any dialogs you receive related to debugging.

3. Enter **90** as the order amount, and you should receive the results shown in Figure 18.13.

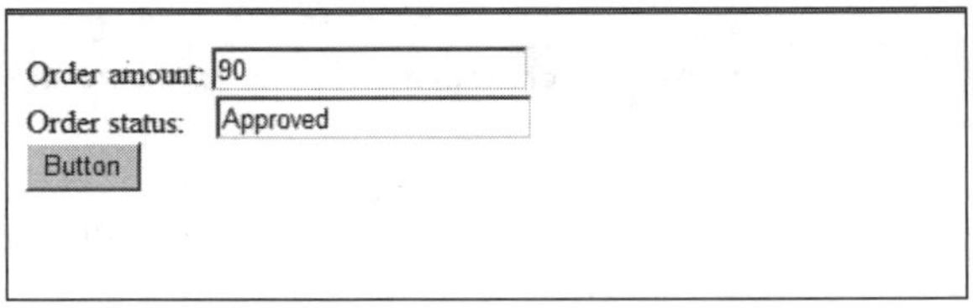

FIGURE 18.13
Approved results
shown on form.

Summary

This hour demonstrated publishing workflows as web services and calling web services from workflows. Then the ability to return SOAP fault from the called workflow was added and the client workflow was configured to receive the SOAP fault. The project structure and the `WebServiceProxy` property were covered next. Finally, the hour wrapped up with a lesson on hosting the WF runtime in ASP.NET.

Workshop

Quiz

1. *What is the purpose of the* `WebServiceInput` *activity?*

2. *What is the purpose of the* `WebServiceOutput` *activity?*

3. *What is the* `InvokeWebService` *activity used for?*

4. *If a workflow throws a SOAP fault, does it raise an exception?*

5. *How does a client maintain context to recall a workflow?*

6. **What is the purpose of the** `InputReceived` **and** `SendingOutput` **properties?**

7. **When must the** `IsActivating` **property be set to** `true`**?**

8. **What function should be performed in** `Gobal.asax` **to improve performance?**

9. **What scheduling service must (should in most cases) be used when hosting the WF runtime in an ASP.NET application?**

Answers

1. It exposes a workflow as a web service.

2. If the web service call is synchronous, there will be a `WebServiceOutput` activity as well that returns the results to the calling web service.

3. To call a web service from a workflow.

4. No, it returns a SOAPFault to the calling workflow that results in a raised exception in the calling workflow.

5. Through a client-side cookie.

6. The first executes before the workflow is invoked as a web service and the latter before the workflow returns a response. The first is bound to the `WebServiceInput` activity and the latter to the `WebServiceOutput` activity.

7. When the `WebServiceInput` activity must instantiate a new workflow instance.

8. Instantiate the `WorkflowRuntime`, so that it is only performed once in the application lifecycle and not on each page request.

9. The `ManualWorkflowSchedulerService`.

HOUR 19

Learning WF-WCF Integration

What You Will Learn in This Hour:

- ▶ Overview of Windows Communication Foundation
- ▶ Exposing WF workflows as WCF services
- ▶ Accessing WCF services from WF workflows
- ▶ Directly Accessing the WF runtime from the WCF host

Overview of Windows Communication Foundation

Before jumping directly into how to use Windows Communication Foundation (WCF) with WF, this section provides an overview of WCF and the next provides an overview of using the two together.

WCF and WF are complementary products that are both part of the .NET 3.0 and 3.5 Frameworks. WCF is Microsoft's distributed computing technology. It is the preferred way to provide and access network endpoints on the Microsoft platform. WCF subsumes all previous Microsoft distributed technologies, including web services, web service enhancements, .NET remoting, and enterprise services. WCF supplies the most thorough web service standard support on the Microsoft platform. WCF can listen for and access network endpoints via HTTP, TCP, named pipes, and just about any other communication protocol.

In the past, enterprise services and .NET remoting were frequently the best choices when communicating behind the firewall, whereas web services were generally best when communicating across the firewall. This required using different programming and security models based on the communication pattern. If the service had both cross-firewall and local clients, this frequently required creating web service and .NET enterprise service or .NET remoting endpoints as well. Even when using web services, you could choose between standard and employing web service enhancement technology (WSE) to gain additional security.

WCF rationalizes distributed computing on the Microsoft platform by providing one programming model and one runtime. It separates the service (the functionality) from the endpoint. The endpoint contains the information necessary to communicate on the wire. A service communicating across the firewall can choose the WCF HTTP binding, which sends standard SOAP over HTTP using basic security. A service also requiring additional security can use the sibling HTTP binding that includes WS* security. Finally a service communicating behind the firewall can utilize the TCP binding that uses compiled SOAP. Therefore, the same service can support all three communication patterns. There needs to be one WCF endpoint created for each communication pattern the service supports. WCF can also use MSMQ when queuing is necessary; it is just another binding. Finally, to streamline endpoint support even more, WCF binding information can be placed in configuration files, allowing the wire format to change without requiring recompilation.

WCF can be hosted in any .NET 2.0 or later application domain, such as a Windows Service, IIS, or Windows Activation Service (improved IIS in Windows 2008) process. The ability to listen across just about any protocol securely and reliably, in any Windows process, and to do so at maximum efficiency makes WCF very powerful. WCF abstracts service functionality from wire format and hosting requirements. There really is no reason not to use WCF for distributed computing on the Microsoft platform. Because of WCF's adept endpoint capabilities, it is commonly referred to as Microsoft's service-oriented technology, with the endpoints being the entry points to the services. As you will see, WF or standard .NET types can provide the logic behind the endpoint.

WF and WCF Overview

Workflows frequently need to be exposed across the network and to access other services on the network. WF can leverage WCF as the endpoint while it provides the logic component of the network service. A customer service, for example, may be exposed as a WCF endpoint and also call out to a credit service. In this case, the WF workflow can be exposed as a WCF endpoint and can utilize WCF to call the credit service as well. WCF is WF's conduit to and from the outside world when working with distributed systems.

WCF provides two activities and hosting capabilities to WF in .NET 3.5 (Figure 19.1). The Send activity provides functionality similar to both the CallExternalMethod activity and the InvokeWorkflow activity. The Receive activity is similar to the HandleExternalEvent activity (and the response portion of the InvokeWorkflow activity). Each activity can be associated with an interface and configured to support synchronous or asynchronous operations. The Send activity, for example can call a method on a service or workflow (that is exposed as a service), pass in parameters, and receive a response, just as a standard method can. The Receive activity provides the same capabilities in the other direction, it receives responses rather than requesting them.

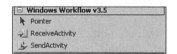

FIGURE 19.1
WCF .NET 3.5
activities.

Having all the flexibility of method calls baked into WF activities that can be used to call services and workflows is quite powerful. It is certainly an improvement over .NET 3.0, where calling to and from the host is not optimum. Workflow to host must be synchronous and host to workflow must use asynchronous events and a special EventArgs-derived payload. Calling workflows is even harder in .NET 3.0, especially to do so synchronously. By and large, the communicating to and from workflows is greatly improved in .NET 3.5. The communication is, however, a work in progress. Correlation (Hour 8, "Working with Parallel Activities and Correlation") is not particularly straightforward to implement at the current time with WorkflowServices.

The third main component of WF-WCF integration is WCF hosting. The WCF Receive activity works in conjunction with the WorkflowServiceHost type to host WF workflows and to create endpoints. These endpoints are called WorkflowServices. When placing a Receive activity on a WF workflow, WCF (or the WorkflowServiceHost type) must host the workflow. Built-in capabilities simplify hosting WCF (and WorkflowServices) in IIS and WAS (IIS in Vista and Windows Server 2008). WCF can also be hosted in Windows Services, Console applications, Windows Forms applications, and other .NET processes, although it is still up to you to manage the lifetime in these applications.

Because of the capability of the Send and Receive activities, the IIS and WAS hosting advantages, and the apparent emphasis toward WCF as a hosting technology going forward, it is reasonable to consider hosting all WF applications as WorkflowServices. Another reason not to host WF in WCF is when using another dedicated WF host product, such as SharePoint or MS CRM. In these cases WCF can still be used to access endpoints, but they are the workflow hosts.

> In .NET 3.0, WF and WCF must be integrated manually. No `WorkflowServiceHost` type or `Send` and `Receive` activities exist. Manual integration is not covered in this book.

There are two workflow-specific projects in the 3.5 Framework. The first contains a sequential workflow project and a WCF contract (interface). The second holds state machine workflows and an accompanying contract. These project types are relevant when exposing a workflow as a service.

The first two exercises in this hour are part of hosting a WF workflow in WCF. They are broken into smaller steps to help digest them.

You begin this hour hosting a workflow in WCF (creating a WorkflowService). You perform this in two steps. First, you use the interface and `Receive` activity prepopulated with the Sequential Workflow Service Library template. This allows you to create functional WorkflowService with minimal work. Then you modify the interface and reconfigure the existing `Receive` activity to use the new interface. The combination of the two parts demonstrates all the standard steps to create a functional WorkflowService.

Next, you learn to access the WF runtime form the `WorkflowServiceHost`. By default, the WF runtime is loaded as part of the `WorkflowServiceHost` under the hood. You will need to access it many times—for example, to register events and add runtime services. Finally, you will call another workflow from a workflow using the `Send` activity.

> WCF is an extremely large subject. Its coverage is limited to that necessary for it to host and be called from WF. If you want more detail on WCF, see *Essential Windows Communication Foundation (WCF): For .NET Framework 3.5* (Addison-Wesley, Steve Resnick, Richard Crane, and Chris Bowen), MSDN, or other sources.

Hosting a Workflow in WCF Using Existing Interface and `Receive` Activity

In this exercise you create a WCF endpoint that hosts a WF workflow. You create a client application to access the WCF host (that runs the workflow). You will leverage the interface and `Receive` activity created by the WCF Sequential Workflow Service Library project to reduce the steps necessary to see a WF workflow run in WCF.

Creating the Solution and Projects

This solution contains three projects. The first holds the WF workflow and contract. The second holds the WCF host, and the third holds the client.

Creating the Solution

Follow the next steps to create the solution.

1. Start Visual Studio 2008. Select File, New, Project.

2. Expand the Project Types and select Other Project Types.

3. Select the Visual Studio Solutions project template.

4. Enter **WcfHostsWfSolution** as the Name.

5. Enter or browse to `C:\SamsWf24hrs\Hours\Hour19LearningWF-WCFIntegra-tion` for the Location.

6. Click OK.

Creating the Sequential Workflow Service Library Project

Follow the next steps to create a Sequential Workflow Service Library project that will hold a workflow ready to be hosted in WCF.

1. Right-click `WcfHostsWfSolution` in the Solution Explorer and select Add, New Project.

2. Expand Visual C# and select WCF (Figure 19.2).

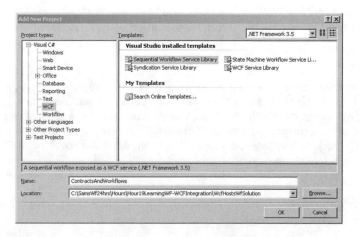

FIGURE 19.2
WCF project types.

3. Select the Sequential Workflow Service Library project template.

4. Enter **ContractsAndWorkflows** as the Name.

5. Leave the default path.

6. Select OK.

Creating the Remaining Projects

Follow the next steps to create the console host and console client project.

1. Create a Console Application project and name it **ConsoleApplicationWcfWorkflowHost**. This project will serve as the WCF Host project.

2. Create a Console Application project and name it **ConsoleApplicationClient**. This is the client that will call the WCF endpoint that hosts the WF workflow.

ABCs of WCF and WF Specific Bindings

WCF endpoints contain an address, a binding, and a contract. The address is the location of the service. The Sequential Workflow Service Library project template created the following address for the Workflow1 service to facilitate testing: http://local-host:8731/Design_Time_Addresses/ContractsAndWorkflows/Workflow1/. Open the App.config file in the ContractsAndWorkflows project and you will see this address in the baseAddresses element. A couple of lines below, the binding is set to wsHttpContextBinding and the contract to ContractsAndWorkflows.IWorkflow1. By leaving the address null, it is created by adding the service name to the baseAddress.

> The bindings dictate the method the service listens for and how it interacts with clients. Change the binding and the service can communicate over a new protocol. You will see at the end of this topic that new bindings were created to permit WCF to host long-running workflows. These bindings permit WCF to retain context across WF workflow persistence points. This exemplifies the power of WCF bindings. They dictate much more than protocols.

These three elements are commonly referred to as the ABCs of WCF. For a WCF client to connect to a WCF host, they must both have identical ABCs. That is, the client connects to the service at the address, over the binding, and via the contract the service specifies. WCF ships with support for a number of bindings. These include the `BasicHttpBinding`, `WsHttpBinding`, and `NetTcpBinding` bindings. The difference between the `BasicHttpBinding` and the `WsHttpBinding` is that the latter includes web services security and reliable message support under the WS* umbrella of standards.

Custom WCF bindings can be created when none of the out-of-the-box WCF bindings work for your scenario. When WCF hosts WF, it needs to maintain session across the workflow persists and activations. Three custom bindings permit WF session state to be managed from WCF: `BasicHttpContextBinding`, `WsHttpContextBinding`, and `NetTcpContextBinding`. As you can see by the name, one is for standard http, another is for WS*-compliant http, and the last is for TCP.

Exploring the `ContractsAndWorkflows` Project and Bindings

The `ContractsAndWorkflows` project contains a WCF interface, a workflow that implements it, and a configuration file that specifies the endpoint information.

Reviewing the Interface

The interface (`IWorkflow1.cs`) has a `ServiceContract` attribute, and its `GetData` operation is decorated with an `OperationContract` attribute (see the next code snippet). The `ServiceContract` attribute informs WCF that this interface can be used to create WCF services. The `OperationContract` attribute states that this operation should be available to service consumers. Operations can exist in a WCF interface that are not available as WCF service operations. Only the operations with `OperationContract` attribute are available. Also, note the standard interface convention. No mandate requires that a synchronous method be used for workflow-host communication and that an asynchronous event be used for host-workflow communication. Any combination of synchronous and asynchronous operations can be used. In this case, a standard synchronous operation delivers the complete roundtrip communication between workflow and host.

```
namespace ContractsAndWorkflows
{
    // NOTE: If you change the interface name "IWorkflow1" here, you must also
update the reference to "IWorkflow1" in App.config.
    [ServiceContract]
    public interface IWorkflow1
    {

        [OperationContract]
```

```
        string GetData(int value);

        // TODO: Add your service operations here
    }
}
```

Exploring the `Receive` Activity

The workflow created by the Sequential Workflow Service Library Project template is prepopulated with a `Receive` activity. The `Receive` activity is used when workflows are hosted in WCF. The `Receive` activity works in conjunction with the `WorkflowServiceHost` type. The `WorkflowServiceHost` type is used when WCF endpoints host WCF workflows. The operations exposed by the `Receive` activity and data it exchanges with clients are specified in an interface.

Follow the next steps to explore the `Receive` activity and its properties.

1. Open the workflow in design mode.

2. Click the `Receive` activity and look at its properties (Figure 19.3).

FIGURE 19.3
Receive activity and its properties.

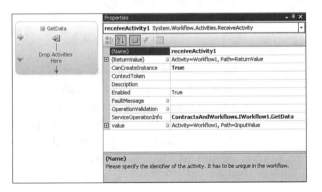

Let's examine each of the `Receive` activity's nongeneric properties starting with `ServiceOperationInfo` and then going from the top down:

▸ **`ServiceOperationInfo`**—Binds the `Receive` activity to a service contract (interface) operation. As you can see, it is bound to the `GetData` operation from the IWorkflow interface that was created with the project.

▸ **`ReturnValue`**—The value returned to the client when the `Receive` activity completes execution. The `Receive` activity is a composite activity, as will be demonstrated in the next section.

▶ **`ContextToken`**—This is used for correlation purposes when the client contacts multiple `Receive` activities on the same workflow. This token ensures that subsequent calls access the proper instance of the workflow. The concept is identical to the `CorrelationToken` used on `CallExternalMethod` and `HandleExternalEvent` activities covered in Hour 8.

▶ **`FaultMessage`**—Allows a fault message to be sent to the client if a problem arises. Returning fault messages is the standard way to return an error to a client when web services are used.

▶ **`OperationValidation`**—Validation logic to be executed before message is accepted. One possibility is to perform role checking.

▶ **`Value`**—The parameter specified in the interface.

The `ContextToken`, `FaultMessage`, and `OperationValidation` properties are not covered in this book. The others are used in this hour.

Click the workflow (not the `Receive` activity), look in the property window, and you will see the `WorkflowServiceAttributes` property. It is a new property that is promoted to the workflow when a `Receive` activity is added. It contains a number of WCF-centric properties, including one that specifies whether exception details are included in faults. These properties are not covered anymore, but you should make a mental note for when you might need them.

Modeling the Workflow

As mentioned, the `Receive` activity is a composite activity. All activities placed in it will be executed before it completes and returns a value to the client.

Follow the next steps to see the default properties and to place a `Code` activity into the `Receive` activity.

1. Open the workflow in code view and you will see `ReturnValue` and `InputValue` properties that were bound to the `Receive` activity `ReturnValue` and `value` properties.

2. Place a `Code` activity in the `Receive` activity. Double-click it and add the following code to its handler:

```
// Set the return value based on the customer number
ReturnValue = InputValue == 1 ? "Good" : "Bad";
```

The workflow is shown in Figure 19.4. The `Code` activity evaluates the value passed in and returns either good or bad based on the value received.

FIGURE 19.4
Workflow with
`Receive` activ-
ity and `Code`
activity placed in
`Receive` activ-
ity.

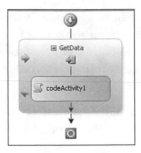

Looking at the `App.config` File

Open the `App.config` file. There is a lot of XML noise. The WCF content is held in the
`system.serviceModel` element. The `Services` element contains the service name
and a `behaviorConfiguration` attribute, which I will explain shortly. The
`baseAddress` plus the address attribute of the endpoint element holds the service
address. In this case the address attribute is blank, so the entire address is held in the
`baseAddress`. The identity element holds the identity and comments you should
read. Finally, the next endpoint element holds the address to the service metadata.
This is where the WSDL can be accessed and will be used to create proxy and an
`App.config` file later.

```
<system.serviceModel>
  <services>
    <service name="ContractsAndWorkflows.Workflow1"
behaviorConfiguration="ContractsAndWorkflows.Workflow1Behavior">
      <host>
        <baseAddresses>
          <add
baseAddress="http://localhost:8731/Design_Time_Addresses/ContractsAndWorkflows/Wo
rkflow1/" />
        </baseAddresses>
      </host>
      <endpoint address=""
                binding="wsHttpContextBinding"
                contract="ContractsAndWorkflows.IWorkflow1">
        <!-- Upon deployment, the following identity element should be removed
or replaced to reflect the identity under which the deployed service runs.  If
removed, WCF will infer an appropriate identity automatically.-->
        <identity>
          <dns value="localhost"/>
        </identity>
      </endpoint>
      <endpoint address="mex"
                binding="mexHttpBinding"
                contract="IMetadataExchange" />
    </service>
  </services>
```

The behavior element contains other information about the service, such as permitting HTTP Get to be used to access the metadata, which allows it to be viewed in a browser.

```
<behaviors>
  <serviceBehaviors>
    <behavior name="ContractsAndWorkflows.Workflow1Behavior"  >
      <serviceMetadata httpGetEnabled="true" />
      <serviceDebug includeExceptionDetailInFaults="false" />
      <serviceCredentials>
        <windowsAuthentication
            allowAnonymousLogons="false"
            includeWindowsGroups="true" />
      </serviceCredentials>
    </behavior>
  </serviceBehaviors>
</behaviors>
</system.serviceModel>
```

Services can be configured in code or via configuration file. The advantage of using a configuration file is that it can be changed without recompiling the service, and potentially done so by administrators. You will use the configuration file created by the WCF Sequential Workflow Service Library project template when creating the host in the next section

Creating the WCF Endpoint and Host

WCF, like WF, can be hosted in any .NET 2.0 or later app domain. The ServiceHost type, contained in the `System.ServiceModel` namespace, is the gateway to WCF, much like the `WorkflowRuntime` type is the gateway to WF functionality. When WCF hosts a workflow, the `WorkflowServiceHost` type, contained in the `System.WorkflowServices` namespace, is used in place of the `ServiceHost` type. The `WorkflowServiceHost` type contains a handle to the WF runtime, thereby permitting a WCF host to run a WF workflow, register runtime events, and add runtime services. The WCF endpoint will be hosted in a Console Application.

You will implement a `WorkflowServiceHost`, set up an endpoint, and allow metadata to be accessed. The endpoint information will be extracted from the `App.Config` file in the workflow project.

Performing Preliminary Setup

Follow the next steps to add references to the assemblies needed to host a WF workflow in WCF. Then reference the project holding the workflow to be run.

1. Click the `ConsoleApplicationWcfWorkflowHost` project in the Solution Explorer.

2. Add references to System.ServiceModel, System.Workflow.Activities, System.Workflow.ComponentModel, and System.WorkflowServices.

3. Add a reference to the ContractsAndWorkflows project.

4. Open Program.cs and add the following using directives:

```
using System.ServiceModel;
using System.ServiceModel.Description;
```

Instantiating WorkflowServiceHost

The WorkflowServiceHost needs to know where to listen (address) and what to listen for (contract or type). All this information will be obtained from the configuration file.

Follow the next steps to move the App.config file from the workflow project into the console host. Then add code to the Program.cs file to instantiate the WorkflowServiceHost.

1. Cut the App.config file from the ContractsAndWorkflows project and copy it into the ConsoleApplicationWcfWorkflowHost project.

2. Now it is time to instantiate the WorkflowServiceHost type and to pass it the type (the workflow). Add the following code to the top of the Main method in Program.cs in the ConsoleApplicationWcfWorkflowHost project:

```
// Instantiate the WorkflowServiceHost and pass it the
// workflow (type) to invoke.
WorkflowServiceHost selfWorkflowHost =
    new
WorkflowServiceHost(typeof(ContractsAndWorkflows.Workflow1));
```

Start, Pause, and Close the Host

Follow the next steps to open the host to start it listening and build the project. The workflow will run in its context. Then you will pause the host while it waits. This must be done, just as with WF, because this is a console application and the console application will complete if not blocked while running workflows (or waiting for workflows to run) that run asynchronously, which is the default.

1. Add the following code to open the host, to pause it, and finally to close it:

```
// Open the service so that it starts listening for client calls.
selfWorkflowHost.Open();
```

```
// Pause the host while it waits for clients to invoke
// workflow through it.
Console.WriteLine("The service is ready.");
Console.WriteLine("Press <ENTER> to terminate service.");
Console.WriteLine();
Console.ReadLine();

// Close the  service.
selfWorkflowHost.Close();
```

2. Build the `ConsoleApplicationWcfWorkflowHost` project.

Running the Host

The host can now be started and the endpoint can begin listening. The WCF host must be running before it can be referenced by the client you will create in the next section, so leave it running when you've completed this section.

Follow the next steps to configure the order the projects should start in and then run the project.

> We will use the multiple startup project option because Visual Studio 2008 is required to use the functionality in this hour.

By the Way

1. Right-click the solution in the Solution Explorer, select Properties, and click the plus sign to expand Common Properties. Select Startup Project, and select the Multiple Startup projects option in the middle of the dialog. Select the `ConsoleApplicationWcfWorkflowHost` project in the list of projects, click the arrow to the right of it, and select Start from the drop-down. Then click OK.

2. Press F5 to start the project (all projects specified to start). You should see the host has started and is waiting to receive a client request that it will, in turn, pass onto the workflow as shown in Figure 19.5.

FIGURE 19.5
WCF Host running.

3. Terminate the `ConsoleApplicationWcfWorkflowHost`.

Creating the Console Application Client

There are two steps to creating the client. The first is referencing the WCF host to build a proxy and a configuration file. The second step is to add the logic to the client to instantiate and invoke the method on the workflow proxy.

Performing Preliminary Setup

Follow the next steps to add referencing and a using directive.

1. Click the `ConsoleApplicationClient` project in the Solution Explorer.

2. Add a reference to `System.ServiceModel`.

3. Add a reference to the `ContractsAndWorkflows` project.

4. Open `Program.cs` and add the following using directive:

   ```
   using System.ServiceModel;
   ```

Adding a Service Reference to the WCF Host

The client needs to reference the service (much the same as a client to an ASMX web service needs to reference the web service). The client may be on the same computer or access the service across the Internet.

Follow the next steps to add a service reference from the client to the host using the `Svcutil.exe` command line utility.

> You can also add a client reference to a service by right-clicking the project and choosing Add Service Reference (similar to adding an ASMX web service reference) or by using the `Svcutil.exe` utility. The first is a little easier but does not offer much control. Therefore, we will use `Svcutil.exe` to add service references in this book.

1. Press F5 to start running the `ConsoleApplicationWcfWorkflowHost`.

2. Select Start, All Programs, Visual Studio 2008, Visual Studio Tools, and Visual Studio 2008 Command Prompt.

3. Enter `cd\SamsWf24hrs\Hours\Hour19LearningWF-WCFIntegration\WcfHostsWfSolution\ConsoleApplicationClient` to go to the client directory.

4. Enter the following command to generate a proxy and a configuration file in the current directory. The HTTP address is taken from the `baseAddress` element of the `App.config` file in the `ContractsAndWorkflows` project and must match the address where the service runs. (Remember the host must be running before you reference it.)

```
svcutil.exe /language:cs /out:GeneratedProxy.cs /config:app.config
http://localhost:8731/Design_Time_Addresses/ContractsAndWorkflows/Workflow1/
```

5. Two files, one named `GeneratedProxy.cs` and the other `App.config` should have been created.

6. Stop the host project from running. You must do this to include the file in the project in a couple of steps.

7. Go back to Visual Studio and click the `ConsoleApplicationClient` project in the Solution Explorer.

8. Click the Show All files icon and the just generated files; a couple of directories should appear in a dimmed format (Figure 19.6). It is a toggle, so click again if you do not see the files.

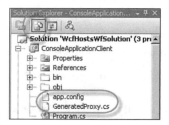

9. Select the `GeneratedProxy.cs` and the `App.config` files. Then right-click and choose Include in Project. They should no longer be dimmed.

FIGURE 19.6
Show All files icon with all files included.

The default behavior of `SvcUtil` is to create a new `ServiceModel` element if there is an existing `App.Config` file and to create a new one otherwise. However, a command-line option exists (`mergeConfig`) that will merge the new endpoints into an existing `ServiceModel` element. You can explore numerous options by entering `SvcUtil` from the command prompt.

Exploring the Generated Files

The `GeneratedProxy.cs`, as the name implies, is a proxy. It is used to call the service. The `App.config` file contains the service endpoint configuration details. Follow the next steps to look at the generated files.

1. Open the `GeneratedProxy.cs` file. Skip down to the public partial class `Workflow1Client`. This is the class you will instantiate in the client, and its `GetData` operation will access the method on the workflow `Receive` activity.

2. Open the `App.config` file. The client's `App.config` file contains bindings and client elements. The binding element specifies the binding to connect to the service—`wsHttpContextBinding` in this case. Other binding-related properties exist, such as the timeout value.

3. The `Client` element at the bottom of the file contains the address, binding, and contract to use to contact the service. These values must match the service values for the client to connect.

Adding Client Code to Call the Service

Now that the client has a reference to the service, follow the next steps to instantiate the proxy and call the service, which will, in turn, call the workflow.

1. Open `Program.cs` in the `ConsoleApplicationClient` project.

2. Add the following code to instantiate an object to call the service, which then invokes the workflow. The address, binding, and contract are retrieved from the configuration file.

```
// Instantiate the WorkflowInterfaceClient from the proxy.
// Endpoint information is retrieved from the config file.
Workflow1Client client = new Workflow1Client();
```

3. Add the following code to call the workflow's `GetData` method, again through the service.

```
// Call the GetData method on the workflow
string status = client.GetData(1);
Console.WriteLine("the status is: " + status);
```

4. Pause the host:

```
Console.WriteLine("Press Enter to terminate the client.");
Console.Read();
```

5. The completed client `Program.cs` `Main` method should look like this:

```
static void Main(string[] args)
{
    // Instantiate the WorkflowInterfaceClient from the proxy.
    // Endpoint information is retrieved from the config file.
    Workflow1Client client = new Workflow1Client();

    // Call the GetData method on the workflow
    string status = client.GetData(1);
```

```
            Console.WriteLine("the status is: " + status);

            Console.WriteLine("Press Enter to terminate the client.");
            Console.Read();
      }
```

6. Build the ConsoleApplicationClient project.

Running the Client

The service should still be running. If not, start it so that the client can access it. Follow the next steps to configure the client project to start in the Multiple Startup projects choice and run the solution.

1. Right-click the solution in the Solution Explorer, select Properties, and click the plus sign to expand Common Properties. Select Startup Project, select the Multiple Startup projects option in the middle of the dialog. Select the ConsoleApplicationClient project in the list of projects, click the arrow to the right of it, and select Start from the drop-down.

2. Click the ConsoleApplicationWcfWorkflowHost project and click the up arrow to the right of the list until it is the first project in the list to ensure it starts first. Then click OK.

3. Press F5 to start the projects. You should see that the client ran and retrieved the status from the workflow (Figure 19.7).

FIGURE 19.7
Console client receives response from the workflow.

4. Stop both the client and host projects.

Hosting a Workflow in WCF: Configuring Receive Activity and Updating Interface

In the previous exercise, you created a workflow, host, and client, and then connected them all. You leveraged the Receive activity, interface, and service created with the Sequential Workflow Service Library project template. In this exercise, you modify the interface, delete the existing Receive activity, add a new Receive activity, and configure the new Receive activity.

Modifying the Interface

WCF interfaces are decorated with ServiceContract and their members with OperationContract, as well as other attributes that delineate they are available to interact with clients. Follow the next steps to decorate the IWorkflow interface as appropriate.

1. Open the IWorkflow.cs file in the ContractsAndWorkflows project.

2. Replace the current GetData method with the following GetStatus method (leave the attribute):

   ```
   string GetStatus(string customer);
   ```

3. Delete the remaining interface content. The IWorkflow1 interface should now look like this:

   ```
   [ServiceContract]
   public interface IWorkflow1
   {
       [OperationContract]
       string GetStatus(string customer);
   }
   ```

> The workflow implements the interface. When configuring the workflow in the next step you will implement the interface. In a nonworkflow implementation, there would be a class that implements the interface.

Configuring the Receive Activity

There should be a red exclamation error mark on the Receive activity, as the method it points to no longer exists. Follow the next steps to delete the existing Receive activity and configure a new one. This will allow you to start from the beginning.

1. Open the workflow in code view and delete the code that initializes the properties and variables. The only code remaining in the class should be the constructor and the code activity handler as shown:

   ```
   public sealed partial class Workflow1 : SequentialWorkflowActivity
   {
       public Workflow1()
       {
   ```

```
            InitializeComponent();
        }

        private void codeActivity1_ExecuteCode(object sender, EventArgs e)
        {
            // Set the return value based on the customer number
            ReturnValue = InputValue == 1 ? "Good" : "Bad";
        }
    }
```

2. Move the Code activity from Receive activity to the workflow.

3. Delete the existing Receive activity, and add a new Receive activity to the workflow.

4. Move the Code activity into the Receive activity you just added.

5. Click on the Receive activity. Then click on its ServiceOperationInfo property and click the ellipsis.

6. The Choose Operation dialog is spawned (Figure 19.8).

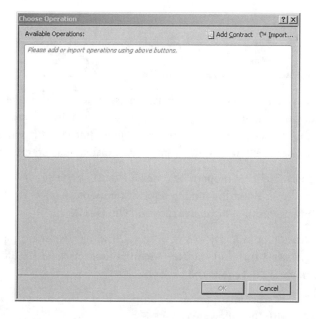

FIGURE 19.8
Choose Operation dialog.

7. Select the Import icon in the upper-right corner.

8. The Browse and Select a .NET Type dialog is displayed. Expand Current Project, select ContractsAndWorkflows, and choose IWorkflow1 in the middle pane. Click OK.

9. You are returned to the Choose Operation dialog, where the GetStatus method shows (Figure 19.9). Only one method is in the interface, so you can click OK. If there were multiple methods, you would choose which one to apply to this Receive activity.

FIGURE 19.9
Populated
Choose Opera-
tion dialog.

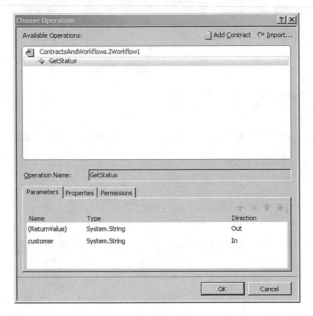

10. Click the CanCreateInstance property and set it to True. This tells WF to start a new instance when a message for this Receive activity is received. If there were multiple Receive activities, the subsequent Receive activities would not invoke a new workflow instance. They would instead use an existing instance.

11. Bind the ReturnValue property to a new field. Click the ReturnValue property. Click the ellipsis, select the Bind to a New Member tab, select the Create Field option button, name it **ReturnValue**, and choose OK.

12. Bind the customer property to a new field. Click the customer property. Click the ellipsis, select the Bind to a New Member tab, select the Create Field option button, name it **Customer**, and click OK.

13. Modify the Code activity handler to compare to a string rather than an int by replacing it with the following code:

```
// Set the return value based on the customer number
ReturnValue = Customer == "1" ? "Good" : "Bad";
```

14. Stop the host if it is still running.

15. Build the entire solution.

The `Receive` activity (therefore service implementation) and interface are now updated.

Rebuilding the Client

In this section, you will update the proxy and change the client to invoke the new method as well.

Rebuilding the Client Proxy

The client proxy is not pointed at the `GetStatus` method. It is still pointed at the `GetData` method contained in the original contract. Follow the next steps to run `SvcUtil` again to update the proxy to point to the correct operation. Then start the host project manually because you do not want all projects to execute.

1. Delete the `GeneratedProxy.cs` and the `App.config` files from the `ConsoleApplicationClient` project by right-clicking them and selecting Delete.

2. Start the host by going to the `C:\SamsWf24hrs\Hours\` `Hour19LearningWF-WCFIntegration\WcfHostsWfSolution\` `ConsoleApplicationWcfWorkflowHost\bin\Debug` directory in Windows Explorer and double-clicking the `ConsoleApplicationWcfWorkflowHost.exe` file.

3. Select Start, All Programs, Visual Studio 2008, Visual Studio Tools, and Visual Studio 2008 Command Prompt.

4. Enter **cd\SamsWf24hrs\Hours\Hour19LearningWF-WCFIntegration\WcfHostsWfSolution\ConsoleApplicationClient** to go to the client directory.

5. Enter the following command to generate a proxy and a configuration file in the current directory.

   ```
   svcutil.exe /language:cs /out:GeneratedProxy.cs /config:app.config
   http://localhost:8731/Design_Time_Addresses/ContractsAndWorkflows/Workflow1/
   ```

6. Terminate the host project. You must do this to include the file in a couple of steps.

7. Go back to Visual Studio and click the `ConsoleApplicationClient` project in the Solution Explorer.

8. New versions of the `GeneratedProxy.cs` and the `App.config` should have been created. If the files are not shown, click the Show All Files icon once or twice until they appear.

9. Select the `GeneratedProxy.cs` and the `App.config` files. Then right-click and choose Include in Project. They should no longer be dimmed.

10. Go to the bottom of the `GeneratedProxy.cs` file and make sure it is invoking the `GetStatus` method and not the `GetData` method. If not, build the solution again, and then go back to step 1 to start over.

Updating the Client to Invoke the New Method

Follow the next steps to update the client to call the `GetStatus` method.

1. Open `Program.cs` in the `ConsoleApplicationClient` project and replace the code that calls the `GetData` method and outputs the results with the following:

```
// Call the GetData method on the workflow
string status = client.GetStatus("1");
Console.WriteLine("the status is from the status method is: " +
status);
```

2. Build the `ConsoleApplicationClient` project.

3. Press F5 to run the solution. The client should access the new updated work-flow, and you should see the result shown in Figure 19.10.

FIGURE 19.10
Client results after changing the `Receive` activity and the interface.

4. Stop the console projects.

Accessing `WorkflowRuntime` from `WorkflowServiceHost`

Even though you have not interacted with the runtime, the workflows in this hour have been run by the WF runtime. The `WorkflowServiceHost` has managed this interaction behind the scenes. At times, however, you need more control of the way workflows are hosted. Registering events with the runtime and adding runtime services, for instance, requires access to the runtime.

In this section, you modify the ConsoleApplicationWcfWorkflowHost host application to retrieve the WorkflowRuntime from the WorkflowServiceHost. Then you register the completed and terminated events and add the tracking service. The only new code is to retrieve the WorkflowRuntime from the WorkflowServiceHost. Registering events and adding services works the same as it does when accessing the WorkflowRuntime directly.

Performing Preparatory Work

Follow the next steps to add references, using directives, and perform other preparatory work.

1. Click the ConsoleApplicationWcfWorkflowHost project in the Solution Explorer.

2. Add a reference to the WorkflowRuntime.

3. Add the following using directives to Program.cs in the ConsoleApplicationWcfWorkflowHost project:

```
using System.Workflow.Runtime;
using System.Workflow.Runtime.Tracking;
```

4. Add the following member variable below the opening class bracket:

```
        static string connectionString = "Initial
Catalog=WFTRackingAndPersistence;" +
            "Data Source=localhost; Integrated Security=SSPI;";
```

Retrieving the WorkflowRuntime

Follow the next steps to access the WF runtime from WCF using WCF's extensibility capability. The WorkflowRuntime is retrieved from the WorkflowServiceHost.Description.Behaviors collection property. Accessing the WF runtime this way conforms to standard WCF extensibility.

1. Add the following code below the line of code that instantiates the WorkflowServiceHost to retrieve the WorkflowRuntime from the WorkflowServiceHost type:

```
        // Retrieve the WorkflowRuntime from the WorkflowServiceHost
        WorkflowRuntime workflowRuntime =
```

```
selfWorkflowHost.Description.Behaviors.Find
<WorkflowRuntimeBehavior>().WorkflowRuntime;
```

2. Add the following code below the code you just added to register the events
   and add runtime services:

```
// Register the workflow events
workflowRuntime.WorkflowCompleted +=
    new EventHandler<WorkflowCompletedEventArgs>
        (workflowRuntime_WorkflowCompleted);
workflowRuntime.WorkflowTerminated +=
    new EventHandler<WorkflowTerminatedEventArgs>
        (workflowRuntime_WorkflowTerminated);

// Add the sql tracking service to the runtime
SqlTrackingService sts = new
SqlTrackingService(connectionString);
workflowRuntime.AddService(sts);
```

3. Add the following handlers below the Main method:

```
static void workflowRuntime_WorkflowCompleted
(object sender, WorkflowCompletedEventArgs e)
    {
        Console.WriteLine("WorkflowServiceHost accessed runtime
completed hander. ");
    }

static void workflowRuntime_WorkflowTerminated
    (object sender, WorkflowTerminatedEventArgs e)
    {
        Console.WriteLine("Workflow terminated");
    }
```

4. Build the `ConsoleApplicationWcfWorkflowHost` project.

Running the Project

Follow the next steps to run the project, and ensure that the `WorkflowCompleted`
handler emitted the content specified in it to the console.

1. Press F5 to run the solution.

2. Go to the host console, and you should see that the workflow completed handler was invoked as shown in Figure 19.11.

3. If you would like, run the WorkflowMonitor (Hour 5, "Creating an Escalation
   Workflow") or look in the database directly to see that the workflow is being
   tracked.

4. Stop both the client and host projects.

FIGURE 19.11
Workflow-
Completed
handler called
from
Workflow-
ServiceHost
hosted
Workflow-
Runtime.

Connecting to a WCF Endpoint from WF

Now it is time to use the Send activity to access a workflow. The workflow with the Send activity will replace the current client that calls the workflow and receives its results. When you use the Send activity to invoke a service, the workflow does not have to run under a WCF host. Moreover, if there are no Receive activities on the workflow, it must not be hosted by the WorkflowServiceHost. Therefore, we must host our new client workflow in the standard WF runtime, where it will access the host workflow that determines the status.

The client workflow accesses the host workflow via its address, bindings, and contract. It can access any endpoint capable of supporting these characteristics. Other possible endpoints include standard WCF services not enabled by workflows and standard web services.

Before continuing, the major Send activity properties are the ServiceOperationInfo property that binds the Send activity to an interface, just as it does for the Receive activity, and the ChannelToken property that points to the EndpointName attribute in the client section of the App.config file. AfterSend and BeforeSend are handlers that can be called before and after the message is sent. Logging and preparation are common uses of these handlers.

Updating the Workflow

In this section, you add a new workflow and configure it to use the Send activity.

Performing Preliminary Setup

Follow the next steps to create a Sequential Workflow Console Application project to host the client workflow.

1. Add a new Sequential Workflow Console Application project and name it **ClientWorkflow.**

2. Add code to pause the host.

Modeling the Workflow

The workflow will initialize a variable in the initial Code activity that will be passed to the service as a parameter. The second Code activity will then emit the results returned from the service to the console.

Follow the next steps to add the activities to the workflow.

1. Open Workflow1 in the ClientWorkflow project in design mode.

2. Add a Code activity to the workflow.

3. Add a Send activity to the workflow below the Code activity.

4. Add a Code activity below the Send activity.

Configuring the Send Activity Step 1

Follow the next steps to configure the ServiceOperationInfo property, which is almost the same as configuring this property on the Receive activity. You will also bind a few properties to send a value to and receive a value from the service.

1. Add a reference to the ContractsAndWorkflows project.

2. Click the Send activity. Then click its ServiceOperationInfo property and click the ellipsis.

3. The Choose Operation dialog is spawned.

4. Select the Import icon in the upper-right corner.

5. The Browse and Select a .NET Type dialog is displayed. Expand the ContractsAndWorkflows project, and choose IWorkflow1 in the middle pane. Click OK.

6. You are returned to the Choose Operation dialog. The GetStatus operation is selected because it is the only operation. Click OK to exit.

7. Bind the ReturnValue property to a new field. Click the ReturnValue property. Click the ellipsis, select the Bind to a New Member tab, select the Create Field option button, name it **StatusValueReturned**, and click OK. This stores the status returned from the called workflow.

8. Bind the customer property to a new field. Click the value property. Click the ellipsis, select the Bind to a New Member tab, select the Create Field option button, name it **CustomerValueSent**, and click OK.

Configuring the Send Activity Step 2: The ChannelToken Property

The ChannelToken property holds the endpoint name of the service the Send activity will invoke. Follow the next steps to populate it with the endpoint name attribute from the client section of the App.config file. This maps the client service parameters (address, binding, and contract) to the Send activity. This is needed because multiple client services may be in one config file. We will use the generated name here, the binding plus the contract, but you are free to change it to a more meaningful name, such as OrderServiceEndpoint.

1. Copy the App.Config file from the ConsoleApplicationClient project to the ClientWorkflow project.

2. Open the App.config file in the ClientWorkflow project. Go down to the client section.

3. Copy the text between the quotes in the name attribute in the client endpoint element (WSHttpContextBinding_IWorkflow1) and paste it in NotePad for use in a couple of steps.

4. The contract attribute in the App.config file must include the project name. To do so, prepend ContractsAndWorkflows to the contract attribute. It is directly to the left of the name attribute. It should look like this when complete:

   ```
   contract="ContractsAndWorkflows.IWorkflow1"
   ```

5. Click the ChannelToken property. Enter **TheChannelToUse**. Then press Enter.

6. Click the + next to the ChannelToken property. Paste the following text you copied from the App.config file in the EndpointName property:

   ```
   WSHttpContextBinding_IWorkflow1
   ```

7. Click the drop-down in the OwnerActivityName property and select Workflow1.

Configuring the Code Activities

Follow the next steps to update the Code activities handlers.

1. Double-click the first Code activity and add the following code to its handler:

   ```
   CustomerValueSent = "1";
   ```

2. Double-click the second Code activity and add the following code to its handler:

```
Console.WriteLine("The service returns the following: " +
StatusValueReturned);
```

3. Build the ClientWorkflow project.

Running the Workflow Client

Follow the next steps to reconfigure the projects to start in the correct order. Then run the solution and the host will return the status to the workflow client.

1. Right-click the solution in the Solution Explorer, select Properties, and click the plus sign to expand Common Properties. Select Startup Project and select the Multiple Startup projects option in the middle of the dialog. Select the ConsoleApplicationClient project in the list of projects, click the arrow to the right of it, and select None from the drop-down. Now set the ClientWorkflow project to start. Then reorder the projects and make sure the ConsoleApplicationWcfWorkflowHost project is first in the list.

2. Press F5 to start the solution; you should see the results shown in Figure 19.12 in the client host Window:

FIGURE 19.12
Workflow client talk to WCF host results.

Summary

In this hour you learned that WCF is complementary to WF. The first is the endpoint and latter the logic. It allows endpoints to be instantiated and called securely, reliably, and at optimum speed. WF can supply application logic and long-running support to WCF endpoints. Alternatively, WF can call out to WCF endpoints. This synergy is likely to increase, with WCF becoming WF's de facto host.

Workshop

Quiz

1. *What three elements do WCF endpoints contain?*

2. *What are the primary functions WCF supplies?*

3. *What two functions does WCF provide WF? And why use WCF for these functions?*

4. *What is the* WorkflowServiceHost *type used for?*

5. *What are the two .NET 3.5 WCF-centric activities, and what is their purpose?*

6. *What are some reasons to retrieve the* WorkflowRuntime *type from the* WorkflowServiceHost *type?*

7. *How do you specify that a service is a WCF contract and that an operation is a WCF operation?*

8. *What is the* SvcUtil *used for?*

Answers

1. Address, binding, and contract.

2. A single unified design-time and runtime experience for building "any" kind of distributed application and the ability to abstract protocols, security, and other operational entities from the service.

3. The ability to host/expose a workflow as a WCF service and to call out to services. WCF alleviates WF from having to build connectivity infrastructure when called by services and calling out to services.

4. To host WF workflows in WCF.

5. The Send and Receive activities. The Send activity calls out to services or endpoints from a workflow. The Receive activity permits a workflow to receive calls from services or endpoints.

6. The general reason is to have more control of the runtime. Specific examples are to register events and add runtime services to the runtime.

7. Attribute the service with [ServiceContract] and the [OperationContract].

8. To create a proxy for the client to call a WCF endpoint and to create the App.config file for the client.

PART V

Custom Activities

HOUR 20

Creating Basic Custom Activities

What You'll Learn in This Hour:

- ▶ Custom activity overview
- ▶ Basic custom activity overview
- ▶ Creating a basic custom activity
- ▶ Creating a compound activity and activity binding
- ▶ Overview of custom basic activity programming model
- ▶ Adding a designer
- ▶ Adding a `ToolboxBitMap` and making it available across projects

Custom Activity Conceptual Overview

You can create your own custom activities in WF. In fact, creating custom activities is as core to WF as any other capability. Therefore, five hours are devoted to them. This section describes the value of custom activities. The next section describes them from a more technical perspective. Then you begin building them.

Following are three reasons to create custom activities:

- ▶ To improve on an out-of-the-box activity for usability reasons
- ▶ To create domain specific activities
- ▶ To create custom control flow patterns.

In the next sections, you'll look at each.

Improve on Out-of-the-Box Activities

In Hour 17, "Learning Advanced Hosting," a third-party–created synchronous `InvokeWorkflow` activity was discussed because many scenarios call for calling workflows and waiting for the called workflow to return a response. Others have modified the `Delay` activity to make it wait until a milestone, rather than waiting for a period of time. Some may even choose to create an entire new set of out-of-the-box (OOB) activities. Improving the OOB activities is a viable scenario for custom activity development, but it is not anticipated to be the primary motivation behind creating custom activities.

Create Domain-Specific Activities

The OOB activities provide general functionality. They are host agnostic and know nothing about any vertical domains or any individual enterprise. Many who use WF will find that its value grows proportionally to the amount of domain activities added. If, for example, you want to use WF to model the credit process, you could use the OOB activities for control flow and then augment them with standard code to perform the actual credit process. Alternatively, you could create `Customer`, `CheckCredit`, `SendNotification`, and other custom activities that express the credit process. In certain situations, when the domain activities are rich enough, they can be used in conjunction with standard control flow activities to permit code-free workflow construction by developers and even business people. For those that use SharePoint workflow, your get to see how different—and in many ways more immediately useful—WF becomes when a number of activities are added with knowledge of the SharePoint domain.

Custom Control Flow Patterns

A large portion of WF's utility and capability to attract a wide range of authors is dictated by its modeling simplicity and capabilities. The `Replicator` activity, for instance, makes it much easier to model *n* number of elements determined at runtime on a workflow. The `EventHandlingScope` activity likewise makes it easier to respond to events while executing a sequential workflow. The `StateMachineWorkflow` allows for an entirely different workflow style. Although the OOB activities offer a solid start, they do not satisfy all possible control flow patterns. They don't even come close. There are numerous other possible control flow patterns. Some can be found at www.workflowpatterns.com, a site that describes 40 or so control flow patterns. Others may be custom to the process and workflow authors of a specific process. In many cases, the maximum benefit will be achieved through a combination of custom domain and control flow activities. The first will bring the domain to WF, and the latter will streamline development and potentially allow less-technical people to create processes.

Custom Activity Technical Overview

Activities are .NET types and have properties and methods, as does a typical class. Activities have their own programming model and life cycle. Their programming model is primarily supported through a number of optional classes that can be associated with an activity via attributes. These optional classes provide custom validation, design, and toolbox support. The activity programming model is very component-centric, wherein an activity is surrounded by a number of support classes that further tailor the activity.

The activity's life cycle is governed by a finite state machine that includes initialized, executing, closed, and other states. One of the main benefits supplied by workflows is long-running transaction state management. The workflow and many of its embedded activities must be able to execute, go idle, and continue execution when an external event arrives. Developers will create queues managed by the workflow runtime to allow activities to go idle, receive information, and to continue execution when the queue is updated via external input or a timer. The activity life cycle is primarily supported through a set of virtual methods contained in the base activity class (covered throughout the next hours).

Finally, activities such as IfElse and While must contain a designer that conveys their capabilities. These activities must also be able to control the execution of their child activities. The capability to create custom activity layouts and control their child activity execution enables the creation of custom control flow patterns. As mentioned before, WF workflows are themselves activities. They, too, carry out their duties by scheduling their embedded child activities, and their look-and-feel is supplied via designers.

Activities that always execute in a single unit in one burst will be referred to as basic activities throughout the next five hours. Basic activities are covered in this hour. Single activities that can execute across multiple bursts are referred to as multiburst activities. Multiburst activities are covered in Hour 21, "Creating Queued Activities," and Hour 22, "Creating Typed Queued and EventDriven-Enabled Activities." Those that control subordinate child execution are referred to as control flow activities. Control flow activities are covered in Hour 23, "Creating Control Flow Activities Session 1," and Hour 24, "Creating Control Flow Activities Session 2."

A fourth type of activity features a control flow activity prepopulated with child activities to save modeling time. This type of activity is referred to as a compound activity and is covered in this hour.

Control flow activities are generally referred to as composite activities. I like control flow better and will use it.

All basic activities are derived (directly or indirectly) from `System.Workflow.ComponentModel.Activity`, and control flow activities from `System.Workflow.ComponentModel.CompositeActivity`. Unfortunately, most of the OOB activities are sealed. The `CallExternalMethod`, `HandleExternalEvent`, and two state machine and two sequential activities are not sealed. When developing custom activities, you will either extend one of the base classes or higher-level nonsealed activities, depending on your needs. A large portion of SharePoint workflow is implemented through a number of `CallExternalMethod`- and `HandleExternalEvent`-derived activities that manipulate SharePoint tasks and other elements.

Basic Custom Activity Overview

This hour walks you through the creation of a custom activity that will retrieve customer data from a SQL table. The first part of the hour involves coding the functionality to retrieve the custom data by overriding the execute method. Overriding the execute method is the only mandatory step when creating a custom basic activity. The second part of this hour demonstrates creating a type of activities referred to as compound activities. You also learn about activity binding and property promotion while creating a compound activity.

The third part of the hour overviews the basic activity programming model that revolves around a series of classes that are associated to the activity via attributes. You will implement the activity designer and activity toolbox icon attributes in this hour. The first controls the look and feel of the activity, and the second controls its toolbox icon and the small icon that appears on the activity itself. After that, you will learn to make the activity available across all projects.

Creating the Solution and Projects

Follow the next steps to create the solution and two projects. The first will hold the custom activity and the second will hold the workflow you place the custom activity on.

Creating the Solution and Projects

The solution will contain two projects. The first will hold the custom activity and the second the workflow you place the custom activity on.

1. Create a new blank solution named **BasicCustomActivitySolution** and place it in the C:\SamsWf24hrs\Hours\Hour20BasicCustomActivity directory (see Hour 2, "A Spin Around Windows Workflow Foundation").

2. Add a Workflow Activity Library (not a Sequential Workflow Library) project named **CustomBasicActivities** to the solution.

3. Rename Activity1.cs to **Customer.cs** in the Solution Explorer.

4. Add a Sequential Workflow Console application project named **CustomActivityTester** to the solution.

5. Add code to pause the host. (See See Hour 3, "Learning Basic Hosting," if you need help.)

Creating the Customer Custom Activity

In this section you create a custom activity and then extend it to receive input. The input is hardcoded originally and then taken from a database.

Setting the Base Activity

Double-click the Customer activity (the .cs file) in the CustomBasicActivities project. You will see that the activity contains a sequence designer capable of holding child activities (Figure 20.1). The activity currently derives from Sequence activity, as shown in the property window and Figure 20.1.

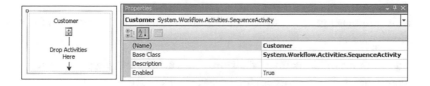

FIGURE 20.1
Default custom activity designer and base class derivation.

The first thing you will do is change the activity to derive from the System.Workflow.ComponentModel.Activity base class because you are creating a basic activity.

Follow the next steps to change the class the activity derives from.

1. Click the `Customer` activity, click in its Properties panel, and click the ellipsis in the Base Class property. Here you can see all the base classes you can derive from when creating a custom activity.

2. Select the `System.Workflow.ComponentModel` and choose the `Activity` type in the middle of the screen (Figure 20.2).

FIGURE 20.2
Base activity
selection form.

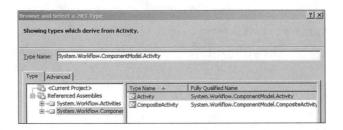

3. Click OK, and the `Customer` activity base class should now be set to `System.Workflow.ComponentModel.Activity`.

Notice that the activity designer now looks like the standard basic activity designer. It is a single unit and cannot contain child activities. This is the default designer associated with activities directly derived from the `Activity` base class.

Overriding the `Execute` Method

For a custom activity to exhibit behavior, you must override its `Execute` method. This is the one mandatory step in custom activity creation.

Follow the next steps to override the `Execute` method.

1. Get to the activity code-beside file by right-clicking the activity and selecting View Code.

2. Notice in the class signature that the custom activity is derived from the base `Activity` class.

3. Add a couple of blank lines below the constructor and type **protected override**, press the spacebar, and select the Execute method to create the execute method shown next:

```
protected override ActivityExecutionStatus
    Execute(ActivityExecutionContext executionContext)
{
    return base.Execute(executionContext);
}
```

4. Replace the code in the method body with the following:

```
Console.WriteLine
        ("I'm printing from within a custom activity's execute
method.");
        return ActivityExecutionStatus.Closed;
```

5. Your Customer class should now look like Listing 20.1.

LISTING 20.1   Customer Custom Activity

```
public partial class Customer : System.Workflow.ComponentModel.Activity
{
    public Customer()
    {
        InitializeComponent();
    }

    protected override ActivityExecutionStatus
        Execute(ActivityExecutionContext executionContext)
    {
        Console.WriteLine
            ("I'm printing from within a custom activity's execute method.");
        return ActivityExecutionStatus.Closed;
    }
}
```

The specifics of the ActivityExecutionContext class and the ActivityExecutionStatus enumerationwill be discussed in Hours 21 and 22. When working with basic activities, it is enough to know that the ActivityExecutionStatus must be returned in closed state so that the activity will complete.

6. Build the CustomBasicActivities project.

You have now overridden the Execute method, instructed it to print a line to the console, and then to return control to the runtime in a closed state. This tells the runtime the activity is finished executing.

Adding the Custom Activity to a Workflow

You will now add the activity to a workflow and run the workflow. The activity is included in a new section of the toolbox named CustomBasicActivities Components (Figure 20.3). The new toolbox section is available to all projects in the current solution. In the upcoming "Adding the Activity to the Toolbox Across Projects" section of this hour, you will learn to make it available to all workflow projects and to change the icon that appears on the toolbox.

FIGURE 20.3
Toolbox with
Customer activ-
ity included.

Follow the next steps to add the Customer activity to the workflow.

1. Set the CustomActivityTester project as the startup project.

2. Drag and drop the Customer activity onto the workflow.

3. Run the workflow, and you should see that the Customer activity printed the content you specified in its execute method to the console (Figure 20.4).

FIGURE 20.4
Workflow with
Customer activ-
ity results.

That's it. You have created a custom activity, placed it on the workflow, and executed the workflow with the custom activity on it. You will create a more useful custom activity as the hour progresses.

Updating the Customer Activity to Receive Input

You update the Customer activity to receive input in this section. First you add a DependencyProperty and then you modify the activity to receive input and print the contents of this DependencyProperty to the console.

Adding a DependencyProperty to the Activity

We need to be able to accept a value and pass it to our Customer activity, which can, in turn, retrieve the correct customer. You will add a new property to the Customer activity that holds the customer number. The property is added and associated to the Customer activity and not to the workflow. The activity will then print this value to the console.

Follow the next steps to create a DependencyProperty.

1. Get to the activity code-beside file by right-clicking Customer.cs and selecting View Code.

2. Move your cursor directly below the constructor, insert a couple of additional blank lines, move your cursor between the lines, right-click, and select Insert

Snippet. Double-click Other, double-click Workflow, and double-click DependencyProperty—Property to insert a new dependency property.

3. You should see the stub dependency property, and the text MyProperty should be highlighted.

4. Enter **CustomerNumber** (replacing MyProperty), and press Enter to leave the wizard.

Updating the Execute Method

Follow the next steps to update the Execute method to use the DependencyProperty you added to the activity.

1. Replace the body of the Execute method with the following:

```
Console.WriteLine("The customer is: " + CustomerNumber);
return ActivityExecutionStatus.Closed;
```

2. Build the CustomBasicActivities project.

Running the Workflow with the CustomerNumber Property

Follow the next steps to run the workflow and populate the CustomerNumber property.

1. Click the Customer activity on the workflow, and you should see the property window shown in Figure 20.5.

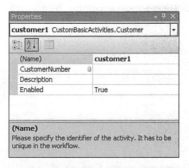

FIGURE 20.5
Customer activity property window.

2. Input the value **MyCustomer** in the CustomerNumber property and run the workflow. You should see the results shown in Figure 20.6.

FIGURE 20.6
Custom activity printing value from property windows.

Updating the `Customer` Activity to Retrieve Information from a Database

The customer number will be manually entered into the `Customer` activity. The `Customer` activity's `Execute` method will now retrieve the customer specified in the property from a SQL database. Finally, the results from the table will be placed in the `Customer` activity's corresponding dependency properties.

Running the SQL Script to Create the SQL Components

Follow the next steps to run a SQL script that will create a CustomActivity database. The database will have one table and a stored procedure. The script needs to be run. The directions that follow show how to run the script in Microsoft SQL Server Management Studio.

1. Open Microsoft SQL Server Management Studio. Select your SQL Server and log in to the dialog.

2. Click File, Open, File, and then open the SQL script `C:\SamsWf24hrs\Hours\Hour20BasicCustomActivity\SQL\CreateCustomAct ivityDatabase.sql`.

3. Click Execute or press F5 to run the query.

4. Verify that the `CustomActivity` database was created and that it holds a `Customer` table and a `GetCustomer` stored procedure.

5. There are three records in the `Customer` table. Customer 0003 is set to always go on hold, customer 0002 evaluates whether to go on hold, and customer 0001 never goes on hold. See Figure 20.7.

FIGURE 20.7
Customer table.

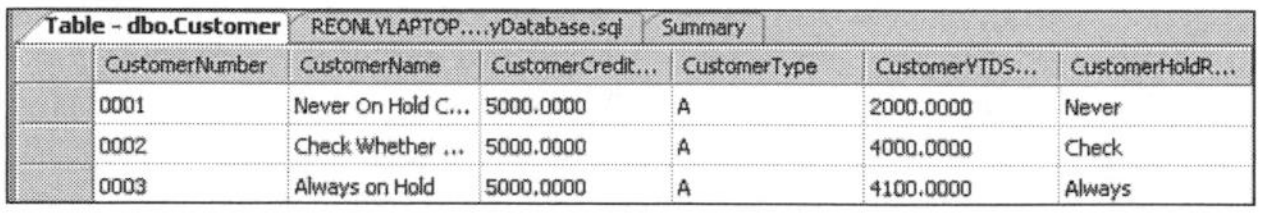

CustomerNumber	CustomerName	CustomerCredit...	CustomerType	CustomerYTDS...	CustomerHoldR...
0001	Never On Hold C...	5000.0000	A	2000.0000	Never
0002	Check Whether ...	5000.0000	A	4000.0000	Check
0003	Always on Hold	5000.0000	A	4100.0000	Always

Adding Additional Dependency Properties

Now you will add `CustomerName`, `CustomerCreditLimit`, and other dependency properties to the `Customer` activity. You'll manually input the customer number into the `CustomerNumber` property, and the other values will be retrieved from a SQL database. Although the customer number would be received from the host system in a real-world scenario, the manual property input is sufficient for demonstrating this activity.

1. Get to the activity code-beside file by right-clicking the Customer activity and selecting View Code.

2. Move your cursor below the CustomerNumber dependency property, right-click, and select Insert Snippet. Double-click Other, double-click Workflow, and double-click DependencyProperty—Property to insert a new dependency property.

3. You should see the stub dependency property, and the text MyProperty should be highlighted.

4. Enter **CustomerName** (replacing MyProperty), and press Enter to leave the wizard.

5. Create additional dependency properties specified in Table 20.1.

TABLE 20.1   Dependency Properties to Add

Name	Type
CustomerCreditLimit	Double
CustomerType	String
CustomerYtdSales	Double
CustomerHoldRules	String

Retrieving Customer from Database

Follow the next steps to update the Execute method to retrieve the customer from the database and store its attributes to the activity dependency properties. You will add quite a bit of code to the Execute method that retrieves a customer from the database and stores the table values to variables. Because it is not WF code, it is not explained.

1. Get to the activity code-beside file by right-clicking the activity and selecting View Code.

2. Add the following using directives:

```
using System.Data;
using System.Data.SqlClient;
```

3. Add the following member variable declaration below the constructor:

```
        private static string ConnectionString = "Initial
Catalog=CustomActivity;" +
            "Data Source=localhost; Integrated Security=SSPI;";
```

4. Replace the contents of the Execute method with Listing 20.2.

LISTING 20.2   Customer Execute Method Retrieves Customer From Database

```
SqlConnection dbConn = new SqlConnection(ConnectionString);
SqlCommand getCustomer = new SqlCommand("GetCustomer", dbConn);

getCustomer.CommandType = System.Data.CommandType.StoredProcedure;
getCustomer.Parameters.AddWithValue("@CustomerNumber",
CustomerNumber);

dbConn.Open();

using (SqlDataReader custReader =
getCustomer.ExecuteReader(CommandBehavior.CloseConnection))
    {
        if (custReader.Read())
        {
            CustomerName = custReader["CustomerName"].ToString().Trim();
            CustomerCreditLimit =
double.Parse(custReader["CustomerCreditLimit"].ToString());
            CustomerType = custReader["CustomerType"].ToString().Trim();
            CustomerYtdSales =
double.Parse(custReader["CustomerYtdSales"].ToString());
            CustomerHoldRules =
custReader["CustomerHoldRules"].ToString().Trim();
        }
    }

Console.WriteLine
    ("The customer number is: " + CustomerNumber);
Console.WriteLine
    ("The customer name is: " + CustomerName);
Console.WriteLine
    ("The customer credit limit is: " + CustomerCreditLimit);
Console.WriteLine
    ("The customer type is: " + CustomerType);
Console.WriteLine
    ("The customer YTD sales is: " + CustomerYtdSales);
Console.WriteLine
    ("The customer hold rules is: " + CustomerHoldRules);
return ActivityExecutionStatus.Closed;
```

5. Build the CustomBasicActivities project.

Running the Workflow with Data Coming from the Database

1. Open the workflows in design-mode and input and input **0002** in the Customer activity CustomerNumber property.

2. Run the workflow. Customer 0002 should be retrieved from the database, and its values output as shown in Figure 20.8.

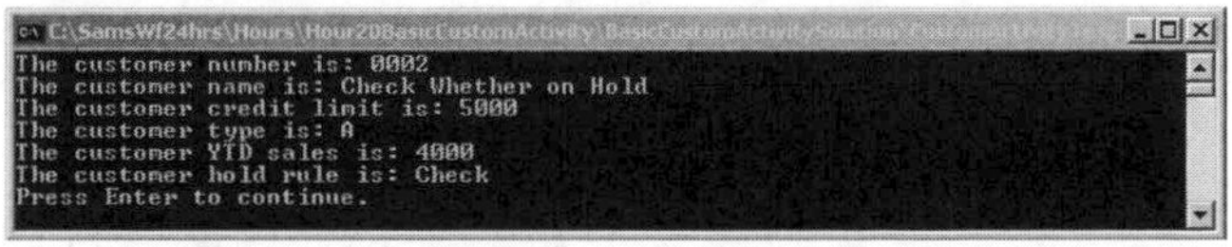

FIGURE 20.8
Get Custom activity printing customer data from database.

Adding Existing Custom `CreditCheck` Activity

The custom `CheckCredit` activity uses the values retrieved by the `Customer` activity and an order amount passed from the host to determine whether the customer passes the credit check. To save time, the `CheckCredit` activity is already created. You have to import it into the project and update the host and workflow to use the new activity.

Import the `CreditCheck` Activity

Follow the next steps to add the existing `CreditCheck` activity to the project.

1. Right-click the `CustomBasicActivities` project, select Add, Existing Item.

2. Browse to `C:\SamsWf24hrs\Hours\Hour20BasicCustomActivity\` `CheckCreditActivity` and select the `CheckCredit.cs` and `CheckCredit.designer.cs` files. Then click OK.

Updating the Host to Pass in the `OrderAmount`

Follow the next steps to update the host to pass the `OrderAmount` to the workflow.

1. Open `Program.cs` and add a parameter above the line that instantiates the WorkflowInstance using the code in the next snippet:

```
// Add the parameters via a dictionary object
Dictionary<string, object> parameters = new
Dictionary<string, object>();
parameters.Add("OrderAmount", 1200);
```

2. Add the parameters to be passed to the workflow by replacing the current lines that instantiate the WorkflowInstance as shown:

```
WorkflowInstance instance =
    WorkflowRuntime.CreateWorkflow(
    typeof(CustomActivityTester.Workflow1), parameters);
```

3. Open `Workflow1.cs` in code-beside view. Then add a DependencyProperty named `OrderAmount` and set its type to double (see Hour 4, "Learning Host-Workflow Data Exchange," if you need help adding a DependencyProperty). This property will retrieve the `OrderAmount` passed in from the host.

Binding the `Customer` Properties to the `CheckCredit` Activity

The `CheckCredit` activity is already constructed and its properties have already been added (Figure 20.9). The `CheckCredit` activity makes credit decisions based on `Customer` activity and workflow data. `ActivityBinding` will be used to update the `CheckCredit` activity's properties. Instead of binding most of the `CheckCredit` activity's properties to the workflow, they will be bound to the corresponding properties in the `Customer` activity. The `CheckCredit` activity also has an `OrderAmount` property that is bound to the workflow `OrderAmount` property that is received from the host. The `CheckCredit` activity's `OnHold` property is updated to Yes if the customer is placed on hold and to No if not. A string is used to allow more information and results other than Yes and No to be stored.

FIGURE 20.9
Binding the
`CheckCredit`
dependency
property to the
`Customer`
credit limit
dependency
property of the
same name.

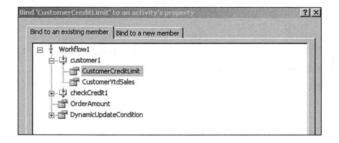

Follow the next steps to bind the `Customer` activity properties to the `CheckCredit` activity's properties.

1. Build the `CustomBasicActivities` project to add the `CreditCheck` activity to the toolbox.

2. Add a `CheckCredit` activity to the workflow below the `Customer` activity.

3. Click the `CheckCredit` activity. Then click the `CustomerCreditLimit` property, click the ellipsis, click the + next to customer1, and select `CustomerCreditLimit` (Figure 20.9). Then click OK.

4. Click the `CustomerHoldRules` property, click the ellipsis, click the + next to customer1, and select CustomerHoldRules. Then click OK.

5. Now bind the `CustomerName`, `CustomerNumber`, `CustomerType`, and `CustomerYTDSales` properties to their corresponding Customer properties.

6. Bind the `OrderAmount` property to the workflow `OrderAmount` property. Click the `OrderAmount` property, click the ellipsis, and select `OrderAmount`. Then click OK.

Adding an `IfElse` to Evaluate Credit Hold Status

Follow the next steps to add and configure and `IfElse` activity to evaluate the `Status` returned from the `CheckCredit` activity.

1. Place an `IfElse` activity below the `CheckCredit` activity. Name the `IfElse` activity **CheckCredit**. Name the left branch **CreditApproved** and name the right branch **CreditRejected**.

2. Click the drop-down in the `Condition` property of the left branch of the `IfElse` activity, select Declarative Rule Condition, click the + that appears next to the Condition property, and enter **CreditHoldRule** in the Condition Name property. Click the ellipsis in the ConditionName property, click the Edit button (to update the CreditHoldRule) and enter the following in the dialog box.

```
this.checkCredit1.OnHold == "Yes"
```

3. Select OK twice to return to the workflow.

4. Add a Code activity to the left branch. Double-click it and add the following code to its handler:

```
Console.WriteLine("Customer is on hold.");
```

5. Add a Code activity to the right branch. Double-click it and add the following code to its handler:

```
Console.WriteLine("Customer is not on hold.");
```

6. Your completed workflow should look like Figure 20.10.

Running the Workflow with the `CheckCredit` Activity

The workflow will now determine hold status. Customer 0001 will never place the customer on hold and 0003 will always place the customer on hold. Customer 0002 will add

FIGURE 20.10
Completed cus-
tom activity
tester workflow.

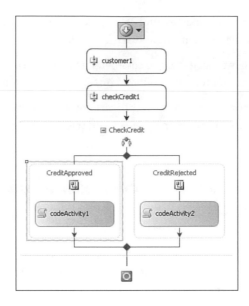

the order amount to the YTD sales, and if the sum is less than the credit limit, the customer will not be placed on hold. Otherwise, the customer will be placed on hold.

Follow the next steps to run the workflow a couple of times for different customers and
evaluate the results.

1. Input **0001** into the `Customer` activity `CustomerNumber` property on the workflow.

2. Run the workflow; the customer should not go on hold, as shown in Figure 20.11.

FIGURE 20.11
Workflow run for
customer set to
never go on hold.

```
C:\SamsWf24hrs\Hours\Hour20BasicCustomActivity\BasicCustomActivitySolution\CustomActivity...  _□×
The customer number is: 0001
The customer name is: Never On Hold Customer
The customer credit limit is: 5000
The customer type is: A
The customer YTD sales is: 2000
The customer hold rule is: Never
Customer is not on hold.
Press Enter to continue.
```

3. Input **0002** into the Customer activity `CustomerNumber` property.

4. Run the workflow; the customer should go on hold because the order amount
(1,200) plus the YTD sales (4000) is more than the credit limit (5,000).

5. Try changing the order amount passed in from the host to less than 1,000 and
running the workflow again if you like.

Adding Event Handlers to Activities

Event handlers can be placed on activities by adding a `DependencyProperty` of type `EventHandler`. The `EventHandler` then appears as a property on the activity when it is placed on the workflow and functions just like the handlers on the `Code`, `CallExternalMethod`, and other WF activities. In this section you create an `EventHandler` typed `DependencyProperty` and then modify the `Execute` method to invoke the `EventHandler`.

Creating the Event Handler

You will add a preprocessing `EventHandler` to the `Customer` activity. We will employ the same terminology used by WF activities that have handlers and name it Invoking, because it executes before the activity executes.

1. Open the `Customer` activity in code view, move your cursor directly below the Customer constructor, insert a couple of additional blank lines, move your cursor between the lines, right-click, and select Insert Snippet. Double-click Other, double-click Workflow, and double-click DependencyProperty—EventHandler (select Event Handler, not Property this time) to insert a new EventHandler dependency property.

2. You should see the stub dependency property, and the text Invoke should be highlighted.

3. Enter **Invoking** (replacing Invoke) and press Enter to leave the wizard. The type is set to `EventHandler`.

The body of the dependency property is an event with `AddHandler` and `RemoveHandler` methods instead of get and set methods. You have now created an event handler that code can be associated with and can execute when you specify.

Modifying the `Execute` Method

Follow the next steps to modify the `Execute` method needed to invoke the handler. The handler will be called at the beginning of the `Execute` method so that it is invoked before the `Custom` activity does its work (retrieves the customer). Conversely, if the handler was placed at the end of the `Execute` method it would support post processing.

1. Add the following code to the top of the `Execute` method in the `Customer` activity class to invoke the event.

```
// Perform preprocessing.
base.RaiseEvent(Customer.InvokingEvent, this, EventArgs.Empty);
```

2. Build the `CustomBasicActivities` project.

You can substitute your activity and dependency property name to use on another activity.

Adding Event Handler and Running the Workflow

Follow the next steps to configure the Invoking property on the Customer activity. Then add logic to the handler that is created and run the workflow.

1. Open Workflow in design-mode and click the Customer activity.

2. Click its Invoking property, enter **PreProcessing**, and press Enter to create the handler.

3. Enter the following code in the handler:

   ```
   Console.WriteLine("I am preprocessing from an event handler.");
   ```

4. Press F5 to run the workflow, and the text from the PreProcessing handler should be displayed along with the other text displayed by the workflow and activity.

Creating Compound Activities

Compound activities are standard WF control flow activities prepopulated with other activities. Retrieving the customer, checking the credit, and then performing actions based on approval or rejection is likely to be a common pattern. Therefore, you will create a CompoundCreditCheck activity that satisfies this scenario in one activity in this section.

Promoted properties allow the properties of child activities to be propagated to their parent. It is common to need to promote properties to the parent when working with compound activities because the child activity properties are locked and not accessible. Promoted properties are demonstrated when configuring the CompoundCreditCheck activity shortly. Property promotion and activity binding can be done only with dependency properties. Neither can be done with standard .NET properties.

Creating and Modeling the Compound Activity

Follow the next steps to create the CompoundCreditCheck activity and populate it with child activities.

1. Right-click the `CustomBasicActivities` project and select Add, Activity.

2. Name the activity **CompoundCreditCheck** and click OK.

3. Add a `Customer` activity to the `CompoundCreditCheck` activity.

4. Add a `CheckCredit` activity below the `Customer` activity.

5. Add an `IfElse` activity below the `CheckCredit` activity. Name the `IfElse` activity **CheckCredit**, the left branch **CreditApproved**, and the right branch **CreditRejected**.

6. Place a `Code` activity in each branch of the `IfElse` activity.

7. The modeled `CompoundCreditCheck` activity should look like Figure 20.12:

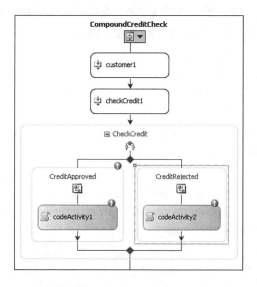

FIGURE 20.12
Modeled Compound-CreditCheck activity.

Configure the `IfElse` Activity

Follow the next steps to configure the `IfElse` activity placed on the `CompoundCreditCheck` activity.

1. Click the drop-down in the `Condition` property of the left branch of the `IfElse` activity, select Declarative Rule Condition, click the + that appears next to the `Condition` property, and enter **CreditHoldRule** in the `ConditionName` property. Click the ellipsis in the `ConditionName` property, click the Edit button (to update the `CreditHoldRule`), and enter the following in the dialog box.

```
this.checkCredit1.OnHold == "Yes"
```

2. Click OK twice.

3. Double-click the Code activity in the left branch and add the following code to its handler:

```
Console.WriteLine("Customer is on hold.");
```

4. Double-click the Code activity in the right branch. Double-click it and add the following code to its handler:

```
Console.WriteLine("Customer is not on hold.");
```

5. Build the CustomBasicActivities project.

Configuring the CheckCredit Activity in the CompoundCreditCheck Activity

Binding is the major component to configuring the CheckCredit activity. First, the CheckCredit activity properties need to be bound to their corresponding Customer activity properties. When that is done, the OrderAmount property needs to be promoted so that it can later be bound to the workflow OrderAmount property.

Follow the next steps to configure the CheckCredit activity on the CompoundCreditCheck activity.

1. Bind the CustomerCreditLimit, CustomerHoldRules, CustomerName, CustomerNumber, CustomerType, and CustomerYTDSales properties on the checkCredit1 activity in the CompoundCreditCheck activity to their corresponding customer1 activity properties.

2. Right-click the checkCredit1 activity and select Promote Bindable Properties. Doing so makes the OrderAmount and OnHold properties become properties of the CompoundCreditCheck activity. These two properties are the remaining CheckCredit properties that were not bound to the customer activity. You will not see the promoted properties on the CompoundCreditCheck activity until placing it on the workflow.

Configuring the Customer Activity in the CompoundCreditCheck Activity

Follow the next steps to configure the Customer activity in the CompoundCreditCheck activity.

1. Right-click the `Customer` activity and select Promote Bindable Properties. This promotes all customer properties, even though only the `CustomerNumber` property is needed.

There is no hard penalty for binding additional properties. If, for clarity or other reasons, binding all properties does not work for you, you can programmatically promote the properties. The details of doing so are not covered in this book. If you are interested, as a starting point, search for `ActivityBind` in `CompoundCreditCheck.Designer.cs` to get an idea about how it works.

---

2. Build the `CustomBasicActivities` project.

Creating a New Sequential Workflow

Follow the next steps to create a new sequential workflow and modify the host to point to the new workflow.

1. Right-click the `CustomActivityTester` project. Then select Add, Sequential Workflow.

2. Name the workflow **CompoundActivityWorkflow** and click OK.

3. Open `Program.cs` and modify it to use `CompoundActivityWorkflow` instead of `Workflow1` by replacing the current line of code that begins with `WorkflowInstance` instance with the following:

```
            WorkflowInstance instance =
                workflowRuntime.CreateWorkflow(
                typeof(CustomActivityTester.CompoundActivityWorkflow),
parameters);
```

4. Open the `CompoundActivityWorkflow` in code view. Then create a dependency property named **OrderAmount** and set its type to double.

Modeling the Workflow with the CompoundCreditCheck Activity

Follow the next steps to add the `CompoundCreditCheck` activity and run the workflow you created in the last section.

1. Open the CompoundActivityWorkflow in design mode and add the CompoundCreditCheck activity to the workflow. What took six activities last section now takes one activity. Moreover, most of the properties including the condition are already set.

2. Click the CompoundCreditCheck activity and you will see that it contains a number of additional properties (Figure 20.13). The CheckCredit promoted properties are prefaced with check_Credit_1 and the ones from the Customer activity are also prefaced.

FIGURE 20.13
Compound-
CreditCheck
activity placed
on workflow and
its properties.

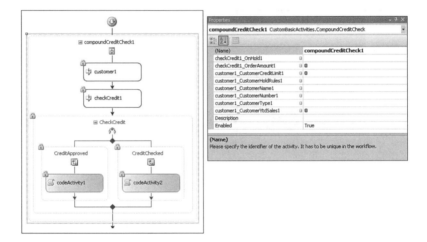

3. Click the CompoundCreditCheck activity. Then click its creditCheck1_OrderAmount property and bind it to the workflow's OrderAmount property.

4. Enter **0002** in the CompoundCreditCheck activity's customer1_CustomerNumber1 property and run the workflow. You should see the results shown in Figure 20.14.

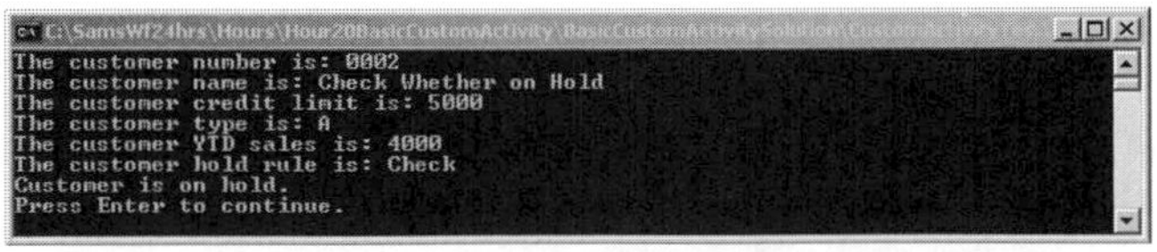

FIGURE 20.14
Workflow results
with Compound-
CreditCheck
activity.

Try entering different customer numbers if you like. The rules should be the same as when you manually build out the workflow using the individual activities.

Activity Programming Model

Activity validation, serialization, design, toolbox support, and code generation are enabled through optional classes that can be associated with the activity via attributes (as shown in Figure 20.15). This hour demonstrates activity design and toolbox support. Activity validation is covered in Hour 24, "Creating Control Flow Activities Session 2."

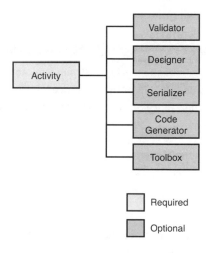

FIGURE 20.15
Custom activity programming model.

Activity validation is for design-time enforcement only. It should be used to validate if a `Condition` property is updated or that the first child of an `EventDriven` activity is a blocking activity. It should not be used to ensure the customer number is valid.

Designer Components

Activity designers control the look-and-feel of activities. The base activity class is associated with the `ActivityDesigner` type by default. This designer produces the standard basic activity designer shape that is now used by the `Customer` and `CheckCredit` activities. This section focuses on `ActivityDesignerThemes`. The activity designer foreground, background, fonts, and icons can be changed via `ActivityDesignerThemes`. The general look-and-feel of an activity designer can be specified via `ActivityDesignerThemes`.

When more precise control is necessary, a number of methods in the `ActivityDesigner` type, such as `OnPaint` and `OnLayoutSize`, allow you to construct the designer look-and-feel from the ground up. Using the methods in the

ActivityDesigner is not covered in this book. See MSDN or other resources if you need more control than that provided by the ActivityDesignerTheme.

Designers are even more important when applied to control flow activities. The designer should convey the activity intent, and it is the designers on a workflow model that make the workflow transparent. For instance, the general function of a workflow with an IfElse and a While activity can be inferred by looking at the designers rendered on the workflow that are associated with these activities.

Creating an Activity Designer Theme

To implement an ActivityDesigner, you must place an ActivityDesigner attribute on the activity class. The attribute must reference a custom class that derives from ActivityDesigner. You then place an ActivityDesignerTheme attribute on the ActivityDesigner class.

Attributing the Customer Activity

Follow the next steps to decorate the Customer activity with a CustomerDesigner attribute.

  1. Add the following attribute above the Customer activity class declaration.

```
[Designer(typeof(CustomerDesigner), typeof(IDesigner))]
```

  2. Your Customer class should now look like this:

```
[Designer(typeof(CustomerDesigner), typeof(IDesigner))]
public partial class Customer : System.Workflow.ComponentModel.Activity
    // Additional code
```

Creating a Customer ActivityDesigner Class

You will not use any of the methods in this class, but the ActivityDesignerTheme is referenced through the designer associated with the activity and not the activity itself. Therefore, follow the next steps to create a blank CustomerDesigner class that the designer theme class can be referenced (attributed) from.

  1. Right-click the CustomBasicActivities project. Select Add, Class, and name it **CustomerDesigner.**

  2. Add the following using directive:

```
using System.Workflow.ComponentModel.Design;
```

3. Specify that the class implements ActivityDesigner by replacing the class declaration with the following code:

```
class CustomerDesigner : ActivityDesigner
```

4. Add the ActivityDesignerTheme attribute by placing the following code above the class declaration:

```
[ActivityDesignerThemeAttribute(typeof(CustomerDesignerTheme))]
```

5. The CustomerDesigner class should look like this:

```
[ActivityDesignerThemeAttribute(typeof(CustomerDesignerTheme))]
class CustomerDesigner : ActivityDesigner
{
}
```

Implementing the Activity Designer Theme

Follow the next steps to create the ActivityDesignerTheme class that will modify the activity designer's appearance.

1. Right-click the CustomBasicActivities project. Select Add, Class, and name it **CustomerDesignerTheme**.

2. Add the following using directives:

```
using System.Workflow.ComponentModel.Design;
using System.Drawing;
using System.Drawing.Drawing2D;
```

3. Replace the class declaration with the following code that implements the ActivityDesignerTheme.

```
public class CustomerDesignerTheme : ActivityDesignerTheme
```

4. Add the following constructor to the CustomerDesignerTheme class in which you will place the design logic in the next step:

```
public CustomerDesignerTheme(WorkflowTheme theme)
    : base(theme)
{
}
```

5. Now alter the activity's appearance by changing its border style, shading, and color by adding the code below the constructor you just added:

```
this.BorderColor = Color.Red;
this.BorderStyle = DashStyle.Dash;
```

```
this.BackColorStart = Color.Aqua;
this.BackColorEnd = Color.Cyan;
this.BackgroundStyle = LinearGradientMode.Horizontal;
```

6. Build the `CustomBasicActivities` project.

7. Open the CompoundActivityWorkflow in design mode, and you should see that the `Customer` activity is now blue. See Figure 20.16, although it does not show the color.

FIGURE 20.16
`Customer` activity with theme applied.

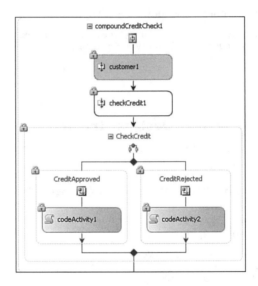

By the Way

If you like, run the workflow again, although it is not necessary because the changes made were design-time only.

ToolboxBitMap Class

The `ToolboxBitmap` type allows a graphic to be associated with an activity. The graphic appears on the toolbox and is embedded in the activity when the activity is on a workflow. The graphic must be 16 × 16 pixels. These characteristics comply with .NET's toolbox graphic rules. There is an existing graphic that meets this criteria that you will use in this exercise. See other resources for instructions on creating a compliant ToolboxBitMap icon. This section covers adding an existing graphic to the toolbox.

Adding Graphic as Image and Associating Class

Follow the next steps to add the existing .jpg file to a new project directory you will create named Resources, and set the file's Build Action property to Embedded Resource.

> The icon shows only on the workflow in this section. It will show on the toolbox as well after the next section, when the item is made available across all projects on the toolbox.

1. Right-click the CustomBasicActivities project and select Add, New Folder.

2. Name the folder **Resources.**

3. Right-click the Resources folder and select Add, Existing Item.

4. Browse to the C:\SamsWf24hrs\Hours\Hour20BasicCustomActivity directory and select the Customer.jpg file.

5. Click the Customer.jpg file.

6. Set its Build Action property to Embedded Resource.

7. Open the Customer activity class in code view. Then add the following code above the class declaration to associate the activity with the customer toolbox icon.

    ```
    [ToolboxBitmap(typeof(Customer), "Resources.Customer.jpg")]
    ```

8. Build the CustomBasicActivities project.

9. Open the Workflow1 in design mode. The activity is unchanged on the toolbox.

10. Add the activity to Workflow1; the activity now has a person with a notepad embedded rather than the standard embedded custom activity graphic (Figure 20.17).

FIGURE 20.17
Customer activity with custom embedded customer graphic.

> If your graphic is named differently from your activity, you will have to use the ToolboxBitmap overload that accepts the assembly and the resource. See MSDN or other sources for details.

Adding the Activity to the Toolbox Across Projects

By default, the activity is available on the toolbox to projects in the current solution. In this section, you learn to make the activity accessible from the toolbox across workflow projects outside of the current solution as well. Installing an item on the Visual Studio toolbox that can be seen across workflow projects is not specific to WF. It requires creating a `.vscontent` file and a `.vsi` file.

Creating the VSContent File

The `.vscontent` file contains the name of the category the toolbox menu item is added to and the name of the DLL in the `FileName` element. The `DisplayName` and `Description` elements are set to Custom Activities. The rest of the information is boilerplate.

Follow the next step to update the `.vscontent` file.

1. Copy the `CustomActivities.vscontent` file shown next from the `C:\SamsWf24hrs\Hours\Hour20BasicCustomActivity` directory to the `C:\SamsWf24hrs\Hours\Hour20BasicCustomActivity\BasicCustomActivitySolution\CustomBasicActivities\bin\Debug` directory.

Creating the VSI file

This file and the DLL must be added to a Zip file. The Zip file is renamed to the `.vsi` extension. This file is then double-clicked to add the item to the Visual Studio toolbox.

Follow the next steps to create the `.vsi` file.

1. Go to the `C:\SamsWf24hrs\Hours\Hour20BasicCustomActivity\BasicCustomActivitySolution\CustomBasicActivities\bin\Debug` directory.

2. Create a new Folder (File, New Folder) named **CustomActivities**. The name of this folder will be the category name the toolbox menu item resides in.

3. Copy the `CustomBasicActivities.dll` file into the CustomActivities directory.

4. Right-click the CustomActivities folder and select Send To, Compressed Zip folder.

5. Drag-and-drop the `.vscontent` file into the Zip file. The Zip file should now have the CustomActivities directory with the `.dll` and the `.vscontent` file.

6. Exit all copies of Visual Studio.

7. Exit from the Zip file and rename it to **CustomActivities.vsi**.

8. Double-click the `CustomActivities.vsi` file, and you should see the following form (Figure 20.18).

FIGURE 20.18
VSI Wizard form.

9. Select Finished and answer Yes to the dialog that warns of a lack of a certificate.

10. If you receive a dialog that Tools.InstallCommunityControls is invalid, click OK and continue.

11. Close the dialog.

12. Open another solution from another hour that has a workflow. Open the workflow. Open the toolbox and the `Customer` activity will reside on the toolbox, even though this project is not in the CustomBasicActivities solution.

13. Add the `Customer` activity to the workflow, and you should see that both the toolbox and the activity have the custom icon you just associated with the `Customer` activity (Figure 20.19):

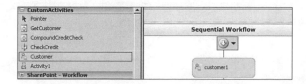

FIGURE 20.19
`Customer` activity on workflow and toolbox with custom icon.

Summary

This hour scratched the surface of what is arguably WF's most powerful feature: custom activities. The `Customer` and `CheckCredit` activities represent custom domain activities that can be combined with other domain activities, such as `GetOrder` to allow common business functions to be molded much more rapidly where they benefit from WF's design-time and runtime capabilities. Then compound activities that allow common activity patterns to be added to the workflow in one step were covered. Finally, changing the activity's appearance and its `ToolboxBitmap` were covered. Event driven and control flow activities are covered in the next four hours.

Workshop

Quiz

1. *What method must you override in an activity for it to do anything?*

2. *What classes allow you to customize the activity look-and-feel?*

3. *When do you use the features in the* `ActivityDesigner` *class?*

4. *When do you use the features in the* `ActivityDesignerTheme` *class?*

5. *How are activity properties made available to the workflow?*

6. *How must the* `Execute` *method be completed?*

Answers

1. Execute.

2. `ActivityDesigner` and `ActivityDesignerAttribute`.

3. Changing the size or painting the activity manually are sample usages. It is generally used in more advanced cases.

4. When you want to change the look of the activity.

5. The dependency properties created in the activity are accessed via the activity name + the property name (for example, `this.getCustomer2.CustomerSales`).

6. Return `ActivityExecutionStatus.Closed`.

HOUR 21

Creating Queued Activities

What You Will Learn in This Hour:

- ▶ Overview of activity life cycle topics
- ▶ Basic queued activity
- ▶ Queued activity from service

This hour covers creating custom activities that execute across more than one burst. Out-of-the-box activities, including the `HandleExternalEvent` and `Delay`, exemplify multiburst activities. In their first burst, they create a queue and register a handler with the queue. They then enter an idle state. When their idle state ends—because of an event receipt or timer expiration—they enter their second burst of execution. These types of multiburst executing activities are vital to WF because through them comes much of WF's ability to provide state support to long-lived processes. You will then enable multiburst activities to be the first child in `EventDriven` activities. `Listen` activity branches and `State` activities are sample `EventDriven` activities.

Following are a couple of figures to give a conceptual understanding of single- and multiburst activities.

Figure 21.1 illustrates the life cycle of a single-burst activity that transitions from initialized to executing to closed.

FIGURE 21.1
Basic activity typical execution.

Figure 21.2 demonstrates the life cycle of a multiburst activity. It sets up a queue in its `Execute` method, idles, and then resumes when the queue is updated.

FIGURE 21.2
Typical multi-
burst activity
execution.

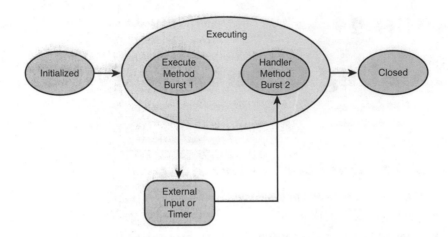

Exploring Activity Life Cycle Topics

Queued activities are very life cycle- and thread-centric. Implementing queued activities requires understanding more of WF's internal operations. Therefore, some of these operations are summarized before we dive into queued activity development. The topics explained in this section are somewhat complex and abstract. If you do not get them on your first reading, go through the exercises and then come back to them. The next two subsections describe the WorkflowQueue type and ActivityExecutionContext, in that order.

WorkflowQueue

All WF host-workflow communication is built on the WorkflowQueue type. The WorkflowQueue type is a named location (or queue) that can respond to events and receive data. When a named queue is triggered, the WF runtime locates the workflow instance associated with the named queue. If the workflow instance is dehydrated in a persistence store, the WF runtime reactivates it. Then the WF runtime delivers the data to the workflow instance.

All WF host-workflow communication is built on this queuing infrastructure, including the ExternalDataExchange communication used throughout this book. The actual named queues receiving the events are hidden from you when using External-DataExchange, Web Services, and Windows Communication Foundation for host-workflow communication.

When working with multiburst activities, you work directly with named queues. There is no abstraction layer built on top of them. The multiburst activities will create a named queue, idle, and then receive the data placed into the named queue.

This hour teaches you to use named queues in the context of multiburst activities. However, what you learn is relevant to using named queues in other scenarios as well. Because all other host-workflow communication capabilities are built on top of named queues, there may be times that one of their implementations does not perform a particular task you need that can be obtained by going directly to the named queues. More so, some prefer to cut out the middlemen and to use the underlying named queues for all host-workflow communication, or to build their own communication abstraction on top.

ActivityExecutionContext

ActivityExecutionContext is the container in which the activity executes. Many of the operations a custom activity performs require it to access the ActivityExecutionContext parameter received in its Execute method. As you saw last hour, custom code can be written in the Execute method that accesses a database and retrieves a customer, for instance. However, many custom activities will use the ActivityExecutionContext for the following reasons:

▶ To access out-of-the-box and custom runtime services (see the "Custom Activity Queued from Service" section) registered with the runtime. The WorkflowQueuingService, for instance, is retrieved from the ActivityExecutionContext to create WorkflowQueue objects when working with multiburst activities.

▶ To allow logic in multiburst activities to process on a different thread while the activity returns control to the runtime (see the "Custom Activity Queued from Service" section).

▶ To move logic from the execute method to services that can be accessed for architectural and maintenance reasons. No samples are directly provided, but the "Custom Activity Queued from Service" section offers the framework.

▶ When working with composite activities (see Hour 23, "Creating Control Flow Activities Session 1," and Hour 24, "Creating Control Flow Activities Session 2") to access and control child activities.

▶ To call its CloseActivity method when working with multiburst and composite activities (see the "Basic Custom Queued Activity" section).

▶ To spawn unique ActivityExecutionContexts and to place them in the ActivityExecutionContextManager collection when creating custom activities that execute the same child activity more than once (for example, While and Replicator). Creating unique ActivityExecutionContexts is not covered in this book.

Overview of Samples

There are four exercises created over the next two hours, the first two in this hour and the latter two in the next, that all build on each other.

The first example creates a very simple queued activity where the host delivers data to the named queue. This is the most simple multiburst activity that you can create.

The second example includes a custom runtime service that processes on a worker thread and, when complete, updates the named queue. This demonstrates using custom runtime services with multiburst activities. The third example extends the second. It accesses a database and uses an EventArgs class to type the data sent from the service to the named queue.

The fourth implements IEventActivity and enables the multiburst activity to be the first child in EventDriven activities. Listen activity branches and State activities are sample EventDriven activities.

> The exercises in this hour and the next use aspects of the Long Running Activity Sample
> (http://www.microsoft.com/downloads/details.aspx?FamilyId=8C2EF231-0622-4BEC-9D35-9E86B64D94C5&displaylang=en) and the FileWatcher SDK sample.

Creating the Solution and Projects

The solution contains two projects. The first holds the custom activity and the second holds the workflow you place the custom activity on. Follow the next steps to create the solution and project.

1. Create a new blank solution named **QueuedCustomActivitySolution** and place it in the C:\SamsWf24hrs\Hours\Hour21QueuedCustomActivities directory (see Hour 2, "A Spin Around Windows Workflow Foundation").

2. Add a Workflow Activity Library (not a Sequential Workflow Library) project named **CustomQueuedActivities** to the solution.

3. Rename Activity1.cs to **BasicQueued.cs** in the Solution Explorer.

4. Add a Sequential Workflow Console application project named **CustomActivityTester** to the solution.

5. Add code to pause the host. (See Hour 3, "Learning Basic Hosting," if you need help.)

Creating a Basic Custom Queued Activity

Finally, it's time to create a queued activity. This activity will create a queue, subscribe to an event on the queue, and create a handler that is invoked when data is received in the queue.

Performing Preliminary Custom Activity Setup

Follow the next steps to set the activity's base type and create a DependencyProperty.

1. Open the BasicQueued activity in design mode. Then click the activity, click the ellipsis in the Base Class property, select System.Workflow.ComponentModel, and select Activity in the middle pane. Then click OK.

2. Right-click the activity and select View Code.

3. Move your cursor directly below the constructor, insert a couple of additional blank lines, move your cursor between the lines, right-click, and select Insert Snippet. Double-click Other, double-click Workflow, and double-click DependencyProperty—Property to insert a new dependency property.

4. You should see the stub dependency property, and the text MyProperty should be highlighted.

5. Enter **CustomerNumber** (replacing MyProperty), and press Enter to leave the wizard.

Override the Initialize Method

The Initialize method is called when the workflow instance is created—or to be precise, when WorkflowRuntime.CreateWorkflow is called. It is not scheduled like the Execute and other methods. It is a good idea to create queues in the Initialize method, in many cases, because it avoids race conditions that can occur if the queues are created when the workflow has already started execution.

Runtime services registered with the WF runtime can be accessed from the Initialize method's IServiceProvider parameter. It is also a good idea to leave the base.Initialize(provider); intact when overriding so that base initialization still occurs.

Follow the next steps to override the Initialize method and create the queue.

1. Add a couple of blank lines below the `CustomerNumber` dependency property you just added and type **protected override**, press the spacebar, and select the Initialize method to create the Initialize method.

   The following method is created:

   ```
   protected override void Initialize(IServiceProvider provider)
   {
       base.Initialize(provider);
   }
   ```

2. Add the following code to the method body below the existing code to retrieve the WorkflowQueuingService from IServiceProvider:

   ```
   // Retrieve the workflow queuing service from the
   IServiceProvider
   WorkflowQueuingService qservice =
       (WorkflowQueuingService)provider.GetService
       (typeof(WorkflowQueuingService));
   ```

3. Add the following code below the code you just entered to create a `WorkflowQueue`:

   ```
   // Create a workflow queue and give it the name of the activity
   // instance on the workflow.
   WorkflowQueue q =
   qservice.CreateWorkflowQueue(this.QualifiedName, true);
   ```

4. The completed `Initialize` method should look like Listing 21.1.

LISTING 21.1   Creating **WorkflowQueue** in **Initialize** Method

```
// Leave base initialization logic.
base.Initialize(provider);

// Retrieve the workflow queuing service from the IServiceProvider
WorkflowQueuingService qservice =
    (WorkflowQueuingService)provider.GetService
    (typeof(WorkflowQueuingService));

// Create a workflow queue and give it the name of the activity
// instance on the workflow.
 WorkflowQueue q = qservice.CreateWorkflowQueue(this.QualifiedName,
true);
```

You just created a `WorkflowQueue` that will later be used to deliver data to.

By the Way

The activity qualified name is used instead of the activity name because using just the activity name is ambiguous when the activity is accessed in a `While` or other activity that may execute it multiple times.

Override the `Execute` Method

Follow the next steps to override the `Execute` method to retreive the `WorkflowQueue` created in the `Initialize` method, register an event with the queue, and return control to the WF runtime in executing state.

1. Add a couple of blank lines below the `Initialize` method and type **protected override**, press the spacebar, and select the `Execute` method to create the `Execute` method.

   The following method will be created:

   ```
   protected override ActivityExecutionStatus
       Execute(ActivityExecutionContext executionContext)
   {
       return base.Execute(executionContext);
   }
   ```

2. Replace the body of the `Execute` method with the following code to retrieve the WorkflowQueuingService from the `ActivityExecutionContext`. The next line will then retrieve the `WorkflowQueue` created in the `Initialize` method from the queuing service.

   ```
           // Retrieve the WorkflowQueuingService from the
   ActivityExecutionContext
           WorkflowQueuingService qservice =
               executionContext.GetService<WorkflowQueuingService>();

           // Retrieve the WorkflowQueue (created in the Initialize
   method)
           // from the WorkflowQueuingService
           WorkflowQueue q =
   qservice.GetWorkflowQueue(this.QualifiedName);
   ```

3. Enter **q.QueueItemAvailable +=** and then press Tab twice to accept the default event signature (below the code you just entered) to register an event and create a handler to the queue. The results should look like this (without the comments):

   ```
           // Register an event for when data is delivered to the queue
           // and create a handler for it.
           q.QueueItemAvailable +=
               new EventHandler<QueueEventArgs>(q_QueueItemAvailable);
   ```

4. Add the following code below the event you just registered (make sure you are not in the handler) to return control to the WF runtime with the activity in the Executing state.

   ```
           // Return control to the runtime in executing state.
           return ActivityExecutionStatus.Executing;
   ```

5. The completed Execute method should look like Listing 21.2.

LISTING 21.2   Retrieving and Subscribing to a `WorkflowQueue` in the
`Execute` Method

```
            // Retrieve the WorkflowQueuingService from the
ActivityExecutionContext
            WorkflowQueuingService qservice =
                executionContext.GetService<WorkflowQueuingService>();

            // Retrieve the WorkflowQueue (created in the Initialize method)
            // from the WorkflowQueuingService
            WorkflowQueue q = qservice.GetWorkflowQueue(this.QualifiedName);

            // Register an event to when data is delivered to the queue
            // and create a handler for it.
            q.QueueItemAvailable +=
                new EventHandler<QueueEventArgs>(q_QueueItemAvailable);

            // Return control the runtime in executing state.
             return ActivityExecutionStatus.Executing;
```

The activity now retrieves the queue created in the `Initialize` method from the
queuing service. Then the activity registers a handler on the queue and returns control to the runtime in executing state. All that remains is to add code to the handler
and update the host program to send data to the queue.

Adding Code to the `QueueItemAvailable` Handler

The `q_QueueItemAvailable` handler is invoked when data is placed in the named
queue. Follow the next steps to update the host program to place data in the named
queue in the next step. The first couple of steps involve retrieving the
`ActivityExecutionContext`, `WorkflowQueuingService`, and the named queue. The
third step, `CustomerNumber = q.Dequeue().ToString();` obtains the data placed in
the queue in the host program.

1. Replace the body of the activity's `q_QueueItemAvailable` handler (generated
   when you created the event) with the following to retrieve the
   `ActivityExecutionContext`:

```
            // Sender contains the activity execution context
            ActivityExecutionContext executionContext =
                sender as ActivityExecutionContext;
```

2. Add the following code below the code you just entered to retrieve the queuing
   service and then the queue from the queuing service:

```
            // Retrieve the queuing service from the activity execution
context
```

```
        WorkflowQueuingService qservice =
            executionContext.GetService<WorkflowQueuingService>();

        // Access the workflow queue the data is delivered to
        WorkflowQueue q =
qservice.GetWorkflowQueue(this.QualifiedName);
```

3. Add the following code below the code you just entered to retrieve the data from the host:

```
        // Retrieve the data from the queue
        CustomerNumber = q.Dequeue().ToString();
```

4. Add the following code below the code you just entered to send the customer number retrieved from the queue to the console:

```
        Console.WriteLine("The customer number is " + CustomerNumber);
```

5. Add the following code below the code you just entered to close the activity. `ActivityExecutionStatus.CloseActivity()` is used instead of `ActivityExecutionStatus.Closed` because event handlers do not permit values to be returned.

```
        // Close the activity
        executionContext.CloseActivity();
```

6. The completed `q_QueueItemAvailable` should look like Listing 21.3.

LISTING 21.3   `QItemEventHandler` Body

```
        // Sender contains the activity execution context
        ActivityExecutionContext executionContext =
            sender as ActivityExecutionContext;

        // Retrieve the queuing service from the activity execution context
        WorkflowQueuingService qservice =
            executionContext.GetService<WorkflowQueuingService>();

        // Access the workflow queue the data is delivered to
        WorkflowQueue q = qservice.GetWorkflowQueue(this.QualifiedName);

        // Retrieve the data from the queue
        CustomerNumber = q.Dequeue().ToString();

        Console.WriteLine("The customer number is " + CustomerNumber);

        // Close the activity
         executionContext.CloseActivity();
```

The examples in this hour all create one queue, and the activities all complete after the second burst. However, activities can create more than one queue and

> execute in more than two bursts. If the QueueItemAvailable handler returns without closing the activity, the activity remains in executing state.

Override the Uninitialize Method

Uninitialize is called when transitioning from executing to closed and permits any cleanup to take place. One common action performed in the Uninitialize method is to delete queues.

Follow the next steps to override the Uninitialize method and delete the queues.

1. Add a couple of blank lines below the q_QueueItemAvailable handler and type **protected override**, press the spacebar, and select the Uninitialize method to create the Uninitialize method.

   The following method is created:

   ```
   protected override void Uninitialize(IServiceProvider provider)
   {
       // Leave base uninitialization logic.
       base.Uninitialize(provider);
   }
   ```

2. Replace the current code in the method body with Listing 21.4.

LISTING 21.4   Deleting Queues in Uninitialized Body

```
// Leave base uninitialization logic.
base.Uninitialize(provider);

// Retrieve the workflow queuing service from the IServiceProvider
WorkflowQueuingService qservice =
    (WorkflowQueuingService)provider.GetService
    (typeof(WorkflowQueuingService));

// Create a workflow queue and give it the name of the activity
// instance on the workflow.
 qservice.DeleteWorkflowQueue(this.QualifiedName);
```

> For brevity, this method will be omitted from subsequent activities in this hour.

3. Build the CustomQueuedActivities project.

Updating Host to Send Data to the Queue

Follow the next step to send the data from the host to the queue to invoke the QueueItemAvailable event handler.

1. Add the following code to the host (`Program.cs` in `CustomerActivityTester`) above the `waitHandle.WaitOne();` line of code:

```
//send some data to the event activity
Console.WriteLine("Enter the customer number: ");
string custNumber = Console.ReadLine();
instance.EnqueueItem("basicQueued1", custNumber, null, null);
```

Running the Workflow

Follow the next steps to run the workflow.

1. Open Workflow1 in design mode and place a `BasicQueued` activity on it.

2. Press F5 to run the workflow. Then enter any customer number when prompted and press Enter.

3. You should see the results shown in Figure 21.3.

FIGURE 21.3
BasicQueued activity on workflow execution results.

Custom Activity Queued from Service

In this section, you create a custom runtime service that will enqueue the customer number to the named queue created in the activity's `Execute` method. It will perform this task in place of the host, which retrieved the customer number in the `BasicQueued` activity (Figure 21.4).

The WF runtime loads workflow instances and then executes the activities on a workflow instance. It is recommended that activities execute quickly and return control to the WF runtime. If an activity conducts work that will not complete very quickly, the activity should employ a custom runtime service to perform this work on another thread. If an activity is waiting on external input or setting up a timer, it should almost always operate on a new thread and return control to the WF runtime. This enables the WF runtime and host application to maximize performance and load the maximum number of workflow instances optimum for the setup. It also allows for dynamic update and other actions to be placed on the workflow instance.

If the activity performs a database call or other task that is not instantaneous but is not necessarily immediate, it still may be best to perform this work via a custom runtime service on a new thread. Doing so may optimize performance because the host

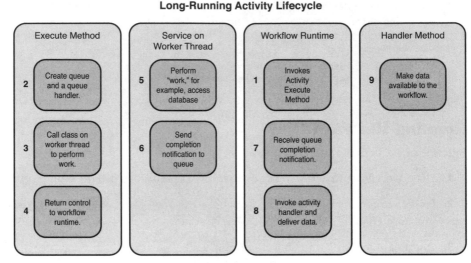

Long-Running Activity Lifecycle

Initialize and other methods omitted for
brevity.

and runtime can load workflow instances based on the optimum threadpool and
other settings.

You will create the CustomerQueuedFromService custom runtime service that operates on the separate thread first. Then you create the
CustomerQueuedFromServiceActivity to call the custom runtime service. This section demonstrates how to create a custom service, access the custom service from the
activity's Execute method, and how to notify the runtime from the service when the
service has completed processing.

Creating the CustomerQueuedFromService Service

The CustomerQueuedFromService includes two methods and one embedded class.
The first method is called on the activity thread and invokes the second method that
does the "database" work on the worker thread. The embedded class holds the information exchanged between the activity and the service.

Preliminary CustomerQueuedFromService Setup

Follow the next steps to create the CustomerQueuedFromService class and
configure it.

1. Right-click the `CustomQueuedActivities` project and select Add, Class.

2. Name the class **CustomerQueuedFromService** and click Add.

3. Add **public** before the class name to make it public.

4. Add the following using directives:

```
using System.Workflow.Runtime;
using System.Threading;
using System.Data.SqlClient;
using System.Data;
```

The service needs access to the `WorkflowRuntime`. The workflow instance will be retrieved from the WF runtime and the data will be enqueued via the workflow instance when the service has completed its work.

1. Add the following constructor below the class declaration opening bracket:

```
// The workflow runtime is being used in this class solely
// to permit data transfer between the workflow isntance
// and the service.
public CustomerQueuedFromService(WorkflowRuntime runtime)
{
    this.runtime = runtime;
}
```

2. Add the following member variable declarations below the constructor:

```
private WorkflowRuntime runtime;
```

Adding `GetCustomer` Method Called from Activity

This method, the `GetCustomerCalledFromActivity` method, is called from the activity on the workflow thread. It then calls the `GetCustomerOnWorkerThread` method that does the actual work on the worker thread.

Follow the next steps to add and code the `GetCustomer` method.

1. Add the following method signature before the ending class bracket:

```
// This is called in the activity thread
public void GetCustomerCalledFromActivity(IComparable
resultQueueName)
    {
    }
```

2. Add the following code to the method to call the `GetCustomerOnWorkerThread` method via the CLR ThreadPool:

```
ThreadPool.QueueUserWorkItem(GetCustomerOnWorkerThread,
```

```
      new CustomerState(WorkflowEnvironment.WorkflowInstanceId,
          resultQueueName));
```

Adding Embedded `CustomerState` Class

Follow the next step to create the embedded `CustomerState` class that stores the information passed between the activity and the service.

1. Add the following class below the method you just added. This class contains the data passed between the two `GetCustomer` methods on different threads. This class is needed because the `QueueUserWorkItem` accepts only one parameter in addition to the method name called.

```
        // This class holds the data passed between the methods called
        // across threads It is required since the QueueUserWorkItem
delegate
        // only accepts one parameter in addition to the method to call.
        private class CustomerState
        {
            public Guid instanceId;
            public IComparable resultQueueName;

            public CustomerState(Guid instanceId,
                IComparable resultQueueName)
            {
                this.instanceId = instanceId;
                this.resultQueueName = resultQueueName;
            }
        }
```

Adding `GetCustomerOnWorkerThread` Method Called from Activity

Follow the next steps to create the `GetCustomerOnWorkerThread` method that does the work and then enqueues the data to the named queue. Doing so will invoke the activity event `QueueItemAvailable` handler you will create in the next section.

1. Add the following method signature below the class you just added:

```
        // Method on donated thread that processes the request
        // while control is returned from activity to workflow.
        private void GetCustomerOnWorkerThread(object state)
        {
        }
```

2. Add the following line of code to the body of the method that produces a hard-coded customer number value:

```
        // Hard-coded customer number
        string customerNumber = "0001 from service";
```

3. Add the following code below the code you just added to retrieve the `WorkflowInstance` from the runtime:

```
// Get the workflow instance Id from the
// CustomerState object.
CustomerState custState = state as CustomerState;
WorkflowInstance wi =
runtime.GetWorkflow(custState.instanceId);
```

4. Add the following code below the code you just added to enqueue the customer number to the activity and invoke the activity handler:

```
// Send the message back to the activity and pass the result
    wi.EnqueueItem(custState.resultQueueName, customerNumber,
null, null);
```

5. The completed `CustomerQueuedFromService` class should look like Listing 21.5.

LISTING 21.5   `CustomerQueuedFromService` Worker Thread Service

```
public class CustomerQueuedFromService
{
  // The workflow runtime is being used in this class solely
  // to permit data transfer between the workflow instance
  // and the service.
  public CustomerQueuedFromService(WorkflowRuntime runtime)
  {
      this.runtime = runtime;
  }

  private WorkflowRuntime runtime;

  // This is called in the activity thread
  public void GetCustomerCalledFromActivity(IComparable resultQueueName)
  {
      ThreadPool.QueueUserWorkItem(GetCustomerOnWorkerThread,
          new CustomerState(WorkflowEnvironment.WorkflowInstanceId,
              resultQueueName));
  }

  // This class holds the data passed between the methods called
  // across threads It is required since the QueueUserWorkItem delegate
  // only accepts one parameter in addition to the method to call.
  private class CustomerState
  {
      public Guid instanceId;
      public IComparable resultQueueName;

      public CustomerState(Guid instanceId,
          IComparable resultQueueName)
```

```
        {
            this.instanceId = instanceId;
            this.resultQueueName = resultQueueName;
        }
    }

    // Method on donated thread that processes the request
    // while control is returned from activity to workflow.
    private void GetCustomerOnWorkerThread(object state)
    {
        // Hard-coded customer number
        string customerNumber = "0001 from service";

        // Get the workflow instance Id from the
        // CustomerState object.
        CustomerState custState = state as CustomerState;
        WorkflowInstance wi = runtime.GetWorkflow(custState.instanceId);

        // Send the message back to the activity and pass the result
        wi.EnqueueItem(custState.resultQueueName, customerNumber, null, null);

    }
}
```

6. Build the `CustomQueuedActivities` project and fix any errors.

Creating the `CustomerQueuedFromServiceActivity` Custom Activity

The `CustomerQueuedFromServiceActivity` custom activity is similar to the `BasicQueued` activity. The difference is that the `CustomerQueuedFromServiceActivity` custom activity retrieves the `CustomerQueuedFromService` from the `ActivityExecutionContext`. Otherwise, the fact that data is enqueued from a runtime service instead of the host does not change the activity.

Preliminary Custom Activity Setup

Follow the next steps to create the `CustomerQueuedFromServiceActivity` and perform some other preliminary work.

1. Right-click `CustomQueuedActivities` project and select Add, Activity.

2. Name the activity **CustomerQueuedFromServiceActivity** and click Add.

3. Open the `CustomerQueuedFromServiceActivity` activity in design mode. Then click the activity, click the ellipsis in the Base Class property, select Sys-

tem.Workflow.ComponentModel, and select Activity in the middle pane. Then click OK.

4. Add a dependency property below the constructor named **CustomerNumber** and set its type to string.

Overriding the `Initialize` Method

Follow the next steps to override the Initialize method and create a queue in it.

1. Add a couple of blank lines below the CustomerNumber dependency property and type **protected override**, press the spacebar, and select the Initialize method to create the Initialize method.

2. Replace the body of the Initialize method with the following code to create the queue. This is identical to the code in the Initialize method of the BasicQueued activity:

```
            // Call base intialize to gain its functionality
            base.Initialize(provider);
            // Retrieve the workflow queuing service from the
IServiceProvider
            WorkflowQueuingService qservice =
                (WorkflowQueuingService)provider.GetService
                (typeof(WorkflowQueuingService));

            // Create a workflow queue and give it the name of the activity
            // instance on the workflow.
            WorkflowQueue q =
qservice.CreateWorkflowQueue(this.QualifiedName, true);
```

Overriding the `Execute` Method

The Execute method now retrieves two services. The first, the WorkflowQueuingService, was retrieved when creating the BasicQueued activity. The latter is the CustomerQueuedFromService service that will retrieve the customer on the worker thread. Steps 1, 2, and 5 are the same in this version of the activity as they were in the BasicQueued activity. Steps 3 and 4 are unique to this version of the activity.

Follow the next steps to create the Execute method.

1. Add a couple of blank lines below the Initialize method and type **protected override**, press the spacebar, and select the Execute method to create the Execute method.

2. Replace the body of the Execute method with the following code that retrieves the WorkflowQueuingService from the ActivityExecutionContext, retrieves the queue from the service, and then registers an event with the queue:

```
// Retrieve the WorkflowQueuingService from the
ActivityExecutionContext
        WorkflowQueuingService qservice =
            executionContext.GetService<WorkflowQueuingService>();

        // Retrieve the WorkflowQueue (created in the Initialize
method)
        // from the WorkflowQueuingService
        WorkflowQueue q =
qservice.GetWorkflowQueue(this.QualifiedName);

        // Register an event to when data is delivered to the queue
        // and create a handler for it.
        q.QueueItemAvailable +=
            new EventHandler<QueueEventArgs>(q_QueueItemAvailable);
```

3. Add the following code below the code you just added to retrieve the custom CustomerQueuedFromService from the ActivityExecutionContext.

```
        // Retrieve the custom CustomerQueuedFromService from the
        // activity execution context.
        CustomerQueuedFromService CustomerQueuedFromService =
            executionContext.GetService<CustomerQueuedFromService>();
```

4. Add the following code below the code you just added to retrieve the custom CustomerQueuedFromService you just created from the ActivityExecutionContext.

```
        // Call the GetCustomerCalledFromActivity method
        // on the custom CustomerQueuedFromService service

CustomerQueuedFromService.GetCustomerCalledFromActivity(this.QualifiedName);
```

5. Add the following code below the code you just added to return the activity in executing state.

```
        // Return control to the runtime in executing mode
        return ActivityExecutionStatus.Executing;
```

Creating and Adding Code to the `QueueItemAvailable` Handler

The QueueItemAvailable handler is the same as the one used in the BasicQueued activity. The fact that the QueueItemAvailable handler is triggered from the custom service instead of the host does not change the way the handler is invoked and receives data from the queue.

Follow the next steps to create the `QueueItemAvailable` handler.

1. Add the handler signature below the method you just created. It must be created manually this time because the event was manually pasted.

```
void q_QueueItemAvailable(object sender, QueueEventArgs e)
{
}
```

2. Enter the following code in the Activity's `QueueItemAvailable` handler:

```
// Sender contains the activity execution context
ActivityExecutionContext executionContext =
    sender as ActivityExecutionContext;

// Retrieve the queuing service from the activity execution
context
WorkflowQueuingService qservice =
    executionContext.GetService<WorkflowQueuingService>();

// Access the workflow queue the data is delivered to
WorkflowQueue q = qservice.GetWorkflowQueue(this.Name);

// Retrieve the data from the queue
CustomerNumber = q.Dequeue().ToString();
Console.WriteLine("The customer number retrieved from the
service is " +
    CustomerNumber);

executionContext.CloseActivity();
```

3. Build the `CustomQueuedActivities` project.

The `CustomerQueuedFromServiceActivity` class should look like Listing 21.6.

LISTING 21.6 `CustomerQueuedFromServiceActivity` That Uses External Service

```
    public partial class CustomerQueuedFromServiceActivity :
System.Workflow.ComponentModel.Activity
    {
        public CustomerQueuedFromServiceActivity()
        {
            InitializeComponent();
        }

        public static DependencyProperty CustomerNumberProperty =
DependencyProperty.Register("CustomerNumber", typeof(string),
typeof(CustomerQueuedFromServiceActivity));

        [DescriptionAttribute("CustomerNumber")]
        [CategoryAttribute("CustomerNumber Category")]
        [BrowsableAttribute(true)]
```

```
[DesignerSerializationVisibilityAttribute(DesignerSerializationVisibility.Visibl
e)]
        public string CustomerNumber
        {
            get
            {
                return
((string)(base.GetValue(CustomerQueuedFromServiceActivity.CustomerNumberProperty
)));
            }
            set
            {

base.SetValue(CustomerQueuedFromServiceActivity.CustomerNumberProperty, value);
            }
        }

        protected override void Initialize(IServiceProvider provider)
        {
            // Call base intialize to gain its functionality
            base.Initialize(provider);
            // Retrieve the workflow queuing service from the IServiceProvider
            WorkflowQueuingService qservice =
                (WorkflowQueuingService)provider.GetService
                (typeof(WorkflowQueuingService));

            // Create a workflow queue and give it the name of the activity
            // instance on the workflow.
            WorkflowQueue q = qservice.CreateWorkflowQueue(this.QualifiedName,
true);
        }

        protected override ActivityExecutionStatus
Execute(ActivityExecutionContext executionContext)
        {
            // Retrieve the WorkflowQueuingService from the
ActivityExecutionContext
            WorkflowQueuingService qservice =
                executionContext.GetService<WorkflowQueuingService>();

            // Retrieve the WorkflowQueue (created in the Initialize method)
            // from the WorkflowQueuingService
            WorkflowQueue q = qservice.GetWorkflowQueue(this.QualifiedName);

            // Register an event to when data is delivered to the queue
            // and create a handler for it.
            q.QueueItemAvailable +=
                new EventHandler<QueueEventArgs>(q_QueueItemAvailable);

            // Retrieve the custom CustomerQueuedFromService from the
            // activity execution context.
            CustomerQueuedFromService CustomerQueuedFromService =
                executionContext.GetService<CustomerQueuedFromService>();

            // Call the GetCustomerCalledFromActivity method
            // on the custom CustomerQueuedFromService service
```

```
CustomerQueuedFromService.GetCustomerCalledFromActivity(this.QualifiedName);

        // Return control to the runtime in executing mode
        return ActivityExecutionStatus.Executing;

    }

    void q_QueueItemAvailable(object sender, QueueEventArgs e)
    {
        // Sender contains the activity execution context
        ActivityExecutionContext executionContext =
            sender as ActivityExecutionContext;

        // Retrieve the queuing service from the activity execution context
        WorkflowQueuingService qservice =
            executionContext.GetService<WorkflowQueuingService>();

        // Access the workflow queue the data is delivered to
        WorkflowQueue q = qservice.GetWorkflowQueue(this.Name);

        // Retrieve the data from the queue
        CustomerNumber = q.Dequeue().ToString();
        Console.WriteLine("The customer number retrieved from the service is
" +

            CustomerNumber);

        executionContext.CloseActivity();

    }
}
```

Updating the Host to Use the New Service

Follow the next steps to register your `CustomerQueuedFromService` with the runtime.

1. Add a project reference from the `CustomActivityTester` project to the `CustomQueuedActivities` project that contains the custom `CustomerQueuedFromService` service.

2. Open `Program.cs` in the `CustomActivityTester` project.

3. Add the following using directive:

   ```
   using CustomQueuedActivities;
   ```

4. Add the following code above the line that starts with `WorkflowInstance` instance to add the custom `CustomerQueuedFromService` you just created to the runtime:

   ```
   // Add the CustomerQueuedFromService to the runtime.
   ```

```
            workflowRuntime.AddService(new
    CustomerQueuedFromService(workflowRuntime));
```

5. Remove the following lines of code from the host because the data is now delivered to the queue via the service and not the host:

```
    //send some data to the event activity
    Console.WriteLine("Enter the customer number: ");
    string custNumber = Console.ReadLine();
    instance.EnqueueItem("basicQueued1", custNumber, null, null);
```

Running the Workflow

Follow the next steps to run the workflow that uses the new custom runtime service you created.

1. Open Workflow1 in design mode, remove the `BasicQueued` activity, and replace it with a `CustomerQueuedFromServiceActivity`. Enter **0001** in the `CustomerNumber` property.

2. Press F5 to run the workflow.

3. You should see the results shown in Figure 21.5.

FIGURE 21.5
Customer-
QueuedFrom
ServiceActi-
vity activity on
workflow execu-
tion results.

Summary

This hour covered creating multiburst activities. In doing so, it touched on queues, the underlying WF WorkflowQueue communication technology. It also showed how to access custom runtime services from within an activity. Queued activities are a critical functional piece of WF because they are paramount to its long-running process capability. Working with queues should also give you a better understanding of how WF works as a whole. Custom runtime services are also integral to WF and you now know there are choices of where to place the custom activity functionality—in the activity or in the runtime service. One or more DLLs registered as custom services can serve as general utility resources across many activities.

Workshop

Quiz

1. *What are workflow queues in WF?*

2. *What other data exchange mechanisms in WF use the queuing technology internally?*

3. *Why is it good to create queues in the* `Initialize` *method?*

4. *Why do some activities return* `ActivityExecutionStatus.Executing` *instead of* `ActivityExecutionStatus.Closed` *from their* `Execute` *methods?*

5. *What is the* `ActivityExecutionContext`?

6. *How is the* `WorkflowQueuingService` *accessed?*

7. *What mechanism is used to know when data is delivered to a queue?*

8. *What does the following code do?* `CustomerNumber = q.Dequeue().ToString();`

Answers

1. A named location where the workflow can receive data.

2. All, whether local service, web services, WCF, or other.

3. It avoids race conditions that can occur when creating them in `Execute` or other methods.

4. To allow the activity to continue processing while returning control to the WF runtime.

5. The container in which activities execute.

6. It is accessed from the `ActivityExecutionContext`.

7. An event is registered on the queue.

8. Retrieves the data placed in the workflow queue.

Creating Typed Queued and EventDriven-Enabled Activities

What You Will Learn in This Hour:

▶ Creating a queued typed activity from service

▶ Creating an EventDriven-enabled activity

This hour builds on the previous hour. In the first exercise, you modify the custom runtime service to deliver typed data to the activity via a custom EventArgs class. In the second you create your own EventDriven-enabled activity that can be placed in a State or Listen activity just like a HandleExternalEvent or Delay activity can.

Creating a Custom Activity that Accesses a Typed Service

This section builds on the CustomerQueuedFromServiceActivity activity created in the previous hour. It will retrieve the customer data from database rather than hard-coding it in the service. The returned data will also be strongly typed by a custom EventArgs class you create. You will start with the activity and service you created in the previous exercise. Although there are not that many new concepts introduced, it demonstrates a valid activity that delegates database retrieval to a custom service on another thread.

Preliminary Project Setup

Follow the next steps to add the custom activity and service from the previous hour. The files have new names to go along with this section, and the activity has been changed to call the new service. Otherwise, they are identical to what you created previously.

1. Open the QueuedCustomActivitySolution in the C:\SamsWf24hrs\Hours\Hour22TypeQueuedAndEventDrivenCustomActiviti es directory. Right-click the CustomQueuedActivities project and select Add, Existing Item.

2. Browse to C:\SamsWf24hrs\Hours\Hour22TypeQueuedAndEventDrivenCustomActiviti es\ExistingFiles, select all three files, and click Add.

Adding the CustomerEventArgs File

The CustomerEventArgs class strongly types the customer data that is exchanged between the activity and the service.

The CustomerEventArgs class is derived from EventArgs and not ExternalDataEventArgs, so there is no WorkflowInstanceId passed to the base class. The workflow instance is provided outside of this class. The class simply holds the customer data. The CustomerEventArgs class is not precreated to give you a chance to see what the class looks like that types the data exchanged, because strongly typing the data is the point to this exercise. The class content is not explained because it is a simple type with three properties.

Follow the next steps to add the CustomerEventArgs class.

1. Right-click the CustomQueuedActivities project and select Add, Class.

2. Name the class **CustomerEventArgs** and click Add.

3. Replace the contents of the entire CustomerEventArgs file with the content contained in Listing 22.1.

LISTING 22.1   CustomerEventArgs Strongly Typed Class

```
using System;
using System.Collections.Generic;
using System.Linq;
using System.Text;

namespace CustomQueuedActivities
{
    [Serializable]
```

```
public class CustomerEventArgs : EventArgs
{
    public string CustomerNumber;
    public string CustomerName;
    public double CustomerCreditLimit;
    public string CustomerType;
    public double CustomerYtdSales;
    public string CustomerHoldRules;

    internal CustomerEventArgs(string customerNumber,
        string customerName,
        double customerCreditLimit,
        string customerType,
        double customerYtdSales,
        string customerHoldRules)
    {
        this.CustomerNumber = customerNumber;
        this.CustomerName = customerName;
        this.CustomerCreditLimit = customerCreditLimit;
        this.CustomerType = customerType;
        this.CustomerYtdSales = customerYtdSales;
        this.CustomerHoldRules = customerHoldRules;
    }
}
}
```

4. Build the `CustomQueuedActivities` project.

Modifying the `CustomerQueuedFromTypedServiceActivity` Custom Activity

The call to the `GetCustomerCalledFromActivity` method has to be changed to pass the customer number to the service because it is used to query the actual customer data. In the previous exercise, a hard-coded customer number was returned. The other changes made use the `CustomerEventArgs` class to type the data and to print the newly retrieved customer data to the console.

Follow the next steps to modify the `CustomerQueuedFromTypedServiceActivity` to use the `CustomerEventArgs` class.

1. Right-click the `CustomerQueuedFromTypedServiceActivity` in the Solution Explorer and choose View Code.

2. Go to the `Execute` method and replace this line of code:
`customerQueuedFromTypedDataService.GetCustomer(this.QualifiedName`
`)`; with the following to pass the `CustomerNumber` to the service as well.

```
customerQueuedFromTypedService.GetCustomerCalledFromActivity(
    this.QualifiedName, CustomerNumber);
```

3. Go to the q_QueueItemAvailable method and replace this line of code: CustomerNumber = q.Dequeue().ToString(); with the following to type the received information:

```
CustomerEventArgs cea = (CustomerEventArgs)q.Dequeue();
```

4. Replace the line of code that writes the customer number to the console with the following to write out the customer information:

```
// Send the customer data to the console
Console.WriteLine("The customber is: " + cea.CustomerName);
Console.WriteLine("The credit limit is: " +
cea.CustomerCreditLimit);
Console.WriteLine("The customer type is: " + cea.CustomerType);
Console.WriteLine("The ytd sales are: " +
cea.CustomerYtdSales);
Console.WriteLine("The customer hold rule is: " +
cea.CustomerHoldRules);
```

Modifying the CustomerQueuedFromTypedService Service

In this section, you modify the CustomerQueuedFromTypedService to retrieve the data from the database and to strongly type it based on the CustomerEventArgs class.

Update the CustomerState Object

Follow the next steps to add a member variable and update the CustomerState object.

1. Open the CustomerQueuedFromTypedService class and add the following member variable below the constructor:

```
private static string ConnectionString = "Initial
Catalog=CustomActivity;" +
        "Data Source=localhost; Integrated Security=SSPI;";
```

Follow the next step to update the CustomerState object.

1. Replace the CustomerState object (nested class) with the following new version that includes the CustomerNumber property now being passed to it:

```
// This class holds the data passed between the methods called
// across threads It is required since the QueueUserWorkItem
delegate
// only accepts one parameter in addition to the method to call.
```

```
private class CustomerState
{
    public Guid instanceId;
    public IComparable resultQueueName;
    public string customerNumber;

    public CustomerState(Guid instanceId,
        IComparable resultQueueName, string customerNumber)
    {
        this.instanceId = instanceId;
        this.resultQueueName = resultQueueName;
        this.customerNumber = customerNumber;
    }
}
```

Updating the `GetCustomerCalledFromActivity` Method to Send Typed Data

1. Replace the `GetCustomerCalledFromActivity` method with the following code that receives the `CustomerNumber` and includes `customerNumber` when instantiating the `CustomerState` object.

```
public void GetCustomerCalledFromActivity(IComparable
resultQueueName, string customerNumber)
    {
        // This is called in the activity thread to get the customer
from the database
        {
            ThreadPool.QueueUserWorkItem(GetCustomerOnWorkerThread,
                new
CustomerState(WorkflowEnvironment.WorkflowInstanceId,
                    resultQueueName, customerNumber));
        }
    }
```

Update `GetCustomerOnWorkerThread` to Send Typed Data

Follow the next steps to change the `GetCustomerOnWorkerThread` method to retrieve the customer from the database and send it to the activity typed by the `CustomerEventArgs`.

1. Replace the body of the `GetCustomerOnWorkerThread` method with the following to initialize the `CustState` object:

```
// Instantiate the CustState object that the
// customer number and workflow instance Id will
// be retrieved from.
CustomerState custState = state as CustomerState;
```

2. Add the following content to the method to retrieve the customer from the database. This code is standard .NET SQL code and is therefore not explained.

```
                        // Retrieve the customer information from the database
                        SqlConnection dbConn = new SqlConnection(ConnectionString);
                        SqlCommand getCustomer = new SqlCommand("GetCustomer", dbConn);

                        getCustomer.CommandType = CommandType.StoredProcedure;
                        getCustomer.Parameters.AddWithValue("@CustomerNumber",
            custState.customerNumber);

                        dbConn.Open();

                        string CustomerName = null;
                        double CustomerCreditLimit = 0;
                        string CustomerType = null;
                        double CustomerYtdSales = 0;
                        string CustomerHoldRules = null;

                        using (SqlDataReader custReader =
            getCustomer.ExecuteReader(CommandBehavior.CloseConnection))
                        {
                            if (custReader.Read())
                            {
                                CustomerName =
            custReader["CustomerName"].ToString().Trim();
                                CustomerCreditLimit =
            double.Parse(custReader["CustomerCreditLimit"].ToString());
                                CustomerType =
            custReader["CustomerType"].ToString().Trim();
                                CustomerYtdSales =
            double.Parse(custReader["CustomerYtdSales"].ToString());
                                CustomerHoldRules =
            custReader["CustomerHoldRules"].ToString().Trim();
                            }
                        }
```

3. Add the following code to the method to retrieve the workflow instance from the runtime:

```
                        // Retrieve the workflow instance
                        WorkflowInstance wi =
            runtime.GetWorkflow(custState.instanceId);
```

4. Add the following code to instantiate a `CustomerEventArgs` object with the customer values returned from the database:

```
                        // Update the eventargs going back to the workflow with the
                        // customer information
                        CustomerEventArgs eventArgs =
                            new CustomerEventArgs(custState.customerNumber,
                                CustomerName,
                                CustomerCreditLimit,
                                CustomerType,
                                CustomerYtdSales,
                                CustomerHoldRules);
```

5. Add the following code to enqueue the typed customer data back to the workflow queue.

```
                    // Send the results back to the workflow queue
                    wi.EnqueueItem(custState.resultQueueName, eventArgs, null,
        null);
```

6. Build the CustomQueuedActivities project.

Updating the Host to Use the Typed Service

1. Replace the line of code that adds the CustomerQueuedFromService service to the runtime with the following to add the CustomerQueuedFromTypedService:

```
                    // Add the CustomerQueuedFromTypedService to the runtime.
                    workflowRuntime.AddService(new
        CustomerQueuedFromTypedService
                        (workflowRuntime));
```

Running the Workflow

Follow the next steps to run the workflow with the strongly typed data.

1. Remove any existing activities from the workflow.

2. Add a CustomerQueuedFromTypedServiceActivity to the workflow, enter **0001** in the CustomerNumber property, and run the workflow.

3. You should get the results similar to Figure 22.1.

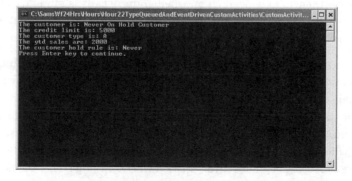

FIGURE 22.1
Customer-
QueuedFrom-
ServiceTyped
Activity
activity on work-
flow execution
results.

You now have a custom activity that retrieves information from the database on another thread while the workflow can be idled. The same pattern can be applied to activities that wait for human input or that perform other actions that take a long time.

Creating an EventDriven Activity

The multiburst activity created in this hour can be placed on a workflow, wait for external input, and receive data in its second burst. However, it cannot yet be the first activity in an `EventDriven` activity, such as a `Listen` activity branch or a `State` activity. This precludes our activity from participating in the canonical wait on external input in one branch and timeout in another branch pattern. It is therefore not yet a complete activity in many ways, because activities that wait on external input frequently need to be placed in `Listen` activity branches and therefore monitored by `Delay` activities.

Many multiburst activities must support being placed on the workflow both independently of an `EventDriven` activity and embedded within an `EventDriven` activity. `HandleExternalEvent` and `Delay` activities, for example, can be placed in `Listen` activity branches or placed directly on the workflow. Activities that can wait on external input but cannot be the first activity in an `EventDriven` activity will be referred to as basic queued activities in this section. Those that can be added as the first activity will be referred to as `EventDriven`-enabled.

The programming model is very different for basic queued and `EventDriven`-enabled activities. This requires that `EventDriven`-enabled activities support two different models. They must support the model used so far throughout this hour, where the activity itself subscribes to the `QueueItemAvailable` event. They must also support a model that delegates subscribing to events to the parent `EventDriven` activity—for example, the `Listen` activity branch.

In this exercise, you create an `EventDriven`-enabled activity that must also be able to operate as a standard queued activity. This requires adding conditional checks that take different actions depending on whether the activity is running as an `EventDriven`-enabled or a basic queued activity. It will run as the first if it is embedded in an `EventDriven` activity and as the latter if it is running standalone.

The `Execute` method must check whether the queue has already been subscribed to, as it will when the activity is running as an embedded activity. If the activity is running standalone, the queues must still be created and events subscribed to in the `Execute` method. To help with this, much of the subscription and queue logic is factored out into `DoSubscribe` and `ProcessQueueItem` methods. The `DoSubscribe` method is called from the `Execute` method when running standalone activities, and from the `IEventActivity.Subscribe` method when running embedded activities.

You will instrument the methods with `Console.Writeline` statements that help understand the different execution patterns of each activity type.

Creating the `CustomerEventDrivenActivity` Custom Activity

The `CustomerEventDrivenActivity` will implement `IEventActivity` because it is required to do so to be an `EventDriven`-enabled activity. The `IEventActivity` interface contains Subscribe and Unsubscribe methods that receive the parent activities ActivityExecutionContext. The custom service and EventArgs classes are the same as their CustomerQueuedFromTypedServiceActivity permutations, so they will be used as is. The EventDriven-enabled activity is very different and will therefore be created from scratch.

Preliminary Custom Activity Setup

Follow the next steps to create the CustomerEventDrivenActivity and set is base type.

1. Right-click CustomQueuedActivities project and select Add, Activity.

2. Name the activity **CustomerEventDrivenActivity** and click Add.

3. Open the CustomerEventDrivenActivity activity in design mode. Then click the activity, click the ellipsis in the Base Class property, select System.Workflow.ComponentModel, and select Activity in the middle pane. Then click OK.

Derive from IEventActivity and IActivityEventListener Interfaces

Next you derive from the IEventActivity and IActivityEventListener interfaces. The first, as already mentioned, allows the activity to be EventDriven-enabled. The second is used by an event that monitors the named queue. It provides another way to accomplish what QueueItemAvailable provided to prior activities last hour.

Replace the class signature with the following that implements the interfaces:

```
public partial class CustomerEventDrivenActivity : Activity,
    IEventActivity,
    IActivityEventListener<QueueEventArgs>
```

Implement the IEventActivity.QueueName

Next, implement the IEventActivity.QueueName property, which stores the queue to listen. This member of the IEventActivity must be implemented when implementing the IEventActivity interface.

Add the following code below the constructor to implement the IEventActivity.QueueName property:

```
private IComparable queueName;

// Required by IEventActivity
[Browsable(false)]
public IComparable QueueName
```

```
{
    get { return this.queueName; }
}
```

Adding CustomerNumber Dependency Property

Follow the next steps to add the CustomerNumber dependency property.

1. Move your cursor directly below the QueueName property, insert a couple of additional blank lines, move your cursor between the lines, right-click, and select Insert Snippet. Double-click Other, double-click Workflow, and double-click DependencyProperty—Property to insert a new dependency property.

2. You should see the stub dependency property, and the text MyProperty should be highlighted.

3. Enter **CustomerNumber** (replacing MyProperty) and press Enter to leave the wizard.

Override the Initialize Method

Follow the next steps to override the Initialize method and initialize the queueName variable.

1. Add a couple of blank lines below the CustomerNumber dependency property and type **protected override**, press the spacebar, and select the Initialize method to create the Initialize method.

2. Add the following code below the code placed in the Initialize method to initialize the QueueName property. The queue will be created in a separate helper method called by both the EventDriven-enabled and basic queued activity implementations.

```
this.queueName = this.QualifiedName;
```

Override the Execute Method

The CustomerEventDrivenActivity.Execute method operates differently depending on whether it is called when the activity is embedded or running standalone. When embedded in an EventDriven activity, the Execute method is not called until after the queue is subscribed to, data is delivered to the queue, and the queue event is executed. This is because the subscription is delegated to its parent EventDriven activity. The Execute method processes the data returned from the service because by the time it is called, the activity's work is done. The custom service has been called and it has returned the data to the activity. Conversely, when the activity executes stand-alone, it operates as it did last hour.

Add the following code to override the Execute method.

1. Add a couple of blank lines below the Initialize method and type **protected override**, press the spacebar, and select the Execute method to create the Execute method.

2. Replace the content of the Execute method that checks if there is processing to be done. If there is none, the activity is closed, which will be the case when called from an EventDriven activity, because the work will already be done.

```
        // If true activity already executed and it will therefore
be closed
        if (this.ProcessQueueItem(executionContext))
        {
            Console.WriteLine("EventDriven-enabled, Execute method:
Returned " +
            "true from ProcessQueueItem.");
            return ActivityExecutionStatus.Closed;
        }
        Console.WriteLine("Standard queued, Execute method " +
        "activity made it past check for EventDriven.");
```

3. Add the following code to begin processing and rerun the activity in executing state, which will be called when the activity is called standalone.

```
        // If this is a standard queued activity, the queue
        // will be created and subscribed to.
        this.DoSubscribe(executionContext, this);

        // Return control the runtime in executing mode
        return ActivityExecutionStatus.Executing;
```

Implement the Subscribe Handler

When the activity is embedded in an EventDriven activity, the IEventActivity.Subscribe method is called in the activity's first execution burst. Therefore, IEventActivity.Subscribe calls DoSubscribe to create the queue and set up the event logic to monitor the queue, as would be done in the Execute method if the activity was running in standalone mode.

To create and code the Subscribe handler, add the following handler to specify what should be done when the queue is updated.

```
        // Create queue and create event logic when activity
        // called from within an EventDriven activity.
        void IEventActivity.Subscribe(ActivityExecutionContext parentContext,
            IActivityEventListener<QueueEventArgs> parentEventHandler)
        {
```

```
        Console.WriteLine("EventDriven permutation in
IEventActivity.Subscribe");
        DoSubscribe(parentContext, parentEventHandler);
    }
```

Creating the `DoSubscribe` Method

This method creates the queue, registers an event with the queue, and calls the custom customer service. It is called from the `IEventActivity.Subscribe` handler when the activity is embedded in an `EventDriven` activity and from the `Execute` method when the activity is standalone. The appropriate `ActivityExecutionContext` (parent `EventDriven` of custom activity) is passed to the method.

Follow the next steps to create and code the `DoSubscribe` method.

1. Add the `DoSubscribe` method signature that receives the proper context and the queue listener:

```
        private Boolean DoSubscribe(ActivityExecutionContext
executionContext,
            IActivityEventListener<QueueEventArgs> listener)
        {
        }
```

2. Create the queue, retrieve the custom `CustomerQueuedFromTypedService`, and call its `GetCustomerCalledFromActivity` method.

```
        Console.WriteLine("In DoSubscribe: Both permutations should
call.");
        WorkflowQueue q = CreateQueue(executionContext);
        q.RegisterForQueueItemAvailable(listener);

        // Retrieve the custom CustomerQueuedFromTypedService from the
        // activity execution context.
        CustomerQueuedFromTypedService customerQueuedFromTypedService =
executionContext.GetService<CustomerQueuedFromTypedService>();

        // Call the GetCustomerCalledFromActivity method
        // on the custom CustomerQueuedFromService service
        customerQueuedFromTypedService.GetCustomerCalledFromActivity(
            this.QualifiedName, CustomerNumber);

        return true;
```

Implementing the `UnSubscribe` Handler

The `IEventActivity.UnSubscribe` handler is called by the `EventDriven` parent activity when the activity is embedded in an `EventDriven` activity. It is called when data is received into the queue. This handler is called instead of the OnEvent handler called for standalone activities.

Add the following handler that executes when the parent EventDriven activity unsubscribes.

```
        void IEventActivity.Unsubscribe(ActivityExecutionContext parentContext,
IActivityEventListener<QueueEventArgs> parentEventHandler)
        {
            Console.WriteLine("Unsubscribe called for EventDriven
perumutation");
            DoUnsubscribe(parentContext, parentEventHandler);
        }
```

Creating the DoUnSubscribe Method

To create the DoUnsubscribe helper method that unregisters the event from the queue, add the following code to unregister the event from the queue:

```
        private void DoUnsubscribe(ActivityExecutionContext context,
IActivityEventListener<QueueEventArgs> listener)
        {
            WorkflowQueuingService qService =
context.GetService<WorkflowQueuingService>();
            WorkflowQueue queue = qService.GetWorkflowQueue(this.QueueName);

            queue.UnregisterForQueueItemAvailable(listener);
        }
```

ActivityListenerEvent

Next, create OnEvent handler that is called for standalone queued activities when data is delivered to the queue. It is a replacement for the QueueItemAvailable handler used in previous activity examples. Most of the work performed is factored into the ProcessQueueItem method.

Add the following OnEvent handler:

```
        void IActivityEventListener<QueueEventArgs>.OnEvent(object sender,
QueueEventArgs e)
        {
            Console.WriteLine("In OnQueueItemAvailable in both cases.");

            // If activity is not scheduled for execution, do nothing
            if (this.ExecutionStatus == ActivityExecutionStatus.Executing)
            {
                ActivityExecutionContext executionContext = sender as
ActivityExecutionContext;
                if (this.ProcessQueueItem(executionContext))
                {
                    executionContext.CloseActivity();
                }
            }
        }
    }
```

ProcessQueueItem **Method**

The ProcessQueueItem method receives the data from the custom service and, in this case, displays it to the console. It is called from the Execute method and the OnEvent handler. It processes when called from the Execute method or from activities embedded in EventDriven activities. It processes from the OnEvent handler for standalone activities. It is called but terminates early when called from the Execute method for standalone activities because the queue is not yet created.

1. Add the following code to create the ProcessQueueItem method:

```
        private bool ProcessQueueItem(ActivityExecutionContext
executionContext)
        {
            Console.WriteLine("In ProcessQueueItem");
            // Retrieve the queuing service from the activity execution
context
            WorkflowQueuingService qService =
                executionContext.GetService<WorkflowQueuingService>();

            if (!qService.Exists(this.QueueName))
            {
                return false;
            }

            WorkflowQueue q = qService.GetWorkflowQueue(this.QueueName);

            // If the queue has messages, then process the first one
            if (q.Count == 0)
            {
                return false;
            }

            // Retrieve the data from the queue
            CustomerEventArgs cea = (CustomerEventArgs)q.Dequeue();

            // Send the customer data to the console
            Console.WriteLine("The customber is: " + cea.CustomerName);
            Console.WriteLine("The credit limit is: " +
cea.CustomerCreditLimit);
            Console.WriteLine("The customer type is: " + cea.CustomerType);
            Console.WriteLine("The ytd sales are: " +
cea.CustomerYtdSales);
            Console.WriteLine("The customer hold rule is: " +
cea.CustomerHoldRules);

            DoUnsubscribe(executionContext, this);
            DeleteQueue(executionContext);
            return true;
        }
```

CreateQueue **and** DeleteQueue **Helper Methods**

Follow the next steps to create CreateQueue and DeleteQueue helper methods that perform the functions their names imply.

1. Add the following two helper methods that create and delete the queues:

```
private WorkflowQueue CreateQueue(ActivityExecutionContext context)
{
    Console.WriteLine("CreateQueue");
    WorkflowQueuingService qService =
context.GetService<WorkflowQueuingService>();

    if (!qService.Exists(this.QueueName))
    {
        qService.CreateWorkflowQueue(this.QueueName, true);
    }

    return qService.GetWorkflowQueue(this.QueueName);
}

private void DeleteQueue(ActivityExecutionContext context)
{
    Console.WriteLine("DeleteQueue");
    WorkflowQueuingService qService =
context.GetService<WorkflowQueuingService>();
        qService.DeleteWorkflowQueue(this.QueueName);
}
```

2. Build the CustomQueuedActivities project.

Running the Workflow

Follow the next steps to create the workflow with your newly created EventDriven-enabled activity.

1. Remove any existing activities from the workflow.

2. Add a CustomerEventDrivenActivity to the workflow, enter **0001** in its CustomerNumber property, and run the workflow.

3. You should get the results shown in Figure 22.2.

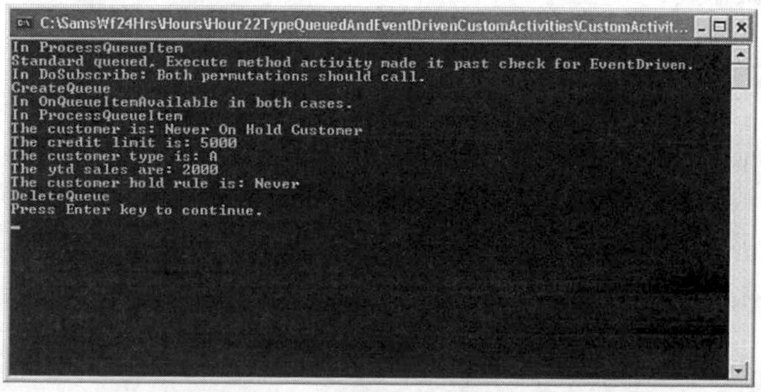

FIGURE 22.2
Customer-
EventDriven-
Activity
standalone activity on workflow execution results.

4. Add a Listen activity.

5. Move the CustomerEventDrivenActivity from the workflow to the left branch.

6. Add a Delay activity to the right branch and set its TimeoutDuration property to **00:01:00**.

7. Run the workflow again and you should get the results shown in Figure 22.3.

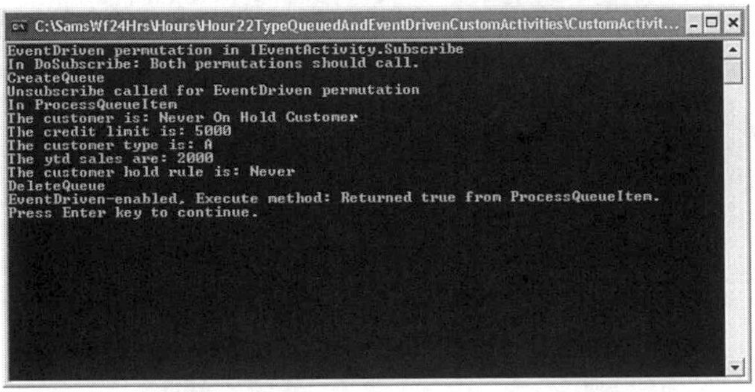

FIGURE 22.3
Customer-
EventDriven-
Activity
activity placed in
EventDriven
activity on work-
flow execution
results.

```
C:\SamsWf24Hrs\Hours\Hour22TypeQueuedAndEventDrivenCustomActivities\CustomActivit...
EventDriven permutation in IEventActivity.Subscribe
In DoSubscribe: Both permutations should call.
CreateQueue
Unsubscribe called for EventDriven permutation
In ProcessQueueItem
The customer is: Never On Hold Customer
The credit limit is: 5000
The customer type is: A
The ytd sales are: 2000
The customer hold rule is: Never
DeleteQueue
EventDriven-enabled. Execute method: Returned true from ProcessQueueItem.
Press Enter key to continue.
```

Summary

This hour covered creating strongly typed queued and EventDriven-enabled activities. The first allows the data that is passed to the workflow from the host to be typed with classes that derive from EventArgs. The latter permits your "queued" activities to be placed in Listen activity branches and other EventDriven activities. You now have all the knowledge you need to create activities that await external stimulus and then send them to the workflow strongly typed. Finally, your activities can participate in the canonical wait for response-timeout pattern. Go and create Customer, CheckCredit, and other activities that receive data from your other systems using this knowledge.

Workshop

Quiz

1. *What is the primary structural difference between the* CustomerQueuedFromServiceActivity *you created last hour and the* CustomerQueuedFromTypedServiceActivity?

2. *What does the following code do?*

   ```
   wi.EnqueueItem(custState.resultQueueName, eventArgs, null, null);
   ```

3. *What does the following code do?*

   ```
   CustomerEventArgs cea = (CustomerEventArgs)q.Dequeue();
   ```

4. **What is the difference between a standard queued activity and an** `EventDriven`**-enabled activity?**

5. **Do** `EventDriven`**-enabled activities have to support one or two programming models to support both being embedded within an** `EventDriven` **activity and also being placed on a workflow in a standalone mode?**

6. **What interface must an** `EventDriven`**-enabled activity derive from?**

7. **What is the purpose of the** `IEventActivity.QueueName` **property?**

8. **When is the** `IEventActivity.Subscribe` **method called?**

Answers

1. The `CustomerQueuedFromTypedServiceActivity` receives strongly typed data from the queue.

2. Strongly types the data in the service that delivers the data to the activity.

3. Retrieves the strongly typed data from the queue in the activity.

4. The latter can be placed in an `EventDriven` activity such as a `Listen` activity branch or a `State` activity.

5. They must support two models. The first is the model used so far throughout this and the previous hour, where the activity itself subscribes to the `QueueItemAvailable` event. They must also support a model that delegates subscribing to events to the parent `EventDriven` activity—for example, the `Listen` activity branch.

6. `IEventActivity`.

7. It is the name of the queue that the `EventDriven` activity listens on.

8. When the `EventDriven`-enabled activity is embedded in an `EventDriven` activity, the `IEventActivity.Subscribe` method is called in the activity's first execution burst.

Creating Control Flow Activities Session 1

What You Will Learn in This Hour:

- ▶ General control flow activity overview
- ▶ Control flow activity: nonexecuting
- ▶ Control flow activity: single child activity execution
- ▶ Control flow activity: executes all children
- ▶ Designer hierarchy overview
- ▶ Control flow activity: add parallel and sequential execution logic
- ▶ Control flow activity: cancellation and early completion
- ▶ Control flow activity: create the `GeneralControlFlowBranch` activity and add a condition

Control Flow Activity Conceptual Overview

This hour and the next cover creating control flow activities. Control flow activities are activity containers that have designers that convey the activity's capabilities and that also have execution logic to carry out these capabilities. Control flow activity designers both illustrate how to use the activity and indicate the activity's function. Control flow activities such as `IfElse`, `Sequential`, and `Parallel` activities all have designers that illustrate how to use them and that convey their function. When placing one of these activities on a workflow, their designers provide general guidelines for populating them with child activities. The other side of control flow activities is execution. When creating custom control flow activities, it is up to you, the control flow activity author, to execute their child activities and to provide rules for this execution.

You can provide any rules you want to determine child activity execution, which means you can create just about any control flow pattern you can think of. The `ConditionedActivityGroup` (CAG), `Replicator`, `EventHandlingScope`, `IfElse`, `While`, and `Parallel` are samples of the different types of control flow activities you can create. As mentioned in Hour 20, "Creating Basic Custom Activities," other possible patterns to implement can be found at the industry standard site, www.workflow-patterns.com, which features more than 40 different patterns. The patterns or activities contained in the Business Process Execution Language (BPEL), a standardized workflow language, can also be supported through custom control flow activities. Yet other possibilities are to create control flow patterns that align with the projects and skill sets of both technical and nontechnical people in your enterprise.

Control flow activities, unlike the compound activities covered in Hour 20, are not prepopulated with all child activities. They are containers for child activities to be placed in on the workflow.

Workflows, such as the `SequentialWorkflow` and `StateMachineWorkflow`, are themselves control flow activities. They also serve as containers that allow child activities to be modeled into them and then execute the child activities at runtime.

A number of elements go into control flow activity creation. This chapter will walk you through a number of the elements while creating a `GeneralControlFlow` activity that can be executed sequentially or in parallel, can complete early, and has conditions on its branches. Designer, validation, and toolbox functions are covered. The activity also supports cancellation, faulting, and compensation, among other features. The activity is flexible and demonstrates many control flow activity concepts that will allow you to create your own powerful control flow patterns.

An activity named `GeneralControlFlow` is developed step-by-step throughout the next two hours. The `GeneralControlFlow` activity not only shows the technical aspects required to build it, but conveys what it is like to build higher-level activities such as the CAG, the `Replicator`, and those found at www.workflowpatterns.com. The `GeneralControlFlow` activity you construct this hour and next will have many, but not all, of the capabilities found in the CAG and `Replicator` activities.

Control flow activities are generally referred to as composite activities. I will use control flow in this chapter because that is the usual purpose of composite activities.

Creating the Solution and Projects

The solution will contain two projects. The first holds the custom activity, and the second holds the workflow you place the custom activity on.

1. Create a new blank solution named **ControlFlowCustomActivitySolution** and place it in the C:\SamsWf24hrs\Hours\Hour23ControlFlowActivitiesSession1 directory (see Hour 2, "A Spin Around Windows Workflow Foundation").

2. Add a Workflow Activity Library (not a Sequential Workflow Library) project named **CustomControlflowActivities** to the solution.

3. Rename Activity1.cs to **GeneralControlFlow.cs** in the Solution Explorer.

4. Add a Sequential Workflow Console application project named **CustomActivityTester** to the solution.

5. Add code to pause the host. (See Hour 3, "Learning Basic Hosting," if you need help.)

Creating the Control Flow Activity

You will progressively create the GeneralControlFlow activity one step at a time in each subsection of this section. You will begin in the first subsection creating the basic shell that will not execute and wind up with an activity that can execute sequentially or in parallel and that supports early termination as the Replicator activity does. You will continue working with the GeneralControlFlow activity next hour, when you will add more advanced conditional logic to its child activities, validation, and other capabilities.

Creating Nonexecuting Control Flow Activity

Finally, it's time to create the GeneralControlFlow activity. In this incarnation, you will derive from the CompositeActivity type and associate it with a SequenceDesigner. The activity will not yet execute.

Set the CompositeActivity Base Type

By configuring the GeneralControlFlow activity to derive from the CompositeActivity base type instead of the Activity base type, the main feature gained is the ability to execute child activities. The CompositeActivity type is associated with the basic single activity rectangular single activity designer. To associate the activity with the SequenceDesigner, open the GeneralControlFlow activity in design mode. Then click the activity, click the Ellipsis in the Base Class property, select System.Workflow.ComponentModel, and select CompositeActivity in the middle pane. Then click OK.

Give the Activity a Designer

The SequenceDesigner is the designer associated with the Sequence activity. It is still rectangular like the basic activity designer, but it allows activities to be added from top to bottom and it expands as necessary the size of its child activities. Designers are covered in more detail in the "Control Flow Activity: Designer Overview" section.

Follow the next steps to decorate the activity with a SequenceDesigner attribute.

1. Right-click the activity and select View Code.

2. Add the following attribute above the class to specify that the activity use the SequenceDesigner:

   ```
   [Designer(typeof(SequenceDesigner))]
   ```

3. Build the CustomControlflowActivities project.

Creating the Workflow

Follow the next steps to add the GeneralControlFlow activity to a workflow and to populate it with child activities.

1. Open the workflow in the CustomActivityTester project.

2. Add GeneralControlFlow activity to the workflow. Notice that it looks like a Sequence activity and would appear (though it will not yet for reasons soon to be explained) to behave like a Sequence activity.

3. Add a Code activity to the GeneralControlFlow activity.

4. Double-click the Code activity and add the following code to its handler:

   ```
   Console.WriteLine("I'm a Code activity in a " +
       "GeneralControlFlow");
   ```

5. The workflow should look like Figure 23.1.

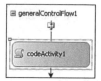

FIGURE 23.1
Workflow with
General-
ControlFlow
activity.

Running the Workflow

The Code activity will not execute because, as the GeneralControlFlow activity author, you are responsible for executing the child activities contained in your activity. The workflow should complete and the code to block your host should be displayed.

Follow the next steps to run the nonexecuting workflow.

1. Set the CustomActivityTester project as the startup project.

2. Run the workflow, and you should see results similar to Figure 23.2.

FIGURE 23.2
Nonexecuting
workflow results.

Adding Single Child Activity Execution

You start down the road to executing child activities in this step. You will override the Execute method, subscribe to the child activity's closed event, and schedule it for execution. You will unsubscribe and close the GeneralControlFlow activity in the handler. This is what control flow activities do—they execute other activities.

Similarities exist between the way control flow activities execute their child activities and the way multiburst activities schedule their long-running work. The notification is different, though, because the WF runtime calls the completion handler itself when control flow activities call their child activities.

Adding Child Activity Execution Logic

The CompositeActivity.EnabledActivities contains all of a control flow activities' child activities. The EnabledActivities property is used by control flow activities to access and execute their children. The first three steps access the first enabled activity and register to the closed event. The fourth step uses the ActivityExecutionContext to execute the child activity. Accessing child activities is another key use of the ActivityExecutionContext.

Follow the next steps to configure the GeneralControlFlow activity to execute a single child activity.

1. Open the GeneralControlFlow activity in code view.

2. Add a couple of blank lines below the constructor and type **protected override**, press the spacebar, and select the Execute method to create the Execute method.

3. Remove the content in the method body.

4. Add the following code to the Execute method to retrieve the first enabled child activity from the GeneralControlFlow activity:

   ```
   // Access the first enabled child activity
   Activity a = this.EnabledActivities[0];
   ```

5. Add the following code to register to the Closed event and to bind it to the ChildActivityContinuation handler:

   ```
   // Subscribe to child activity closed event
   a.Closed += ChildActivityContinuation;
   ```

6. Add the following code to tell the WF runtime to execute the child activity:

   ```
   // Schedule child activity for execution
   executionContext.ExecuteActivity(a);
   ```

7. Add the following code to return control to the WF runtime in the executing state. Just as with multiburst activities, the activity is returned in executing state and is closed in the handler.

   ```
   // Return control to workflow in executing state
   return ActivityExecutionStatus.Executing;
   ```

8. The completed Execute method should look like this:

   ```
   protected override ActivityExecutionStatus
   Execute(ActivityExecutionContext executionContext)
   {
       // Access the first enabled child activity
       Activity a = this.EnabledActivities[0];

       // Subscribe to child activity closed event
       a.Closed += ChildActivityContinuation;

       // Schedule child activity for execution
       executionContext.ExecuteActivity(a);

       // Return control to workflow in executing state
   ```

```
        return ActivityExecutionStatus.Executing;
    }
```

Adding the `ChildActivityContinuation` Handler

When the first child activity completes execution, the WF runtime will invoke the `ChildActivityContinuation` handler. The handler will unsubscribe to the `Closed` event and close the `GeneralControlFlow` activity.

Follow the next steps to create the `ChildActivityContinuation` handler.

1. Add the following code to create the `ChildActivityContinuation` handler signature:

```
// Handler for executed children
void ChildActivityContinuation(
    object sender, ActivityExecutionStatusChangedEventArgs e)
{
}
```

2. Add the following code to the handler you just created to retrieve the child activity that just completed executing from the `EventArgs` passed to the handler:

```
// Access the child activity that just completed
Activity a = e.Activity;
```

3. Add the following code to unsubscribe to the closed event for the child activity that just completed executing:

```
// Unsubscribe to the closed event
a.Closed -= ChildActivityContinuation;
```

4. Add the following code to retrieve the `ActivityExecutionContext` and use it to close the `GeneralControlFlow` activity:

```
// Retrieve the AEC and close the activity
ActivityExecutionContext executionContext =
    sender as ActivityExecutionContext;
executionContext.CloseActivity();
```

5. The completed `ChildActivityContinuation` should look like this:

```
// Handler for executed children
void ChildActivityContinuation(
    object sender, ActivityExecutionStatusChangedEventArgs e)
{
    // Access the child activity that just completed
    Activity a = e.Activity;

    // Unsubscribe to the closed event
    a.Closed -= ChildActivityContinuation;
```

```
        // Retrieve the AEC and close the activity
        ActivityExecutionContext executionContext =
            sender as ActivityExecutionContext;
        executionContext.CloseActivity();
    }
```

6. Build the `CustomControlflowActivities` project.

Running the Workflow

Follow the next steps to run the workflow, which will now execute a single child activity. It will do so because the `GeneralControlFlow` activity tells the WF runtime to execute the child activity.

1. Run the workflow and you should see the `Code` activity execute as shown in Figure 23.3.

FIGURE 23.3
One activity executing workflow results.

2. Add another `Code` activity to the `GeneralControlFlow` activity below the first `Code` activity. Then double-click it and add the following code to its handler:

```
Console.WriteLine("I'm the second Code activity in a " +
    "GeneralControlFlow");
```

3. Run the workflow again and you should see the same results you saw when the workflow had only one `Code` activity. The second `Code` activity should not execute because you only instructed the WF runtime to execute one child activity. You will rectify this in the next section.

Executing All Child Activities

In this step, you tell the WF runtime to execute all child activities by iterating through the `EnabledProperties` property in the `Execute` method. Then you modify the `ChildActivityContinuation` handler to check that all children are completed before closing the `GeneralControlFlow` activity. This step is necessary because the

`ChildActivityContinuation` handler is called after each child completes execution, and the `GeneralControlFlow` activity should not be closed until all its child activities have completed execution.

Updating the `Execute` Method to Process Multiple Children

Follow the next steps to add a `foreach` statement to the `Execute` method that will iterate through all enabled activities. Otherwise, there are no changes.

1. Open the `GeneralControlFlow` activity in code view.

2. Add the following code to the top of the `Execute` method to create a `foreach` loop that will iterate through all child activities:

   ```
   // Iterate through all child activities
   foreach (Activity a in this.EnabledActivities)
   {
   }
   ```

3. Delete this line of code: `Activity a = this.EnabledActivities[0]` and its associated comment because the activities will be accessed in the `foreach`.

4. Move the following lines of code into the `foreach` statement.

   ```
   // Subscribe to child activity closed event
   a.Closed += ChildActivityContinuation;

   // Schedule child activity for execution
   executionContext.ExecuteActivity(a);
   ```

5. The `Execute` method should now look like Listing 23.1.

LISTING 23.1   `Execute` Method That Executes All Child Activities

```
    protected override ActivityExecutionStatus
Execute(ActivityExecutionContext executionContext)
    {
        // Iterate through all child activities
        foreach (Activity a in this.EnabledActivities)
        {
            // Subscribe to child activity closed event
            a.Closed += ChildActivityContinuation;

            // Schedule child activity for execution
            executionContext.ExecuteActivity(a);
        }

        // Return control to workflow in executing state
        return ActivityExecutionStatus.Executing;
    }
```

Updating the `ChildActivityContinuation` Handler

The `ChildActivityContinuation` handler now needs to check that all children have executed before closing the `GeneralControlFlow` activity.

1. Add the following code before the `executionContext.CloseActivity` line of code to iterate through all child activities:

```
foreach (Activity eachActivity in this.EnabledActivities)
{
}
```

2. Insert the following code into the `foreach` statement to check if the current activity iteration is closed. It returns with the activity still in executing state if it finds any child activities that are not closed.

```
if (eachActivity.ExecutionStatus !=
ActivityExecutionStatus.Closed)
        return;
```

3. The `ChildActivityContinuation` handler should now look like Listing 23.2.

LISTING 23.2   `ChildActivityContinuation` Handler That Executes All Child Activities

```
// Handler for executed children
void ChildActivityContinuation(
    object sender, ActivityExecutionStatusChangedEventArgs e)
{
    // Access the child activity that just completed
    Activity a = e.Activity;

    // Unsubscribe to the closed event
    a.Closed -= ChildActivityContinuation;

    // Retrieve the AEC and close the activity
    ActivityExecutionContext executionContext =
        sender as ActivityExecutionContext;

    foreach (Activity eachActivity in this.EnabledActivities)
    {
        if (eachActivity.ExecutionStatus !=
ActivityExecutionStatus.Closed)
            return;
    }
    executionContext.CloseActivity();
}
```

Running the Workflow

Both Code activities should now execute. Run the workflow, and you should see that both Code activities execute as shown in Figure 23.4.

FIGURE 23.4
All activities exe-
cuting workflow
results.

You now have created a functional control flow activity. It overrides the `Execute` method. In the overridden method it schedules child activities for execution and subscribes to their closed event. It then returns control to the WF runtime in executing state. You also created a `ChildActivityContinuation` handler that is invoked by the WF runtime when child activities are closed. There are many more control flow activity options—some of which will be explored in this chapter—but what you have created serves as a solid start.

Designer Hierarchy Overview

Custom control flow activities frequently require a designer that conveys the control flow activity intent. WF features a collection of designers that convey and that are used by its out-of-the-box (OOB) activities. The `Parallel` and `IfElse` activities, for instance, both use the `ParallelActivityDesigner`. You can use this designer as well, when creating a custom control flow activity with similar semantics.

WF designers are supported by a hierarchical class structure. The `ActivityDesigner` is at the top of the WF designer hierarchy. It is both the simple rectangular designer associated with basic activities that does not accept child activities and the designer from which all other WF designers are derived. The `CompositeActivityDesigner` is one step up the designer hierarchy, and it serves as the basis for all designers that can accept child activities. At the next level resides the `FreeformActivityDesigner` and the `StructuredCompositeActivityDesigner`. The `FreeFormDesigner` allows activities to be placed anywhere on the design surface. It is used by the state machine workflow and can be derived from and extended to create a freeform flow charting designer and other designers that benefit from a freeform design surface.

The `StructuredCompositeActivityDesigner` serves as the basis for WF's designers that dictate where activities are placed and automatically connect them. The two strands that meet this condition are the `ParallelActivityDesigner` and the `SequenceDesigner`. The `ParallelActivityDesigner` is used by the `IfElse` and `Parallel` activities. The `SequenceDesigner` and designers derived from it are used by the `Sequence` activity, `SequentialWorkflow` activity, and other sequentially oriented activities.

The `Parallel` activity allows multiple branches to be added side by side. The branches are supported through `SequenceDesigners`. Therefore, the `Parallel` activity presentation is supplied by the aggregate of the `ParallelActivityDesigner` and one or more SequenceDesigners. Even control flow activity designers are simply rectangular shapes. The ParallelActivityDesigner places its branches side by side, whereas the Sequence activity places its branches (or activities) from top-to-bottom. So when you create a control flow activity, you must plan both its designer look-and-feel and how it will organize its child activity designers.

In the next step you will associate your activity with the ParallelActivityDesigner because it is the most appropriate for the GeneralControlFlow activity. The fact that it can execute in parallel and you will later make its branches conditional leads to the choice of the ParallelActivityDesigner. This is so, even though the GeneralControlFlow activity will retain a sequential execution option.

Adding Parallel Execution Option

As mentioned previously, a control flow activity may schedule its child activities for execution in just about any way. In this step, you will dive into altering the way child activities are scheduled by adding parallel and serial execution options to the GeneralControlFlow activity.

Sequential or parallel execution options are relevant only when the activity's immediate child activities are themselves control flow activities. Let's look at the existing Parallel activity to see why. Parallel activity branches are themselves Sequence activities that may contain one or more child activities. It is the Sequence activity's children (and the Parallel activity's grandchildren) that execute in parallel when the parallel option is selected. If sequential execution is selected, all child activities in the first Sequence activity are executed, then all the child activities in the second, and so on. The sample workflow at the end of this exercise will be reconfigured to demonstrate this concept.

Adding a Dependency Property to Specify Execution Type

Follow the next steps to add the ExecutionMode DependencyProperty.

1. Open the GeneralControlFlow activity in code view.

2. Move your cursor directly below the constructor, insert a couple of additional blank lines, move your cursor between the lines, right-click, and select Insert Snippet. Double-click on Other, double-click Workflow, and double-click DependencyProperty—Property to insert a new dependency property.

3. You should see the stub dependency property, and the text MyProperty should be highlighted.

4. Enter **ExecutionMode** (replacing MyProperty) and press Enter to leave the wizard.

Adding Parallel and Sequential Execution to the `Execute` Method

Two common patterns can be employed when scheduling activities. The first, the parallel pattern, schedules all child activities for execution in the `Execute` method. It then alternates execution of its children activities. The second, the sequential pattern, schedules one child activity for execution in the `Execute` method, and then schedules subsequent children in the closed child handler. This way only one activity is scheduled at a time.

Follow the next steps to modify the `Execute` method to support both sequential and parallel execution.

1. Add the following `IfElse` below this line of code:
   `executionContext.ExecuteActivity(a);` in the `Execute` method. This code exits the `foreach` after one child is executed, which should happen when sequential `ExecutionMode` is specified:

```
if (ExecutionMode == "Sequential")
{
    // Only need the first to executed if executing
    // sequentially
    break;
}
```

2. The completed `Execute` method should look like Listing 23.3.

LISTING 23.3 **`Execute` Method That Supports Both Parallel and Sequential Execution**

```
    protected override ActivityExecutionStatus
Execute(ActivityExecutionContext executionContext)
    {
        // Iterate through all child activities
        foreach (Activity a in this.EnabledActivities)
        {
            // Subscribe to child activity closed event
            a.Closed += ChildActivityContinuation;

            // Schedule child activity for execution
            executionContext.ExecuteActivity(a);

            if (ExecutionMode == "Sequential")
            {
                // Only need the first to execute if executing
```

```
            // sequentially
            break;
        }
    }

    // Return control to workflow in executing state
    return ActivityExecutionStatus.Executing;
}
```

Adding Sequential Execution Option to the Handler

When executed in parallel, the child completion handler unsubscribes to the closed event for the just completed child activity and then checks whether all child activities are completed. If so, the parent activity is closed. When executed sequentially, the handler executes child activities that remain in Initialized state as well, because only the first child activity is executed in the Execute method. The remaining child activities remain in Initialized state when exiting the Execute method.

Follow the next steps to modify the ChildActivityContinuation handler to support both parallel and sequential execution.

1. Add the following code below the line of code that begins with ActivityExecutionContext executionContext to process sequentially executing activities:

    ```
    // Execute Sequentially
    if (ExecutionMode == "Sequential")
    {
    }
    ```

2. Add the following code to the if statement you just added to locate and execute the next activity in Initialized state:

    ```
    // Locate and execute next activity in initialzed state
    foreach (Activity eachActivity in this.EnabledActivities)
    {
    }
    ```

3. Insert the following code into the foreach statement you just added to subscribe to the closed event of the current child activity, schedule it for execution, and return control the WF runtime with the activity still in executing state:

    ```
            if (eachActivity.ExecutionStatus ==
    ActivityExecutionStatus.Initialized)
            {
                // Subscribe to child activity closed event and
    execute it
                eachActivity.Closed += ChildActivityContinuation;

                executionContext.ExecuteActivity(eachActivity);
    ```

```
                                // return from handler with activity still in
          executing state
                                return;
                            }
```

4. Add the following code above this line of code:

    `executionContext.CloseActivity();` to process activities executing in parallel:

    ```
            // Execute In Parallel
            if (ExecutionMode == "Parallel")
            {
            }
    ```

5. The existing `foreach` statement above the `if` statement you just added should be placed in the `if` statement (the one you just added).

6. The completed `ChildActivityContinuation` handler that supports both parallel and sequential execution should look like Listing 23.4.

LISTING 23.4   `ChildActivityContinuation` Handler That Supports Both Parallel and Sequential Execution

```
          // Handler for executed children
          void ChildActivityContinuation(
              object sender, ActivityExecutionStatusChangedEventArgs e)
          {
              // Access the child activity that just completed
              Activity a = e.Activity;

              // Unsubscribe to the closed event
              a.Closed -= ChildActivityContinuation;

              // Retrieve the AEC and close the activity
              ActivityExecutionContext executionContext =
                  sender as ActivityExecutionContext;

              // Execute Sequentiall
              if (ExecutionMode == "Sequential")
              {
                  // Locate and execute next activity in initialized state
                  foreach (Activity eachActivity in this.EnabledActivities)
                  {
                      if (eachActivity.ExecutionStatus ==
ActivityExecutionStatus.Initialized)
                      {
                          // Subscribe to child activity closed event and execute it
                          eachActivity.Closed += ChildActivityContinuation;

                          executionContext.ExecuteActivity(eachActivity);

                          // return from handler with activity still in
          executing state
                          return;
                      }
              }
```

```
            }
        }

        // Execute In Parallel
        if (ExecutionMode == "Parallel")
        {
            foreach (Activity eachActivity in this.EnabledActivities)
            {
                if (eachActivity.ExecutionStatus !=
ActivityExecutionStatus.Closed)
                    return;
            }
        }

        executionContext.CloseActivity();
    }
```

Configuring Activity to use `ParallelActivityDesigner`

Follow the next steps to configure the `GeneralControlFlow` activity to use the `ParallelActivityDesigner`.

1. Replace the current attribute that specifies the `SequenceDesigner` with the following attribute that specifies the `ParallelActivityDesigner`:

   ```
   [Designer(typeof(ParallelActivityDesigner))]
   ```

2. Build the project.

3. Open the workflow in design mode, and the `GeneralControlFlow` activity should now reflect the new parallel designer, as shown in Figure 23.5.

FIGURE 23.5
GeneralContr-
olFlow activity
now configured
to use
ParallelActi-
vityDesigner.

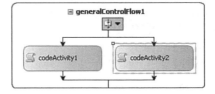

Updating the Workflow

So that both the sequential and parallel execution patterns can be demonstrated, Sequence activities will be added to the `GeneralControlFlow` activity and Code activities to the Sequence activity.

Follow the next steps to update the workflow.

1. Open the workflow in design mode.

2. Delete the current `GeneralControlFlow` activity.

3. Add a new `GeneralControlFlow` activity.

4. Add a `Sequence` activity to the `GeneralControlFlow` activity.

5. Add another `Sequence` activity to the `GeneralControlFlow` activity to the right of the one you just added (hover to the right of the existing branch but within the `GeneralControlFlow` activity to add it).

6. Add two `Code` activities to the `Sequence` activity in the left branch.

7. Add two `Code` activities to the `Sequence` activity in the right branch of the `GeneralControlFlow` activity (Figure 23.6).

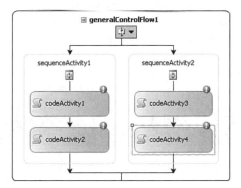

FIGURE 23.6
`GeneralContr-olFlow` activity populated with `Sequence` and `Code` activities.

8. Double-click the first `Code` activity in the left branch and add the following code to its handler:

```
CodeActivity ca = sender as CodeActivity;
Console.WriteLine("Left-hand branch, activity name:" +
ca.Name);
```

9. Double-click the second `Code` activity in the left branch and add the following code to its handler:

```
CodeActivity ca = sender as CodeActivity;
Console.WriteLine("Left-hand branch, activity name:" +
ca.Name);
```

10. Double-click the first `Code` activity in the right branch and add the following code to its handler:

```
CodeActivity ca = sender as CodeActivity;
Console.WriteLine("Right-hand branch, activity name:" +
ca.Name);
```

11. Double-click the second `Code` activity in the right branch and add the following code to its handler:

```
CodeActivity ca = sender as CodeActivity;
Console.WriteLine("Right-hand branch, activity name:" +
ca.Name);
```

Running the Workflow

Follow the next steps to run the workflow twice, once with the `GeneralControlFlow` activity configured to run sequentially and once in parallel.

1. Click the `GeneralControlFlow` activity on the workflow and set its `ExecutionMode` property to **Sequential**.

2. Press F5 to run the workflow and you should see that the `Sequence` activity in the left branch executes all its activities, and then the `Sequence` activity in the right branch does the same. There is no interleaving. Check the numbers of the `Code` activities to verify. Mine are 1, 2 in the left branch and 3, 4 in the right branch. See Figure 23.7.

FIGURE 23.7
GeneralContr-
olFlow execut-
ing sequentially.

3. Click the `GeneralControlFlow` activity and set its `ExecutionMode` property to **Parallel**.

4. Press F5 to run the workflow and you should see that the activities execution is interleaved, because the `GeneralControlFlow` activity executes in parallel. In my case, the order is 1, 3, 2, 4. See Figure 23.8.

FIGURE 23.8
GeneralContr-
olFlow execut-
ing in parallel.

Adding Cancellation and Early Completion

Many approval scenarios can complete before all responses are received. The precise reason depends on the business rules. Some processes may be considered complete when a specified percentage of responses (for example, 66% or 90%) are received. Others may be considered complete when over half approve or reject the item being reviewed.

This section contains simple logic to test the number of `GeneralControlFlow` activity branches completed versus a new property that contains the number of branches that should be executed. If the number of executed branches equals the number of branches to execute, the GeneralControlFlow activity completes, even though it may have additional branches.

The GeneralControlFlow activity cannot complete until all its children are in some combination of Closed and Initialized states. The GeneralControlFlow activity will likely have activities in executing state when its ExecutionMode property is set to Parallel and its BranchesToExecute property is set to a value less than its total number of branches. To close a control flow activity such as the GeneralControlFlow activity, the executing child activities must be closed first by calling ActivityExecutionContext.CancelActivity.

If the ExecutionMode property is set to Sequential, the child activities of branches not yet executed would be set to Initialized because each branch is scheduled for execution right before it executes. You do not need to modify their Initialized state because they do not prevent the parent control flow activity from closing.

By the Way

Updating `ChildActivityContinuation` Handler to Check for Early Termination

Follow the next steps to modify the ChildActivityContinuation handler to check for early completion.

1. Open the GeneralControlFlow activity in code view.

2. Add a dependency property below the constructor named **BranchesToExecute** and set its type to int.

3. Add the following member variable below the constructor that will track the number of GeneralControlFlow activity branches executed:

    ```
    int BranchesExecuted = 0;
    ```

4. Add the following code to the ChildActivityContinuation handler below this line of code: ActivityExecutionContext executionContext to increment the number of branches executed:

    ```
    // Number of branches executed
    BranchesExecuted++;
    ```

5. Add the following code to the ChildActivityContinuation handler below the code you just added to check for early completion:

    ```
    // Check if early termination is required
    if (BranchesExecuted == BranchesToExecute &&
    BranchesToExecute != 0)
    ```

```
                     {
                     }
```

6. Insert the following foreach statement into the if statement you just added to iterate the child activities:

```
foreach (Activity eachActivity in this.EnabledActivities)
{
}
```

7. Insert the following if statement into the foreach statement you just added, which checks for currently executing activities:

```
if (eachActivity.ExecutionStatus ==
    ActivityExecutionStatus.Executing)
{
}
```

8. Insert the following code into the if statement you just added to schedule the currently executing activity for cancellation:

```
// Schedule executing activites for cancellation.
executionContext.CancelActivity(eachActivity);
```

9. Build the project so the new property will be available to the workflow.

If any child activities were still executing when the early completion threshold was reached, they are scheduled for cancellation. Parent activities can request that their child activities be executed and canceled.

By the Way

> A bug was discovered with this code too late to fix before publishing. If you set the ExecutionMode property to Sequential, it will no longer terminate early as it should. There will be a fix posted by the time you are reading this book on my website at www.reassociates.net.

Updating and Running the Workflow

Follow the next steps to update and run the workflow that will cancel selected activities because of early termination.

1. Add a Delay activity to the top of each GeneralControlFlow activity branch.

2. Set the TimeoutDuration property on the Delay activity in the left branch to 00:00:10 and the one in the right branch to 00:01:00.

3. Set the GeneralControlFlow activity's BranchesToExecute property to 1 and make sure its ExecutionMode property is set to **Parallel.**

4. Run the workflow and (after a little pause because of the Delay activity) you should see that only the first branch executes, as shown in Figure 23.9.

C:\SamsBook\Chapters\Chapter21ControlflowActivities\ControlFlowCustomActivitySolution\...
Left-hand branch, activity name:codeActivity1
Left-hand branch, activity name:codeActivity2
Press any key to continue.

FIGURE 23.9
GeneralContr-
olFlow early
completion
results.

5. Run it again and set breakpoints on the cancellation code if you like to see cancelation in action.

Creating GeneralControlFlowBranch and Adding a Condition

You will now add conditions to the GeneralControlFlow activity branches. If the condition evaluates to true, the branch is executed, otherwise it is not. Each branch will be evaluated, and it is possible that multiple branches will evaluate affirmatively. Because all branches that evaluate affirmatively are executed, the activity is analogous to the switch statement commonly found in programming languages. However, the activity can execute the branches in parallel, which most programming languages cannot do.

The condition must be set on each branch, so a new activity must be created. The GeneralControlFlowBranch activity will be created. It is essentially a Sequence activity with an additional property of type ActivityCondition. The GeneralControlFlow activity will then be modified to evaluate this property. When evaluated positively, the branch will execute; otherwise, it will not.

Performing Preliminary Activity Setup

Follow the next steps to create the GeneralControlFlowBranch activity.

1. Right-click the CustomControlflowActivities project and select Add, Activity.

2. Name the activity **GeneralControlFlowBranch**.

   It should derive from the Sequence activity, which is the default.

Adding the Condition Property

Follow the next steps to add a Condition property to the GeneralControlFlowBranch activity. This Condition will be evaluated to determine whether or not the branch should execute.

1. Open the `GeneralControlFlowBranch` activity in code view.

2. Add a new dependency property below the constructor named **Condition** and set its type to **ActivityCondition**.

3. Build the CustomControlflowActivities project.

4. Open the workflow in design view and add a `GeneralControlFlowBranch` activity to the top of the workflow.

5. Click it, and you will see it holds a `Condition` property (Figure 23.10) that looks and behaves like the conditions on other WF activities.

FIGURE 23.10
GeneralContr-
olFlowBranch
activity with con-
dition property.

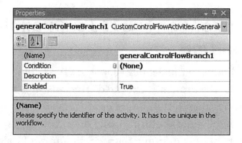

6. Remove the `GeneralControlFlowBranch` activity you just added from the workflow. You will reconfigure the workflow and run it with `GeneralControlFlowBranch` activities shortly.

Modifying the `GeneralControlFlow` Activity to Evaluate the Condition

Follow the next steps to modify the `GeneralControlFlow` activity's `Execute` method needs to evaluate the `GeneralControlFlowBranch` activity's `Condition` property.

By the Way

> In the next hour you learn to create attached properties that do not require that a specific child activity be placed in a parent for the condition to be evaluated. The activity will function similarly to the CAG activity, where any child activity is evaluated.

1. Open the `GeneralControlFlow` activity in code view.

2. Add the following code to the top of the `foreach` in the `Execute` method to check if the condition evaluates to `true`:

```
if (a.Condition.Evaluate(a, executionContext))
    {
    }
```

3. Move all original code in the foreach into the If statement you just added.

4. Replace the foreach line of code with the following that iterates the
GeneralControlFlowBranch activities that have the Condition property:

```
foreach (GeneralControlFlowBranch a in this.EnabledActivities)
```

5. The updated Execute method should look like this:

```
protected override ActivityExecutionStatus
Execute(ActivityExecutionContext executionContext)
{
    // Iterate through all child activities
    foreach (GeneralControlFlowBranch a in this.EnabledActivities)
    {
        if (a.Condition.Evaluate(a, executionContext))
        {
            // Subscribe to child activity closed event
            a.Closed += ChildActivityContinuation;

            // Schedule child activity for execution
            executionContext.ExecuteActivity(a);

            if (ExecutionMode == "Sequential")
            {
                // Only need the first to execute if executing
                //   sequentially
                break;
            }
        }
    }
}
```

Updating the Workflow

Follow the next steps to reconfigure the workflow to use the new
GeneralControlFlowBranch activity. The first step is to delete the current
GeneralControlFlow activity because its child activities are currently Sequence
activities. Sequence activities do not have a Condition property, so the
GeneralControlFlow's current branches cannot be evaluated. As mentioned, this
limitation is solved when using attached properties later in the hour.

1. Open the workflow in design mode.

2. Add a new GeneralControlFlow activity to the workflow.

3. Add two GeneralControlFlowBranch activities to the GeneralControlFlow
activity.

4. Move the Code activities from the original GeneralControlFlow activity to the
new one in the corresponding branches.

5. Delete the original `GeneralControlFlow` activity.

6. Click the left branch of the `GeneralControlFlow` activity.

7. Click the drop-down in the `Condition` property and select Code Condition.

8. Click the + at the left of the `Condition` property, enter **TrueCondition** in the `Condition` property, and press Enter.

   You are placed in the `TrueCondition` handler.

9. Hardcode the Code Condition to return `true` by entering the following in the handler:

   ```
   e.Result = true;
   ```

10. Click the right branch of the `GeneralControlFlow` activity.

11. Click the drop-down in the `Condition` property and select Code Condition.

12. Click the + at the left of the `Condition` property, enter **FalseCondition** in the `Condition` property, and press Enter.

    You are placed in the `FalseCondition` handler.

13. Hardcode the Code Condition to return `false` by entering the following in the handler:

    ```
    e.Result = false;
    ```

Running the Workflow

Follow the next steps with the `GeneralControlFlowBranch` activity.

1. Run the workflow, and you should see the following results with only the left branch executed because only the left branch should evaluate to `true` (Figure 23.11).

FIGURE 23.11
Workflow with one branch evaluating to `true`.

```
C:\SamsBook\Chapters\Chapter21ControlFlowActivities\ControlFlowCustomActivitySolution_custom...  _ □ ×
Left-hand branch, activity name:codeActivity1
Left-hand branch, activity name:codeActivity2
Press any key to continue.
```

2. Change the second branch `Condition` property to point to `TrueCondition`.

3. Run the workflow again, and both branches should execute.

Summary

Control flow activities are generally engrained into a workflow product. The fact that WF allows you to create your own custom control flow activities prevents you from having to depend on which control flow patterns Microsoft deems important. This hour walked you through a powerful control flow activity and intended to demystify complex control flow patterns. They are simply made of conditions, execution modes, subscribing to child handlers, and a few other elements. In the next hour you will learn to create custom activity validation and other functions that support custom activities.

Workshop

Quiz

1. *What is the* `EnabledActivities` *property used for?*

2. *What is the difference between the* `SequenceDesigner` *and the* `ParallelActivityDesigner`*?*

3. *What is the purpose of the next two lines of code?*

    ```
    a.Closed += ChildActivityContinuation;
    executionContext.ExecuteActivity(a);
    ```

4. *John adds a custom activity, derives from* `CompositeActivity`, *and attributes it to use the Sequence Designer. Will the activity execute?*

5. *Why is the following code placed in the* `Execute` *method of an activity that executes sequentially and not one that executes in parallel?*

    ```
    if (ExecutionMode == "Sequential")
    {
        // Only need the first to execute if executing
        // sequentially
        break;
    }
    ```

6. *How do you add a* `Condition` *property to a custom activity?*

7. *How do you ensure that only activities that evaluate to* `true` *are scheduled?*

Answers

1. It holds all enabled child activities and is frequently iterated through to execute all `Child` activities.

2. Child activities are vertically placed in the SequenceDesigner and horizontally in the ParallelActivityDesigner.

3. To subscribe to an activity's Closed event and schedule the activity for execution with the runtime. When the runtime completes executing the child, the ChildActivityContinuation handler is invoked.

4. No, the Execute method must be overridden, and the child activities must be scheduled for execution.

5. Only the first child activity should be scheduled in the Execute method when the parent activity is configured to execute sequentially. The remaining activities are then scheduled in the handler. When slated for parallel execution, all child activities are scheduled in the Execute method.

6. Add a DependencyProperty to the activity of type ActivityCondition.

7. Call the custom activity's Condition.Evaluate method and pass the activity and execution context as parameters (this assumes the ActivityCondition-typed property is named Condition).

HOUR 24

Creating Control Flow Activities Session 2

What You Will Learn in This Hour:

- ▶ Control flow activity: add custom designer
- ▶ Control flow activity: `ToolBoxItem`
- ▶ Control flow activity: custom validation
- ▶ Control flow activity: attached properties
- ▶ Implementing compensation
- ▶ Activity life cycle artifacts

In this hour, you extend the activity you worked on the previous hour. You start by adding a custom designer that allows you to specify the look-and-feel and to control its design-time validation. You prepopulate the branches in the activity using the `ToolBoxItem`. You then learn to further validate the activity at design-time by adding custom validation. Then you use attached properties that allow all child activities to be evaluated, not just ones populated with `GeneralControlFlowBranch` activities. Finally you wrap up by adding compensation and reviewing the activity life cycle.

Enhancing the `GeneralControlFlow` Activity

You need to create a custom designer for the `GeneralControlFlow` activity. The custom designer is used to control the way the activity is interacted with at design-time.

Adding a Custom Designer

The custom designer you apply to the GeneralControlFlow activity is derived from ParallelActivityDesigner. The OnCreateNewBranch method is overridden so that GeneralControlFlow activity branches can be added to the GeneralControlFlow activity via its shortcut menu. The CanInsertActivities is overridden to ensure that only GeneralControlFlowBranch activities are added to the GeneralControlFlow activity.

Adding and Setting Up the Class

Follow the next steps to add a class in which you will code the custom activity designer.

1. Right-click the CustomControlflowActivities project and select Add, Class.

2. Name the class **GeneralControlFlowDesigner**.

3. Add **:ParallelActivityDesigner** to the right of the class name to derive from the ParallelActivityDesigner type.

4. Add the following using directives:

   ```
   using System.Workflow.ComponentModel.Design;
   using System.Workflow.ComponentModel;
   using System.ComponentModel;
   ```

Overriding the OnCreateNewBranch Method

Follow the next steps to override the OnCreateNewBranch method to return a GeneralControlFlowBranch activity.

1. Add a couple of blank lines after the opening class bracket and enter **protected override**. Press the spacebar and select the OnCreateNewBranch method to create the OnCreateNewBranch method.

2. Remove the content in the method body.

3. Add the following code to the OnCreateNewBranch method to add a GeneralControlFlowBranch activity:

   ```
   return new GeneralControlFlowBranch();
   ```

Override the CanInsertActivities Method

Follow the next steps to override the CanInsertActivities method to enforce that only GeneralControlFlowBranch activities are added.

1. Add a couple of blank lines and type **protected override**, press the spacebar, and select the CanInsertActivities method to create the CanInsertActivities method.

2. Add the following code to the top of the CanInsertActivities method to ensure that only activities of type GeneralControlFlowBranch are added:

```
foreach (Activity a in activitiesToInsert)
{
    if (!(a is GeneralControlFlowBranch))
    {
        return false;
    }
}
```

Telling the GeneralControlFlow Activity to Use the Custom Designer

Follow the next steps to decorate the GeneralControlFlow activity with a GeneralControlFlowDesigner attribute to associate it with the new designer.

1. Open the GeneralControlFlow activity in code view.

2. Replace its ParallelActivityDesigner attribute with the following:

```
[Designer(typeof(GeneralControlFlowDesigner))]
```

3. Build the CustomControlflowActivities project.

Testing the New Designer

Follow the next steps to test the new designer you created by adding legal and illegal activities to it.

1. Open the workflow in design mode.

2. Right-click the GeneralControlFlow activity and select Add Branch. A new GeneralControlFlowBranch will be added, as shown in Figure 24.1.

3. Delete the branch you just added.

FIGURE 24.1
Add
`GeneralContr-
olFlowBranch`
to
`GeneralContr-
olFlow` activity
by right-clicking it.

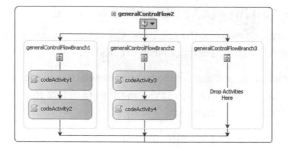

4. Try to add a Sequence activity (or any activity other than the `GeneralControlFlowBranch`) to the `GeneralControlFlow` activity; it will not let you.

Adding `ToolBoxItem`

The `IfElse` and `Parallel` activity both have two branches when placed on the workflow. This is more convenient and contributes to their look-and-feel. In this step, you create a new class derived from `ActivityToolboxItem` and attribute the `GeneralControlFlow` activity to point to the new custom class.

Adding the Class

Follow the next steps to add the new class that will derive from `ActivityToolboxItem`.

1. Open the `ControlFlowCustomActivitySolution` in the `C:\SamsWf24hrs\Hours\Hour24ControlFlowActivitiesSession2` directory.

2. Right-click the `CustomControlflowActivities` project and select Add, Class.

3. Name the class **GeneralControlFlowToolBoxItem**.

Add Code to the Class

The overridden `CreateComponentsCore` method instantiates a `GeneralControlFlow` activity and adds two `GeneralControlFlowBranch` activities to it. Otherwise, most of this code is boilerplate and is therefore not explained in detail.

Follow the next steps to code the `GeneralControlFlowToolBoxItem` class and associate it with the `GeneralControlFlow` activity.

1. Replace the code in the `GeneralControlFlowToolBoxItem` class with the following code that adds two `GeneralControlFlowBranch` activities to the

GeneralControlFlow activity when the GeneralControlFlow activity is added from the toolbox:

```
using System;
using System.Collections.Generic;
using System.Linq;
using System.Text;
using System.Workflow.Activities;
using System.Workflow.ComponentModel.Design;
using System.Runtime.Serialization;
using System.ComponentModel.Design;
using System.ComponentModel;
using System.Workflow.ComponentModel;

namespace CustomControlflowActivities
{
    class GeneralControlFlowToolBoxItem : ActivityToolboxItem
    {
        public GeneralControlFlowToolBoxItem(Type type)
            : base(type)
        {
        }

        private GeneralControlFlowToolBoxItem(SerializationInfo info,
StreamingContext context)
        {
            this.Deserialize(info, context);
        }

        protected override IComponent[]
CreateComponentsCore(IDesignerHost host)
        {
            CompositeActivity activity = new GeneralControlFlow();

            activity.Activities.Add(new GeneralControlFlowBranch());
            activity.Activities.Add(new GeneralControlFlowBranch());

            return new IComponent[] { activity };
        }

    }
}
```

2. Add the following attribute to the GeneralControlFlow activity to tell it to use the custom ToolBoxItem:

   ```
   [ToolboxItem(typeof(GeneralControlFlowToolBoxItem))]
   ```

3. Build the CustomControlflowActivities project so that the activity will be updated when you test it on the workflow.

Testing the `GeneralControlFlowToolBoxItem` Class

Follow the next steps to add a `GeneralControlFlow` activity to the workflow and see it prepopulated with `GeneralControlFlowBranch` activities.

1. Open the workflow in design mode.

2. Add a `GeneralControlFlow` activity to the workflow. It should be prepopulated with two `GeneralControlFlowBranch` activities, as shown in Figure 24.2.

FIGURE 24.2
GeneralCon-
trolFlow
placed one work-
flow with
ToolBoxItem.

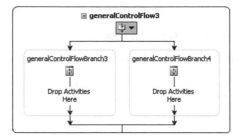

3. Delete the `GeneralControlFlow` activity you just added from the workflow. There is no need to run the workflow because it is a design-time change.

Adding Custom Validation

Two of WF's main objectives are to enable more spontaneous application logic creation and to diversify the application logic creation market. XAML-only workflows can be executed without compilation and writing code. Technically savvy business-people can create XAML-only workflows using the SharePoint Designer in SharePoint workflow, for example. In addition, dynamic update allows running workflow instances to be changed. Although powerful, these capabilities are also dangerous. What if, for example, a workflow model, although syntactically correct, is obviously erroneous? Maybe the workflow model contains a custom start transfer activity but does not implement its complete bank transfer cohort.

Custom activities can be associated with classes that derive from `ActivityValidator` or `CompositeActivityValidator`. These derived classes can traverse the entire workflow model. Therefore, the validation logic contained in a start transfer activity can search the workflow model for a complete transfer activity, and if not found, the WF validation logic throws an exception.

Validation is called on when workflows are loaded, compiled, or dynamic update is applied. A workflow cannot be run or changed without passing validation. Validation should be used to check the workflow model and its design-time properties. It should not, for example, be used to ensure that the customer number passed to a workflow is correct. This is not a design-time error, but rather caused by the specific data sent to a specific workflow instance. Either the workflow or the host application should validate the customer number at runtime.

We will employ validation to ensure that the ExecutionMode property is set to either Sequential or Parallel, to ensure that the BranchesToExecute is larger than or equal to 0, and to ensure that only GeneralControlFlowBranch activities are added to the GeneralControlFlow activity.

Adding and Seting Up the Class

Because we are validating a control flow activity, we will derive from CompositeActivityValidator for reasons explained shortly. If validating a basic activity, derive from ActivityValidator, which is similar but has no child activity validation capability.

Follow the next steps to add the custom validation class.

1. Right-click the CustomControlflowActivities project and select Add, Class.

2. Name the class **GeneralControlFlowValidator**.

3. Add **:CompositeActivityValidator** to the right of the class name to derive from the CompositeActivityValidator type.

4. Add the following using directives:

   ```
   using System.Workflow.ComponentModel.Compiler;
   using System.Workflow.ComponentModel;
   ```

Overriding the `Validate` Method to Validate the Properties

It is your job to locate any errors and populate a variable of type ValidationErrorCollection with them. Each entry to ValidationErrorCollection must contain a description and an error number provided by you. You must also call its base.ValidateProperties method so that validation is called on all the control flow activity's child activities. If any errors are returned in the ValidationErrorCollection variable, WF raises an exception and the workflow is invalidated.

Follow the next steps to override the Validate method and validate the GeneralControlFlow activity's properties.

1. Add the following code inside the class you just created to override the `Validate` method:

```
public override ValidationErrorCollection Validate(
    ValidationManager manager, object obj)
{
}
```

2. Add the following code to the method body so that base validation is called on all `GeneralControlFlow` activity child activities:

```
// Leave the base error validation intact
ValidationErrorCollection errorCollection =
    base.ValidateProperties(manager, obj);
```

3. Add the following code to create a `GeneralControlFlow` object from the `obj` parameter:

```
GeneralControlFlow generalControlFlow =
    obj as GeneralControlFlow;
```

4. Add the following `if` statement to ensure that validation occurs only when the activity is on a workflow and not when the activity itself is being compiled when the property will rightfully be null:

```
// A null parent signifies the activity is being compiled
// and validation should only occur when being placed on a
workflow
// and not when the activity is being compiled.
if (generalControlFlow.Parent != null)
{
}
```

5. Add the following code inside the `if` statement you just added to update the `errorCollection` variable if the `BranchesToExecute` are less than 0.

```
// Ensuring BranchesExecute >= 0
if (generalControlFlow.BranchesToExecute < 0)
    errorCollection.Add(new ValidationError
        ("BranchesToExecute must be larger than or equal to
0", 1));
```

6. Add the following code below the `if` statement you added a couple of steps ago to update the `errorCollection` variable if the `ExecutionMode` is not Sequential or Parallel:

```
// Ensuring ExecutionMode is set to Sequential or Parallel.
if
(!(generalControlFlow.ExecutionMode.Contains("Sequential")
    ||
generalControlFlow.ExecutionMode.Contains("Parallel")))
```

```
errorCollection.Add(new ValidationError
("Execution mode must be sequential or parallel", 1));
```

Validate the Child Activity

Follow the next steps to ensure that the `GeneralControlFlow` activity holds only activities of type `GeneralControlFlowBranch`. This validation may seem redundant, because we already enforce that only `GeneralControlFlowBranch` activities are added to the `GeneralControlFlow` activity in the custom designer. However, designer validation is enforced only when the workflow is constructed graphically. If the author directly edits the XAML or code, the designer validation will not be called on. Therefore, at many times, validation such as enforcing which child activities a parent will accept should be performed in the designer and in code validation. The first prohibits the child activity from being inserted in the first place. And the latter produces a red exclamation mark over the activity and works no matter how the workflow is constructed.

1. Add the following code below the code you added in the previous step to ensure that only `GeneralControlFlowBranch` activities are inserted as child activities.

```
// Ensuring that only GeneralControlFlowBranch children
// are added.
foreach (Activity a in
generalControlFlow.EnabledActivities)
    {
        if (!(a is GeneralControlFlowBranch))
        {
            errorCollection.Add(new ValidationError
                ("Can only add GeneralControlFlowBranch
activities.", 1235));
        }
    }
```

2. Add the following code outside of the `if generalControlFlow.Parent != null` statement to return errors, if any:

```
return errorCollection;
```

3. The completed `Validate` method should look like Listing 24.1.

LISTING 24.1   `GeneralControlFlow` Activity `Validate` Method

```
public override ValidationErrorCollection Validate(
    ValidationManager manager, object obj)
{
    // Leave the base error validation intact
    ValidationErrorCollection errorCollection =
        base.ValidateProperties(manager, obj);
```

```
         GeneralControlFlow generalControlFlow =
             obj as GeneralControlFlow;

         // A null parent signifes the activity is being compiled
         // and validaiton should only occur when being placed on a workflow
         // and not when the activity is being compiled.
         if (generalControlFlow.Parent != null)
         {
             // Ensuring BranchesExecute >= 0
             if (generalControlFlow.BranchesToExecute < 0)
                 errorCollection.Add(new ValidationError
                     ("BranchesToExecute must be larger than or equal to
0", 1));

             // Ensuring ExecutionMode is set to Sequential or Parallel.
             if (!(generalControlFlow.ExecutionMode.Contains("Sequential")
                 || generalControlFlow.ExecutionMode.Contains("Parallel")))
                 errorCollection.Add(new ValidationError
                 ("Execution mode must be sequential or parallel", 1));

             // Ensuring that only GeneralControlFlowBranch children
             // are added.
             foreach (Activity a in generalControlFlow.EnabledActivities)
             {
                 if (!(a is GeneralControlFlowBranch))
                 {
                     errorCollection.Add(new ValidationError
                         ("Can only add GeneralControlFlowBranch
activities.", 1235));
                 }
             }
         }

         return errorCollection;
     }
```

Associating the Custom Validator with an Activity

Follow the next steps to decorate the GeneralControlFlow activity with the
GeneralControlFlowValidator attribute.

1. Open the GeneralControlFlow activity in code view.

2. Add the following class attribute:

    ```
    [ActivityValidator(typeof(GeneralControlFlowValidator))]
    ```

3. Build the CustomControlflowActivities project.

Testing the New Validation

Follow the next steps to test the custom validation you just created.

1. Open the workflow in design mode.

2. Click the `GeneralControlFlow` activity.

3. Enter **Seq** in the `ExecutionMode` property and the red exclamation mark should appear (Figure 24.3).

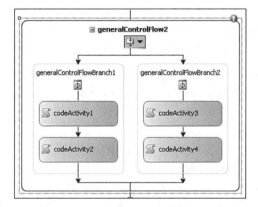

FIGURE 24.3
Validation error (red exclamation mark) shown when `BranchesToEx-ecute` less than 0.

4. Enter **Sequential** in the `ExecutionMode` property and the red exclamation mark should disappear.

5. If you like, open `Workflow1.designer.cs` and add a non-`GeneralControlFlowBranch` activity to the `GeneralControlFlow` activity; the red exclamation mark will reappear.

Adding Attached Properties and the `ActivityCondition` Type

Attached properties allow parent activity properties to be propagated to child activities. The `ConditionedActivityGroup` (CAG), for instance, propagates its condition property to its child activities. This propagated property is evaluated on each branch to determine whether the branch should execute. This is the case no matter which child activity (`Sequence`, `Code`, and so on) is inserted into the CAG. In this step you change the `GeneralControlFlow` activity to use attached properties. This allows child activities to virtually acquire these properties while placed in the

GeneralControlFlow activity, again just like activities placed in a While or CAG activity "acquire" condition properties. Doing so eliminates the requirement to create a custom child activity each time an activity needs to project properties on a child activity.

Four steps are required to implement attached properties in WF:

1. Create a customized or attached DependencyProperty (details soon).

2. Create a class that extends IExtenderProvider, which marshals the property between the parent and child activities.

3. Create a custom designer that displays the attached property in the property window.

4. Access the attached property from the GeneralControlFlow activity, which is different than when accessing a standard dependency property.

It is not trivial to implement attached properties. A Microsoft Program Manager has created a sample that we will largely follow to implement them. Most of the code is boilerplate, and you do not need to modify it much to use on different activities and properties. The first step, creating the attached property itself, changes the most and is therefore explained in the most detail. The other more stable steps, creating the IExtenderProvider and the designer specifics, are not covered in detail. The focus is on what needs to be changed so that you can use them with other activities and properties and take advantage of attached properties in your applications. See www. dennispi.com/2006/03/getting-dependencyproperty_03.html if you want more details.

Attached properties are another reason to use dependency properties.

Creating Attached Dependency Property

The dependency property you will create to serve as an attached property will call the DependencyProperty.RegisterAttached method instead of the DependencyProperty.Register method used by standard dependency properties. Its setters and getters will be static methods that work with the object type. They cannot be typed to an activity because it is unknown what activity or type they will be projected on.

Follow the next steps to create the attached property.

1. Open the GeneralControlFlow activity in code view.

2. Create a standard dependency property named Condition below the constructor and set its type to ActivityCondition.

3. Change `DependencyProperty.Register` to
`DependencyProperty.RegisterAttached` in the dependency code initiation
as shown:

```
public static DependencyProperty ConditionProperty =
    DependencyProperty.RegisterAttached("Condition",
    typeof(ActivityCondition), typeof(GeneralControlFlow));
```

4. Delete the remaining portion of the dependency property.

5. Add the following static method that can be called by the child activity to get
the condition property:

```
public static object GetCondition(object dependencyObject)
{
    return ((DependencyObject)
      dependencyObject).GetValue(ConditionProperty);
}
```

6. Add the following static method that can be called by the child activity to set
the condition property:

```
public static void SetCondition(object dependencyObject,
    object value)
{
    ((DependencyObject)dependencyObject).SetValue(
      ConditionProperty, value);
}
```

7. The completed attached property should look like Listing 24.2.

LISTING 24.2   **Attached Dependency Property**

```
public static DependencyProperty ConditionProperty =
    DependencyProperty.RegisterAttached("Condition",
    typeof(ActivityCondition), typeof(GeneralControlFlow));

public static object GetCondition(object dependencyObject)
{
    return ((DependencyObject)
      dependencyObject).GetValue(ConditionProperty);
}

public static void SetCondition(object dependencyObject,
    object value)
{
    ((DependencyObject)dependencyObject).SetValue(
      ConditionProperty, value);
}
```

Creating Class that Extends `IServiceProvider`

Follow the next steps to create and code a class that implements `IServiceProvider` to project the `Condition` property onto its child activity.

1. Right-click the `CustomControlflowActivities` project and select Add, Class.

2. Name the class **`ConditionPropertyExtenderProvider`**.

3. Add the following using directives:

   ```
   using System.Workflow.ComponentModel;
   using System.ComponentModel;
   ```

4. Add **`:IExtenderProvider`** to the right of the class name to implement the `IExtenderProvider` interface.

5. Add the following class attribute to tell the extender provider class the name of the property to service:

   ```
   [ProvideProperty("Condition", typeof(Activity))]
   ```

   The attribute is obviously specific to the property being attached.

Add `GetCondition` and `SetChild` Methods

Follow the next steps to create methods that retrieve and set the `Condition` property on the current activity if its parent is the `GeneralControlFlow` activity.

1. Add the following code to the class to call the `GetCondition` method that returns the `Condition` property if the parent activity is a `GeneralControlFlow` activity:

   ```
           public ActivityCondition GetCondition(Activity theActivity)
           {
               if (theActivity.Parent is GeneralControlFlow)
                   return
   theActivity.GetValue(GeneralControlFlow.ConditionProperty)
                       as ActivityCondition;
               else
                   return null;
           }
   ```

   Only the code that references the `GeneralControlFlow` activity and the `ConditionProperty` is specific to the activity and condition. The other code is boilerplate.

2. Add the following code to call the `SetCondition` method that returns the `Condition` property if the parent activity is a `GeneralControlFlow` activity:

```
public void SetCondition(Activity theActivity, ActivityCondition
value)
    {
        if (theActivity.Parent is GeneralControlFlow)
            theActivity.SetValue(GeneralControlFlow.ConditionProperty,
value);
    }
```

Again, only the code that references the `GeneralControlFlow` activity and the `ConditionProperty` is specific to the activity and condition. The other code is boiler-plate.

Implementing the `IExtenderProvider.CanExtend` Method

Follow the next steps to determine whether the current activity's parent activity is `GeneralControlFlow` activity, and if so to allow it to be extended.

1. Add the following code to implement the `IExtenderProvider.CanExtend` method to check whether the activity's parent is a `GeneralControlFlow` activity:

```
bool IExtenderProvider.CanExtend(object extendee)
    {
        return (extendee is Activity) &&
            (((Activity)extendee).Parent is GeneralControlFlow);
    }
```

2. Build the `CustomControlflowActivities` project.

Modifying the Custom Designer

Follow the next steps to modify the custom designer to show the attached `Condition` property.

1. Open the `GeneralControlFlowDesigner` designer class.

2. Add the following using directive:

```
using System.ComponentModel.Design;
```

3. Add the `Initialize` method in Listing 24.3 to the `GeneralControlFlowDesigner` class that is all boilerplate other than two calls to `ConditionPropertyExtenderProvider`:

LISTING 24.3   Attached Property Activity Designer **Initialize** Method That Projects the **Condition** Property

```
protected override void Initialize(Activity activity)
{
    base.Initialize(activity);

    IExtenderListService extenderListService =
        (IExtenderListService)GetService(typeof(IExtenderListService));
    if (extenderListService != null)
    {
        bool foundExtender = false;
        foreach (IExtenderProvider extenderProvider in
            extenderListService.GetExtenderProviders())
        {
            if (extenderProvider.GetType() ==
typeof(ConditionPropertyExtenderProvider))
                foundExtender = true;
        }

        if (!foundExtender)
        {
            IExtenderProviderService extenderProviderService =

(IExtenderProviderService)GetService(typeof(IExtenderProviderService));

            if (extenderProviderService != null)
            {
                extenderProviderService.AddExtenderProvider(new
ConditionPropertyExtenderProvider());
            }
        }
    }
}
```

4. Build the `CustomControlflowActivities` project.

Modifying **Execute** Method to Evaluate the Attached Property

The `Evaluate` method on the `Condition` property is called differently when accessing it on an attached property; otherwise, the concept is the same: call evaluate and see if the branch should execute.

Follow the next steps to modify the `GeneralControlFlow` activity's `Execute` method to work with attached properties.

First the `Condition` property is retrieved. Then the call to the `Evaluate` method is from the `Condition` property and not the activity. When using a standard property, the `Condition` property is accessed via the activity.

1. Open the `GeneralControlFlow` activity in code view.

2. Replace the `foreach` line of code at the top of the `Execute` method with the following code that loops through activities, specifically `GeneralControlFlowBranch` activities.

```
foreach (Activity a in this.EnabledActivities)
```

3. Add the following code to the top of the `foreach` in the `Execute` method to retrieve the `Condition` property by calling the `GetValue` method you added when creating the `Condition` property:

```
// Retrieve the activity condition form the Condition
property
ActivityCondition ac =
    (ActivityCondition)a.GetValue(ConditionProperty);
```

4. Replace the current line of code that calls `Evaluate` through the activity (`if (a.Condition.Evaluate(a, executionContext))`) with the following code that calls it through the `Condition` property:

```
if (ac.Evaluate(a, executionContext))
```

5. Build the `CustomControlflowActivities` project.

Remove the `GeneralControlFlowBranch` Validation

Follow the next steps to remove the validation that enforces that only `GeneralControlFlowBranch` activities are added to the `GeneralControlFlow` activity, because attached properties allow for any child activities to be added.

1. Open the `GeneralControlFlowDesigner` class.

2. Remove the `CanInsertActivities` method.

3. Open the `GeneralControlFlowValidator` class.

4. Remove the `foreach` and the code within it that ensures only `GeneralControlFlowBranch` activities are added.

5. Open the `GeneralControlFlow` activity in code view and remove the `ToolBoxItem` class attribute. It is appropriate to prepopulate the parent activity only when the child activities are confined to specific type.

6. Build the `CustomControlflowActivities` project.

Updating the Workflow

1. Delete the current `GeneralControlFlow` activity from the workflow.

2. Add a new `GeneralControlFlow` activity to the workflow.

3. Add a `Sequence` activity to the left branch and a `Code` activity to the right branch (remember to hover).

4. Click the `Sequence` activity branch, and you will see a `Condition` property. Then click the `Code` activity branch, and you will see a `Condition` property (Figure 24.4).

FIGURE 24.4
Code activity with attached Condition property.

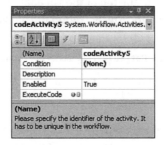

5. If you would like, add activities to the `Sequence` activity, update the `Condition` properties, and then run the workflow.

Reviewing Activity Life Cycle Artifacts

WF activities have an official life cycle tracked by an enumeration, additional handlers related to this life cycle, and optional handlers.

Activity Life Cycle and the `ActivityExecutionStatus`

WF activity execution is governed by a finite state machine (Figure 24.5). The activity will always be in one of the states. The standard activity execution path has been from `Initialized` to `Executing` to `Closed` for most activities we have worked with the last three chapters. One activity in this chapter also entered the `Canceling` state. The two other possible activity states are `Faulting` and `Compensating`. Let's take a brief look at how each state is entered:

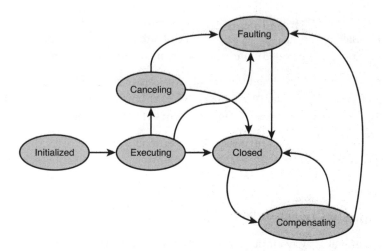

FIGURE 24.5
Activity life cycle
and transitions.

The `Initialized` state is entered when the host calls
`WorkflowRuntime.CreateWorkflow`. At this time all workflow activities are initialized.

The `Executing` state is entered when the parent activity calls the
`ActivityExecutionContext.ExecuteActivity` method. The one exception is that
the root activity is executed (or scheduled for execution) when
`WorkflowInstance.Start` is called.

The `Canceling` state occurs when parent activity calls
`ActivityExecutionContext.CancelActivity` or when a control flow activity faults.
In our early completion activity earlier in the hour, we saw that a control flow activity will cancel one or more of its child activities when they are in the executing state
and the activity is ready to close. The base `Cancel` method handler is called for these
activities; if you need to perform additional cleanup, you can override the `Cancel`
method. We will not do this.

The `Faulting` state is entered when an unhandled exception occurs in an activity.
More precisely, the faulting state is entered when an unhandled exception occurs in
any of the activity life cycle states (handlers) with the exception of Initialized, which
raises an exception to the host starting the workflow. When a basic activity faults,
the default behavior is to call `ActivityExecutionContext.Closed` and pass the
exception to the parent activity. When called on a control flow activity, the default
behavior is to cancel the currently executing child activities first and then close and
pass the exception to the parent activity. It has to do this to be able to close. We will
not override the default fault handling.

The Compensating state is entered when a downstream activity invokes the compensation handler for the current activity. Unlike all other states, compensation takes place on activities in a closed state. You will create a compensation handler shortly.

The Closed state is called when the activity requests to be closed, either by returning ActivityExecutionStatus.Closed from the Executing, Canceling, or Faulting methods, or by calling ActivityExecutionContext.Closed from a handler. Only the activity may close itself.

The ActivityExecutionStatus enumeration mirrors the activity life cycle. There is one entry for each life cycle state.

Other Activity Handlers

These additional activity virtual methods that may be overridden are not part of the activity life cycle but can be invoked at various points of the life cycle. The OnActivityExecutionContextLoad handler is called each time the activity is loaded, which may occur multiple times if the activity is persisted. The OnActivityExecutionContextUnload is conversely called each time the activity is unloaded. The OnClosed and Uninitialized methods are called when the activity is closed.

Implementing Compensation

There is no default compensation in WF. Activities that want compensation must implement the ICompensateableActivity.Compensate method. Basic activities can have compensation logic stored in the ICompensateableActivity.Compensate method. Control flow activities can have both the Compensate method and a Compensation Handler associated with them.

Overriding the Default Compensation Handler

In this section, you will implement the ICompensateableActivity.Compensate method. You are not associating any specific custom compensatory logic with the activity and therefore will simply return ActivityExecutionStatus.Closed. If there was compensation logic you wanted executed each time this activity was compensated, it would be placed here. By adding the method and returning closed, you allow for a custom Compensation Handler to be associated with the activity. This allows the workflow author to choose what compensation logic the activity should receive for that specific workflow model.

Follow the next steps to add a Compensation Handler to the GeneralControlFlow activity.

1. Go to the workflow and right-click a `GeneralControlFlow` activity.

2. Notice it has no View Compensation Handler option.

3. Replace the `GeneralControlFlow` class signature with the following, which also implements the `ICompensateableActivity.Compensate`:

   ```
   public partial class GeneralControlFlow : CompositeActivity,
   ICompensatableActivity
   ```

4. Go to the end of the class and insert the following method:

   ```
   // Make the activity compensation-eligible.
   ActivityExecutionStatus ICompensatableActivity.Compensate(
       ActivityExecutionContext executionConttext)
   {
       return ActivityExecutionStatus.Closed;
   }
   ```

5. Build the `CustomControlflowActivities` project.

6. Go back to the workflow, right-click the `GeneralControlFlow` activity, and notice there is now a View Compensation Handler option (Figure 24.6). This activity may now have compensation handlers associated with it.

FIGURE 24.6
Activity compensation handler option shown.

See Hour 16, "Working with Exceptions, Compensation, and Transactions," for additional compensation coverage.

Summary

This hour concludes the five-part series on custom activities. The first hour in the series covered basic activities, the second two multiburst activities, and that last two control flow activities. This hour built on the `GeneralControlFlow` activity you started last hour. It already could execute in parallel, terminate early, and have conditions applied when `GeneralControlFlowBranch` activities were placed in it. This hour you added validation, designer support, and learned to apply conditions to any child activity among other items. Finally, as stated before, the capability to add control flow patterns to WF allows patterns found at www.workflowpatterns.com, BPEL, and other places to be added to WF by you, third parties, and Microsoft over time.

Workshop

Quiz

1. *What function does the* `ActivityToolboxItem` *serve?*

2. *When is validation invoked in WF?*

3. *Is WF validation better suited for ensuring that a* `Condition` *property is set or ensuring that a customer exists?*

4. *Is validation limited to the current composite activity?*

5. *Why was an attached property used to apply the condition at the end of the hour instead of a standard* `DependencyProperty`*?*

6. *What functions does a custom designer support?*

Answers

1. It permits a composite activity to be prepopulated with child activities when dragged onto the workflow designer from the toolbox. It is useful for activities such as `IfElse` and `Parallel`, which both have two branches added when placed on the workflow, which improves comprehensibility and speeds up usage.

2. When workflows are loaded, compiled, or dynamic update is applied.

3. Normally, for ensuring a condition is set, because this generally occurs at design time. Checking that a customer exists, on the contrary, is generally a runtime event.

4. No, it can crawl the entire workflow. Doing so allows it to ensure required activity pairs (`BeginTransfer`, `EndTransfer`) and other workflow-level rules are enforced each time and place that validation is invoked.

5. Attached properties permit any child activity of a parent activity, such as the `GeneralControlFlow` activity, to be evaluated.

6. They allow for design-time validation and to control the look and feel of an activity.

Index

X

Y-Z

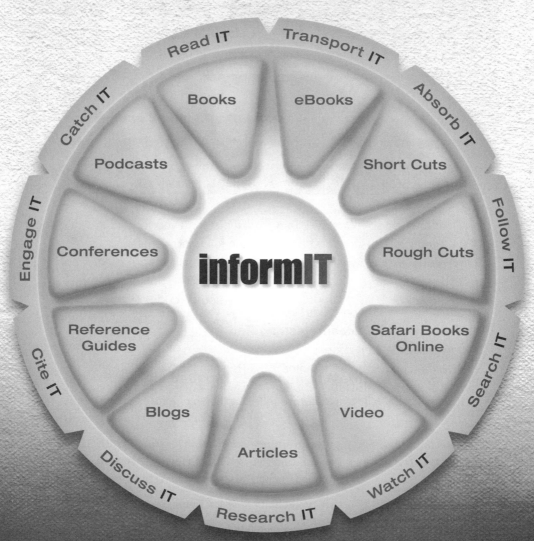

FREE Online Edition

Your purchase of **Sams Teach Yourself Windows Workflow Foundation in 24 Hours** includes access to a free online edition for 45 days through the Safari Books Online subscription service. Nearly every Sams book is available online through Safari Books Online, along with more than 5,000 other technical books and videos from publishers such as Addison-Wesley Professional, Cisco Press, Exam Cram, IBM Press, O'Reilly, Prentice Hall, and Que.

SAFARI BOOKS ONLINE allows you to search for a specific answer, cut and paste code, download chapters, and stay current with emerging technologies.

Activate your FREE Online Edition at www.informit.com/safarifree

> **STEP 1:** Enter the coupon code: FBEHMZG.

> **STEP 2:** New Safari users, complete the brief registration form.
> Safari subscribers, just log in.

If you have difficulty registering on Safari or accessing the online edition, please e-mail customer-service@safaribooksonline.com